MARION KAPLAN

———————

THE PORTUGUESE

THE LAND AND ITS PEOPLE

PENGUIN BOOKS

PENGUIN BOOKS

Published by the Penguin Group
Penguin Books Ltd, 27 Wrights Lane, London W8 5TZ, England
Penguin Books USA Inc., 375 Hudson Street, New York, New York 10014, USA
Penguin Books Australia Ltd, Ringwood, Victoria, Australia
Penguin Books Canada Ltd, 10 Alcorn Avenue, Toronto, Ontario, Canada M4V 3B2
Penguin Books (NZ) Ltd, 182–190 Wairau Road, Auckland 10, New Zealand

Penguin Books Ltd, Registered Offices: Harmondsworth, Middlesex, England

First published by Viking 1991
Published in Penguin Books 1991
3 5 7 9 10 8 6 4 2

Printed in England by Clays Ltd, St Ives plc

Eu gosto deste país, nunca pensei que este país fosse insignificante, e mesmo que o seja em comparação com outros, é o meu país, não é o simples facto de ter aqui nascido, é muito mais simples, é que tudo aquilo que sou é daqui que vem, o meu modo de entender o mundo criou-se aqui, para o bem e para o mal, o positivo e o negativo, o bom e o medíocre, enfim, foi aqui que eu me fiz.

José Saramago

(I like this country. I have never thought this country insignificant even compared with others. It is my country, not for the simple reason that I was born here. It's much simpler than that. Everything I am and was, my very understanding of the world, all that I did, for good or ill, positive or negative, worthwhile or mediocre, was here.)

I sit every day in the sun. That's why we're here, isn't it?

A foreign resident

Contents

List of Photographs

Section One

1 The Belém tower, Lisbon
2 Lisbon: alongside elegance there is a build up of human pressure, an endless preoccupation with housing
3 *Casa do Povo* (House of the People), a social centre that is a feature of virtually every town and village
4 In the Beira town of Idanha-a-Velha (once the Roman Egitania) a travelling salesman displays his wares on the steps of the *pelourinho*, town pillory.
5 Between the boulders is the home of an elderly resident of Monsanto. The Misericórdia charity organization is delivering a hot lunch
6 The northern town of Amarante
7 Alentejo homestead
8 Slate rooftops in Piódão
9 *Espigueiros*, corn stores, at Soajo
10 Faro: the future looms in building styles
11 In an Algarve village: a meeting of the ways
12 *Moliceiro* regatta (once they gathered weed for fertilizer) in the Aveiro lagoon
13 Folk art and humour ('Living alone sets me to thinking') on the swan's neck prows of the *moliceiros*
14 *Dia dos Rapazes*, 'day of the boys', a wintertime *festa* in Trás-os-Montes villages when boys don masks and devilish disguise
15 Rite of passage: masked boys in robes of rags 'terrorize' village girls in the far north
16 Art in *azulejos*: the ornamental façade of the tilemaking Viúva Lamego factory in Lisbon

All photographs by Marion Kaplan

List of Maps

Provinces

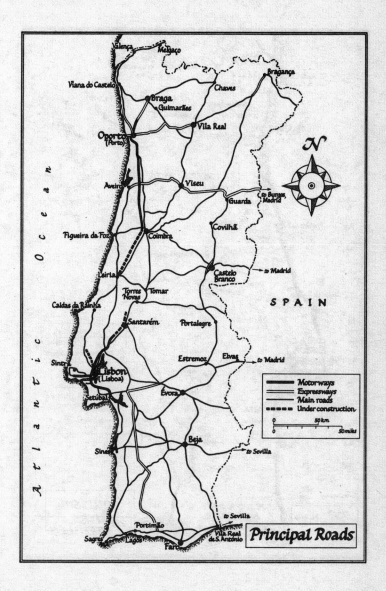

Valença
Melgaço
Bragança
Viana do Castelo
Chaves
Braga
Guimarães
Vila Real
Oporto
(Porto)
Aveiro
Viseu
Guarda
*to Burgos,
Madrid*
Covilhã
Figueira da Foz
Coimbra
Leiria
Castelo
Branco
to Madrid
Torres
Novas
Tomar
S P A I N
Caldas da Rainha
Santarém
Portalegre
Estremoz
Elvas
to Madrid
Sintra
Lisbon
(Lisboa)
Setúbal
Évora
Sines
Beja
to Sevilla
A t l a n t i c   O c e a n
to Sevilla
Portimão
Sagres
Lagos
Vila Real
de S. António
Faro

	Motorways
	Expressways
	Main roads
	Under construction

0   50 km
0   50 miles

Principal Roads

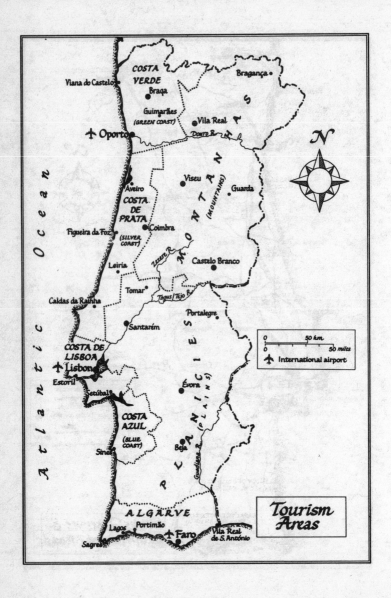

Tourism
Areas

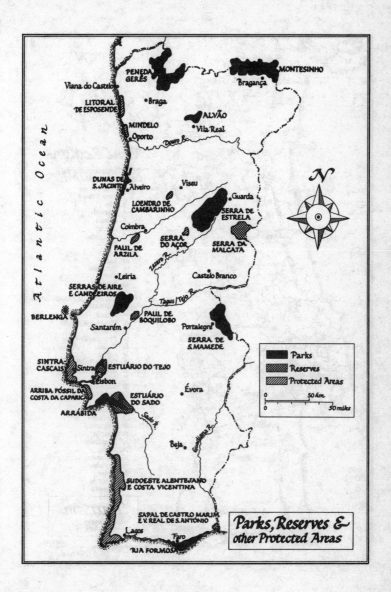

Parks, Reserves & other Protected Areas

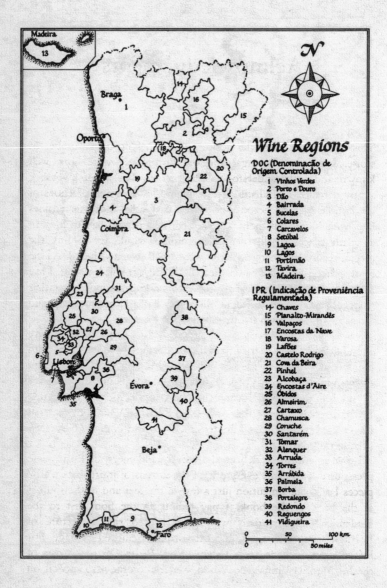

Wine Regions

DOC (Denominação de Origem Controlada)

1 Vinhos Verdes
2 Porto e Douro
3 Dão
4 Bairrada
5 Bucelas
6 Colares
7 Carcavelos
8 Setúbal
9 Lagoa
10 Lagos
11 Portimão
12 Tavira
13 Madeira

IPR (Indicação de Proveniência Regulamentada)

14 Chaves
15 Planalto-Mirandês
16 Valpaços
17 Encostas da Nave
18 Varosa
19 Lafões
20 Castelo Rodrigo
21 Cova da Beira
22 Pinhel
23 Alcobaça
24 Encostas d'Aire
25 Óbidos
26 Almeirim
27 Cartaxo
28 Chamusca
29 Coruche
30 Santarém
31 Tomar
32 Alenquer
33 Arruda
34 Torres
35 Arrábida
36 Palmela
37 Borba
38 Portalegre
39 Redondo
40 Reguengos
41 Vidigueira

Acknowledgements

This book arose from the notion, after working on a number of stories here, <u>that Portugal and the Portuguese were both well known and little understood.</u> The picture was a patchwork: a sunny country, a fatalistic nature, memories of empire, echoes of revolution, historic heroes like Vasco da Gama, modern heroines like Rosa Mota. But there were so many gaps: you had to look in so many places to fill them. I thought I would try to link the pieces, record the changes, relate what I had seen and heard. As the book proceeded, I learned a great deal, and am still learning. I say this not so much as an excuse for errors and omissions but rather to point out that, <u>in Portugal, discovery has a larger meaning and more possibilities than I anticipated</u> when I began.

I made my discoveries with a good deal of help: initially, long ago and far away in Africa, from Mário Sampaio; much later, with the encouragement of the late Bill Whitehead, in New York; from the well-informed corps of foreign correspondents in Lisbon, above all Jill Jolliffe; with the generosity and consideration of Margarida Sarda, director and editor of *Selecções do Reader's Digest*. (For material I have used from articles I did for the *Digest* and *National Geographic* I thank the editors.)

I owe an enormous debt to the voluble and energetic Portuguese press; unable to name every one of the dozens of journalists whose pieces I clipped, I mention just a few in my text and in the sources at the back of the book. I pay tribute in the book list to the academics and historians who gave me so rich a picture of Portugal's impressive past and extraordinary cultural heritage. For information on wine areas I thank Eng. Pedro Castro e Costa of the Instituto da Vinha e do Vinho. Material on the map appears on pp. 30–31 with the kind cooperation of António Martins Mourão of the Comissão Nacional para as Comemorações dos Descobrimentos Portugueses. To my long-time agents in London, Camera Press, goes my continuing appreciation of their efforts, and to Tony Cooke in particular many thanks for fine printing.

I thank the staff of the Press Room in Lisbon for stout assistance on request, and *Turismo* personnel across Portugal for a generous supply of leaflets, lists, information and, in Aveiro, a sumptuous cruise on the tranquil lagoon. In Oporto, my thanks go especially to my friend Maria de Fátima Marques Pinto. I am grateful for hospitality bestowed by the Douro world of port wine and the green region of *vinho verde*.

Here in the Algarve I thank friends for friendship, and Elisabete Viegas especially for lightening my efforts to learn the language of Camões. To Constantino José Marrachinho at Loução Filho, Lda., in Faro, I am grateful for processing my black and white negatives, to the staff of Photoclik, especially Dina Coelho in Loulé, for constant concern for my colour work. To Fernanda and José Martins, the best neighbours anyone could have, a thousand thanks for years of kindnesses. And to Eric Robins for his infinite patience, among so many virtues, my gratitude and love.

Marion Kaplan
Loulé, 1991

A note on spellings, Portuguese words, and place-names

I have tended towards Portuguese spellings for people and places. Yet the *infante* Dom Henrique, son of Dom João I and his English queen, Philippa, will always be for me Prince Henry the Navigator. *Infante* is the child of kings, *Dom* and *Dona* honorifics for royalty and rank. In the north, I again think of Porto as Oporto. Maps at times show both. Portuguese expressions I translate in the context. The index also helps to clarify Portuguese phrases or repeated sets of initials.

This is not a guidebook, there is no gazetteer – nor, in the main body of the book, do I make practical travel suggestions. (I compensate a little in an appendix.) But I have, nearly everywhere, given a rough direction for the places that I write of – at times well off the beaten track – making it relatively easy for even first-time travellers in Portugal to find them.

1 The enduring appeal

There are countless reasons for coming to Portugal – my own list began with a peaceful setting at the water's edge of a crowded Europe and grew to epic length. From the time of the Phoenicians, who came for commerce in the first millennium BC, this small country has endured and enjoyed an endless flow of visitors – soldiers and crusaders, merchants and traders, brides and pilgrims, priests and nuns, the faithful and the faithless, politicians and diplomats, master builders and humble labourers, poets, writers and artists, restless travellers, romantic adventurers and sun-seeking tourists.

They came in search of gold and mineral wealth, to marry and settle. They came in times of daring exploration, an unparalleled age of discovery, expanding empire and vast wealth. They came in times of war – between nations, between brothers, civil, colonial. They experienced earthquake, witnessed arrant autocracy, absolute dictatorship, a peaceful revolution and the crises and curves of democratic government.

Now, since Portugal has entered the European Economic Community, new invaders come for commerce. Some of us come from countries where we were called European but really were not. Many come also to explore old and graceful cities, towns and villages, to delight in the natural splendours of beautiful landscapes, to eat well and to drink splendid wines. Many more come in search of sunshine, gleaming beaches, a clean sea. In tourism's bland prose, paradise is promised; for some, perhaps, it is here. The Portuguese offer a courteous and unsurprised welcome. The frontiers of their country have been virtually the same since it became a sovereign kingdom in 1139. They have seen it all before; history, it has been said, is prophecy in reverse.

On the map of Europe Portugal is to be found down in the left-hand corner, small, slender and inconspicuous. Blue ocean rims the west and south. Rivers to the north and east divide Portugal from – and bind it to – the bulk of Spain. These vital rivers, the Minho, the Douro and the Guadiana, are part frontier, part peaceful waterway. The Tejo, or Tagus, longest of all, 626 miles or just over a thousand kilometres, belongs to both, girdling the Toledo of El Greco and Cervantes and harbouring, at its mouth, the Lisbon of Vasco da Gama and Camões. The Iberian peninsula is geographically united, historically related, emotionally widely separate.

Portugal is modest and unassuming on the map, pleasingly patterned with numerous smaller rivers, highlands and green valleys and, to the south, in the Alentejo, a great, rolling plain. No more than 350 miles long and 140 miles wide, it measures in area 34,216 square miles (88,684 square km), less than three quarters of the size of England. Bigger countries often seem crimped and mean, crammed with smoking industry and tired, pale people. In Portugal there is such grandeur, such an extraordinary sense of space, that maps appear puzzlingly out of scale. Vistas sprawl to distant horizons. The air is clear. Beaches, pale and glowing, have no end. The mountains – rugged, wildly beautiful and unhostile – seem to touch the roof of the sky, though none is higher than 2,000 m. From the southern hill where I live the night sky is satin smooth and so diamond bright that it is easy to imagine I can touch the stars and wrap myself in the glittering canopy. And if in the real world there is the dirt of ages and the crude detritus of modernity, roadside dumps and negligently drifting garbage, acid rain is still barely more than a menace, and many of the rivers are sweet and clean.

The fast-growing eucalyptus, its two faces showing paper and pulp profits and rural decline, ranges over huge areas on a scale that deeply troubles environmentalists. But here still are silver-green olive trees, marching in great armies over soft-edged hills, meadows of cork oaks with their colour-coded trunks, sprawling vineyards – brown and bony, leafy and green, or a blaze of red and gold according to the season.

Wild landscapes are bleakly theatrical, bursting in spring into gawdy palettes of wild flowers. Birdsong trills jauntily in the air, the music of goat bells rings across the pastures. Solitary wolves still survive in dark forests, lynx prowl silently in tangled thickets, boars roam open heathland and subversively raid farmers' crops. Eagles and vultures soar over tall cliffs, moon-faced owls roost in convent ruins.

Old churches and great castles are rooted in the terrain like ancient rocks. Villages built of stone cling to steep hillside and broad plain. Cities across the country were full of life and noise and colour a thousand years ago, from Braga, Oporto and Coimbra in the north, to Lisbon – for northerners this is already the south – Évora and Beja in the Alentejo and Faro on the south coast.

Here too are the Portuguese people, more than ten million of them, the number rising steadily as health care and the quality of life improve and emigrants return to their homeland with a sense of optimism and excitement that they had never believed possible. Sometimes, the optimism is misplaced, expectations set too high. In quiet villages, people living with dignity in old ways have small regard for the newly settled emigrant in his big, conspicuous house. But all Portuguese, many of the youngsters with ambitious enthusiasm, accept that change is in the air, new trends – and pressures – reshaping old ways. Portugal, whose dark era of more than forty years of dictatorship ended in the peaceful revolution of 1974, is noisily pounding at the doors of the technological age.

Not every Portuguese wants a computer or a car telephone or even a car, though the young, smart, prosperous city family regards a car as a fact of life and views costly gadgets with keen interest. Already, traffic congestion is acute in places, the accident rate appalling and, with services unable to keep pace with an expanding society, standard telephones are liable to frequent breakdown and slow reconnection. The dream, above all, for many Portuguese, is to have their own home, with running water and a modern tiled bathroom. They aspire to honest work with decent pay, good education and job opportunities for their children. Only in the context of a nation emerging from a long sleep are these aspirations at all remarkable; but for many, until now, they were unattainable.

Even now, with a surging economy and a society in which old families and new rich are both unashamed to be seen enjoying their wealth, the basic conditions of a healthy, happy life are for many painfully elusive.

'Portugal has lost, one hopes for ever, its image as a country stopped in time and history,' said Mário Soares, a popular president, in May 1988. For decades this had been the picture: Europe's poorest country, a society paralysed, inward-looking, backward, dull. A foreign film producer, delighting in photogenic settings and good-natured people, found a symbol for Portugal in a Lisbon bar: a clock on the wall that ticked its way – backwards. A neighbour of mine, a kind man with all the rigid caution of an old-fashioned farmer, insists that the two worst things that have happened in Portugal in recent years have been the revolution of 25 April 1974 and entry into the EEC. Yet Portugal is also the land of the bold explorers and mariners who discovered two thirds of the world, mapped its seas, its skies, its continents, masterfully established the first and greatest of the modern empires, the last to be disbanded. In the sixteenth century, Portugal was the richest, most powerful nation on earth, Lisbon the richest capital. Although wealth and power vanished, Portugal's impact and influence stayed strong; the Portuguese language today is spoken by nearly 200 million people.

Portugal is again looking out and reaching out – not to empire but to cultural and commercial contact. Again, other countries in Europe and across the world are enthusiastically looking in. Portugal's best-loved geographer, Orlando Ribeiro, who walked the wildest, remotest landscape to take its measure, came to view his land not as a simple gift of nature but as a portion of space fashioned by generations, imprinted with the stamp of many different influences. And, over the centuries, the appeal of this ancient land for others has been strong.

Carthaginian armies, around 200 BC, passed their winters in the Algarve – the southern region's mild winters today attract legions of golfers and platoons of athletes escaping from the ice and snow of northern Europe. Greeks followed briefly. For Strabo the map of Iberia had the shape of an outstretched bull's hide; he never visited it himself, but wrote – as others would do – from travellers' reports. The Iberia of the Greeks became the Hispania of the Romans and by 60 BC Lisbon – Olisipo – was the western capital of the Roman empire. Julius Caesar named the city Felicitas Julia, a graceful tribute considering how long – two centuries – and how bitterly the Romans had fought to establish their authority.

In the heathlands, forest and mountains that were the wild domain of fiercely unwelcoming Celtiberians and Lusitanians, a Lusitanian leader, Viriato, skilfully held off the Romans for eight years, between 147 and 139 BC, by a series of bold and cunning strategies. Unable to capture him among the rugged crags and slopes of his mountain fastness in the Mons Herminius – today it bears the sweeter name of Serra da Estrela, 'mountains of the stars' – and unable to beat him honourably, the Romans bribed assassins to murder him. More than that of any Roman, the name of Viriato has endured in the Iberian peninsula over the centuries. He was Portugal's first true national hero, loved and admired with the passionate fervour only focused now on champion football players – with which, as it happens, Portugal is well endowed.

Yet the Romans left a valuable legacy: a network of roads, the basis of the motorways and expressways linking Portugal today with Spain and all Europe; the Portuguese language, a Romance tongue deriving from Latin; a tradition of fine cities – Conimbriga among them – and civilized rule within a legal framework.

Christianity came, in diverse doctrines that were viewed by opposing camps with rigid intolerance – Priscillian, a young man from Galicia whose teachings influenced many devotees including a bishop of Braga, was condemned and burned to death for heresy. But even as the first bishops busily travelled from council to council a force of four Germanic barbarian tribes stormed into Iberia from across the Pyrenees.

Against the Vandals, Visigoths, Alans and Swabians (or Suevi), who, Caesar noted, wore animal skins and little else, Christianity held its own, flourished and spread, even among the pagan invaders. The Swabians and Visigoths, in a confused pattern, were around until 711; then, as good Catholics, they too were pushed aside by invaders striking from north Africa in Islam's forceful surge from the Middle East. For all their differences, these invaders were afterwards simply and evocatively known as Moors.

The Moors, only recently inspired to a powerful faith in Allah by his prophet, Muhammad, who died in 632, took to Iberia with marked enthusiasm. Over more than four centuries different groups of Muslims, primarily the Berber Almoravids and Almohads, held power – not without a ceaseless Christian struggle to remove them. Among the more unexpected of their attackers were Viking pirates who appeared from the icy north in the ninth century and terrorized Lisbon and Silves – then Chelb or Shalb, the Moors' southern capital. Their random attacks only ended when a Viking fleet was beaten off and destroyed in the River Arade near Silves by the son of the emir, Abdel Rahman III, in 966.

In 1147, in Lisbon, following a seventeen-week siege, Dom Afonso Henriques, Portugal's first king, led a dramatic assault on the Moors in the city's supposedly impregnable castle, aided by English, German, Fleming and French crusaders. They were an unsavoury, mercenary lot. Disgusted, the king had first tried persuasion, sending Bishop Pedro Pitões of Oporto and Archbishop João Peculiar of Braga to negotiate a surrender. The response was recorded by an English crusader. It was long, composed and clear: 'How many times in your memory have you come hither with pilgrims and barbarians to drive us hence? . . . Go away, for you shall not enter this city but by the sword.'

Eventual victory for King Afonso Henriques was sullied by the greed, drunken loutishness and savage tactics of many of the 13,000 soldiers fighting in the name of Christ. In one of their grosser acts, they stuck on poles around the castle walls, where they could best be seen by the anguished defenders, the heads of eighty Moors captured in Almada, south of the Tejo. The Portuguese prefer to recall the strength and valour of their own heroic Martim Moniz, the king's boon companion who, as legend relates, held open a castle gate even as Moors hacked and speared him to death.

Not all the crusaders were villains. Some Portuguese still regard drunkenness as the English vice but one Englishman, Gilbert of Hastings, became Bishop of Lisbon. Another Englishman, a fair-minded priest signing himself only as R, told a friend whose name appears as Osb (Osbern?), in a long letter in Latin, how successfully things turned out, eventually, for the Portuguese king. Conquest of the Moors was the foundation of the kingdom of Portugal and the castle of São Jorge its first and oldest monument. In 1249, armies of King Afonso III completed the conquest in Portugal by their victory at Faro, although the Moors held on in Spain for another two and a half centuries.

The Moors departed with the utmost reluctance. Some stayed, some became Christian. Their Mudéjar artistry became an integral part of Portuguese indigenous style. King João I, expanding the old Moorish palace at Sintra early in the fifteenth century, ordered tiled walls and cool courtyards from Moorish artisans living untroubled under Christian rule. The palace became his favourite residence and a summer home for succeeding generations of kings and queens.

Except in the north, the Moors had a profound influence in Portugal. In 1515–21, Francisco Arruda, one of Portugal's finest architects, ignoring French, Italian or Spanish styles, created the enchanting Belém tower set like a chess piece on the banks of the Tejo. The style is called Manueline, after the reigning king, but Arruda was an admirer of Moorish artistry, and had travelled in north Africa to study it; his exquisite fantasy, crowned with Byzantine cupolas, was of Moorish inspiration. Its famous outline has become virtually the logo of Lisbon, a symbol of the discoveries, an emblem for all Portugal.

The Moorish heritage is strongly visible today in great fortifications and fine, unfussy buildings, as well as in numerous architectural touches, from the distinctive Algarve filigree chimneys to the glorious *azulejos*, or tiles, which ornament countless churches, palaces, *solares* (manor-houses) and ordinary homes. At Mértola, on the Guadiana, which the Romans called Myrtilis, a Muslim mihrab was found inside the square, battlemented church. In many summer-crowded property developments and villas the architecture is of Moorish or mock-Moorish derivation. Often, it is horribly out of keeping with the landscape, without proportion or balance, but, as tourism expanded and building boomed, the style, like any other, acquired its own inherent good and bad qualities – mostly bad. Lack of control or plan, profiteer developers' bulldozer instincts, the bursting 1980s pace of expansion were all negative influences.

Yet in the south the Moors are almost a physical presence: in the name – Algarve is *al-gharb*, 'the western land', which included Al-Andalus, or Andalucia, and Al-Faghar, today's Algarve – in the faces and fatalistic nature of the people; in the fields and plantations of sweet oranges, succulent figs and almonds that they loved so much; in the great stones of unmortared walls in valleys speculators have not yet reached. Moorish place-names are common – the Christian shrine of Fátima bears a Muslim name and its roots are tangled in tales of Moorish princesses; it is the hand of Fátima which you see on so many door knockers. Moorish terms are still used in measures – an *almude* for enologists today signifies 25 litres, some farmers still sell their cork or their almonds by the *arrôba* (15 kg), an easy basketful.

Horticultural skills came from the Arabian Yemenites, a cultured people who made eleventh-century Silves an illustrious city ten times richer and grander than Lisbon, with sumptuous palaces and mansions, and lively bazaars. Their gifts included fine poetry and philosophy. According to the Muslim geographer, Idrisi, they 'were elegant in manner and eloquent of speech'.

In Portugal today, a nation rich in poets and with a deep respect for poetry, scholars lament that too little note is taken of the great Islamic poets like Al Mu'Tamid, who was born in Beja and became emir of Seville, his friend, Ibn Ammar from Estombar, or the mystic Al Oriani, teacher of Ibn Arabi, among the great mystic philosophers of Islam. For most Portuguese, these names are no more than echoes from the past; there is Muslim poetry enough in the grandeur of old stone. As for Silves, it is now a modest town beside a silt-choked River Arade. A cathedral enhances its dignity. Battle cries are stilled. The sounds which echo loudest from the great red sandstone walls of the Moors' castle today are the rock rhythms of summer beer festivals.

The wrenching of power, the use, abuse and passing of power, are headlined throughout history by battles, wars, sieges – the stuff of blood-stirring narrative. The shifts and movements of people, their trade and commerce, intellectual and social development, are end-lessly interwoven.

By the twelfth century Portugal was astir and Portuguese merchants were already trading with England and Italy. By the thirteenth, Portugal was bubbling with activity. King Dinis, a far-sighted, thoughtful and constructive ruler, who reigned from 1279 to 1325, brought to Portugal new faces and new ideas. His father, King Afonso III, conqueror of the last Moorish strongholds, had spent much of his youth in Paris and had married Matilde, a countess of Boulogne – from whose family his own ruling House of Burgundy was descended. Dinis had a French as well as Por-tuguese tutor. His approach was so modern and open-minded he appointed a Genoese as admiral of his fleet.

By the reign of King Fernando (1367–83), Lisbon was a booming port. The horrors of plague – the Black Death of 1348, which had reduced the Portuguese population to less than a million – were well in the past. The chronicler Fernão Lopes wrote that at times 450 ships lay in the Tejo river. Daily, more ships arrived in Lisbon with travellers and traders eager to sell and to buy, to exchange goods and ideas, to work. Among them were Milanese, Genoese, Catalans and Majorcans, many of them Jews.

The origin of the first known Jewish communities is obscure but Jews were prominent and influential in medieval Portugal. Dom Dinis appointed the chief rabbi administrator of his treasury. They were physicians, astrologers, artisans and tax collectors, an activity as unpopular then as now. They were, it was recognized, the world's finest map-makers.

The Infante Dom Henrique, son of King João I, better known as Prince Henry the Navigator, instigator of the great discoveries, in-vited to Portugal and took with him to Sagres Jehuda, the son of the greatest of all cartographers, Abraham Cresques. Cresques, a Jew from Palma in Majorca, where there was a famous map-making school, had produced in about 1375 a magnificent Catalan atlas for the king of Aragon. It was given to Charles V of France, and survives as one of the most strikingly beautiful medieval chart collections.

In the 1480s Jews in Faro, Leiria and Lisbon set up the first printing presses in Portugal; the first eleven published works, beginning in 1487 with the *Pentateuch*, printed by Samuel Gacon in Faro, were in Hebrew. Jews living in Portugal and Jews from Moorish north Africa channelled information, formally and informally, between the Christian and Muslim worlds. In 1488 King João II used two Jews, Rabbi Abraham of Beja and José de Lamego, as emissaries in his grand schemes to find the unknown land of Prester John.

But as in Spain, Portuguese Jews suffered from the over-zealous piety of Spain's Catholic rulers, Ferdinand and Isabella who, from the moment of the triumphant conquest of the Moors in Spain in 1492, were determined to expel all Jews. The name of their inquisitor-general, Torquemada, still sends shivers of horror across the centuries.

Some 60,000 Spanish Jews were allowed into Portugal on a temporary basis – in addition to 600 wealthy families who had already purchased the right to settle from Dom João II. From Salamanca came the astronomer and mathematician Abraham Zacuto; his *Almanach Perpetuum*, printed in Leiria, contained tables enabling mariners to find their latitude at sea by declination of the sun. Translated by his pupil, Joseph Vizinho, from Hebrew to Latin and tested by Vizinho on a voyage in 1485 along the coast of Guinea, they were the basis of the system used by the Portuguese for many years. When Vasco da Gama's fleet of four ships left Lisbon in July 1497 to search for the route to India, the declination tables prepared by Zacuto were among his navigational aids.

Dom João II was an imaginative and forceful king, a builder of empires, for the ordinary Portuguese – the nobles feared and disliked him – a 'perfect prince'. When he died in 1495 he was succeeded by Dom Manuel, his twenty-six-year-old cousin who was also his wife's brother. King Manuel, with an eye to the whole peninsula, had one immediate concern: to marry the Spanish rulers' eldest daughter, Isabel. There was a condition: Manuel must rid his land of Jews.

Extremely reluctant to part with a valuable section of his community, King Manuel, dubbed 'the Fortunate' for the great wealth that came to him from Portugal's discoveries, prevaricated. He ordered a few brisk baptisms, forcibly converted a number of Jews and declared that only unbaptized Jews need leave. As some 20,000 made preparations to sail a deal was struck: Jews who accepted conversion could stay for twenty years, a period later extended for a further sixteen years. Among the Jews who scorned the offer was Abraham Zacuto.

The Jews who stayed, now called New Christians, were not left in peace. Though New and Old Christians intermarried freely, the Jewish presence was not forgotten, either in Portugal or abroad. Minor intolerance was transformed by the Portuguese Inquisition – even crueller, it was said, than the Spanish – into a reign of monstrous terror. Thousands were tortured, thousands more left to rot in prison cells. Some 1,500 were garrotted or burned at the stake. An *auto-da-fé* was public entertainment. In 1573, the wilful king, Sebastião, watched in Évora, where the Holy Office had thirty-seven years earlier opened its first Portuguese branch, the burning of seventeen people. For the years between 1540 and 1765 archives hold records – incomplete – of over 36,000 cases. The Portuguese Inquisition was only suppressed in 1820.

In Portugal today there is a small active religious Jewish population. Several towns – Guarda, Bragança, Castelo de Vide, Trancoso, Viana do Castelo, Lamego – have remnants of a Jewish quarter (*Judiaria*), and synagogues. In the Templars' town of Tomar the fourteenth-century synagogue contains a museum named after Abraham Zacuto. A conspicuous heritage of the New Christians is family names meaning a plant or animal or bird. These families have long been Catholic – as are, nominally, the 'secret Jews' in Belmonte, a Beira town south of Guarda and birthplace of Pedro Álvares Cabral, discoverer, in 1500, of Brazil.

The Belmonte community, for generations married and buried by the Church, still clings to its Jewish origins. 'There are 120 of us,' a sprightly hides and skins merchant, Júlio Mendes Henriques, told a visiting cultural group one October day. 'We hope to build our own synagogue, to have weddings performed by a rabbi. The Judaic idea is alive and growing. We celebrate holy days, the *dia puro*, Yom Kippur. I am fifty-three now but, some time, I and others will be circumcised. We are preparing ourselves.' A year later, I learned that more than thirty men and boys had in fact been circumcised there by 'a Jewish specialist who came from Lisbon'.

In the eighteenth century, Belmonte had a considerable population of Jewish traders and craftsmen – Jews were never farmers. The name given to the Jewish quarter was Marrocos. New Christians came to be called Marranos – still to modern Jews a derogatory term. Jews were also called *rabinos*, a word close to rabbi. For many years people believed that Jews had tails. Perhaps the idea prevailed as much by linguistic chance as through anti-Semitism: the word for tail in Portuguese is *rabo*.

There are other intriguing footnotes to the story of the Portuguese Jews. Like many other Portuguese, they migrated to the lands discovered and colonized by the Portuguese explorers. In Brazil, Jews practised their religion openly when the Dutch occupied Recife in 1630; they departed when the Dutch did, in 1654. Some went to the Netherlands to join Portuguese Jews already there, others to New York, the first Jewish community – of twenty-three refugees – to settle there.

Of the Portuguese Jews in Amsterdam, research into the Lopes Suasso family suggests that Francisco Lopes Suasso, banker to William of Orange, also used the wealth of his father, António, to finance William's voyage from The Hague to Torbay in the Glorious Revolution of 1688, in which the Catholic James II was replaced by his Protestant daughter Mary and her Dutch husband – one of the landmarks of constitutional monarchy and political democracy in Britain.

In the Second World War, despite orders from Salazar that none of the Jews desperate to escape from Hitler's armies should be allowed to enter neutral Portugal, Aristides de Sousa Mendes, who was the Portuguese consul-general in Bordeaux in June 1940, in three days and nights issued thousands of visas to the refugees. This quiet hero, Portugal's Raoul Wallenberg, was recalled to Lisbon and dismissed. He never held public office again, and he died poor and disgraced in 1954. In 1988, democratic Portugal published a law that posthumously reinstated Sousa Mendes in the diplomatic corps. It was voted unanimously by the National Assembly, the members rising to their feet to honour him. In 1989, President Soares offered a grace-note: an apology to the Jews, on behalf of Portugal, for their persecution by the Inquisition.

The Muslims had been vanquished in battle, the Jews forcibly melded into the Christian population or deported. But each had made an indelible mark on the Portuguese corpus – which is staunchly Christian, proudly nationalistic and openly hospitable, characteristics derived in part from geographical accident, in part from kingly foresight – or caprice.

Royal marriage alliances brought new blood and new ways into the land at its highest level. Portuguese kings and queens – whether from cold ambition, genuine cultural aspiration or the casual exercise of power – brought about a cosmopolitan atmosphere that made it relatively easy for newcomers to make their mark. Portuguese students were sent abroad to be educated. Europe's greatest scholars and artists were invited to Portugal; many came and were made welcome.

The different styles, fostered and approved by Portuguese kings, made for a rich and harmonious culture. Legend, here and there, provides a touch of drama and conflict in matters of imported skills. In the building of the Santa Maria da Vitória monastery church at Batalha, the story goes, an architect who may have been Irish, David Huguet, modified the inspired plans of the master architect Afonso Domingues and twice caused the chapter-house dome to collapse. Domes never did become popular in Portugal.

Santa Maria da Vitória is a *promessa*, the splendid consequence of a vow made by King João I before the battle of Aljubarrota on 15 August 1385, in which Portugal won a decisive victory over Spanish forces. Extra pungency is added by the revelation that the architect, the aged Afonso Domingues, who successfully completed this masterpiece, was blind. At the centre of his airy and delicate founder's chapel – the Capela do Fundador – like a flower cluster in stone, is the canopied tomb of Dom João, hand in hand with his English queen, Philippa of Lancaster.

The Portuguese have brilliantly demonstrated their superb architectural and stone-cutting skills in great structures that endure across continents, the monuments of faith and of empire. Quick to absorb the best of foreign influences and to appreciate the craftsmanship commissioned by kings, they involved themselves in fine building from earliest times, their work reflecting, more than any foreigner's, the needs, moods and yearnings of the Portuguese people. The Portuguese, a strongly individualistic people, have from the beginning been absorbed by their own society. So have others: the foreigner was always here, contributing to an architectural sequence that flowed from Romanesque at the end of the eleventh century to Gothic in the twelfth century; Manueline – late Gothic – led to Renaissance, mannerist in the sixteenth century, the profusions of baroque, which included rococo and Joanine (from Dom João V, who adored it), the clear Greco-Roman lines of neo-classical in the eighteenth century and the harmonious mixtures of nineteenth-century eclectic.

Portugal was born as a kingdom under the cross of Christ and foreign monks were among its earliest creative builders; in the north, French influence appeared in architecture in the fourteenth century with the Cluny and Cistercian Orders. Dominicans served at Batalha even as work was continuing. The monastery is unfinished to this day, yet is considered to be among the greatest Gothic masterpieces of Portugal and all Europe.

Across the centuries the French presence has been wide-ranging. In the sixteenth century the Norman sculptors Nicolas (or Nicolau) Chanterène and Jean de Rouen, whom the Portuguese call João de Ruão, were the shining lights of a Coimbra school of sculpture and were credited with bringing ornamental Renaissance art to Portugal. Chanterène worked in one exquisite, monumental or notable church after another – the beautiful Jerónimos monastery at Belém in Lisbon, Coimbra, Caldas da Rainha and Évora, where he lived for several years and where the Renaissance spirit in letters was already well established. In Sintra, his alabaster altarpiece, carved in 1532 for Dom João III, has as its setting a chapel in the fantastic, golden-domed, comic-opera Pena palace, which was built by a German architect, Baron von Eschwege, between 1840 and 1849 for Ferdinand of Saxe-Coburg-Gotha, consort of Queen Maria II – Maria da Glória to her Portuguese subjects.

Enterprising Germans – from 13,000 crusaders to the bronzed sun worshippers on the Algarve and Alentejo beaches – have always headed to Portugal with enthusiasm. Germans printed some of Portugal's earliest books and sailed with the Portuguese explorers. German hired soldiers died among the Portuguese in their battles;

the German military genius, General von Schomberg, came to Portugal in 1660 to train the Portuguese to win them. The Marquis of Pombal appointed a German, Count von Schaumburg Lippe, to command the army. Germans entered commerce and studied nature. Alfredo Keil (1854–1907), of German parents, artist and musician, composed the song that became the national anthem.

The German-born architect, Johann Ludwig, trained in Italy and, as João Ludovice, worked for the Jesuits in Lisbon. He designed the grandiose monastery-palace of Mafra for King João V. Built between 1717 and 1735, the vast rectangular block, celebrating – at horrendous cost – the birth of a child to João's Austrian queen, required a work-force that at one period was a mighty army of 45,000 craftsmen, stonemasons and labourers. The child, a girl, grew up to become queen of Spain. The first-born son died; the surviving heir, José, born in 1714, preferred Belém, riding, the opera. The huge monastery is heavily overpowering, with overtones, in a minor key, of Spain's Escorial – indeed it is music rather than its magnificent baroque library that alleviates the atmosphere of this extravagant monument to a king's glory. As well as occasional orchestral concerts, a resounding carillon rings out at times from Mafra's great bells. The bell-ringer is often Francisco Gato, an airline pilot who learned to play the bells at his father's knee. Considerable strength is needed – one well-known *carilhonista* used to strip down to shorts and used thick leather gloves to protect his hammering hands. The bells came from a foundry near Brussels, the cost of a single carillon of fifty bells a fortune in gold. 'So cheap?' Dom João V allegedly exclaimed. 'I'll take two.'

Pink, pale and exquisite, the rococo palace at Queluz is perfumed femininity to Mafra's stern monkishness. Built by the Portuguese architect Mateus Vicente de Oliveira and completed in 1752, it was later extended by a French artist, Jean-Baptiste Robillon, who also created the formal gardens. The palace – Portugal's charming miniature Versailles – was the favourite residence of King João VI.

But even Mafra's Ludwig/Ludovice had his lighter side, which can be seen in the graceful *palacete*, now the Solar do Vinho do Porto, the Lisbon home of the Oporto-based Port Wine Institute.

*

Portugal's justifiable pride in its rich culture encompasses the foreign contribution as much as national art. Now and again a voice arises critical of Portugal's leaning towards European culture – imported ideas and customs have corrupted Portugal, traditionalist voices thunder. Others, modern and broadly humanist, argue that the links should be stronger; in the seventeenth and eighteenth centuries they would have been sneered at as being *estrangeirados* ('foreignized'). Yet foreign links were there from long before and, after all, it is the art itself that matters. Was Boitac, the architect, French? His origin remains a mystery. What is important is that his work – at the Jerónimos monastery and elsewhere – is glorious in style and elegant in proportion.

As well as contributing to Portugal's national culture, foreign architects have also had a hand in its defence: the system of fortification thought out by the seventeenth-century military engineer, Sébastien Le Prestre de Vauban, was promptly incorporated by the Portuguese into some of their own ancient forts and castles. To the north and east the fortifications at Valença and Almeida are as daunting as the day they were completed; Marvão, on its eastern heights looking down on Spain, is dramatically safeguarded by Vaubanesque ramparts.

A fine French artist who worked in Portugal was Jean Pillement (1728–1808). His decorative painting is to be seen in Oporto's Soares dos Reis Museum; in panels set into the backs of chairs now in Lisbon's Ajuda Palace, but once aboard the ship which carried Dona Maria I and the Prince Regent, Dom João, to exile in Brazil in 1807 in the face of the French advance; and in Sintra *quintas* (manor-houses). On the walls of the Hotel Palácio dos Seteais in Sintra are paintings in the style of Pillement, including, with wonderful incongruity, the walls of the TV room. Two of Pillement's paintings, oil on canvas, record the drama of rescue and recovery in 1786, after being wrecked off Peniche, of the Spanish treasure-bearing warship, the *San Pedro de Alcântara*. In the 1980s a French marine archaeologist, Jean-Yves Blot, with his Portuguese wife, Maria Luísa, headed an international team of experts in research for Portugal's National Museum of Archaeology and Ethnology.

France, in its enthusiasm for Portugal, has bestowed more than art and expertise. One French princess, Marie-Françoise of Savoy – Maria Francisca to the Portuguese – married two successive Portuguese kings: poor incapable Dom Afonso VI in 1666 and, after this marriage was annulled and the king dethroned in 1667, his brother Dom Pedro II. French interests were patently paramount again when Napoleon, provoked by Portuguese support of the English at the beginning of the nineteenth century, ordered some 24,000 French troops under the command of General Andôche Junot to invade. For the French, in what became the Peninsular War, the experience was profitless: a miserable defeat by Portugal's English ally, Sir Arthur Wellesley, later the Duke of Wellington, and subsequent humiliations. The Portuguese, for their part, despite an alliance dating to 1373, were less than pleased to be seen as dependent on the English.

For subsequent French visitors, the past was put aside. Portugal, after all, offered an intriguing culture and great natural beauty. Charles Bonnet explored enthusiastically. A civil engineer specializing in geology, he produced in 1850 a geological map of the Algarve, which laid the foundations for experts today. He fell in love with Loulé, where he settled in 1860 and died in 1867. Valéry Larbaud considered Lisbon's riverside Terreiro do Paço – now the Praça do Comércio, but still often called by its former name – '*la plus belle place d'Europe*'. Simone Weil, radical and mystic, travelling with her parents in 1935, was enthralled with the sight of devout fisherfolk in a religious procession.

For others in the thirties, their palate was paramount: French cuisine was on offer, along with Portugal's distinctive regional cooking. French chefs ruled the kitchens of leading restaurants, including Lisbon's most renowned and most gorgeously decorated restaurant, Tavares Rico, the haunt for many years of the literary world. Portugal's own master chef, João Ribeiro, who for twenty-five years from 1936 was head chef in the classic Aviz Hotel (now closed), trained in the French tradition.

A meal is ephemeral, too quickly a fading memory. Travellers come and go. Even the horror of war fades. The best known of all French visitors to Portugal left landmarks of engineering construction. Before he achieved world fame with his Paris tower,

Alexandre-Gustave Eiffel built six laced metal bridges in northern Portugal. The first, in 1876–7, an elegant arched railway bridge spanning the River Douro in Oporto, was named after the queen, Dona Maria Pia, and was still in use well over a hundred years later. In Lisbon's Baixa, linking the central city area to the Carmo convent ruins and the neighbourhood above, is Eiffel's *elevador*, a metal passenger lift like a grey turret, all French charm and *folie*.

Eiffel plainly liked variety – at an early stage he was involved in the design of the Statue of Liberty. His skills are admired in Angola. His metalwork supports the roof and adorns the galleries of the Sala de Portugal, a large hall in Lisbon's Sociedade de Geografia. His most unlikely project is probably Portugal's most interesting garage, the Auto Palace in Lisbon's Rua Alexandre Herculano.

The Portuguese have long been accustomed to foreign contact. A few study it. At the Sorbonne University, Dr José Saldanha studied relations between Portugal and France. 'For France, Portugal, living back to back with Spain, is the Atlantic frontier of Europe. Arranged marriages across the centuries ensured a diplomatic link. Portugal traded with England but stayed linked to France mainly through culture. So close was this in the nineteenth century that, for instance, Portuguese literary works were advertised in France.' At times, even today, Portuguese specialists write in French – Dom Diogo de Bragança, a descendant of the last royal line, wrote a treatise in the 1980s in French, for a French publisher, on equestrian dressage. Another link stretches across sea and space to the French satellite tracking station on the remote Açores island of Flores.

Italians, too, came eagerly to Portugal. Before the Portuguese made their discoveries across the oceans of the world, Genoa, and then Venice, were Europe's mercantile capitals. A Genoese community existed in Lisbon in the twelfth century. Later, as the Portuguese were expanding their interests along the African coast, Genoese sailors seemed to be everywhere. Assuming he was Genoa-born, a matter of some dispute, one of them was Cristóvão Colombo, better known as Christopher Columbus – a seaman, scholars believe, in the Portuguese fleet commanded by Diogo de Azambuja which voyaged to Mina (now in Ghana) in 1481.

Another notable Italian visitor was Amerigo Vespucci, from a distinguished family in Florence; his name is everlastingly linked to the discovery of America. Although, as a geographer, he lived and worked in Spain, he was admired in Portugal and, in 1501, he sailed under the Portuguese flag.

Yet another Italian, a young Venetian, Alvise Cadamosto, served Prince Henry the Navigator. He undertook a commercial voyage aboard a caravel with a Portuguese sailing-master that sailed from Sagres in March 1455. Portuguese explorers had already charted the route – to Madeira, the Canary Islands of Tenerife and Gomera (still inhabited by the naked, painted, aboriginal Guanche cave-dwellers of mysterious origin) and on to the African coast. His value to Portugal and posterity is in the vivid record he kept of the voyage and of the sexual habits and strange ways of the peoples he encountered.

Later, in 1519, when the Portuguese navigator, Fernão de Maga-lhães, or Magellan, set sail – under Spanish auspices – on the first circumnavigation of the world, it was an observant Italian, Antonio Pigafetta, who kept a detailed journal of the long and harrowing voyage. A long connection with Rome and its popes ensured close contact between Portugal and Italy – Italians were even involved in the design of Lisbon's cool and lovely gardens. Perhaps it was as much Portugal's congenial environment as its neutral status in the Second World War that led Italy's last king, Umberto, to seek exile close to Lisbon after his forty-six-day rule ended sharply in 1946. He lived with his family in a pink-walled mansion in Cascais, Vila d'Itália, for thirty-six years, popular doyen of several dispossessed European royals for whom, as their crowns gathered cobwebs, Portugal was a sunny sanctuary.

Portuguese architects took inspiration from Italian Renaissance, baroque and neo-classical art, blending and contrasting them with Gothic and with Portugal's own distinctive Manueline, or late Gothic, style, which lavishly encompasses sea-related themes. The style was borrowed and revamped by Luigi Manini when, in the late nineteenth century, he designed the Buçaco Palace, now a hotel, for the royal family. Manini, a scene-painter in Lisbon's bewitchingly splendid São Carlos opera house, all curl and swirl and many-layered boxes, was clearly used to romantic, and florid, set pieces.

Of sterner stuff was Filippo (or Felipe) Terzi, an Italian from Bologna brought to Portugal by the Spanish king, King Philip II, after his invasion of Portugal in 1580. Portugal's rage over its brief loss of independence has barely dimmed after four centuries, but nevertheless Terzi's work at São Roque and São Vicente de Fora in Lisbon, Setúbal castle, and in Coimbra and Tomar, is profoundly admired.

But of all the Italian artists and architects who came to Portugal one captivating Tuscan figure stands out: Niccolò – or Nicolau – Nasoni, who came to live in Oporto in 1725 at the age of thirty-four and died there in 1773. In his years in Portugal he left his exuberant mark upon the land: in Oporto he created two beautiful palaces – one now the Museum of Ethnography and History, the other, Freixo, on the banks of the Douro. He designed the Clérigos church with its tall tower – the tallest in the land – and certainly inspired the odd belfry that juts like a feather on a bonnet from the otherwise unremarkable city hall. His light-hearted flourishes add grace and charm to this ancient, grey, river-misted city on the steep slopes of the Douro.

Nasoni also designed the *solar* – manor-house – of Mateus, close to Vila Real. In one room is displayed the masterwork of José Maria de Sousa Botelho, diplomat and grandson of the first owner of this lovely house: a connoisseur's edition of *Os Lusíadas* by the epic poet Luis de Camões, the greatest literary work in the Portuguese language. Two of the illustrators, among the leading French artists of the time, were François Gérard and Évariste Fragonard. Nasoni's baroque building has the greater visibility: the Mateus mansion appears on the label of the cleverly marketed, extensively exported *rosé* wine, with which it has otherwise no connection.

Of the many excellent wines in Portugal only one, port, has direct foreign antecedents, grape-variety apart. The English association with port is a long and colourful story. A 1703 treaty between Portugal and England gave Portugal priority in buying English wool; England would buy Portugal's best wine. The wines, from the mountainous upper reaches of the River Douro, were dry and harsh to British palates. In 1676, so the story goes, two young wine shippers from Liverpool, attempting to stabilize the wine for transport to England, added brandy – and created port.

English port-wine buyers explored the Douro valley with the colonial fervour applied to darkest Africa. A dedicated pioneer, Joseph James Forrester, in 1855 was made a baron for his determined fight to preserve the quality of the wine. He had spent a dozen or more years mapping the river and the wine district. It was a sad irony, therefore, when in May 1861 he was drowned in the fearsome rapids of the Douro before it was dammed – dragged down, it was said, by the weight of a purse of gold coins at his belt. The author Camilo Castelo Branco, renowned for his coruscating pen, unkindly chose to view Forrester's death as the river's vengeance and was far more distressed to learn that, though Dona António Adelaide Ferreira, founder of the port-wine house of Ferreira, had survived the disaster of an overturned boat, a cook, Gertrudes Engrácia, 'a treasure of culinary joys', had been engulfed.

For a time, the English, from Oporto on the north bank near the Douro's mouth and from their lodges at Vila Nova de Gaia opposite, dominated the port-wine trade. Fierce eighteenth-century competition mellowed to a cordial, dynastic, tradition-bound – but efficient – association of shippers with names like Taylor, Croft, Cockburn, Symington and Graham. Dutch and German houses made port, too – Kopke was founded in 1638 by Nicolau Kopke from Hamburg, who arrived in Portugal as consul-general to the Hanseatic League – but for a long time were coldly viewed as outsiders.

Portuguese firms like Ferreira and Cálem joined this eminent company, matching them for quality and prestige. Today's port, a fortified wine rich in colour, aroma and taste, is a distinguished product far from its rough beginnings. Several of the wine-tasters – on whose skills fortunes depend – are Australian.

English and Portuguese these days companionably don the robes and share the duties of a port-wine brotherhood, the Confraria do Vinho do Porto, established in 1983 primarily through the efforts of Robin Reid of Croft's. Even the once exclusive Britishness of the weekly luncheons in the British Association's granite Factory House – constructed by British consul John Whitehead to his own design between 1786 and 1790 – has been relaxed in recent times as Portuguese have been appointed directors in British houses.

Additionally, takeovers by conglomerates, national and international, have broken the pattern.

Port is still sometimes called the Englishman's wine and ordinary Englishmen, with an appreciation of a fine tawny and noble vintages, can become misty-eyed over port's luscious body and richly developed bouquet. France, as it happens, buys more port, mainly ruby, than the English and shippers in the late 1980s noted with satisfaction a growing American interest in the top-quality range.

At Taylor, Fladgate & Yeatman, founded in 1692, it is recalled that there was an American partner, Joseph Camo, in the company at a time when Napoleon's army was attacking Oporto. As a neutral, he was able to protect at least some of Taylor's precious stock. Portwine historian Charles Sellers described him as 'a typical American, full of energy, fertile in resource and never wanting in pluck'. He was the only American ever to have worked in port in Oporto.

Americans too have close ties to Portugal. American engineers designed the impressive bridge across the Tagus at Lisbon completed in 1966. At 2,277.64 m (7,473 ft), it was for some time the longest suspension bridge in Europe. Today banks with American names compete in an open market. Americans, with an air-force base in the Açores and more than a hundred companies operating across the land, were investing in the late 1980s in chemical and pharmaceutical products, agriculture and horticulture, glass and ceramics, in real estate – land and buildings - in automobile plants and parts and services, in advertising, computers and high technology, soft drinks and fast food. American business noted what its ambassador to Portugal called (in 1988) a 'new dynamism' – high economic growth, a rising per capita income, declining unemployment and falling inflation. In that year alone, American direct investment in Portugal was $130m. In 1990 the United States President George Bush complimented Portugal on its 'tremendous progress in overthrowing a dictatorship, consolidating democracy . . . standing as an inspiration and an example to Eastern European countries'. Relations were better than ever. Bankers paid smiling visits – David Rothschild one of them. John Kenneth Galbraith, in Portugal for a seminar, cheerfully discussed economic theory with a Portuguese economics professor of different views.

American musicians, grand old names in entertainment like Ray Charles, Ornette Coleman, Tony Bennett, Nina Simone, Tina Turner, are booked by the Estoril Casino and commercial organizers. (The Portuguese, not at all partisan, also invite dancers from Leningrad and Cuba.) Screen stars come to Portuguese film festivals – Robert Mitchum, in his seventies, astonishing Portuguese film fans with his indifference to the cinematic art. Sports stars come, including the glamorous giants of basketball, the Harlem Globetrotters. Their jolly encounters with eager Portuguese basketball players confirm that basketball is not yet one of Portugal's prime sporting accomplishments. But, as the Portuguese learned centuries ago, expertise can be bought, and rangy black Americans come on contract to play for Portuguese teams.

American tourists fly into Portugal at the rate of some 200,000 a year; through emigration, many have Portuguese family links. And many elderly Americans, responding to the beauty of the country, the sense of security it offers and the natural courtesy of most Portuguese, have retired here.

The English never left. Clinging purposefully to their essential Englishness, whole colonies grew old, died and were buried 'in some corner of a foreign field that is for ever England'. In Lisbon, the English cemetery is in Estrela, overlooked by the British Hospital in what one travel book describes as 'the ideal situation'.

Some Oporto families of English origin can look back on six generations in Portugal. Many of them still preserve, along with their Douro *quintas*, traditional ways and traditional hospitality. Through the centuries, the English came in a virtual non-stop stream. Along with the textile-makers and glass-makers and pioneering wine merchants, writers and poets came to rest and rhapsodize – wealthy William Beckford, Robert Southey, the inimitable Lord Byron, Sacheverell Sitwell (on whose death, in 1988, at ninety, arose comment on his taste for drinking *rosé* in winter), pale and suffering Henry Fielding, who lasted two months, died on 8 October 1754, and lies somewhere in the Estrela cemetery. A monument put up long after his death appalled Dorothy Quillinan, Wordsworth's daughter, who saw it in 1846 – 'a huge ungainly thing ... on a spot selected by *guess*. The bones it covers may possibly have belonged to an idiot.'

Dorothy Quillinan remarked, as have other travellers, on the large numbers of dogs. How incredulous she would be at the growing interest in national breeds like the big, handsome Serra da Estrela and Rafeiro do Alentejo, the hunting pointer-like Perdigueiro and the fishermen's one-time hard-working water-dog, the broad-footed Cão d'Água, now an aristocratic domestic pet. The Princess Rattazzi, pithily observant diarist of nineteenth-century Portugal, noticed too the large number of cats – 'indispensable furniture in Portuguese homes', as they still are. A territorial black cat I knew, a beguiling, golden-eyed mix of wild and affectionate, had an instant selective response to the sound of cracking almonds.

Sir Richard Fanshawe, British ambassador to Portugal in 1662, thought Lisbon 'with the river the goodliest situation that I ever saw'. Lord Tyrawley, ambassador from 1724 to 1741, took to Portugal so wholeheartedly he went home with three 'wives' and fourteen illegitimate children. All the romantics adored Sintra, the cool and pretty hill town near Lisbon; Sintra was close and an easy journey. It is only fairly recently that the hinterland has become accessible; despite the national *pousadas* (state-owned hotels), the growing numbers of small hotels (*estalagens* and *residenciais*) and the extremely agreeable manor-houses open to guests under the *Turismo de habitação* scheme, most visitors stay in cities and resorts. The Douro only thirty years ago was a river of dangerous rapids. In the Alentejo of 1835 George Borrow, zealous missionary and sharp-eyed writer, encountered a goatherd carrying wolf-cubs. That this was the stuff of fairy-tales was not unnoticed by the great Danish story-teller, Hans Christian Andersen, who journeyed here in 1866.

Today the heaths and forests of the broad Alentejo have been tamed and cultivated. Wild creatures are still hunted, but alongside the Portuguese farmers there are now farmers and horticulturalists from England, Germany, Holland and Scandinavia. In Beja, the German Air Force operates an 800-hectare training base. South of Beja the British, whose investment in Portugal in the late 1980s doubled and redoubled, were deep in the Neves Corvo copper mines, the richest in Europe. Foreigners are investing in the land, in commerce, in tourism, in the future of Portugal – in 1990 at new record-breaking levels. The American giants searched for oil in vain for years. A Finnish multinational is still prospecting.

New business is coming from within the EEC and outside it – Norwegians, among others, constructed a well-planned tourist development in the Algarve and started a salmon-breeding project to the north. Millionaires' yachts sail in summer to Portugal. Stavros Niarchos and Gianni Agnelli came here to enjoy the sun and sniff the breeze; the Italian magnate Carlos de Benedetti launched a holding company. The Japanese, whose entire overseas trade Portugal dominated in the sixteenth century, have purchased grandly eccentric *quintas* in Sintra. A Chinese group based in Macau decided to build a textiles factory. Mighty supermarkets – hypermarkets – appeared on city outskirts; one of the wealthiest investors was a Portuguese emigrant who had made it rich in Brazil. In 1988, when Marks & Spencer opened its first franchised Lisbon store, Portugal's growth rate was put at 152 per cent a year, 16 million visitors crossed the borders and well over 100,000 foreigners were resident in Portugal. (By 1990 foreign residents numbered around 170,000.) It did not escape the attention of most that Portugal had the lowest wages and the lowest cost of living in Europe.

Polished jetsetters with expensive tans and designer gear come to see and be seen. Hitch-hikers come too, free of responsibility and short on cash. To the Portuguese they are *turismo de pé descalço* 'barefoot tourists', but no unkindness is intended, except by meaner spirits or a few short-sighted officials. For all too many *camponeses* (country people) poverty is no disgrace but a natural condition.

Nobody can quote a precise figure for foreign residents; the authorities sternly regard perhaps 60,000 of them as illegal. But the Portuguese have always enjoyed dialogue, and admired things and people from outside. Eça de Queiroz, an eloquent nineteenth-century novelist, gently mocked the wealthy Jacinto for sweating blood over his studies on to fine quality imported paper and satirizes the desire for fine foreign possessions. Never having had a large enough population to make cultural isolation practicable or appealing – Henry the Navigator, in the early fifteenth century, invited Flemings to settle in the Açores islands – the Portuguese nearly always welcome the foreigner with cordiality. Prince Henry himself brought to his court Jews and Muslims, Catalans, Genoese and Venetians, Scandinavians and Germans and, as his captains made progress, African tribesmen. They were the Algarve's first international community.

For the foreigner who comes to contribute, to profit or for heedless pleasure, Portugal's appeal stays strong. A new orchestra formed in 1988, the Nova Filarmonia Portuguesa, attracted American, English, Czech, Bulgarian, Hungarian as well as Portuguese musicians; together, they made good music. Their backers and sponsors, too – their *fundadores, incentivadores, promotores, dinamizadores* – were thoroughly international. The philanthropist Calouste Gulbenkian, whose oil wealth funded a superb museum, a symphony orchestra, dance and choral companies and numerous cultural, social and educational enterprises of inestimable value to Portugal, was an Armenian. In football, Portugal's heroes include Brazilians – around eighty played in first-division teams in the 1990 season; trainers, at times, are Swedish and English.

Most English people and other foreigners head for the alluring Algarve, where many in recent years have bought holiday homes. Here are *charcuteries, pâtisseries*, tasty English pies and German-baked bread. Scandinavians run a long-established plant nursery. At the São Lourenço cultural centre the directors, a German and his French wife, relaxedly present exhibitions of good art and informal concerts.

There are doctors, dentists, medical specialists, solicitors, accountants and estate agents of many nationalities. Other foreigners have found a niche as pool cleaners or plumbers. Two Englishwomen became chimney sweeps. An imaginative English couple offered a travelling magic show. An English company organizes funerals. Muslims, too, are back in the land they love. A Saudi Arabian prince, cousin to the king, eager to invest in Portugal, began with a luxury hotel; other Arab investors followed.

Life at times borders on the frenetic. Noise, heat, traffic, crowds press on the nerves. Over-strained services – water, electricity, telephones – cannot always cope. But for most holiday-makers the pleasures of the Algarve match or exceed expectations and most resident foreigners view the drawbacks as the price they pay for sunshine; life is fun – and much easier than in their home country. And, away from the brasher resorts, away from busy roads and road works, building sites, expanding towns, the cacophonous machinery of modern times, Portugal retains a sense of privacy, tranquillity and space. Across the country old ways, customs and tastes endure. Witches and superstition survive, oxen still haul crescent-shaped fishing boats from the sea and give their docile strength to pulling gnarled wooden ploughs. The old and the outdated, the homespun, the poor, are soothingly picturesque yet also a true reflection of much of Portuguese life.

The Portuguese face change and the future with some doubts but considerable dignity. For themselves and their visitors they preserve, with increasing care, their *patrimônio* (heritage): imposing castles and elegiac churches, art treasures in paintings and tiles and stone, traditions in architecture, folk *festas*, music and drama – which often cost nothing, or not much, to see.

To holiday-makers, Portugal offers a rich and tangible past as well as sunshine and long, clean, seductive beaches. Many visitors cheerfully bypass culture to bask beside their hotel pool or on the uncrowded beaches, or play golf, but the Portuguese legacy extends to everyone in the daily spectacle of street and market-place, in generous food and good wine, in the morals and manners of the Portuguese.

They do not always have the graces of the salon – there are men who spit, fishwives who scream, motor cyclists who display macho with deafening resonance. But then the Portuguese might balk at foreigners' quirks, or their clubbiness, or the way foreigners have moved, and are moving, smoothly into what was once called trade and commerce and is now the economy; they do not like the tragic intrusion of foreign-peddled drugs, or of foreigners who walk the streets mindlessly displaying bare flesh, who impose on livelihood, culture, and the ways and values of the land. In the end it is as it always was, a bargain – mutual need and stimulation, compliments paid and returned. The large majority of Portuguese are open-hearted, easy-going and tolerant. They possess an independence of spirit, a natural courtesy, a genuine hospitality and kindliness in which fortunate strangers are, for the most part, and as ever, warmly enfolded. Portugal's appeal for the foreigner endures.

2 From the end of the world

There was a time when Portugal was the boldest and most formidable nation on earth. For a century and a half, from the mid fifteenth to the late sixteenth century, Portugal was the supreme power across the oceans of the earth. Its wealth, from its dominions and from monopolies across the globe, was dazzling, the grandiose effect of the grandest of causes: discovery.

The Portuguese were the first Europeans to open the way into the Atlantic, to sail down western Africa, to cross the Equator, to round the Cape of Good Hope, to reach India by sea from the west. They were the first westerners in Ceylon, Sumatra, Malacca, Timor and the spice islands of the Moluccas, the first Europeans to trade with China and Japan, and to see Australia, more than two hundred years before Captain Cook. To the west, the first to set a foot in south America, they discovered Brazil.

A Portuguese, Fernão de Magalhães – Ferdinand Magellan – ignored the dissuasions of the Portuguese ambassador of the day and led the first, Spanish-sponsored, circumnavigation of the globe between 1519 and 1522, though regrettably he did not survive it. Earlier, other Portuguese had explored the north Atlantic. Columbus, a careful record-keeper, alludes to a voyage from the Açores in about 1450, by Diogo de Teive and his son, João. It is thought that they discovered the Newfoundland Grand Banks whose icy waters gave the Portuguese the *bacalhau* (cod) they love so much, still called *o fiel amigo* (the faithful friend).

Labrador – named after João Fernandes, a farmer, or *lavrador*, from the Açores islands – Newfoundland and Greenland all saw Portuguese mariners under their own, the Spanish or the English flag, at the beginning of the sixteenth century; João Fernandes, the

Portuguese believe, also sailed with the Genoese John Cabot, in his 1497 voyage under the patronage of Henry VII of England. The famous 1502 Cantino map shows that the Portuguese had already found Florida. In 1525, sailing like Magellan under the Spanish flag, the Portuguese captain Estêvão Gomes explored the east American coast down to Chesapeake Bay; in 1542, João Rodrigues Cabrilho was charting the coast of California.

'God gave the Portuguese a small country as cradle but all the world as their grave,' observed the eloquent seventeenth-century Jesuit, Padre António Vieira, himself a revered Portuguese. The Portuguese are proud of the achievements of any Portuguese any-where and, earlier than anyone, they were everywhere. And, their anguish fed by frustration, they grieve still for explorers who were swallowed by the sea and neglected by history.

In the ranks of Portuguese heroes are the noble João Vaz Corte Real, governor in the 1470s of Terceira island in the Açores, and his two sons, Gaspar and Miguel Corte Real. All three, from as early as 1472, when João Corte Real returned to the islands from the 'Terras de Bacalhau', explored the north American coast. In 1500 Gaspar claimed a considerable part of it for the king of Portugal. Gaspar embarked on a further voyage in the spring of 1501 but disappeared without trace. His brother, Miguel, sailed out of Lisbon in May 1502 to look for him.

The years passed. Miguel, like his brother, disappeared. His name was discovered, carved with the arms of Portugal and a date – 1511 – on a great boulder called the Dighton Rock at the mouth of the Taunton river, near Boston, Massachusetts. Many Por-tuguese view the rock as evidence that Miguel Corte Real was marooned for ten years on the north American mainland. But if he was the first European in America there was neither celebration nor honours; his, like countless others, was a voyage without return.

'The discovery of America and that of a passage to the East Indies by the Cape of Good Hope are the two greatest and most important events recorded in the history of mankind,' declared Adam Smith, the political economist. To the Portuguese, the tri-umph of their vast maritime accomplishments is shadowed by the

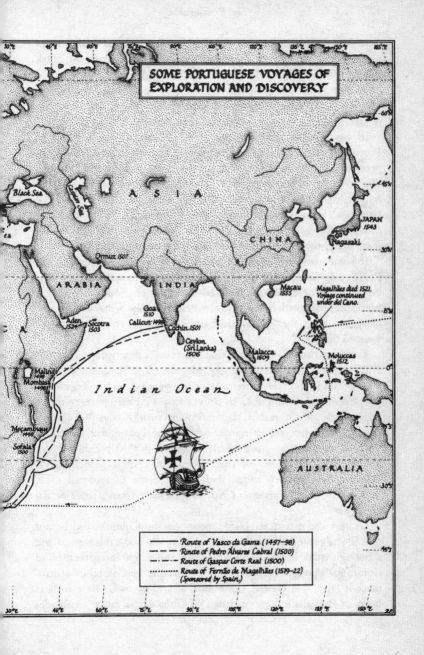

SOME PORTUGUESE VOYAGES OF EXPLORATION AND DISCOVERY

Black Sea

Caspian Sea

A S I A

ARABIA

CHINA

JAPAN 1543

Nagasaki

Ormuz 1507

INDIA

Macau 1555

Magalhães died 1521.
Voyage continued
under del Cano.

Aden 1524
Socotra 1503

Goa 1510

Calicut 1498

Cochin 1501

Ceylon
(Sri Lanka)
1506

Malacca 1509

Moluccas 1512

Malindi 1498
Mombasa 1498

Indian Ocean

Moçambique 1498

Sofala 1500

AUSTRALIA

Route of Vasco da Gama (1497–98)
Route of Pedro Álvares Cabral (1500)
Route of Gaspar Corte Real (1500)
Route of Fernão de Magalhães (1519–22)
(Sponsored by Spain)

obscurity of their westward voyages and the singular achievement of Columbus. At times there are wistful echoes, even, of Mark Twain who joked: 'It was wonderful to find America, but it would have been more wonderful to miss it.' (He once visited the Açores and found the islands backward and boring. There was nowhere, in fact, he thought more wonderful than America.)

In his lifetime and for ever after Columbus was a thorn in Portuguese flesh. There are Portuguese historians who, while appreciating the incalculable results of his epoch-making 1492 voyage, like it to be remembered that Columbus learned his seamanship largely from the Portuguese, that he went no further than the Caribbean in his greatest voyage and, to his death, believed he had touched the golden shores of India. Portuguese navigators, for their part, knew where they were heading – and got there.

If some scoff at Columbus, there are also hints of regret. The Portuguese king, João II, for all that Columbus was married to a good Portuguese woman, disliked his ambition, found his project preposterous, heeded his court mathematicians who – rightly – disagreed with the figures, and turned him down. The honours went to Spain.

But from the world of academe has come a new view on the old saga – that Columbus, generally considered to be Genoese-born, was Portuguese. The Florentine cosmographer Paolo Toscanelli, who encouraged Columbus to believe in a westward passage to the Indies, thought Columbus, then living in Portugal, was Portuguese. Several solid researchers agree. And as the Portuguese began, in 1988, a twelve-year programme celebrating the five hundredth anniversary of the era of discoveries, an earnest academic, Dr Mascarenhas Barreto, added fuel to the flame of national pride with his book, *O Português Cristóvão Colombo Agente Secreto do Rei Dom João II*.

Despite the provocative title, pronouncing Columbus to be not only Portuguese but a spy for King João, the book is a serious and thorough work based on long research and a new interpretation of Columbus's personal cipher. Genoa's claim to be Columbus's birthplace is false, it is argued. Columbus, according to Dr Barreto, was born in the small Alentejo town of Cuba as Salvador Fernandes

Zarco, an illegitimate son of the Infante Dom Fernando, who was the nephew and heir of Dom Henrique – Henry the Navigator. And as the maternal side of the family was descended from New Christians, this means that Columbus, the red-headed mystic, would be Jewish, too.

Intriguing theories to one side, all seafaring nations recognized Portugal's skills of seamanship. Among voyagers from other lands eager to learn from Portuguese experience was Francis Drake. Rounding the globe in his *Golden Hind* in 1577–80, he enlisted the Portuguese Nuno da Silva as pilot.

On land and river as well as by sea the Portuguese were vigorous explorers. Diogo Cão, who discovered the Zaïre river in 1482 and planted the first of several claim-staking stone pillars, carried back to Portugal with him four black hostages who had the good fortune to be treated as ambassadors instead of slaves. Taken back on a subsequent voyage, they impressed the Bakongo with their *fidalgo* (grandee's) clothes, their Portuguese speech and, no doubt, their Christian faith.

Pêro da Covilhã was a young Portuguese fluent in Arabic and with a gift for languages. Sent east in 1487, by King João II to find the source of the rich trade in spices, he travelled first to Rhodes, and then to Alexandria in Egypt. Disguised as a Muslim, he was soon noting the cinnamon, pepper and cloves, and the fleets of traders and merchants, in Aden, Cannanore, Calicut and Goa in south-west India, Ormuz at the entrance of the Persian Gulf, and Sofala, an important port in what is now Moçambique. There he learned of the great island of Madagascar, which the Moors called the 'Island of the Moon'.

Back in Cairo after three years of journeying, his report made to the king through João's Jewish emissaries, he acted as guide for one of them – the Rabbi Abraham – as far as Aden and Ormuz, and then sailed to Jedda. Confident that his disguise remained impenetrable, he daringly visited those most sacred of Muslim cities, Mecca and Medina. But Afonso de Paiva, who had travelled with him as far as Aden, had died somewhere in Africa in the attempt to track down the mysterious Christian emperor, Preste-João, or Prester John. Covilhã's orders were to complete that mission, so the intrepid traveller loyally made his way to the mountainous territory of the fabled emperor, pausing only at the St Catherine monastery in Sinai for a Christian blessing.

Covilhã was the first European to see Ethiopia. He was warmly received by the emperor, not Prester John but Eskander, and well liked. But, as with many other adventurous foreigners later, he was forbidden to leave. His extraordinary travels came to an end, though not, it appears, his gift to adapt and beguile. Covilhã married an Ethiopian woman, settled into family life, and was still alive and well thirty years later, according to another hardy traveller, Padre Francisco Álvares, a priest from Coimbra on another harrowing diplomatic mission to the daunting land of the Christian emperor in Africa.

Portuguese explorers travelled Africa extensively. From 1505 onwards Portuguese were establishing themselves in south-eastern and central Africa; Gaspar da Veiga explored the Zambezi river in 1530; Lake Tana, Africa's highest lake and source of the Blue Nile, was first reached by Gaspar Pais in 1603; another Pais, Pêro, was the first foreigner to see the Blue Nile falls in 1618. Nearly two hundred years before Livingstone, a Jesuit priest, Padre Jerónimo Lobo, crossed Africa, virtually unnoticed. Colonial fervour in nineteenth-century Africa was the setting for explorations as arduous and thrilling to the Portuguese as those of Livingstone and Henry Morton Stanley, whose crossing of the continent from the east, completed in 1877, inspired Alexandre da Rocha Serpa Pinto, a major in the Portuguese army, to make a crossing from the west. A separate and slower exploration made by two naval colleagues, Hermenegildo Brito Capelo and Roberto Ivens, from the Angola coast to Moçambique across terrain where no European had ventured before, received considerable scientific acclaim.

These men are heroic figures to the Portuguese, their prowess recorded in the history books, their names remembered on patterned street tiles in every town and city across the land. Women, of course, were there, too – at times, like Antónia Rodrigues from Aveiro, say the chroniclers, donning men's clothes to fight in battle. And if the praises for the world-shattering voyages of Bartolomeu Dias round the cape of Africa and of Vasco da Gama across the Indian Ocean to India sound loudest in the hymning of the Portuguese discoverers, there were many more whose achievements were significant.

'The noble island of Cipangu' – Japan – was described by Marco Polo, illustrious thirteenth-century Venetian traveller, in the massively influential report of his travels which he called *Description of the World*. It was this book, first printed in 1483, that inspired Columbus, who had a copy of his own, to his 'Enterprise of the Indies' and his dreams of discovering Cipangu. But even Marco Polo never saw Japan and his information on the sea distance from Cathay (China) to Cipangu was wrong. From Europe, it was the Portuguese who, venturing east from India, got there first and soon dominated its trade.

In India, Bengal was visited by Portuguese in 1576, and the area was extensively explored after 1628 by an Augustine priest, Sebastião Manrique. From India missionaries travelled to China – through Tibet. A Portuguese priest, Padre António de Andrade, was the first European to set eyes on Lhasa, Tibet's remote and impressive capital, in 1624. Another priest, Bento de Góis, who died in China in 1602, had crossed the Himalayas to get there.

'The lesson of history teaches us to have pride in the past and modesty in the present,' sighs Armando Martins Janeira, a Portuguese diplomat who adored the Orient. Former glories cannot hide the mediocrity of today, he sadly observed, lamenting that, in the late 1980s, Portugal was the only European country in which there was no serious study of the culture of the Orient – where, up to the eighteenth century, Portuguese remained the *lingua franca*.

As Portugal looks back on its extraordinary achievements, its celebrations are tinged with yearning and a somewhat querulous frustration. How could this small nation have attained such grandeur – and how could its fall have been so great?

In Portugal, echoes from the past resound in every city, every village, across the land. Perhaps the first trumpet blast for a heroic age was sounded in the cool green hamlet of Ponte de Mouro on northern Portugal's Minho frontier close to Monção. Here, on 1 November 1386, in a luxurious tent captured from the Castilian

king in the battle of Aljubarrota, Portugal's King João I, Master of
the Order of Avis, met England's John of Gaunt, Duke of Lancaster, the fourth son of Edward III. In their negotiations for John of
Gaunt's invasion of Castile, to which he had some claim by marriage, it was agreed that King João would marry one of John's two
daughters. João chose Philippa, the elder of the two and, for those
times, at twenty-six, closer to perpetual spinsterhood.

The marriage was happy and fruitful: Philippa gave to King João
and Portugal six sons and two daughters. The first-born son and
daughter died in infancy. Of the surviving sons, each with intelligence and talent, the third was Henry, born in Oporto on 4 March
1394.

It was in Sintra, in the Moorish palace where the royal family
liked to pass the summer, that a plan was conceived to cap King
João's prosperous reign with the acquisition of the Muslim port of
Ceuta on the coast of Morocco. Dom João himself had suggested a
tournament; good horsemanship was a fundamental of court life.
His sons urged him to consider taking Ceuta instead; Duarte, heir
to the throne, was twenty-one, fair-haired Pedro twenty and the tall,
dark Henry eighteen.

A council meeting held in Torres Vedras confirmed the plan; on
a wall among tiny houses below the ruined castle a small sign
marks the place. Preparations for invasion began. The prime task
was to build a fleet in Oporto. The loyal townspeople backed the
still mysterious cause with enthusiasm. Giving up all their fresh
meat to be salted for the campaign, they left themselves only the
offal. To this day the *portuense*, the people of Oporto, call themselves
tripeiros (tripe-eaters). The fleet was ready to sail in July 1415;
twenty gleaming galleys, in a total force of 240 ships, flew Prince
Henry's new banner with its motto *Talent de bien faire*.

In August 1415, in Ceuta, Prince Henry, who would never sail
further than this, finally smelled the warm winds of Africa,
savoured the holy joy of conquest over the infidel and saw, with
considerable interest, the rich booty such enterprise provided. Portuguese looters, seeking gold, also found fine oriental carpets and
wall hangings, warehouses of wheat, huge quantities of pungent
spices, the pepper, cinnamon, cloves and other costly seasonings

that meant so much to the peoples of Europe in an age when most food was basic, unpalatable and dull. There was no coffee or tea as yet; fresh meat was limited, salt-dried meat sinewy. Spices injected taste and disguised rot. For some, they were a cure in sickness; for others they enhanced life, and virility, in health.

Henry was back in Ceuta three years later and made diligent inquiries concerning the hinterland and the camel caravans that crossed it. The interior of Africa, the extent of it, the seas around it were mysteries. A few fishermen and merchant adventurers had wandered offshore, impelled by wind, current or curiosity. There were islands, it was known. Legend attributed to them mellifluous names – Antillia, the Isle of Seven Cities, the Fortunate Isles. But there were also fearsome stories of boiling oceans, mighty whirlpools, man-eating sea monsters. No educated person now believed the earth was flat, but what lay beyond the near horizons no one knew. Maps gave hints and half truths, idealizations and exaggerations, wild guesses and wonderful art. To Prince Henry, above all, they gave inspiration – and provoked thought.

For his valour in the taking of Ceuta Prince Henry had been knighted by his father, King João, and dubbed Duke of Viseu. Instead of settling in that cool, hilly and agreeable town, set among the damp pine forests and granite swoops and hollows of the Beira Alta region of central Portugal, or touring the grand cities of Europe with his popular, sociable brother Pedro – whose new title was Duke of Coimbra – Henry turned his face to the south and rode to the seaward limits of the land, to the bleak and windswept promontory of Sagres, that lies at the south-westernmost tip of Europe.

It is a sombre place, even in sunshine. Waves crash against towering, storm-grey cliffs, spray bursting in shrouds of white lace. Wind and sea hiss and groan in eerie duet. Portugal's five hundred miles of coastline embrace great cliffs, rugged promontories, sea-sculpted caverns and numberless weird rock formations. Most haunting of them all is the strange, jutting, throne-like rock below the lighthouse off Cape St Vincent.

. To the north, cliffs fold like repeating mirror images into the distance; at times fishermen, mere specks, stand precariously at the

exposed edge. They seem relaxed and contemplative and foolishly
daring; it is a long way to fall for a fish. Close to Sagres, the two
promontories protect a bay like the horns of a bull. South-east of
Sagres a small harbour provides greater safety from the prevailing
northern winds, which the Portuguese call *nortadas*.

The cape is named after a martyred priest, St Vincent, buried
here in the year 304 – the Romans called it 'Promontorium Sacrum'.
So revered was the place that Christian monks, even through Moorish times, were tolerated at the shrine. Ravens, it was said, had
followed the ship that brought the bones to Sagres, the sacred
promontory. When, in 1173, the relics of St Vincent – *São Vicente* –
were taken up the coast to Lisbon by order of Portugal's founding
king, Afonso Henriques, ravens again flew in close escort. St Vincent was proclaimed patron saint of Lisbon, whose city crest
includes the ship-guarding ravens.

Sailors say São Vicente, seated on his stark throne, attended by
sea-birds, blesses them as they pass. Now, some two hundred ships
a day round the cape, where the rock stands as signpost and
monument to mariners. To the ancients the cape marked *o fim do
mundo* – the end of the world. For the brave explorers Prince Henry
sent to sea it was their last glimpse of Portugal, land and home.

Henry himself spent little time in brooding. He had been
educated in the chivalric ideals of the military Order of Christ, of
which he was governor and administrator. He also held authority,
among his titles, as governor of the Algarve. From the town of
Lagos, from lodgings at nearby Raposeira and eventually in his
own Vila do Infante, he undertook a tenacious search of seaways to
the south, backed by a systematic study of cartography, nautical
science, such as it was, and ship design.

Modern historians, doubting the familiar account, say that despite
the great stone *rosa dos ventos*, the fort and the geographic allure of
the promontory, Sagres may not have been the setting of a formal
school of navigation. The wind rose, or compass rose, that you can
see there was discovered and restored only this century. Its origins
are obscure. Of the Vila do Infante there is only the chronicler's
patchy account. But certainly Henry created a centre of research,
collected all the available books, maps and pilots' manuals and

invited the finest cartographers and most knowledgeable sea captains to his side.

Romantic myth blurs fact and fallacy, but it is Sagres which symbolizes Portugal's reaching out from the medieval to the Renaissance era, the pure search for knowledge, the study of the skies and the charting of the seas, the measured relation between distance and time – all the paradoxes that are today the commonplaces of the science, and adventure, of space.

The information that Henry sought was desperately hard to acquire. The ocean was uncharted, and although the compass, the hourglass and the astrolabe were used, in practice they were fragile and, on rolling decks, gave inaccurate readings. Seamen were superstitious and fearful, their ships unsuitable for ocean voyaging, with square sails that handled easily enough in a favourable wind but poorly in a contrary one. The little *barinel*, square-rigged with two masts, also required oarsmen. Ships had ventured out before Prince Henry began his quest; none had returned with anything more rewarding than fish, rumour and tall mariners' tales.

The very first ships – square-rigged *barcas* – that Henry launched, brought results, though not at all in the way he had hoped. The *barcas* returned, from the waters off Morocco, having sighted nothing. One ship, it seemed, had been lost in a gale. But though blown far off course, the ship later returned to Sagres with thrilling news of discovery. The two captains, João Gonçalves Zarco and Tristão Vaz Teixeira, youthful retainers in Henry's entourage, reported that they had landed at a small, uninhabited island some 400 miles to the south-west. They had named it Porto Santo in thanks for their safe landfall, taken aboard fresh water and found their way home. The year was 1419.

Henry promptly ordered the two young squires back to Porto Santo to plant crops and cultivate the island. With them he sent Bartolomeu Perestrelo, the Portuguese son of an Italian-born father. Initial settlement failed, it seems, because the rapidly increasing progeny of a pregnant rabbit they had taken with them devoured the existing vegetation and every green shoot that appeared. Later, Perestrelo would overcome these initial errors and misfortunes; he was also to become father-in-law to Christopher Columbus.

In the mists of legend and chroniclers' accounts lay the next revelation, the island of Madeira. Discovery, or rediscovery, is credited to Zarco and Vaz Teixeira. A cloud hung in the sky to the south-west of Porto Santo, they told Prince Henry. Though their sailors feared it marked the edge of eternal darkness, Henry persuaded his two captains to investigate. The cloud hung like a thick curtain. As they approached, they heard the roar of breakers and were on the point of retreat when the curtain lifted and they saw a shining bay set below a high green mountain.

Madeira, meaning wood in Portuguese, was the name chosen by the young mariners when they saw how densely forested was the lovely island they had found. Again they started settlement with error and misfortune – a fire purposely lit to clear space for planting spread hopelessly out of control. It lasted, according to report, a biblical span of seven years. Yet profit grew from disaster: in a rich soil the ashes fertilized abundant crops.

With the approval of his father, who held supreme authority over all his son's ventures, Prince Henry energetically organized, from mainland Portugal, the cultivation and colonization of Madeira, a true Atlantic prize. He shipped in Malvoisie vines from Crete and sugar cane; he selected the grain for plantations of wheat and barley, and the best available cattle. Among the first settlers were families from the Algarve and, initiating a practice that became common later when manpower shortage was even more acute, *degredados* (convicts) from the prisons of Lisbon. So strong was the settlers' pioneering spirit that the first boy and girl born in Madeira were christened Adam and Eve.

The Açores islands, nine green gems forming an archipelago 400 miles long and a third of the way across the Atlantic, were the next jewels in the Portuguese crown. Certainly some had been sighted before Santa Maria, in the east, was found by Diogo de Silves in 1427. (Credit for the discovery has also been given to another Portuguese, Gonçalo Velho Cabral.) The largest island, São Miguel, 55 miles (88 km) to the north, was already being settled in 1439. The two tiny islands to the west, Corvo (meaning 'raven') and Flores ('flowers'), were discovered in about 1450 by Diogo de Teive. Their high, wind-carved cliffs, according to Professor J. H. Parry in *The Discovery of the Sea*, mark the true extremity of Europe.

*

The name Açores, or Azores, given to the group by Cabral, means goshawks, which he saw flying high in the sky. Here, some said, were the Fortunate Isles of the Romans (though the Canaries, too, seem to fit map and fable). The strange silhouette of these beautiful volcanic islands sparked argument about their origin. Often quoted is Plato's account of a sunken empire, Atlantis, lying beyond the Pillars of Hercules – Gibraltar.

Legend illuminates the Sete Cidades ('seven cities') crater on São Miguel with its twin lakes, one blue, the other green – formed, goes the tale, from the parting tears of a princess and her shepherd lover. In the centre cluster of islands are Terceira, the felicitous Graciosa, São Jorge, Faial and Pico ('peak'), which is named for its splendid mountain rising to 7713 ft (2351 m), higher than anywhere in mainland Portugal.

Prince Henry, with his usual efficiency, saw to the colonization of the islands, offering land to Flemish farmers to bolster the numbers. The islands soon became ports of call for European seafarers. Christopher Columbus paused at Santa Maria on his return to Spain after discovering the New World in 1492; a mean story has it that he failed to pay his water bill.

From the proceeds of the ventures he sponsored and, later, licensed to eager merchants – many from Lagos, which in time became his prime ship-building yard and main commercial centre – Prince Henry received a one-fifth share. He had a keen eye for profit but remained throughout his life a solitary and ascetic figure, piously eager to combat Muslim infidels and passionately determined in the pursuit of knowledge. And for all the success of island ventures to the west, the focus of his ambition was fixed to the south.

The first barrier was a point called Cape Bojador ('the jutting cape') less than a thousand miles from Sagres but the limit of geographical certainty. Beyond Bojador lay all the myths and terrors of the Sea of Darkness. For nineteen years Henry sent out ship after ship – until at last Gil Eanes, one of his courtiers, reported that he had sighted the cape and seen with his own eyes the boiling waters of the mariners' tales. As always, Henry was persuasive.

'There is no peril so great,' the chronicles quote him as saying, 'that the hope of reward will not be greater.' In 1434 on his second try, Eanes – and a remarkably courageous crew – stayed off the coast and sailed their *barca* past the dreaded cape without mishap. For Prince Henry the only trophy was a desert plant dug from a sandy shore. The true prize was the breaking of the deadlock of fear and superstition.

Now the coast of Africa – still undefined – was open. Eanes was promptly sent back, accompanied by Prince Henry's cup-bearer, Gonçalves Baldaya, in a second ship, a *barinel*. Inching down the coast they saw footprints. Within a year Baldaya, on his second voyage, had reached what they later hopefully called Rio de Ouro, the river of gold. But there was no gold; the sole reward for all the enterprise of Prince Henry and his men was a barrel or two of seal oil.

By 1441, when Nuno Tristão, a young squire in Prince Henry's service, made the first of a series of voyages down the African coast, there was a new impetus and a new ship, the caravel, to speed the explorers' voyages. The caravel transformed exploration. The Italian adventurer, Cadamosto, who undertook voyages for Prince Henry and for himself, pronounced it the handiest vessel afloat. Even Columbus had an affection for his little caravel, *Ninã*, that he did not feel for the *Santa Mária*, his flagship.

The caravel was inspired in part by the cargo-carrying *caravelas* which sailed on the River Douro – Henry would have been familiar with them from his childhood in Oporto – and partly by the Arab dhow with its lateen, or triangular, sails, used in eastern oceans since ancient times. The caravel, with two or even three raked masts, was fully decked, with a raised stern. Its hull, with a pronounced sheer, was of pine on a straight oak keel. The lateen rig – later, bigger caravels added a square sail and topsail – made the caravel much easier to sail into the wind than the square-rigged *barca*. The first caravels, about 60 feet long, carried crews of around twenty. With no accommodation, they slept where they could on or below deck; the captain and shipmaster had the use of a small poop cabin astern.

Gradually, aids to navigation were improved. Navigators, guided by the Pole star, used to dead reckoning and familiar with the compass, now began to establish their position with the quadrant, the astrolabe adapted for use at sea, and its simplified version, the *balestilha*, a cross-staff which enabled them to calculate latitude from the angle of the horizon to the sun. Celestial tables and charts became increasingly detailed, and each voyage of exploration provided new information for the prince and his cartographers.

Nuno Tristão, on several voyages between 1441 and 1446, sailed past Mauritania, past the Senegal river, and up to and along the River Gambia – where he was killed, with several of his shipmates, by the poisoned arrows of unfriendly Africans. It was a sad day, but it was scarcely surprising: Portuguese discoverers were soon followed by commercial traders from Lagos; sailors' haphazard kidnappings of Moors and blacks for booty and information had already moved on to the vastly profitable business of slavery.

The chronicler records that Prince Henry, mounted on a fine horse, attended a sharing out of slaves in Lagos, and he describes the grievous weeping and groaning as 'fathers were parted from sons, husbands from wives, brothers from brothers'. Henry gave away his one-fifth share, forty-six slaves, and apparently 'reflected with pleasure on the salvation of these souls which otherwise would have been lost'.

Slavery was not his objective. Indeed, Portuguese kings tried, somewhat weakly, to stop it. What interested Henry greatly was that the caravel that took his faithful Nuno Tristão on his last voyage could be sailed home after sixty days by a crew of only five survivors, mainly ships' boys of tender age. Ships and seamanship were close to his dry heart and, by the time that heart gave out, on 13 November 1460, Portuguese mariners had reached the growling mountain of Serra Leão (Sierra Leone) on Africa's west coast and had found the eastern group of Cape Verde islands. Madeira was booming, peaceful relations had been established with the Gambian people of the poisoned arrows through the tact of sea captain Diogo Gomes, and a busy trading post had been established on the island of Arguim in what is today Mauritania.

In the evergreen saga of Portugal's discoveries the role of Prince Henry is viewed at times with scholarly scepticism. It was with the approval of his father, King João I, that Henry could be so assertive, it is said. Or it was his brother, Prince Pedro, regent after their brother Duarte's death in 1438, who sponsored much of the exploration; or that privately funded merchants deserve greater credit. Or that Prince Henry, with other preoccupations in Lisbon, with the Muslims of north Africa, with the Canary islands – to which Castile then had uncertain rights – with his brothers' family crises, was less than single-minded in his endeavours at Sagres.

He was thought to have died a virgin; his body was clothed in a horsehair shirt. Yet he spent heavily on his enterprises and left huge debts at his death. His courageous mariners had brought him strange trophies: fresh ostrich eggs, dried elephant meat, a little gold, a lion – which he gave to an Englishman living in Ireland – and a few hapless Africans. It is surely the very complexity of his life that attracts argument.

Yet Prince Henry was unquestionably the organizer, the mover, the *impulsionador* – a wonderful Portuguese word – of Portuguese exploration. He was navigator not of any single ship but of the Age of Discovery itself, for, above all, he kindled a flame that in the years to come would light the path of Portuguese mariners to the far corners of the earth.

Portuguese kings and princes were not operating in a vacuum of purely domestic aspiration. Their deeply held Christian ideals were under siege in the world they knew. In 1453 Constantinople had fallen to the Turks under Mehmed II – the great-grandfather of Suleyman the Magnificent, born in 1494. Suleyman was only four years old when Vasco da Gama, the sea route to India gloriously attained, was outflanking Islam on foreign shores (though even he, in strange new places, was confused by Hindus). In 1522, the year that Magellan's little ship, *Victoria*, had circled the globe, Suleyman seized Rhodes. Conflict exploded and burned across Europe. The Ottoman empire was the strongest force on land. But, for a surprisingly long time, small Portugal dominated the seas.

At the time of Henry's death his nephew, Dom Afonso V, was king. Without the same interest as his uncle in what still seemed a slow pace of exploration, he passed much of his reign in planning expeditions against Morocco. His main prize was the recovery, in

1464, of the bones of Henry's brother, Prince Fernando, who had become hostage to the Moors in a mishandled campaign in Tangier in 1437. Poor Fernando was horribly treated by the fanatical king of Fez. When he finally died in 1443, his body was hung, head down, from the city walls.

Afonso was nicknamed 'the African' for his efforts in north Africa. Only in 1469 did he pursue Henry's objectives in Africa – by contract with a merchant from Lisbon, Fernão Gomes. Gomes had exclusive rights to trade along the Guinea coast providing he also covered 100 leagues, or about 300 miles, of new territory each year. Five years later, the huge western bulge of Africa was familiar, the western Cape Verde islands as well as São Tomé and Principe had been discovered – and still Africa stretched on to the south.

In 1481 King Afonso V died – in the Sintra palace where he was born – and was succeeded by his son, Dom João II, who, from a young age, had been imbued with his great-uncle Henry's passion for exploration. For the last seven years João, determined and ambitious, had held responsibility for trade and discovery. He now gave considerable thought and energy to discoveries beyond anything Henry had contemplated. The groundwork had been laid. Dom João, demanding secrecy among his captains and pilots, for where Portugal showed the way others were quick to follow, prepared his strategy – for India.

First, to give protection to Portuguese seafaring and trading in west Africa Dom João ordered that a fort should be constructed; in 1482 São Jorge da Mina – Elmina – was built in the Gold Coast, now Ghana, under the supervision of Diogo de Azambuja, the soldier and diplomat – whose fleet may have included Christopher Columbus as a seaman.

Then, from Lisbon, Dom João dispatched navigators including the excellent Diogo Cão – certainly a nickname, for *cão* means dog – down and farther down the African coast; Cão himself, in three remarkable voyages, extended Portuguese authority – indicated by stone markers (*padrões*) – a further 6,000 miles, to Cape Cross, as well as into the Congo river region.

He was followed, in a carefully planned expedition of two caravels and – for the first time – a store ship, by Bartolomeu Dias.

That same year, 1487, Dom João sent Pêro da Covilhã and his colleague, Paiva, eastward on travels that he hoped would lay bare two great mysteries of the age: the source of eastern spices and the whereabouts of Prester John.

Bartolomeu Dias was the navigator who broke the last barrier along Africa's interminable coast by sailing around its thrusting toe. Taking a route across the Gulf of Guinea, he bypassed Elmina and sailed along the coast as far as Luderitz Bay, battling for much of the way against the prevailing southerly winds. From Luderitz Bay the chronicles have him dramatically driven south for thirteen days in tempestuous seas. Modern mariners believe Dias deliberately stood seaward and then south. When at last westerly winds appeared Dias sailed east and, finally, north.

Dias made landfall at today's Mossel Bay, where the natives were not friendly and threw stones; in return, it seems, Dias killed one with an arrow, an unhappy beginning. He continued up the coast to the Great Fish River, but near here, against his own urging, his crew demanded that they turn back for the long haul home. A document was prepared and signed confirming each man's decision. On the return voyage Dias saw for the first time the cape that he had turned – memorably for ever after the Cape of Good Hope. (What is now Cape Agulhas, the southernmost point, he named after the Irish St Brennan.) The route to the east was open.

By any standard of skill and navigational judgement, the land-mark voyage was a brilliant achievement, yet it was little ap-preciated by Dom João, who had set his heart on India and the spice routes. Dias, hoping to please his sovereign by easing the costs of the voyage, had picked up some gold and a few slaves from the African coast and ferried home a pilot, Duarte Pacheco Pereira – later the author of a notable cosmographical treatise – who had been stranded on an island. When Dias, back in Lisbon in December 1488, presented his charts to Dom João, among those present was Christopher Columbus, still despairingly seeking spon-sorship for the enterprise that would make him Admiral of the Ocean Sea.

There was no quick sequel to the rounding of the cape. Around

1491, perhaps, Covilhã's report, brought by the Jewish emissaries, would have been in Dom João's hands. For others, perhaps for Dom João, it became clear that Dias and his exhausted crew had turned back a few days' sailing from Sofala, where Covilhã had stayed – a fingertip from circumnavigation of that enormous, daunting, African continent.

King João and other Portuguese were not much excited by the Columbus voyage of 1492 or impressed by his thirty-three days at sea from the Canaries to the Bahamas in a fair wind. Dom João put in a claim for the island. The matter was resolved with Spain's rulers, Ferdinand and Isabella, in the earth-dividing Treaty of Tordesillas of 1494: all lands found west of a demarcation line, drawn 370 leagues to the west of the Cape Verdes, would belong to Spain and all lands east of it to Portugal. It was an odd treaty for there was no way to measure longitude or set a precise line – yet it worked.

A policy of secrecy regarding the Portuguese discoveries is known to have been adopted, in varying degrees, by Prince Henry, King João II – *senhor de todos os segredos*, lord of all the secrets – and, after his early death in 1495, by his successor, the ambitious King Manuel, whose mind was on conquest. Pilots were told to keep silent in front of foreigners. Charts were kept under lock and key. The chronicles have surprising gaps. Portugal, with reason, feared that its prizes would be snatched away.

The policy, or conspiracy, of silence could explain the route of Bartolomeu Dias; also why King João appeared to know of the islands that Columbus discovered, and other mysteries. The Portuguese made many unannounced voyages – and, no doubt, findings. Scholars, nose to paper, like to have dates and facts. Yet clues are there and, as Alan Villiers observed, after the rigours of a cod-fishing voyage with a Portuguese fleet: 'In the great maritime history of Portugal there is no need to invent voyages.'

No secrecy attended the ceremonial departure, in 1497, of Vasco da Gama on his epic voyage for India. Now Dom Manuel I, at twenty-six, was king; he was the son of Prince Henry's heir, Fernando; the only son of King João II had died in a riding accident. Manuel's inheritance encompassed the incomparable seafaring lore systematically garnered by his visionary forebears and their brave sea captains. Even the endless outlay, the expense, was no worry, for at last, from west Africa, there was gold to pay for it. Manuel was 'the Fortunate'; and perhaps it was fortunate that, as kings went, though he was capricious and adored the pomp and power of monarchy, he had – say the chroniclers – likeable qualities, too.

Seamen for their part knew from experience the risks from hostile or waterless shores, the hazards of angry winds and strong currents, the discomfort and tedium of life at sea. They had seen the North Star fade in the horizon and found new security in the Southern Cross. They were confident of their own seafaring capability; most were born in the ports and fishing villages of Portugal. They were men well tested but they did not yet know the hideous torment of long-distance voyagers – scurvy.

For Vasco da Gama's expedition two *naus* of about 100 tons, the *São Gabriel* and *São Rafael*, were specially built under the supervision of Bartolomeu Dias. They were solidly constructed, square-rigged ships more suited to long distances than the nimble little caravel, although a 50-ton caravel, the *Berrio*, sailed with them. A 200-ton store ship completed the small fleet. The ships carried provisions for three years, guns and gunners, interpreters, musicians and priests, and a few convicts, as was now standard practice, for high-risk duties. (History records that some survived and prospered.)

The fleet was ably manned by a crew of 170, including Diogo Dias, a brother of Bartolomeu, and Paulo, the sweet-tempered older brother of the authoritative Vasco da Gama. As leader of the expedition, the stocky, black-bearded Vasco da Gama – born in Sines in 1460 or thereabouts, a gentleman of wide-ranging abilities in the young king's household – would prove brilliantly competent, of sound judgement, cautious and courteous with potential allies, hot-tempered and savagely harsh when opposed. Everything, it seemed, had been thought of, including trading goods and simple gifts – beads and brass basins, cheap cloth and woollen caps. It was these that nearly proved the undoing of the great enterprise.

The voyage was boldly venturesome from the start. The course chosen by Vasco da Gama was a wide swing from near Sierra Leone through the open Atlantic to bring him to a bay, St Helena, just above what is now Cape Town. He was ninety-three days at sea, without sight of land. The navigation, over some 3,500 miles of open sea, was complex. It was an astonishing feat, regarded by modern mariners as one of the greatest in ocean voyaging.

The native people of South Africa, the Khoi, were as unfriendly to Vasco da Gama as they had been to Dias: a *padrão* set up at Mossel Bay was torn down even as the fleet weighed anchor. Further on the Portuguese, because it was Christmas, called the coast Natal, its name today. Vasco da Gama's ships were the first from Europe ever to sail up the east African coast. They encountered suspicion, hostility, deception. Many seamen were ill with scurvy. Vasco da Gama sailed cautiously in search of fresh water and food, Christians and a pilot to take them to India. In Malindi they found all they needed. Their Arab pilot, the elderly and experienced Ahmed Ibn Majid, was even piously pronounced by a Portuguese chronicler to be Christian.

The passage to India, the most fateful in history, was uneventful. It lasted twenty-six days. Vasco da Gama anchored off Calicut, on the Malabar coast, on 18 May 1498. As he had brought no splendid gifts, he did not impress the Hindu ruler, the sophisticated Zamorim, and first contacts soon soured. After three months, in heavy monsoon rains, Vasco da Gama sailed for home. Contrary winds, the malevolence of petty Muslim rulers, the depredations of scurvy, slowed the journey. Paulo da Gama, taken ill near the end, died in Terceira in the Açores. His grief-stricken brother delayed his own return but at last, in September 1499, two of the four ships, the square-rigged *São Gabriel* and the little caravel *Berrio*, received a jubilant welcome in the Tejo river at Lisbon. Of the 170 mariners who had sailed out in the summer of 1497, only 55 came home.

Even before a stone of the glorious Jerónimos monastery at Belém, built by King Manuel in thanksgiving, had been laid, new fleets were sailing for India. In 1500 Pedro Álvares Cabral led a fleet of thirteen ships, sailing in a south-westward swing so wide he came upon Brazil. Claiming it for Portugal, and leaving behind a few *degredados*, he carried on to India. Ten days' sailing from Brazil, the fleet was struck by a sudden storm. Four ships were lost; captain of one was Bartolomeu Dias, the discoverer of the cape for which they were bound.

*

Today the great fleets have gone and Portugal's merchant navy is unimpressive, yet the Portuguese still head out to sea in brightly painted fishing boats, motoring from modern ports or pushed out in pounding surf. All along the coast and on the rivers are the descendants of discoverers and the boatbuilding skills of the men who created the caravel. Of today's active, hard-working boats none is lovelier than the *meia-lua*, the half-moon – high-prowed surfboats which still ride the west-coast surf. The Douro preserves its port-ferrying *barco rabelo*, the Aveiro lagoon the swan-necked, weed-collecting *moliceiro* – seeing a fleet of these stately craft under sail in a saint's day regatta is like watching rare birds fly. On the Tejo are a few treasured broad-beamed cargo barges, flower-patterned *fragatas* and *varinos*. The days of sail are kept alive by the navy's sailtrainer, *Sagres*, a magnificent three-masted barque, the Cross of Christ on each of its ten square sails, and the elegant *Creoula*, a four-masted, steel-hulled schooner – as *bacalhoeiro*, pride of the fleet that once carried 3,000 men each year to the cod-rich waters of the Grand Banks.

Soon out of step with the times, however, the *Creoula* was left in dock to rust. Slowly, she was brought back to life by the Portuguese Sail Training Association, Aporvela – whose members designed two graceful replica caravels, *Bartolomeu Dias*, which sailed from Portugal to Mossel Bay in 1988 to commemorate Dias's great voyage five hundred years earlier, and *Boa Esperança* ('Good Hope').

Portugal's discoveries changed the shape of the world. The established geography based on the thinking of Ptolemy, a second-century Greek living in Egypt, was transformed. Access to India by sea from the west ended the Muslim monopoly of spices and toppled the merchant traders of Genoa and Venice. The Persian Gulf, the Red Sea and the Mediterranean, and the caravan routes that linked them, lost their validity. Lisbon, with its sea bridge to India and the rich commerce of the Orient, with its links to Brazil, to Madeira and to Africa, was the main port, the busiest marketplace, the treasure-house of Europe.

At home the discoveries, and the colonization – and evangelization – that followed them, channelled national energy, purpose and will. What began with the purposefulness of Prince Henry, the fortitude, ability, urge for profit and plain curiosity of his mariners, ended in empire and the high peaks of glory. From a summit, the only possible direction is down. Such a sprawling empire could never have been sustained – Portugal's population was never higher in those times than one and a half million, too low and too extended to hold off hungry opposition. The Dutch and the English, particularly, were soon nibbling at Portugal's rich cake.

The Portuguese look back with pride on that grand era, though many among this easygoing people rather wonder how they did it – and most choose to ignore the brutality and greed of the slave trade. As celebrations of the five-hundredth anniversary of the Age of Discoveries got under way, after a fitful start marked by bickering and controversy that had commentators deploring the state of their nation, the nation's leaders worry that there is too much looking back, too little looking ahead. The Portuguese should throw off old ways of thinking, their habit of systematic opposition to progress, they cry. Even as the communications services announced overdue improvement to the telephone system and the arrival of portable telephones, the Portuguese were still heatedly, loudly and at length, discussing the Inquisition, the truth of the conspiracy of silence, who really discovered America, the legacy of empire and their own extraordinary past as interpreted by their own passionate, gifted, oracular and opinionated historians.

Now Portugal has embarked for territory as challenging, perhaps, as those other, distant lands: the community of Europe. 'The present does not conflict with the past, but rather grows from it,' Mário Soares, as president, stated reassuringly. He had himself fought hard to persuade the Portuguese of the merits of EEC membership.

But in Portugal it is easy to confuse present with past, for they are interwoven and time is nothing. Although through youthful initiative the present is reaching out to the future, the past is inescapable. Portugal still governs a remnant of empire in Macau, the arrangement with China an echo of the deal that was struck around 1557. Its conscience over East Timor, seized and oppressed by Indonesia, its sense of post-colonial concern in Africa, its urge for continued links of culture and trade wherever Portuguese is spoken, are not put aside under new pressures. The Portuguese flag still flies over the ruggedly beautiful islands of the Açores, autonomously governed like the flourishing and prosperous Madeira with its 'free zone' enticing new commerce. Over on little Porto Santo, Prince Henry's first Atlantic trophy welcomes tourism and faces time-share developments with equanimity.

Nearer to Lisbon, Sines, dominated by a great oil-tanker terminal, would probably not be recognized by Vasco da Gama, who was born there and became admiral of the Indian, Arabian and Persian Seas and a viceroy of India. In Sabrosa, above the River Douro, the name of Fernão de Magalhães appears in modest lettering on the street where he is thought to have been born. Old stone, the chatter of old folk, a worn escutcheon, are his memorial here. A profounder compliment was paid by astronomers who named the galaxies nearest to our own the large and small Magellanic Clouds after the man who saw them first in the globe-encircling voyage that established the dimensions of the earth, a tribute stirringly echoed by the United States in 1989 when they launched the spacecraft *Magellan*, the first to explore the solar system in a decade, on its journey to the planet Venus. Belém rejoices in its own inestimable beauty, successfully ignoring the modern protuberances on its skyline. Sagres, where exploration and discovery began, is still ruled by the wind and sea.

The coast of Portugal, birthplace of countless mariners whose bones have merged with so many seas, survives human assault with grace and forbearance. Each summer, in a contest run by a national newspaper, *Diário de Notícias*, children on crowded holiday beaches sculpt from sand, not sandcastles, but bullfighters and goalkeepers, and Prince Henry and Bartolomeu Dias, as vividly as if they knew them – and they do.

3 Kings, queens and castles

Portugal's green and red flag flies bravely above the great keep and granite towers of Guimarães castle. Youngsters, heedless of history, romp on the grass below. Lines of chattering schoolchildren tramp the castle's inner parapets – a school tour, with ice-cream to follow.

These children are the future citizens of a country which was born at that very spot, the bright flag the republican symbol of nationhood for which Guimarães was the royal cradle – and flying this day, as it happens, in honour of the poet, Luís Vaz de Camões (c. 1524–80), whose epic *Os Lusíadas* is the ultimate expression of all Portugal's pride, glory and sense of loss.

Lusus was the companion of Bacchus, the legendary first settler of Portugal. The bravest people in Iberian history were those of Roman Lusitania. Myth, historical account, lyrical poetry record the feats of the 'sons of Lusus' – the Portuguese.

Here in Guimarães, in about 1109, it is said, a son, Afonso Henriques, was born to Count Henry of Burgundy and his wife, Teresa, the illegitimate daughter of the king of Castile, Alfonso VI. Her dowry, extending to Coimbra and the Mondego river, included all the land between the Minho and Douro rivers, a place called Portucale.

Count Henry died when his son was no more than five. In 1128 Afonso Henriques, whom the chronicles describe as a man of giant stature, immensely strong and with a flowing beard, seized power from his regent mother and her lover, Fernando Peres, and dispatched them to exile in Galicia. The date marks the dawning of Portugal. By 1139 his troops, hailing his leadership in the battle of Ourique, against the Moors, were calling him king. Legend elaborates victory: on the battlefield somewhere to the north of the

Alentejo town of Ourique, on the day of Santiago, 25 July 1139, Afonso Henriques had a vision of Christ. The Portuguese were the chosen people 'who would reap for Him a great harvest in different regions'. A glorious destiny, they believed, was assured.

Afonso Henriques was formally acclaimed King of Portugal in 1143 in the church of Santa Maria de Almacave, Lamego, at the first gathering of the Cortes, a parliament representing nobles, clergy and *povo* (the people). A Visigoth crown was placed on his head. The event was described in a twelfth-century document found at Alcobaça in the seventeenth century – and pronounced a forgery, a poor copy made for contemporary reasons of succession. So fact is only probability; the first steps of Portugal's long road are paved with many such brittle fragments.

By 1143, the young king's realm reached the Tejo. Against a tribute of four ounces of gold a year and a declaration that he would be liegeman to St Peter and the Pope, Dom Afonso Henriques won recognition of Portugal's independence from the Holy See.

He had still to win the prize he desired most of all: Lisbon. An attempt to take Lisbon by force with a few passing crusaders in 1140 had failed. The Moors had invaded Portugal in 711 and were proving difficult to dislodge. Leiria kept changing hands. Coimbra, on the north bank of the Mondego, had been won back from the Moors in 1064 and was Dom Afonso Henriques's capital and campaign base.

In March 1147, by surprising the defenders, he won the important town of Santarém, guardian of the Tejo river valley. The arrival in Oporto only two months later of 164 ships sailing to the Holy Land with a rowdy assortment of crusading soldiery from England, Germany, Flanders and Boulogne was the weapon he needed (theirs were giant catapults and siege towers) to force the Moors from their citadel in Lisbon.

After the fall of Lisbon the fortresses of Almada, Palmela and Sintra fell quickly. Later, in 1158, it took a siege of two months to win the key to the south, the castle at Alcácer do Sal, which rose grandly above the River Sado. The Moors retook it in 1191 and lost it for good in 1217. Conquest of such imposing strongholds, it is clear from the merest glance, requires a mighty fist. In one seemingly impregnable fortification after another, preserved, restored or in ruins, is the evidence still of Dom Afonso Henriques's amazing achievement.

But there is more than that to consider: the great castles, the tremendous walls, those towering ramparts, were there long before Dom Afonso Henriques came and conquered. Hilltop forts dotted the landscape as long ago as the fifteenth century BC, when Celts fought Iberians. Merchant Phoenicians visited peaceably around the eleventh century BC. Carthaginians and Greeks drove away the Phoenicians. Greeks reorganized the existing fortifications, which in turn were demolished, expanded or modernized by invading Romans between 218 BC and AD 400. Then came Vandals, and Visigoths, and Christianity.

War eased to peace and the growth of settled communities – the Portuguese thrived before Portugal existed. Seeking security, they turned Roman forts into fortified villages. In the eighth century came the Moors and their fine building; in the twelfth, the pugnacious King Afonso; then dynasties of kings and queens of a unified nation – the first, the oldest, in Europe. In libraries and archives are treaties and documents to delight and tantalize historians – or spark controversy. To a knowledgeable eye all of this history is written in the stones.

The heritage for modern Portugal is a bountiful cross-culture of nearly two hundred medieval castles, coastal fortresses, fortified cities and sundry centuries-old watch-towers. Additionally, there are megalithic *antas* (dolmens) and more than forty small *castros* and larger *citânias*, prehistoric fortified towns of what is called the *castreja* culture, lasting from about 800 BC to AD 200.

The extensive Iron Age *citânia* of Briteiros, between Braga and Guimarães, with its lively suggestion of day-to-day bustle, is the biggest and best known. Excavation began in 1875, under Dr Francisco Martins Sarmento, and lasted eight years. He died in 1899 and serious excavation was only resumed in 1930. Inevitably there were puzzles: strange stones, mysterious granite structures – crematorium or heated bath-house? Discussion continues, the expression of opinion as much normal Portuguese polemic as traditional academic debate.

Of the castles a number, like the once-crucial Alcácer do Sal, are little more than ruins, gaunt sculptures on a silent hill. Granite and limestone blocks, great walls and massive arches have been tumbled by earthquakes or long ago abandoned – the invention of artillery and gunpowder in the fourteenth century altered the nature of warfare for ever. But many castles have been conserved and half a dozen have been transformed into stylish and soothingly comfortable *pousadas*.

These state-owned castle hotels are in Óbidos, Estremoz, Setúbal, at nearby Palmela – crouched like a great stone beast on the high rocky peninsula south of Lisbon – and at Vila Nova de Cerveira in the far north beside the quiet-flowing Minho. At Marvão to the east, where the castle looks disdainfully down on Spain, a nine-room seventeenth-century mansion, expanding carefully into neighbouring houses, is tucked neatly below the castle within its stout outer walls. At Almeida in the west and Valença in the far north, *pousadas* lie within the angled walls of frontier fortifications, stout bulwarks against enemy assault.

In all of them – silent sentinels guarding a tranquil valley or castles resounding with visitors' clamorous voices – are phantoms from across the ages. Armies battled, but there were also times of peace, of exploration and expansion. Several rulers between the thirteenth and sixteenth centuries built, or rebuilt, handsome castles. But none compares with King Dinis, who inherited the throne in 1279 at the age of eighteen and ruled with bursting energy and rare imagination until his death in 1325.

He was an accomplished poet and did much to develop and propagate the Portuguese language; he founded Coimbra University – it started in Lisbon. He nationalized Church authority. The Castile-founded Order of Calatrava had already become the Portuguese Order of Avis; Dinis gave national status, along with the castle of Palmela, to the Order of Santiago and, when Philip le Bel of France persuaded Pope Clement V to suppress the rich and powerful Order of the Knights Templar, he grasped the opportunity to create from the order, established in Portugal since the 1120s, the entirely Portuguese Order of Christ. The rights and resources of each of these military–religious orders, whether headed by a grand master, governor or administrator, were vested – most usefully, as Prince Henry the Navigator would prove – in the royal family, later narrowed to the Crown.

Dom Dinis was concerned with the improvement of crops and raising production of wheat and barley, and tried to persuade his court that farming was not demeaning. He expanded commerce by authorizing some forty local fairs. He planted forests, devised systems of law, trade and administration – and, with an eye to Castile, he ordered the construction of castle after castle, fort after fort.

His hand is in great frontier fortifications and small town defences across the land and through the alphabet, from Alcoutim on the Guadiana river to Valença on the Minho, from Alegrete to Vila Viçosa; in Alfaiates, within the bulwarks of Almeida, in the empty wall of Arraiolos, in Beja's sturdy keep, in Campo Maior, Castelo Bom, Castelo Rodrigo – and in Castelo de Vide, where his marriage to the saintly Princess Isabel of Aragon was arranged.

They married in the castle town of Trancoso in 1282 and chose Leiria with its imposing castle as their main residence. They spent summers in cool Sintra in the palace of the former Moorish governor, a custom adopted by generations of succeeding royalty, and they must surely have remarked on the view from the mountaintop Moorish castle, whose tidy silhouette today is nineteenth-century primping.

Queen Isabel was the perfect, loving wife for her able husband. Legend and the chronicles of Rui de Pina elaborate on her humility, charity and virtue. Miracles occurred: she cured the sick; gold coins in her apron cascaded to the ground as fragrant roses. Dom Dinis expressed his feelings with his usual practicality: he bestowed on his wife, as gifts, the lands and revenues of several towns including Trancoso – an anniversary gift – Abrantes, Porto de Mós, Leiria and, after refurbishing its castle, the little gem of Óbidos, the walled town which Dom Afonso Henriques had snatched from the Moors.

Queen Isabel died in 1336 in the eastern fortified town of Estremoz; the *pousada* created here from the great rugged castle bears her name. In 1625, for her selfless dedication to God and the poor, she was canonized as Rainha Santa Isabel, the Holy Queen. Dom Dinis, the poet king who spent his life crafting a well-ordered nation, won a less exalted title: *O Rei Lavrador*, the Farmer King.

Not all the castles of Dom Dinis are still standing and none looks quite the way he left it. One of the most visible sits at Évora Monte above the busy road linking Évora and Estremoz. A dandy little castle built in 1306, it has four chubby round towers within protective walls and bears flourishes in the Manueline style from 1516. The earthquake of 1531 caused considerable damage. The castle, restored within a few years, was the setting for an eventful signing party, the Convention in 1834 that ended absolute rule and brought peace to the country after years of internal strife.

Suddenly, quite recently, it was painted custard yellow. Fancy lighting was installed. The bedizening of a national monument occasioned some protest, but not much, especially as the yellow faded. The Portuguese have been building castles, and rebuilding them, for more than a thousand years. Restoration always arouses criticism (as does the lack of it) for *patrimônio cultural*, the national heritage, is taken seriously. But they have in Portugal – and have had across a large expanse of the world – many other castles. The most striking thing about them, apart from impressive stonework, is their emphatic diversity.

A fortified castle had been built at Tomar, founded in 1162 by Gualdim Pais, companion-at-arms of King Afonso Henriques and Grand Master of the Templars. With the disbanding of the Templars, the brand new but unsurprisingly similar Order of Christ was given headquarters facing the Guadiana river and Spain at Castro Marim, in the Algarve, in the massive castle built by King Afonso III, father of Dinis. They were there from 1319 until 1356, when they returned to Tomar.

Within Tomar's twelfth-century walls are the splendours of the sixteen-sided *charola*, the original rotunda church where the knights attended mass on horseback, the sixteenth-century cloisters of the Convento de Cristo monastery and the most elaborate and ornate church window in Portugal – the Cross of Christ and of the Order of Templars is its plainest feature. At Castro Marim, high ruined walls overlook salt-pans, a modest, well-made town and a nature reserve. EEC membership has transformed old longings to reality with a bridge across the Guadiana river where, for as long as anyone can remember, sturdy ferry boats coped with the increasing traffic.

Along the Algarve, an ancient string of defences – a eighteenth-century map shows forty-six maritime forts – has left its stony imprint on main towns like Tavira and Faro as well as on diminutive Cacela Velha, inland Salir and Aljezur, taken from the Moors in 1249 and supposedly their very last foothold in the Algarve. The gates, legend suggests, were opened to the Portuguese commander, Paio Peres Correia, by a Moorish maiden in love with one of his knights.

Chivalric orders are not quite gone. The Templars, formally banned in 1312, have an entirely modern 1984-registered presence in Portugal. The order's declared objectives include serving the poor of Jesus Christ and battling against practices offensive to the modern Christian. Now and again they hold elaborate investitures.

Gualdim Pais, whose founding of Tomar was the most significant step – for modern Portugal – in a constructive career, built another castle, the enchanting Almourol, which sits lightly on a tiny island in the Tagus river not far from Tomar. In this magical place, emerging from river mist and rainbows at sunrise, haunted in the evening by aimless young soldiers from the training camp at Tancos, it is not surprising that legends of giants and knights and princesses abound. One tells of a princess's passion for her father's Moorish slave. Her sighing ghost, it is said, can still be seen by moonlight. At Dornes, a minuscule village seeming to rise from the dammed Zêzere river it is the pentagonal tower beside the church that is said to have been built by Templars.

At Vila da Feira the castle seems to have come straight out of a fairy-tale, with its four conical chimneys flanking a sturdy keep. A fifteenth-century fantasy, rising from an eleventh-century structure, it was built, records indicate, on a temple to a local god. The castle has an unusual deep well with a linked stairway. Rumours persist of mysterious underground passages and hidden treasure.

Pointed towers, shaped like Feira's, with gleaming green tiles, cap the odd castle that perches above Porto de Mós in Leiria province. Built by King Sancho I at the beginning of the thirteenth century, it was altered by the determined Dinis and re-altered, restored, re-done, in subsequent epochs. With its arched entrance and balconies above, the castle is an eye-catching curiosity bearing little resemblance, for sure, to the original military construction.

Castles long ago changed character. But those masterpieces of military architecture are no mere relics. Even in the tiny village of Sortelha, in the district of Terreiro das Bruxas, 'place of the witches', in Guarda region, where an ancient and impressive castle is built snugly into huge rocks within a ring of walls, life goes on – amid uproar at times, for Sortelha's primary school is only steps away from the castle's powerful keep.

Children, shops, normal daily life, are also to be met with at Marvão, set high – 2,828 ft, 862 m – above a spectacular escarpment only 6 km from Spain. A medieval walled town, open to the skies, with a dominating castle and intricate fortifications, it is a peaceable kingdom unmarred by modern blemishes. Even the *pousada* blends discreetly into the whitewashed houses. The Moors were here – evicted by Dom Afonso Henriques – in 1166, and Dom Dinis, wary for his defences. Now, the loudest noise most days is the chirping of caged birds.

At Lindoso, at the stark and mountainous north-east frontier, sheep and long-horned cattle graze the slopes below the castle – its keep dates from the time of Dom Dinis – wandering among the eerie cluster of tomb-like *espigueiros*, corn stores from the eighteenth and nineteenth centuries. At Sabugal, below the muscular keep, and giving the castle a cheerful, homely look, there is sometimes laundry drying on a line. The picture-book castle at Penedono is linked to the story of Álvaro Gonçalves Coutinho who, with other *fidalgos*, sailed to England in the reign of King João I and his English queen, Philippa, to joust for the honour of twelve English ladies.

At Bragança in the north, the castle's wooden door, viewed from the *pousada*, has the gleam, at sunset, of purest gold. Far to the south, in Loulé, it appeared that there was neither gold nor glamour in the plain-spoken castle with its 1940s battlements. Earthquake, as elsewhere, had uprooted stone and murdered history. Yet modern researchers quickly found a touch of Roman, and Moorish walls. In a town captured from the Moors in 1249, whose charter came from King Afonso III, father of Dinis and ultimate conqueror of the Moorish Algarve, it could hardly have been otherwise.

Coastal fortifications were the keen concern not only of Portuguese kings but of the Spanish who ruled Portugal between 1580 and 1640. In places, what Dom João III and his widow had begun, the Spanish Philip II completed. The 'key to the kingdom' was the powerful fort of São Julião da Barra at the entrance to the Tejo. Among those whom it deterred was Francis Drake, leading against Spain in 1589, less than a year after the celebrated defeat of the Spanish Armada, a fleet greater than the Armada's. Drake's expedition was a ruinous failure. Half his men, more than 8,000 soldiers and sailors, died of disease or deserted. The British ignominy was in time forgotten. In Salazar's day the fort was used to offer hospitality to guests, including General Eisenhower and Field-Marshal Montgomery.

The castles, usually on top of a hill, physically loom over numerous cities, towns and villages in Portugal (with the conspicuous exception of the castle at Lousã, south of Coimbra, which sits in a snug, forested valley where a pilgrimage route adds to its singularity). But to many Portuguese they are a natural part of the scene and virtually invisible; except for youngsters in love, there is no reason to go there.

For every castle there are at least three churches. There is often a *pelourinho* – an ancient stone post, or pillar, that marks the town's foundation, its first square, its pillory. Castle towns, sharp-edged by a scalpel sun, bright light accentuating sliding shadows, have their dim musty stores and bland self-service shops, hump-backed ovens, bakeries and pastry shops, and anonymous *tascas* where men can retreat for a *bagaço* – a tot of something strong, stimulating and cheap. There may be a town garden where old folk can sit, and a bandstand, perhaps. There is an open space for markets, fairs and festivals. There is a primary school, post office, police station and fire brigade. Somewhere, there will be a football field.

There is, of course, a town well or fountain. But if basic drains is a leading item on many town councils' action list, close behind is a newer, truer, status symbol, a public swimming-pool. In the Alentejo, south of Évora, a road sign on the outskirts of Portel, ignoring this pleasant town's fine castle and several churches of artistic merit, announces only: PISCINA. Public pools, enormously popular, are now common. Ancient towns categorized as *cidades* (cities) may lack a bookshop but the sports complex is growing in size and ambition and a heated, covered, swimming-pool projected.

Not everyone in Portugal looks towards the sea or has even seen it – even in the Algarve only half of all *algarvios* live on the littoral and three quarters of the region is still agricultural. The great discoveries, the patient decades of exploration, were led by lands-men. Despite heavy emigration there were always more people dependent on agriculture than on fishing and the sea; there still are. Small inland towns are perfectly aware of their priorities – as were, in more threatening times, the rulers of Portugal.

Portugal's castles are their evocative legacy. Terrible battles were fought around them and blood spilled on their stones. Centuries of kings, queens, heroes and plain folk passed through their portals. In Lisbon, within the majestic walls of São Jorge, daring explorers were honoured, criminals – and the innocent – imprisoned, great plays performed, inspiring poetry recited. There is still a grand *sala* for meeting, and a restaurant for eating. Water tinkles in weathered fountains. Children climb unwarlike cannons and veterans of real wars bang down their dominoes. Families stroll under tall trees and admire the peacocks and swans and bright-plumed birds that cackle and cry over oldest Lisbon. Below the broad ramparts lies the sprawling capital, a magnificent jigsaw in river-misted greys and earthy reds with the River Tejo for a frame. The power and the glory, the practical defences, the threat and challenge that São Jorge and all Portugal's splendid castles represented are gone; in their place is immortality.

Dom Afonso Henriques, Portugal's first king, lived to be nearly eighty, an astonishing age for those times. He died on 6 December 1185, and was buried in the church of Santa Cruz, Coimbra. He had ruled for fifty-seven years. He had made himself king, and

Portugal a kingdom – defying his cousin, Alfonso VII, in Spain, who had assumed no less a title than emperor. He vanquished Moorish strongholds across the country: Beja and Évora, Moura and Serpa came into his fold – briefly, for the Moors were far from finished. From these Alentejo campaigns emerged Portugal's own El Cid, the mysterious Geraldo Sem Pavor, Gerald the Fearless, who fought prodigiously for Christian, for Moor – perhaps, historians suggest, by agreement with his king – and for himself. Like El Cid, Afonso Henriques had been knighted in the Spanish town of Zamora.

Portugal came into being by the strong arm of its first king, a man who was audacious, astute, ambitious and of immense personal courage – and who could cheerfully break his promises, and tear up treaties as it suited him. Oliveira Martins, the nineteenth-century historian whose renown in Portugal is only exceeded by the redoubtable Alexandre Herculano, was never constrained by false reverence. No man deserves greater respect in the very soul of the Portuguese than its first king, he wrote in a clear-eyed portrait. Portugal became fact 'thanks to the valiant, mediocre, tenacious, brutal and perfidious character of Afonso Henriques'.

Except in fables, no one pretends that the power of kings derives from qualities that are entirely virtuous. In Portugal, in the three hereditary dynasties of monarchs, the Houses of Burgundy, Avis and Bragança, who ruled Portugal until 1910 – except for the sixty-year period of rule from Spain, which the Portuguese do their utmost to forget – there was much earnest and constructive rule that enhanced Portugal's internal development, external expansion and overall well-being.

But in these long centuries there was also perfidy, murder and madness, sagas rich in intrigue, feuding and foul deeds. There were strange and unhealthy marriages, creeping illness, horrible death. As for royal genealogy, so numerous were the bastards that not even the inestimable Oliveira Martins could keep track.

Afonso Henriques had retained his French connection by marrying Mafalda, daughter of the count of Maurienne and Savoy. Initiating a string of Iberian alliances that were often of only brief duration, he married off two of his daughters, Urraca to Fernando

II of Leon and Mafalda to Alfonso, the king of Aragon. All three of his bastard sons did well: two fought in Portugal's army, the third enjoyed the position – possibly too well for he had to resign – of Grand Master of the Military Order of St John of Jerusalem.

His oldest son became King Sancho I of Portugal. Long before his father's death Sancho had led campaigns to oust the Moors and, after their initial defeat at Silves – when, once again, English crusaders broke the terms of the Moors' retreat in a frenzy of plunder, rape and massacre – promptly and prematurely declared himself 'King of Portugal and of the Algarve', a title that endured to 1910 and the end of monarchy. Yet he found time to make music with his court – he was said to be a fine lyric poet – and to father several children, nine from his wife, Dulce of Barcelona, and at least two others. He also made a great deal of money from trade, mainly from Flanders. He died extremely rich, aged fifty-seven, in 1211.

By his will huge quantities of gold coin, as well as lands, properties, castles, furniture, jewels, cloth and all the rest of his worldly goods were widely, and specifically, distributed. Among bequests to the Church and the religious orders was a sum to the Cistercians at Alcobaça to build a leper house. Leprosy, thought to have entered Portugal with the crusaders, had the ring of horror to it then as later. Dom Sancho could not have known that his heir, Afonso II, whose childhood illnesses had left him with the unflattering nickname 'the Fat', would eventually die of this terrible disease, although not before marrying a Castilian princess and having four children.

His son, thirteen-year-old Sancho II, inherited, in 1223, nothing but trouble – from the Church which had excommunicated his father and only agreed to bury him on rigorous conditions, from the court and its intrigues and, ultimately, from his own much cleverer brother, yet another Afonso, who had been raised and educated in Paris. Poor confused Dom Sancho was scarcely married, in his thirties, before his wife was snatched away so that there could be no heir, and he himself was ultimately hounded out of Portugal and died in Toledo in 1248.

A resumed crusade led by the knights of the Order of Santiago had made headway against the weakening Moors, forcing them from Mértola, Tavira and Cacela. The reconquest in Portugal was triumphantly completed with the capture of Faro and the last Algarve strongholds in 1249 under the new king, Dom Afonso III. The Moors, after more than five centuries, were vanquished. And if, these days, there is nothing of the Muslim grandeur of Granada, no mosque as sublime as Córdoba, no city with the Moorish splendour of Seville, the Portuguese have no regrets: Portugal had won the unity that Spain would not have until 1492.

In Faro today, steps away from cheerful shopping areas and promenades, the city walls still stand. Within them is a quiet world of old stone, the *Sé* (cathedral) with orange trees lining the *largo* in front, the bishop's palace, the city museum and library, narrow streets of small homes and cottages. Through a small and unpretentious archway with none of the lovely proportions of the main Moorish entrance, is the sea – and, unexpectedly, a railway track set at the shoreline. At intervals diesel trains shuffle by. A minuscule bridge spans the low channel between lagoon and cosy harbour with the station just beyond. The railway links coastal towns with the national network, and Spain.

If the Portuguese, a relaxed, self-confident people, have a single national complex, it is over Spain, their only neighbour, five times as big, and inescapable. Rails and roads and the full panoply of modern communications and trade link the two nations, yet a barrier divides them that is invisible, intangible, perhaps even indestructible.

'There exist difficulties in relations,' Portuguese and Spanish deputies to the European Parliament cautiously admitted after a couple of years of EEC membership. From a military officer it came straight from the heart. 'We were taught to hate Spain,' said Major Vítor Alves, born in 1935 and one of the prime movers in the 1974 revolution. God is a Spaniard, declare Portuguese farmers, bemoaning a cruel turn of fate. From Spain, it is said, come neither good winds nor good marriages.

To the Romans, Visigoths and Muslims, Portugal and Spain were a single entity. Wrenched apart by King Afonso Henriques, the separate kingdoms maintained links through centuries of royal intermarriage. In 1253 Portugal's Dom Afonso III, to gain recognition of his sovereignty of the Algarve, arranged to marry a daughter of King Alfonso X of Castile. That she was still an infant and he already married did not appear to trouble anyone except his French wife – and she, fortuitously, died five years later.

King Dinis, son of Dom Afonso, and his bride, the young and pious Isabel of Aragon, had two children. He, less virtuous than she, also fathered – according to the chronicles – seven other children upon seven different mothers. Titles and favours granted to the illegitimate sons provoked jealousies that only the saintly Queen Isabel was able to calm. Differences with Castile were resolved by treaty, confirmed in the usual way: Dom Dinis married off his daughter, Constança, and his son, who would become Afonso IV, to the Castilian king and his sister.

As king, Afonso IV, inevitably entangled with factions in Spain, thought to play the game by the same rules. Yet his daughter, Maria, was abandoned by the Castilian king like the pawn she was and his son and heir, Pedro, though married into Castile, found true love with a Galician lady in his wife's court, Inês de Castro. The awful story of Pedro and Inês is one that every Portuguese schoolchild knows: her brutal murder by three advisers of Dom Afonso IV, the frightful revenge of Dom Pedro on the two killers he eventually caught – their hearts drawn from their bodies, one from the chest, the other from the back – and the grisly crowning of Inês's long-dead corpse.

King Pedro I is 'the Justicer'. His dreadful vengeance on Inês's murderers was only one of many violent punishments; his main preoccupation, his consuming passion, was the administration of justice. To the eminent Herculano he was a madman with lucid intervals. Yet although his justice was often harsh, ordinary people – the *povo* – respected him for it, and his reorganization of jurisdiction gave Portugal a solid and unified structure. For the iconoclastic Oliveira Martins, if Afonso Henriques was the founding bandit chief, stern Dom Pedro I is the father of the Portuguese family.

True love has a fitting forever-after ending in finely carved twin tombs set whitely in the transept of Alcobaça Abbey where Dom Pedro and Inês were placed 'foot to foot', as he commanded – a king's spatial measure, for they are several feet apart – so that the first thing he might see, come the Resurrection, was the face of his beloved. But as in any grand tale of passion and horror there remains a small mystery: the fate of Inês's third killer, who was never found.

His name was Diogo Lopes Pacheco. A beggar helped him escape, in one version. He hid in the stony villages of the mountainous Beira – Piódão, perhaps. Families with the Pacheco name around there are numerous, and Pachecos have served their country honourably. Yet family pride is a peculiar thing: convinced they are descended from the third assassin, Pacheco families blithely gather on a Sunday in June to celebrate his escape from the king's fury with jugs of wine and a jolly picnic.

The eldest son of Dom Pedro, rich, handsome and feckless, became King Fernando I in 1367. He muddled through his reign, even as Lisbon was growing in importance, devoting much of his time and energy to hunting and fornication. With Portugal caught between rivalries in Spain, he first agreed to marry a princess from Aragon, then declared for a daughter of Henry of Trastamara – Henry II of Castile. Finally he married – in the old Templar church at Leça do Bailio, near Oporto, since he rightly suspected disapproval in Lisbon – the ambitious niece of his Portuguese adviser, Leonor Teles, who was already married.

For Portugal's rulers up to now the way had been clear: betrothals, marriages of convenience and alliances binding Portugal to the ruling houses of Spain – *tal pai, tal filho*, like father, like son. The pattern was marred only by the aspirations and claims of royal bastards, the convoluted intrigues in the various courts and, in 1383, the end of a direct male line.

That year, twelve-year-old Beatriz, Dom Fernando's heiress, had married the recently widowed Juan I, now king of Castile (having already been promised to the English prince, Edward, when she was ten and he six and then to a young son of Juan). By the terms of the marriage contract Beatriz would succeed to the Portuguese throne and Juan bear the title, as consort, of 'King of Portugal'.

Dom Fernando's youthful bloom had faded into weak-kneed

apathy. With his sudden death six months later, Juan rashly ordered the Portuguese to proclaim Beatriz queen, at the same time adding Portugal's arms to his own standard. Supported by pro-Castilian churchmen and some of the landed aristocracy, he entered Portugal, assumed authority from Leonor, the *governador* widow of Fernando – and soon dispatched her to Castile.

The Portuguese were outraged at the presumption, although less than unhappy to see the departure of an unpopular woman. There was tumult in the streets of Lisbon and confusion across the land. Who had a rightful claim? Who could be king? Most conspicuous was Dom João, the Grand Master of the Order of Avis and illegitimate son of King Pedro. João had vented his rage at court intrigues by killing the Galician adviser, and lover, of Leonor. Storming the cathedral, a Lisbon mob hurled the Spanish bishop from its tower. João had patriots on his side. This was a revolution, the first popular revolt in Europe. The people of Lisbon appealed to him to become defender of the realm. Both sides made preparations for war, the Portuguese cause backed by town and country folk with grievances against Castile. On 6 April 1385, the twenty-seven-year-old João was proclaimed King João I and a new dynasty, the House of Avis, created on a foundation of popular support.

The strength of those foundations was put to the test late in the afternoon of 14 August, near Porto de Mós. Dom João, together with his close friend and military commander, *Condestável* (Constable) Nun' Álvares Pereira from the Alentejo, deployed the Portuguese forces and a support troop of English archers so skilfully that, although heavily outnumbered – by more than 20,000 to less than 10,000 – they quickly vanquished the Castilian enemy. Their victory in the battle of Aljubarrota gave the Portuguese two centuries of independence, reinforcing national unity in a more equably, more commercially structured society – merchants had backed João, nobility opposed him, including a brother, killed in the action, of Nun' Álvares Pereira. Aljubarrota remains a landmark not only in the history of the Portuguese but in their perception of Spain.

In a light-hearted Algarve–Andalusian debate more than six hundred years later, a Portuguese politician and member of the European Parliament could say: 'In Portugal *antiespanholismo* [an anti-Spanish attitude] is cultivated . . . A Portuguese who dares to show open cooperation with Spain can be accused of being a bad Portuguese, even a traitor.' Is this an exaggerated view? Possibly not. The Portuguese have long memories. 'Since Aljubarrota,' he declaimed, 'Portugal has lived under the terror of Spain.' But the time had come 'to conquer these demons. After all, our independence is no longer in danger.'

The gathering was friendly, one of many cultural encounters held in the first years of EEC membership. In the euphoria of incoming floods of money, Spain and Portugal were like two new boys arriving at school on the same day who shake hands and decide to be friends. Their prime ministers, of different political stance and viewpoint, engaged in discussions in evident amity – one newspaper commented that these mini-summits were becoming something of a bore, and that Aljubarrota had at least been livelier. In a cartoon comment on this mutual warmth, Spain's *El País* showed Iberia as two faces smiling benevolently at one another.

The protocols and accords multiply, along with cultural, environmental, educational, sporting and social exchanges, though economic imbalance causes alarm. Which, in the context of long-standing mutual dislike, was more of a shock – Spanish troops taking part in Portuguese manoeuvres, or Paulo Futre, a Portuguese football star, winning brilliant victories for a Spanish team? Earnest efforts are consistently made to impress on young Iberians the importance of good neighbourliness but the thrilling exploits of the past, and the gorier stories, are the basis of patriotism and not to be ignored. Portuguese are brought up on the classic accounts of their remarkable history. A favourite story is about the baker of Aljubarrota, Brites de Almeida, a formidable woman who stoutly defended her town in battle by laying into the Castilian army with her long baking spoon. She killed seven Castilians and, with the true spice of horror, baked them in her oven.

The happy marriage of Dom João I and his English wife, Philippa, astonished the Portuguese, not through any lack of admiration for her – she was very well liked – but for the virtue that entered royal life. Dom João's first love had been a *donzela nobre*, a damsel named Inês Pires by whom he had two children, Afonso –

who became the Count of Barcelos and, in his old age, the first Duke of Bragança, hard, shrewd and immensely rich – and a girl, Brites. After marriage to Philippa, Dom João 'in the vigour of life,' wrote a Portuguese historian, 'got no bastards. What a singular change in our court customs.' Numerous courtiers and their ladies were chastened into marriage. It was their chattering over his embracing a court lady in the Sintra palace, allegedly, that provoked Dom João to order a ceiling there to be repainted to show a flock of magpies.

Por bem, the magpies declare; Dom João's motto is repeated on his tomb. It was true that he always meant well. He was a straightforward man, lucky in his friends, his wife, his children. His friends – the scholarly Dr João das Regras, who was his adviser, and the able *Condestável* Nun' Álvares Pereira – had won him a throne, a battle and lasting security. (They became even closer with the marriage of Álvares's daughter, Brites, to Dom João's illegitimate son, Afonso. Her dowry formed the basis of the wealthy ducal House of Bragança.) Queen Philippa gave her husband, and Portugal, an enduring alliance with England and, through her brilliant and devoted children, the intellectual thrust that powered Portugal out of the obscurity of the Middle Ages into the sunlight of the Renaissance.

Of the *infantes* (princes), Duarte, the introspective heir, wrote a book, *Leal Conselheiro*, 'Loyal Counsellor'; Pedro travelled widely, sending home the latest maps and works of literature and geography. He was the cleverest and brightest spirit of his family, though solitary, brooding Henry, mainspring of Portugal's great discoveries, won greater fame. Isabel, the only daughter, married the flamboyant Duke of Burgundy, Philip the Good, but always propounded her family's cause. Dom João's illegitimate daughter, Brites, married Thomas FitzAlan, Earl of Arundel and, as a widow, another English nobleman.

The princes married unusually late or not at all. First to marry was the fourth son, João, who, by special dispensation, married his niece Isabel, daughter of his half-brother, the Count of Barcelos. Duarte and Pedro married princesses of Aragon from contesting families. The marriage, not so much later, of Pedro's daughter,

Isabel, aged eight, to Duarte's heir and child king, Afonso V, aged ten, led only to inter-family squabbles and tragedy.

The first cruel blow to strike the family was the death from the plague of Philippa, on the eve of the departure of her sons for Muslim Ceuta – where they won their knighthood with swords she gave them on her deathbed, along with a fragment of the True Cross. (The pure theatre of the deathbed scene, and Philippa's last composed words to her sons, comes from the vivid chronicles of Eanes de Zurara.) Her husband, Dom João, survived to the age of seventy-six. He died in 1433, on the anniversary of the battle of Aljubarrota, with four of his sons at his bedside. His great friend, Nun' Álvares Pereira, had spent many years of his life building the Convento do Carmo in Lisbon. He renounced his titles, entered the Carmelite Order and died, two years before Dom João, as Frei Nuno de Santa Maria – Brother Nuno.

King Duarte I reigned only five years and died, it was thought, from grief over the dreadful fate of his youngest brother, Fernando, delivered as hostage to the Muslims after the ill-judged 1437 expedition against Tangier, Ceuta was the prize the Muslims demanded. It was never conceded; Fernando, after six years of imprisonment and vengeful cruelty died in Fez. His sufferings, the abuse of his body, became blistering literature. Through the intrigues of his half-brother, the Count of Barcelos, Pedro too met a violent death – in the brief battle of Alfarrobeira, north of Santarém, shot through the heart in the first flurry of arrows aimed by the forces of his son-in-law, the young King Afonso V.

Afonso's reign was confused and undistinguished. His attentions were divided between Africa – where he recovered the bones of his uncle, Fernando – the complex manoeuvres of Spanish factions and his own family. He knighted his son, Dom João, the 'Perfect Prince', amid the carnage of victory in the Moorish fortress at Arzila, and he did take some interest in the increasingly successful explorations. He was 'the African', but he could have been called by many other names and probably was. In the succession claims in Spain he took the opportunity, as a widower and ignoring bitter opposition from the Portuguese, to marry his own niece, Joana,

the daughter of his sister, Joana, who had married Henry IV of
Castile. Now, to Portuguese disgust, he called himself King of
Castile.

Factionalism led to war. Dom Afonso's forces were defeated in a
long and bloody battle in Toro in 1476. The victors were the
redoubtable Ferdinand of Aragon and Isabella of Castile who had
married in 1469. Seeking support from France, Afonso appeared to
be overcome by the folly of his actions and went into hiding,
declaring only that he wished now to be a monk. He was soon
found and persuaded to return to Portugal. He decided to abdicate
but, before the Cortes were gathered, died morosely in 1481.

His son was now King João II – vigorous, clear-headed, ambitious, dynamic. He had experience of government and long before
had assumed responsibility for the explorations proceeding rapidly
down the coast of Africa. As king, he decided to solidify Portugal's
claims on the coast against numerous prowling trading ships.
(Lisbon merchants were happy to hear that the entire crew of a
ship from Flanders had allegedly been eaten.) Dom João ensured
that the trading-post at São Jorge da Mina was well fortified.

Under the command of Diogo de Azambuja two 400-ton cargo
ships and nine caravels set sail for Africa. (One captain was Bartolomeu Dias who would be the first to round the southern cape.)
The ships carried five hundred soldiers and a hundred or so stonemasons and carpenters as well as construction materials and cannon.
Dom Diogo obtained permission from the African chiefs at Mina –
they could hardly have refused – to build a castle-warehouse and
church. In this way Portugal constructed the first of many castles
and forts outside its own small country, each plainly signalling
national determination – eventually across a huge empire – to take,
hold and protect the gains of a formidable enterprise.

Dom João had all the qualities of kingliness. He clarified rights
and corrected abuses. He asserted his grip on the nobility through
revision of a law, the *Lei Mental*, conceived by King João I and
enacted by the succeeding Dom Duarte, that each nobleman should
pay homage in order to have his titles and grants of land confirmed.
(This useful law lasted until 1832.) Sensing threat, he found an

excuse for the execution on a charge of treason of the current Duke of Bragança (whose vast estates were restored to the Crown). He dealt with a plot against him by summoning, and stabbing to death, the Duke of Viseu, his cousin and his brother-in-law. The duke's younger brother, Manuel, Duke of Beja, remained loyal to Dom João – an early stroke of fortune for he later succeeded him.

As a boy of sixteen João had married the twelve-year-old daughter, Leonor, of his uncle Fernando. Their only son, Afonso, in a familiar alliance, married the eldest daughter of the Catholic monarchs in Spain. A year later, in 1491, on a June day when his father was enjoying a swim in the Tejo at Santarém, Afonso was thrown from his horse and died. Dom João also had a bastard son, Jorge, who was given titles but was not made heir, largely due to Leonor's stout defence of the interests of her brother Manuel.

Dom João had faced plots in his family, the enmity of nobles and the anti-Jewish hysteria of Spain. As Islam surged, he hungered obsessively for contact with the legendary Christian land of Prester John. Determinedly, he pursued the search for a route to the spices of the Indies and was not surprised that Columbus – wherever his westward voyage had taken him – had not found it. After decades of Portuguese persistence, Bartolomeu Dias, in his rounding of Africa's cape, had shown the way.

Dom João died in 1495 at the brink of glory, aged only forty. The stated cause of death was dropsy but there were strong hints of poison – a Venetian spy reported that everyone knew the king's enemies wanted to kill him; even his wife appeared at King João's deathbed only by order of her brother, the heir Dom Manuel. Dom João had been ill for some time. Doctors tried different remedies, including the medicinal waters of Caldas de Monchique. Whatever their benefit for other sufferers – they have given comfort since Roman times though it is not now claimed that they help kidney ailments – the Monchique waters only aggravated the king's pain. He died at Alvor, and if the nobility were glad of it, ordinary people mourned. Barbers stopped work for six months in a concerted effort to make nobles display a grief they did not feel (long hair and a beard were signs of mourning). The king was buried in Silves cathedral – a stone marks the place. Four years later his remains were transferred to Batalha, and splinters from the original coffin of the once Perfect Prince became treasured relics.

Manuel, as king, completed the grand design conceived by Prince Henry and elaborated by King João II. His father was the adopted son and heir of Prince Henry; his cousin and brother-in-law, Dom João II, despite a passion for secrecy, had kept him fully informed. Dom Manuel's symbol, for he was as demanding and ambitious as his predecessor, was the armillary sphere, a hollow globe used by astronomers. Yet his first act as king promoted domestic peace: he returned their lands and properties to the Bragança family. Many towns, too, received new, confirmed or revised charters.

Abroad, with the sea route to India at last attained by Vasco da Gama, King Manuel I gave himself the title: 'King, by the Grace of God, of Portugal and the Algarves, both this Side of the Sea and beyond it in Africa, Lord of Guinea and of the Navigation, Conquest and Commerce of Ethiopia, Arabia, Persia and India'. Today, a modest statue stands in the small town of Alcochete, where the king was born, on the unfashionable southern shore of the Tejo estuary. Cobbled waves roll at the king's feet. A palm tree bows his way. Steps away, fishing boats tie up to a homely jetty. Yet fact outgrew hyperbole: the true empire and the seas it dominated soon stretched beyond the grand title. As discovery became conquest and trade expanded, castles and fortresses sprouted. Some began as modest factories, or trading stations, and were later strongly fortified. Great fleets left Lisbon, their declared object neither conquest nor occupation but protection of the sea routes.

The Portuguese had strong leaders – the first viceroys and governors, Francisco de Almeida, Afonso de Albuquerque and Vasco da Gama himself were brilliant and authoritative men. It was very quickly clear that protection could not be achieved by unassertive means, and the forts rose fast. In these demanding times no one was a slouch. At Kilwa, even captains and *fidalgos* – the chronicle reports – pushed barrows while soldiers, sailors and stonemasons prepared mortar and cut and laid stone; the fortress was pronounced secure, the walls sufficiently high, in sixteen days.

In Morocco, the Portuguese already held fortresses in Ceuta, Alcácer-Seguir, Arzila and Tangier. More were built – notably, at

Azammur and Mazagão (today's El-Jadida). They rose in west and east Africa and, as the Portuguese forcefully disposed of opposition, in strategic coastal positions from Ormuz at the mouth of the Persian Gulf down the Malabar coast of India and across to Macau and the Moluccas. Many of them still stand – huge, strong, powerfully impressive, but they are no longer on guard.

In Ghana children frolic on the wooden boats below the walls of Axim and tourists, as well as Ghanaians, admire Elmina. Fort Jesus in Mombasa is museum as well as tourist feature. Modern Morocco and Portugal are amicable business partners, the Moroccan forts a symbol for both of bloodier times. Goa was annexed by India in December 1961; the great fort of Diu stands mighty still. In Macau, the fortress was tastefully converted to a luxurious *pousada*. In Ethiopia, seventeenth-century Portuguese influence lives on among the royal castles of Gondar and the stone charm of King Fasiladas's private swimming-pool.

4 Empire, earthquake and the argument of tyrants

King Manuel I lived his life richly and to the full, the extraordinary architecture he encouraged in Portugal a graphic signal of his taste and the times. Wealth floated in on the Tejo tides in seething abundance: spices from the east – pepper, cinnamon, nutmeg, cloves – and gold from Africa, sugar from Madeira (and soon from Brazil and São Tomé), cargoes from every foreign port. Some ships carried slaves; the demand from developing sugar plantations would turn an already brutal trade (of perhaps 150,000 slaves shipped from Africa in the second half of the fifteenth century) into a barbarous and heavy multinational traffic that persisted into the nineteenth century.

Dom Manuel's viceroys and captains sent exotic gifts – among them five elephants, 'four males and a female', wrote the chronicler Damião de Góis, describing the grand processions of Dom Manuel and his entourage through Lisbon and the countryside. Behind the elephants pranced a finely caparisoned horse ridden by a Persian with a leopard on the crupper. Far in front, so that the elephants could not see it, went a rhinoceros and its Indian trainers.

To mark the election of Pope Leo, Dom Manuel sent one of the elephants, the horse, its Persian attendant and the leopard as gifts. The trappings were sumptuous and the presentation in Rome a huge success, especially when the elephant sprayed water over many cardinals and other guests. Later, Dom Manuel sent the pope more gifts, including the rhinoceros. Sadly, the ship foundered in a storm. The rhinoceros carcass was found on a beach; it was stuffed with straw and sent to Rome. Albrecht Dürer saw it and made it the subject of one of his most famous engravings.

There were, as time passed, many more shipwrecks and far

greater losses than one unfortunate rhinoceros. Thousands of men (and a few women) made the long, slow journey to India – more than six months from Lisbon to Goa. A round voyage, with a standard stopover in Goa, took at least a year and a half. Conditions were appalling: always there was overcrowding, foul drinking water, crudely inadequate sanitation. As many as half of the six hundred to eight hundred passengers, who were supposed to take their own food, died of dysentery, scurvy, typhus, one fever or another or, if the ship called at Moçambique, of malaria. '*Ao cheiro desta canela, o reino nos despovoa,*' mourned poet Sá de Miranda – 'At the scent of this cinnamon, the kingdom loses its people'.

In the reign of Dom Manuel there were more than 250 sailings from Lisbon to India. The ships now were square-riggers, to begin with of some 400 tons. As the years passed, bigger and bigger ships were built, of 1,000 tons and 1,600 tons and larger still for greater carrying capacity. Ponderous at best, ill-equipped to beat off predators (the Dutch and English were later quick to snatch at any advantage) the great galleons, among the most beautiful ships ever built, sank by the score.

Afonso de Albuquerque, governor of India, was himself shipwrecked, immediately after the Portuguese conquest and sacking of Malacca in 1511. Sailing for India aboard his flagship, *Flor de la Mar* ('Flower of the Sea'), he was caught in a storm off Sumatra. The governor and his captains survived on a raft. The galleon, and all its treasure of gold, including the golden throne of the sultan of Malacca, precious stones and bronze cannon, sank to the bottom – 'the greatest wealth ever lost in a single shipwreck,' wrote Gaspar Correa, a chronicler of the eastern empire. The wreck was located only in 1988; the value of the treasure was estimated at over $3bn.

King Manuel desired more than vast wealth, dominance across distant seas and the rare and exotic prizes of empire. He wanted Spain, and hoped by the magic of marriage alliance to bring all Spain into his empire. The price was high, for Spain's Catholic monarchs demanded expulsion of the Jews from Portugal as a condition. Manuel was certainly persistent: he married three Spanish brides. The first was Isabel, oldest daughter of Ferdinand and

Isabella, and the childless widow of Afonso, son of Dom João II, whose place he had assumed as heir. When Isabel – and an infant son – died, Dom Manuel married her sister, Maria, who gave him ten children. Last, when he was once again, at forty-nine, a widower and the Iberian picture had changed, Manuel was so smitten by the young woman contracted to marry his own son and heir that he married her himself. Leonor, his third bride, was his niece-by-marriage and sister of Charles, the new king of Spain; Charles, the first Habsburg on the throne of Spain, was soon to be elected Emperor Charles V of the Holy Roman Empire.

From this marriage a daughter was born – Maria, who, though rich and beautiful, never married because, it was said, of what her dowry could do to the national treasury. Perhaps her beauty was not entirely wasted; some thought she was the muse, the romantic inspiration, for Camões. As for Dom Manuel's ambitions, in the end, through a stroke of historic irony, precisely the opposite of his grand scheme occurred. When the male line of Avis died, Spain claimed Portugal.

King Manuel I died aged fifty-two in 1521 of a fever, 'a sort of lethargy', and was succeeded by his son, King João III, at nineteen so diffident that everyone was astonished when he seduced a lady-in-waiting of his former fiancée and new stepmother Leonor. The child born of the encounter was the first royal bastard in years. Yet dutifully, and for the usual reasons of restoring peace – what endlessly fractious, suspicious and grasping neighbours these two extraordinary Iberian nations proved to be – he married Catarina, another sister of Charles V; Charles in turn married João's sister, who now became the Empress Isabel.

The reign of Dom João III saw significant changes for the Portuguese. Lisbon was growing, the countryside emptying. The ships sailed out to India – one fleet of them in 1524 with the retired and ageing Vasco da Gama, Admiral of the Indies, as second viceroy – but trading wealth was disappearing into the hands of foreign merchants and bankers and profits on spices were now low. Looking elsewhere, Dom João granted great coastal sections of Brazil to Portuguese *donatários* (proprietors), to occupy and settle. French and then English pirates harassed both Spain and

Portugal on the western sea routes. Leonor, King Manuel's widow, married King François I of France, who declined to restrain French privateers with the famous words: 'I should very much like to see the clause in Adam's will which excluded me from the partition of the world.' (He had once dubbed Dom Manuel 'the grocer king'.)

Religious schisms were shaking Europe apart. Martin Luther in 1520 burned the papal bull condemning his doctrines. In Portugal Dom João, urged by his zealous brother, Henrique, Archbishop of Évora, won the pope's consent to institute the Inquisition. Rome itself was about to be sacked, victim of the war between Charles V and François I. The old yearning for Prester John vanished when an ambassador from Ethiopia was presented to the court, his letters addressed to the late King Manuel. In these years, too, the Society of Jesus appeared in Portugal – Dom João chose Simão Rodrigues, the first Portuguese follower of St Ignatius, as a tutor for his son. Within a short time the Jesuits dominated education in Portugal and, led by a Basque priest who became St Francis Xavier, gained even greater authority through forceful and far-reaching mission work abroad.

Dom João III reigned for thirty-six difficult years, attempting to maintain the policy of the Avis kings of avoiding foreign entanglement and to take up arms only against the infidel. He had ten children; nine died. The one survivor, also João, lived long enough to marry Juana, the daughter of Charles V, but died early in 1554. A few days later his widow gave birth to a son, *o Desejado*, the much desired, Sebastião. When Sebastião was three, Dom João suddenly died of a stroke.

Sebastião grew up wilful, stubborn, foolish and, if the passionately cherished independence of the Portuguese had not hung on his health and head, he might have been decently ignored. He enjoyed hard exercise, yet it seemed something was wrong where it mattered most – his sexual organs. There was talk of marriage to Mary Queen of Scots, or to a daughter of Spain's King Philip II; nothing came of it. (Portuguese patriots blame only Philip.) Sebastião's head became filled with the crusading ardour of his forebears. At the age of twenty-four he led an unwilling army in an absurdly mismanaged holy war against strong Muslim forces in north

Africa. At the battle of Alcácer Quibir on 4 August 1578, he was quickly killed and the Portuguese army destroyed. Some 8,000 Portuguese died in the battle, another 15,000 were helplessly taken prisoner.

Portugal was stunned; Camões, whose exalting poem, *Os Lusíadas*, had been published in 1572, lay ill in hospital. 'And so I shall end my life,' he wrote, 'and all will see that I loved my country so that not only was I content to die on her soil, but die with her.'

Sebastião living was inept, flighty and arrogant, Sebastião dead an instant hero. But was he dead? Who had seen him die? A naked body had been found and buried, Lisbon learned nearly three weeks later, in the governor's house in Alcácer. What happened to his fine armour, his sword, his standard? Who was the caped figure that silently entered Arzila among a group of Portuguese who got away? In the profound shock of appalling defeat, many Portuguese people – superstitious, religious, premonitory and inexhaustibly prolix – chose to believe that Sebastião would reappear to lead the nation to glory.

Legends grew and were most wonderfully elaborated. Much was made of rambling verses on a prophetic theme, *trovas*, written by a cobbler in Trancoso; they were banned by the Inquisition and became even more popular. Around the obstinate head of the living Sebastião had whirled the vital question of succession. Now, for many, the messianic dream – it came to be called *sebastianismo* – was the only escape from the logical end to all those endogamous, near-incestuous marriages: the rightful claims of Spain.

A last desperate effort was made to keep Spain at bay. Henrique, sixty-six years old, a cardinal and Grand Inquisitor, was the only surviving son of King Manuel. He was proclaimed king, and offered to seek papal dispensation so that he could marry. A suitable bride, in terms of continuity of the monarchy, was available: the thirteen-year-old daughter of the Braganças. From Spain, Philip II easily obstructed the match: he bribed as many Portuguese as possible through his agent, Cristóvão de Moura, confidently insisted on his own claim through his Portuguese mother (his Portuguese wife, Maria, daughter of Dom João III, and their mad son, Don Carlos, were dead) and – for many Portuguese the supreme inducement – promised to pay the balance of the enormous ransom Morocco was demanding for Portuguese prisoners.

For Portugal, the irony was bitter. During King Sebastião's reign Portuguese settlement in Macau had been accepted by the Chinese emperor. Portugal's empire, bound across distant seas by a chain of forts and lively trading centres, had never been greater. Yet Portugal was broke, its wealth dispersed in the attempt to sustain its sprawling domains and finally wasted on a futile expedition. Recovering Sebastião's body – if it was his – had cost a fortune. Families had sent money and jewels towards the ransom of the eighty or so nobles still held in Fez. Some, though not all, had been released. Thousands of Portuguese soldiers, along with Portugal's ambassador, who offered himself as hostage, failed to make it home; many were enslaved.

The Cardinal-King Henrique died on 31 January 1580. Sebastião would live on in glorious memory; Henrique was angrily condemned by plain folk, the *povo*, to live in hell for suggesting that Philip had a stronger claim than one last Portuguese possibility, Dom António, the prior of Crato, a bastard son of a brother of King João III. At a meeting of the Cortes, the *povo* insisted they would rather die than welcome Philip II. But as pressure from Philip intensified and new offers were made – including autonomous rule – the country divided. As Spanish forces entered from the east, Santarém pronounced António king. He entered Lisbon briefly but was forced to flee as Spanish troops arrived. He won patriotic support in Coimbra and in Oporto. His last Portuguese refuge was the Açores, where the wild bulls of Terceira island were usefully brought into action against invading Spanish forces. Although António's cause as pretender was taken up by England's Queen Elizabeth, all efforts failed and he finally died in France in 1595.

Between 1580 and 1640 three Spanish kings, Philip II, III and IV, ruled the peninsula. European power shifted dramatically in those years; 1588 saw the defeat of Spain's Invincible Armada, more by wind and weather, most historians agree, than by Sir Francis Drake. Many of the ships in that fleet were built in Lisbon and manned by

Portuguese. But Spain's enemies were imposed on Portugal: first, Portuguese ports were closed to English ships and then, in 1594, Philip banned the Dutch, seizing some fifty ships lying in the Tejo. The Dutch retaliated by heading directly to India, guided by a Dutch trader who had travelled aboard Portuguese ships. By 1602 both England and the Dutch had an East India Company and Portugal's eastern monopoly was shattered.

None of the Philips spent much time in Portugal. Philip II had been declared King Philip I of Portugal in the convent at Tomar in March 1581, and returned to Madrid in February 1583. It was the only journey in his life outside Spain. Advisers counselled him to make Lisbon his capital. Had he done so, the Portuguese story would be vastly different. But he did not. His son, Philip III, who inherited in 1598 territory greater than any single ruler before or since, made a short visit in 1619. Philip IV took virtually no interest in Portugal at all.

In 1640 a group of Portuguese conspirators persuaded a reluctant and cautious Duke of Bragança, a man whose pleasures were music and hunting, to become king. The family was the wealthiest in Portugal, with vast properties and numerous titles; an earlier Bragança had been a legitimate claimant. Details of the conspiracy were kept from the duke – not even the plotters were confident. Yet all went much as planned: on 1 December, early in the morning, they charged the palace in Lisbon – the governor was the Duchess of Mantua – shot her scheming secretary, Miguel de Vasconcelos, and tossed him out of the window. Spanish garrisons in the Tejo and coastal forts surrendered. The Duke of Bragança left his life of ease in Vila Viçosa to be acclaimed King João IV in Lisbon on 15 December. Supporting him to the hilt was his wife, yet another Spanish lady, Luisa de Guzmán, sister to a powerful Andalusian duke.

The first of December, the day of the overthrow of Spanish rule in 1640, is now a national holiday. Speeches are made. The present Duke of Bragança, a well-liked country gentleman, addresses a modest group of ardent monarchists. That he is heir to a non-existent throne is not the point. What is sparklingly clear in the flow of words is that never again will the Portuguese allow their independence to be taken from them. That the manifold demands of modern nationhood turn true independence to a fine abstract and that Spain, especially, is imposing new stresses upon small Portugal in the name of EEC economics is in this context ignored.

The Portuguese now had Dom João IV as their king and were the masters of their own destiny, but in fact they had little to celebrate. Although the Jesuit Padre António Vieira insisted that it was Dom João, not Sebastião, who was the redeemer-king, the reign consisted of a series of cautious steps, guided by Padre Vieira, to recover whole chunks of empire – the Dutch were now in Brazil and west Africa as well as to the east – to win influential allies, to rebuild national forces and to secure the frontier against Spain. In exchange for financial assistance in developing Brazil, Dom João restored to the New Christians property which had been seized by the Inquisition. Such pragmatism did not preclude his dedicating his crown, in 1646, to the Blessed Virgin (kings were never crowned again), nor from attending Inquisition burnings; the victim of one *auto-da-fé* was a northern nobleman who had promoted Dom João's restoration across Europe. An early threat was a palace plot linked to Spain, which was resolved by beheading three of the plotters – nobles who had been among the first to swear their loyalty, along with the young son of a duke who refused to denounce his father. Six commoners who had been implicated were hanged – as was, a few years later, an insufficiently calculating assassin who had been paid by Madrid to shoot the king during a religious procession.

Though much troubled by gout and saddened over the death from an illness of his adventurous oldest son, Teodósio, in 1653 – the youngster had left court to join the Portuguese forces in the Alentejo – Dom João died peacefully in November 1656. His patient reconstruction had been remarkably successful. If separation differences with Spain seemed for the present insoluble, the Dutch, to his delighted surprise, had been forced out of Brazil (and Angola) by rebellious Portuguese. Treaties had been signed with France and Holland, and with Charles I of England in 1642 and Oliver Cromwell's Commonwealth in 1654, reviving and significantly strengthening the Anglo-Portuguese alliance formed in 1373 and confirmed by the Treaty of Windsor in 1386, a year before the marriage of King João I to Philippa of Lancaster.

But now, while English merchants in Portugal celebrated the considerable privileges of favoured-nation status, ranging from religious liberty and their own burial-ground to low taxes and their own appointed judge, another marriage was in the air, a brilliant coup for Dom João's Spanish widow, Luisa, who had become regent after his death. The heir was her thirteen-year-old son, Afonso, unfortunately incapacitated physically and mentally by what his doctors called a *febre maligna*. He had a brother, Pedro, five years younger, and an older sister, born 1638, called Catarina. The two boys would become kings of Portugal. Catarina, for whom marriage with France's Louis XIV had seemed the likeliest possibility, became, as Catherine of Braganza, Queen of England.

Catherine's marriage to Charles II in May 1662 gave Portugal another treaty of alliance, ten warships and two regiments each of cavalry and infantry – 2,000 men, with horses, arms and supplies. They arrived in time to assist Portuguese forces in beating back the Spaniards from Évora and winning the crucial battles of Ameixial, Castelo Rodrigo and Montes Claros (vividly recorded on tile panels in the Palácio de Fronteira). In 1668, Spain, much weakened – clinging only to Portugal's north African seedbed of empire, Ceuta – at last recognized Portugal's independence. For Spain, after sixty years of dominating Portugal's possessions across the world, Ceuta – grimly Spanish to this day – was no grand prize.

The marriage gave England the largest royal dowry (two million cruzados, some £300,000) that had ever been conceded, trading rights with all Portuguese territories, Tangier and, as an afterthought, Bombay, which King Charles promptly handed to the East India Company for an annual rent of £10. (Tangier was abandoned in 1684.) It also introduced the English to an inestimable ritual of civilization: the drinking of tea, a five o'clock custom of Catherine and her court.

The young woman born in the great ducal palace at Vila Viçosa (where portraits showing dark eyes and slender elegance indicated a greater allure than English prejudice suggests) left her mark, too, on the north American continent. Two years after the wedding, the

British purchased New Amsterdam from the Dutch, and changed its name to New York after the king's brother, the Duke of York. A borough of the city called Kings County in honour of Charles is better known as Brooklyn; another borough, in tribute to Catherine was – and is – Queens.

The marriage of Catherine, diffident and Catholic, to the 'merry monarch' gave England no heir – Catherine suffered four miscarriages while Charles II, for his part, took solace elsewhere so vigorously that five of England's twenty-six dukes are descended from his mistresses. But when Catherine's earnest Catholicism and lack of English, which she never did learn, subjected her at times to hostility, Charles stood by her. She remained in England as dowager queen after his death and only returned to Portugal in 1692 on the death of his successor, King James II. She spent most of the last years of her life in Lisbon, in the palace of Bemposta, today a military academy with her coat of arms above its gate. She died in 1705.

Royal marriages in Portugal meanwhile had their own piquant aspects. Princess Marie-Françoise of Savoy married two Portuguese kings, Catherine's two brothers, in turn. And if the prime motive for the first match, with poor paralytic Afonso, was to assert French influence on Portuguese policy, the second motive (the first was unchanged) for the match with Pedro, five years younger, strong and passionate, might well have been love. In the convoluted palace plots and sub-plots, among Shakespearian characters spurred by lust for power, envy, hope and despair, by patriotism, maternal ambition, madness and grief, love was the only missing ingredient.

In the first years of the reign of Dom Afonso VI, with his mother as regent, the adolescent Afonso shocked the court by taking up with street gangs and choosing a conniving best friend from among them. His mother, thinking ahead, installed Pedro in a separate household but was herself banished from court and ordered to a convent in a coup instigated by a courtier, the Count of Castelo Melhor. Afonso ended the regency; Castelo Melhor, assuming the archaic title of *escrivão da puridade* (literally 'scribe of purity', it simply means the king's private secretary), ruled for the king, determined the forceful – and effective – policy against Spain and set the terms that ended the restoration wars. He copied the authoritative style of Richelieu in France and he arranged Afonso's marriage with Marie-Françoise, a proxy wedding sealed by contract in Paris in June 1666. But, in the end, he was undone by French intrigue. He fled to Buçaco, hid in the dense forest, and ultimately established himself in England at the court of Queen Catherine.

The royal drama was building to its tragic climax, with Afonso as victim. With Castelo Melhor out of the way, Marie-Françoise locked herself in a convent, and requested the annulment of the marriage. Pedro moved into the royal palace. Smooth-talking nobles persuaded Afonso to hand the reins of government to his brother. In the Cortes held in January 1668, the three estates, commoners, clergy and nobles, agreed that King Afonso must go and that the queen, for her 'great virtues and the necessity of succession', should stay. (Had she departed, Portugal would have been obliged to repay her dowry.) Pedro became prince regent, the royal marriage was annulled on the grounds that it had never been consummated and Pedro promptly married his sister-in-law.

Afonso had intended, in his vague way, to retreat to the great Bragança estates. Instead, he was shipped off to the Açores but, when a plot was discovered to restore him, he was brought back to closely guarded seclusion within the royal palace at Sintra. The worn paving stones of the room which was his prison until his death in September 1683 are there for tourists to see today, grim token of a deposed king's nine years of despair and misery.

On the death of Afonso, his brother at last became King Pedro II. His queen, their wife, lived to enjoy her regained title for only three months. From the marriage had been born one child, a daughter called Isabel Josefa, now fourteen. A French marriage planned for her had failed to materialize; before she died, at thirty-one, King Pedro had a new family and a male heir – and, such was his luck, a glittering new source of income from Brazil: gold.

Pedro I had been 'the Justicer', an authoritative all-powerful king who ruled with an iron rod as lawmaker and judge. By the time of Dom Pedro II, more than three hundred years later, the supremacy of kingship had become diffused. The king was now titular head of an increasingly complex modern state with officials representing the Crown in functional posts across the country. From Portugal's earliest days, the king's direct link with his subjects had been through the three estates of the Cortes. Their main role was to raise funds or armies, to confirm an heir or a kingly desire. Often, they raised issues – King João II was presented with a list of 173 problems and complaints by the Cortes in 1481. Later, with all Portugal frantic for the proper upbringing of the fatherless Sebastião, the Cortes in 1562 implored his regent mother to ensure he grew up as a good Portuguese: 'Let him dress Portuguese ... eat Portuguese, ride Portuguese, speak Portuguese, all his acts be Portuguese, and thus you will accustom him to have great love for the kingdom and its affairs.' Their advice through the centuries was often ignored; after 1697, they were never called again.

Dom Pedro II, who had seized the crown, was the first absolute monarch. His reign had begun in high drama and the shrill echoes of family strife; it closed in the sturdy embrace of profitable commerce. Portugal, pressed by a sagacious superintendent of finance, the Count of Ericeira, began to develop its own tariff-protected textile and glass industries. (The drama had not ended; fifteen years after his appointment, he committed suicide.) Two more treaties with England were signed, one the notable Methuen Treaty of December 1703, providing preferential trade terms for British textiles in Portugal and Portuguese wines in England. The treaty is credited with stimulating the port-wine trade – at the lasting cost, some say, of sufficient home-grown wheat. Inevitably, there was a fresh involvement with Spain – the War of the Spanish Succession, in which Portugal sided with Britain in supporting a Habsburg, rather than Bourbon, claimant, an issue which, for the Portuguese, was peculiarly satisfying as, for the moment, Spain offered no threat.

King Pedro, after his French wife's death, had taken a German bride, Maria Sophia Elizabeth, from the Palatinate. An heir, the future Dom João V, was born in October 1689 and was followed by four more children. (In the old tradition, Dom Pedro had additionally fathered bastard children.)

The sobriquets which Portuguese kings have been given – pithy, one-word descriptions – are not always kind (Dom Afonso II is *o Gordo*, 'the Fat') and not always accurate (the wretched, captive Dom Afonso VI, in whose name Portugal won resounding victories over Spain, is *o Vitorioso* and his pitiless brother, Dom Pedro II, is *o Pacífico*). Dom Pedro's son, João, who succeeded when he died in 1706, is *o Magnânimo* but also, with reason, *o Magnífico*.

The reign of King João V restored to Portugal the image of a wealthy, powerful state not known since the heady days of King Manuel – though it was France's Louis XIV, the Sun King, whom Dom João chose as model. Initial finds of gold in Brazil were followed by the discovery of even richer deposits and a rush of prospectors. The Crown held a one-fifth entitlement, always underpaid due to evasion and smuggling; rules and penalties were eventually relaxed to ensure the gold flowed directly to Portugal. This practical approach was rewarded in 1728: diamonds were discovered in the same Minas Gerais area and revenues from Brazil became even more bountiful.

Brazil gave to the Portuguese monarch what his own country could never do: absolute power, vast wealth and excellent credit. Early in his reign, with the gold flow still sluggish, the wages of the army – still vainly engaged in the anti-Bourbon struggle – were unpaid for eleven months. Dom João's expenditure was enormous throughout his life. In one ambitious project after another, bills were left unpaid for months or years. In the gigantic monument of the monastery-church at Mafra, most wildly extravagant of all, gold was transmuted into stone, a father's vow into a punitive colossus. In 1720 the French ambassador confided to his king that Mafra would never be finished as all the money in the Iberian peninsula could not pay for it. Lisbon was bankrupt, and 45,000 workmen had been paid little, late or not at all – but the basilica was consecrated in 1730 and the entire structure completed by 1735. Statistics are offered: among them 5,200 doorways, 2,500 windows, the costly bells, the monastic cells. The greatest wonder within the massive pile is the superb rococo library shining with a golden light. Here at last, among the thousands of books, are the whiffs and echoes of struggling, thinking, warm-blooded humanity.

The celebrated library of the University of Coimbra grew from Brazilian gold and Dom João's lofty cultural inclinations. Scholarship flourished under his patronage. He encouraged writers and historians; numerous important books were published – on the Portuguese language, poetry, culture and the genealogy of the royal house. From the king's cook came new editions of the first major work on Portuguese food, *Arte de Cozinha*. (Dom João's brother, Francisco, liked his food so well he ate fourteen lobsters at a sitting, and died of indigestion.) He instituted a Royal Academy of History in Lisbon, exempting its members from censorship by the Inquisition. He took an educated interest in the sciences, sent students abroad, built hospitals at home. His fondness for the baroque style has left its distinctive mark not only on such ancient cities as Oporto, Braga and Guimarães, and on numerous fine houses and churches, but also in small Alto Alentejo towns like Crato, Fronteira, Monforte and Alter do Chão. On the outskirts of Alter do Chão, too, are the stables and green fields of the Coudelaria de Alter, the national stud founded by Dom João V in 1748 to ensure the purity and quality of Portugal's own handsome, sweet-natured Lusitanian horses.

As it often does, the image of wealth shone brighter than the reality. Once more there were Spanish marriages – of Dom João's son and heir José, to Mariana Vitória, the fourteen-year-old daughter of Philip V of Spain and his ambitious wife, Isabel Farnese, and of Dom João's oldest daughter, Maria Bárbara, to the Spanish heir, later Fernando VI; the heavy cost was paid by a *donativo*, a 'voluntary' tax raised largely from Brazil.

The huge Aqueduct of Free Waters, 109 arches across 18.5 km, striding across Alcântara like a lean grey giant to provide Lisbon with drinking water, was paid for by the *povo* through a tax on the city's meat, olive oil and wine. Unusually, the clergy were required to pay, too. The brilliant engineering was the work of Manuel da Maia, with Custódio Vieira as architect; Lisbon's city museum displays their drawings. The aqueduct was largely constructed between 1732 and 1748, and was completed in 1835. Even William Beckford, whose susceptibilities lay elsewhere, was deeply impressed.

The aqueduct performed a social service. Dom João V, Portugal's own Sun King, was a cultured and impressionable man with a genuine concern for those in need: for many years he gave gold coins to the deserving during twice-weekly audiences, the *magnânimo* side of his nature. He had come to the throne at seventeen, well educated in the classics, in languages, in mathematics. He had, like so many kings, a love of music, especially of opera – Lisbon opera came to be widely admired – and church ritual. To ecclesiastical affairs, one way and another, he devoted much of his attention.

Throughout Portugal's long history, relations between Rome and each devoutly Christian Portuguese king had seldom been warm, since both were determined to hold and assert authority in matters relating to the Church. Over the centuries, through expanding and contracting empire and the missionary dominion of the Company of Jesus, the essential issues had changed little. The tie was symbiotic: each needed the other. Dom João was required, as earlier kings had been, to take up arms against the infidel: with Portuguese help, the Turks were defeated in the 1717 battle of Matapan.

In return Dom João won the status of patriarchate for his own chapel and for some of the Lisbon parishes. Determined that Lisbon would rank with the highest Catholic courts of Europe, he persisted over years of sharp differences with one pope after another until his patriarch was also a cardinal and he himself elevated above his own nobles with the title *O Rei Fidelíssimo* ('Most Faithful King').

Dom João was not, however, a faithful husband. He had numerous *amours*, among them Dona Leonor Clara whose husband, snatching up their children, left home – the Palácio da Terrugem in Oeiras – in disgust. But his most bizarre extra-marital activities conveniently linked his passion for the Church and his prodigal endowment of religious establishments with a long and intimate relationship with the nuns of Odivelas convent. The arrangement was open, widely known and appeared to disturb no conscience. Once, the nuns of Odivelas, to everyone's surprise, marched on Lisbon – but they were protesting about an entirely unrelated matter, the return to their convent of a New Christian nun absolved by the Inquisition. The king, disliking rebellion in any form, had them chased back by his cavalry. Nuns, it seems, were restless: at least two other convents revolted within a period of a few years.

From Dom João's ardour at the nunnery, three sons were born – António, in 1714, to a French nun; Gaspar, in 1716 – he became archbishop of Braga, as had a bastard of his grandfather; and, in 1720, José, who was appointed Inquisitor-General. From infancy they were called *os meninos da Palhavã* ('the children of Palhavã'), the Lisbon palace where they grew up – the name lives on in the Spanish embassy, a Metro station, a neighbourhood burgeoning into the Wall Street of Portugal. (Odivelas, on the northern out-skirts of Lisbon, survives, too, in part: the tombs of King Dinis, who founded the convent around 1295, and his natural daughter are there.) The mother of José was Madre Paula who, above all others, was King João's dearest love.

Only kingly lustre made the affair notable; the Church was an integral part of the social and political fabric. Virtue was esteemed but concupiscence not uncommon. History records hundreds of other instances of human failing, from archbishop to lowly priest and nun, in the churches, monasteries and convents of Portugal, as elsewhere.

The affairs of the country had shifted to a system that held the roots of modern bureaucracy. Secretaries and ministers reported to the king who, in his later years, suffered from epilepsy and, despite the solace of the Church, could think of little but his own mortality. His Brazilian-born secretary, Alexandre de Gusmão, described to him the effect of his ministers' apathy: '... many lands usurped, others untilled, and many roads impassable ... many great places almost deserted, with their manufactures ruined and lost ...' Clearly, in what the king's own chronicler grandly declares a Golden Age in Portugal, opportunities had been missed.

Was one of them man-powered flight? Gusmão had a brother, Bartolomeu, a Jesuit priest, who invented a flying machine, a rudimentary aerostat which he called *Passarola*, 'Big Bird'. Displayed in the presence of the king on 7 October 1709, it rose into the air to some height. The public, enthralled, nicknamed Padre Bartolomeu de Gusmão '*Voador*' ('flyer'). The king, though he treated the inventor kindly, making him a member of his Royal Academy of History, did not offer to sponsor Padre Bartolomeu's ideas and theories on 'navigating by the element of air'. He died at the age of thirty-eight, after harassment from the Inquisition, in Toledo, Spain, in 1724.

For most of us, Portuguese is a difficult language, long Portuguese names hard to remember and hard to pronounce. The man born as Sebastião José de Carvalho e Melo of a minor rural family in 1699 became Count of Oeiras in 1759 and a marquis in 1770. It is as the Marquês (Marquis) de Pombal that he is known to history, his name feared, reviled, cursed and hated – and admired and honoured as Portugal's greatest statesman. No one forgets Pombal. No one dared ignore him.

Dom João V respected his abilities but did not like him. Pombal, over six feet tall and of striking looks, had, reflected Dom João, '*cabelos no coraçao*' (a hairy heart). The barb, if peculiar, was apt: there was an ambivalence about Pombal, a dangerous unpredictability. Appointed as envoy to the Court of St James in London by Dom João in 1738, he was smoothly affable. He was a loving husband and family man – a first marriage, an adventurous elopement, had ended with his wife's death; he married again, an Austrian to whom he was lastingly devoted. Returning to Portugal a few months before Dom João's death, he was – for twenty-seven years – a brilliant, imaginative and industrious secretary of state, and then chief minister to the supine, pleasure-loving King José I. To those who opposed him he was an implacable enemy, a merciless and sadistic tyrant.

Dom João died in 1750, his passing eased by the pious rituals that had gladdened his life. The new king, José, was thirty-six, genial and indulgent. He enjoyed cards and horse-riding, adored the opera even more than his father had done, and was unexceptionably devout. He himself was father, by his wife, Mariana Vitória, of four daughters – the oldest, sixteen, a future queen, Maria I. Dom José had been excluded by his father from any active role in government and was now well content to leave the day-to-day affairs of the country to Pombal, willingly endorsing all papers presented for his signature.

How fair the prospect seemed, how glowing the future. Lisbon, crammed with a population of 270,000, prospered on the hills that rose beside the river Tejo. Then, quite suddenly, the ancient city that war had never touched, was annihilated.

On the morning of All Saints Day, 1 November 1755, when candles were lit and the churches full, Lisbon was struck by an earthquake of such terrible force that some 30,000 people died in the collapsing buildings, in fires, in the flood wave of the Tejo river. 'One moment has reduced one of the largest Trading Cities to ashes,' wrote a surviving merchant. The earthquake, and the series of shocks that followed it, destroyed almost all of Lisbon – its churches, palaces, splendid buildings, fine town-houses and numberless humbler dwellings.

'Itt began like the rattleing of Coaches . . . I look about me and see the Walls a shakeing and a falling down then I up and took to my heells, with Jesus in my mouth,' a young nun wrote to her mother. An English merchant, who had time to snatch up his wig and his hat, described the 'Spectacle of Terror and Amazement', the 'Gatherings of Crowds about Priests and Friars, all falling on their Knees, kissing the Earth, beating their Breasts, slapping their Cheeks, and crying out for Absolution, which was granted in general Terms to Hundreds of them at once'.

Another survivor recalled with dread 'every stone in the walls separating each from the other, and grinding, as did all the walls of the other houses . . .' At the river mouth a sea captain watched in horror how 'the water rose in five minutes about sixteen feet, and fell in the same time for three times'. As his own ship quivered and shook he could hear the dreadful cries from the wretched citizens of a ruined city. A letter tells of the fires that 'raged for nine days and nine nights with incredible fury'. Nothing was left 'but desolation and sorrow'.

Although north Portugal was little affected by the 1755 earthquake, the shock was severe through the Alentejo region right down to the coastal towns of the Algarve some 200 miles away. A

great city and much of the country was devastated, a whole culture
lost – public and private papers, libraries, precious objects and
paintings, as well as traders' goods and funds. The king and his
family camped in tents in gardens at Belém, which had been spared
the ferocity of the city shocks, though Dom José's beloved new
opera house had collapsed like a shell. Pombal, his own Oeiras
palace undamaged, sagely moved to a hut. Many survivors took to
the crowded roads. Others managed as best they could, sleeping in
fields and ruins. The dead were buried and looters hanged.

Lisbon was not unused to earth tremors, or earthquakes, but the
earthquake of 1755 was a calamity of such awesome dimensions
that Portugal suffers from it still. The Portuguese speak constantly
of the Great Earthquake as if it had just occurred; they speak of it
even as a frighteningly memorable, and personal, experience. In
some ways it is. When the Chiado shopping area in the heart of
Lisbon burned in the summer of 1988, it was not just an unfortunate
and costly fire but a deeply felt private tragedy constantly compared
with the Great Earthquake.

The shock was felt as far as France, the action of the tidal wave
as far as the Caribbean. But the earthquake had a much greater
impact on Europe than a momentary seismic spasm, for it struck at
the Enlightenment concept of the benevolence of nature (much as
the atomic bomb in a later age would end any idea of the benevolence of science). 'Never before has the Demon of Fear so quickly
and powerfully spread throughout the land,' Goethe would proclaim. The Revd John Wesley ruminated in his *Serious Thoughts
Occasioned by the Great Earthquake of Lisbon* on the king's supposed
'large building filled with diamonds, and more gold stored up,
coined and uncoined, than all the other princes of Europe together'.
Dr Johnson wearied of hearing of the Lisbon earthquake. Voltaire
found in it inspiration for a pessimistic poem as well as a vital
strand in the horrid adventures of his *Candide*. Madame de Pom-
padour, it was said, gave up rouge for a week. In religious, superstitious Portugal, argument raged. The theme of divine punishment
was much laboured; but it was also observed that most of those
who perished were virtuous church-goers and that among the first

buildings to fall were the palace of the patriarch and the Inquisition.

Ashes cooled, life began again. The British Parliament voted a gift of £100,000 and sent food, pickaxes and shovels. The upper city, the Alfama and Bairro Alto, were hardly damaged. Within a month, on 4 December, Manuel da Maia, whose aqueduct had withstood the shocks unharmed, presented a dissertation on reconstruction. Pombal dissuaded the king from making Coimbra his capital or moving to Brazil; a new Lisbon would be created in the dust and ashes of the old. Plans by the architect Eugénio dos Santos were chosen – and when he died in 1760 Carlos Mardel, with his own innovative ideas, took over. The most radical urban renewal project of eighteenth-century Europe was under way.

The Baixa, the lower city, is today *Lisboa pombalina*, not because of a specific Pombaline architecture but for its unity, style and proportion. The houses in the simple grid plan are neo-classical, with only three basic variations in their exterior design, which the personal whims and flourishes of modern commerce have not modified greatly. At the time, some thought the plan monotonous, yet an architect in Oporto admired it so much that he proposed to Pombal that the entire country be replanned and rebuilt to the same *quadrícula* scheme. Vila Real de Santo António in the earthquake-damaged Algarve was conjured into a jaunty echo of the Baixa, but fortunately the thought went no further and the individuality of Portugal's resplendent cities survived.

Not even Lisbon was fully rebuilt in Pombal's lifetime: the huge triumphal arch dominating the Praça do Comércio, its columns each made of a single stone, was not completed until 1873. Of greater priority to Pombal, and ceremoniously installed on the centre of the same square on 20 May 1775 with the aid of a specially designed lifting machine, was an imposing statue of Dom José mounted on his favourite horse, Gentil. The royal horseman and sculpted stone base were the work of Joaquim Machado de Castro. The statue gained a green patina in time but the English have always called the Praça do Comércio Black Horse Square, a name that puzzles the Portuguese; a Lusitanian horse is either the rich brown or bay of the Alter Real of the once-royal stables or a light grey – never black.

The Portuguese have tolerated English idiosyncrasies for centuries. The ties of trade and alliance are strong. Pombal, as envoy in England, observed how much better treated were the English in Portugal than the Portuguese in England, a situation that some say has not wholly changed. That he admired the British commercial and maritime skills was not at all appreciated by the merchant houses – the factories – in Portugal, whose independent ways and trade preferences Pombal sharply curbed. Yet, for all the cries of woe and ruin, in the five years after the earthquake trade with Britain did better than it had in years. British merchants complained, survived and prospered. Those who criticized Pombal did not.

In his determination to control the commerce of the kingdom and its colonies, Pombal created chartered companies in Brazil and Asia, in tobacco, fishing and whaling, and, arousing wide discontent, port wine. The General Company for the Cultivation of the Vineyards of the Upper Douro, which was founded in 1756, defined the areas from which the wine could be drawn. Out of chaos came order, from the wildly dramatic plunging hills of the Douro valley increased production of the 'precious nectar', and from the world a new respect for *porto* (port wine). Unlucky growers along the Tejo and Mondego rivers had their own vines ruthlessly hauled out. (Today, the EEC has suavely adapted Pombal's rigorous controls.)

When the Lisbon Chamber of Commerce, the Mesa do Bem Comum, questioned the founding of the Brazilian company, Pombal had the chamber dissolved and several members imprisoned or exiled. When Oporto taverners protested against the Douro wine company, seventeen of them were hanged, and another hundred and sixty sent to the galleys, imprisoned, fined and deported. When shots were fired at King José, wounding him slightly as he returned home one night, Pombal used the attempted assassination to assert his own unrivalled power. Pombal loathed the nobility for ignoring him and the Jesuits for their strong influence and supposed riches. He accused the aristocratic Távora family – known to be furious that the king was amorously pursuing the young Marchioness – and managed to implicate the Jesuits as well. Troops surrounded Jesuit colleges. The Duke of Aveiro, the Marquises of Távora and Alorna and several counts were arrested. Servants of the noble families were tortured. A dreadful, barbaric blood-letting on a Belém scaffold in January 1759 began with the beheading of the elder Marchioness of Távora, continued with the principal members of the family and their servants being broken on the wheel, strangled or beheaded, and ended with the burning of one alleged assassin, the entire scaffold and the ghastly array of mangled corpses. In September, the Jesuits were expelled from Portugal. A renowned Jesuit, the old and eccentric Padre Malagrida, was found guilty of treason, blasphemy, impiety and false prophecy (a brother of Pombal was now Inquisitor-General) and was garotted and burned in a particularly well-attended *auto-da-fé*.

Who really shot at the king was never established. The Society of Jesus was expelled from France and Spain and suppressed by the pope in 1773. Despite all their knowledge and experience, the Jesuits did not foresee the draconian fate Pombal imposed on them. Even when the papal ban was lifted, they never recovered their former strength.

Pombal, all opposition dead, banished or terrorized, now set about redesigning the entire education system. He created grammar schools and reformed Coimbra University. He established laboratories, botanical gardens, an observatory, even a special college for the nobility with a curriculum ranging from languages, ancient and modern, to astronomy, physics, navigation, architecture, fencing and dancing. The mighty Inquisition became a paltry state department and public *autos-da-fé* ceased overnight. Most galvanizing of all Pombal's achievements, slavery was banned in Portugal, discrimination by colour was forbidden in the Asian territories and, in 1773, the iniquitous legal requirement of 'purity of blood' for holders of office and the socially poisonous distinctions between Christian and New Christian were abolished.

In 1775, Pombal summarized for the king the triumphs of his reign – improved literacy, expanded industry, burgeoning culture, prosperity. A redesigned Lisbon, of charm, grace and harmonious architecture, had emerged out of ruin and disaster. The Seven

Years War between France and England (1756–63) had not, for Portugal, despite a Bourbon invasion, ended unsatisfactorily. In 1759 French ships had been blasted from Portuguese waters by Admiral Edward Boscawen and Pombal had dispatched an enraged response. King José's daughter, Maria, now twenty-six and with no suitable spouse in sight, married her amiable uncle Pedro in 1760.

In 1776 Dom José fell ill. His dying wish was to see his grandson, José, married. A wedding was swiftly arranged – with the boy's remaining aunt, Maria Benedita. On 24 February 1777 the reign of King José came to an end and, with it, the enlightened despotism of the Marquis of Pombal. On 5 March, Pombal was dismissed and the prisons opened; as hundreds of wan survivors of his tyranny celebrated, he was banished to the small castle town of Pombal. Required to defend himself, he showed that the king's signature had authorized all his actions. He died aged eighty-three, his mind still vigorous, on 8 May 1782.

His achievements recognized and admired, Pombal today stands grandly atop a pillar in the centre of Lisbon. Placing him there was no simple matter. The first stone was laid in 1882, the centenary of his death, in the presence of royalty. In 1926 the stone was ceremoniously relaid – Portugal had become a republic guided by President Bernardino Machado. The monument was finally inaugurated in 1933, delayed by a series of tribulations – monarchist conspiracies, republican quarrels, coups and countercoups, world war, armed insurrection and the assumption of power in Portugal by a military dictatorship. From his eminence Pombal surveys broad avenues and streaming traffic, a city in a rush, whose buildings bear the marks of election posters and the spray of graffiti, the free expression – eloquent if not elegant – of a disputatious people in a lively, fast-changing, democratic nation.

5 Plots, shots and silences

Democratic notions of government by the people and for the people, Thomas Jefferson's 'sacred and undeniable truth' that all men are created equal, were not at first well received in Portugal. The road to the Second Republic, born in 1974, is circuitous, spattered with blood, damp with the flood of fine phrases, shadowed by phantoms and, in places, savagely holed by demagoguery and fascism. Not everyone agrees the road is now running straight and true, or even in the right direction. Only in the last few years of this hard-won republic, since 1987, have the Portuguese people experienced majority party rule by a democratically elected government. The challenges and criticisms hurled from left, right and centre are – democracy's paradox – the building blocks of a vigorous new society.

To the autocratic Marquis of Pombal the Declaration of Independence on 4 July 1776 by Great Britain's North American colonies demanded an unequivocal response: Portuguese ports were closed to North American ships and they were to be viewed as pirates. 'Such a pernicious example should induce the most uninterested rulers to deny all help and favour, directly or indirectly, to some vassals who have so publicly and formally rebelled against their natural sovereign.'

Within a year, the government of Queen Maria I, which included, despite Pombal's fall from power, some of his ministers, was dealing equably with Benjamin Franklin. In the War of Independence (1776–83) Portugal managed to remain neutral and uninvolved – and to profit from burgeoning cotton plantations in Brazil. The British, denied North American cotton, promptly looked to the south. The sanctity of commerce seemed the overriding principle.

Yet although the powerful truths of the New World were contagious, their force only struck Portugal two years after the French Revolution.

Portugal's ambassador in Paris, along with other embassies, had not been much alarmed by the storming of the Bastille on 14 July 1789; the raising of the *tricolore* flag of revolution, the exulting anger of the mob, seemed an entirely internal matter. That there had been an almighty explosion casting sparks across the globe quite escaped his notice. King Louis XVI, after his attempted flight in June 1791, had sent a letter to all the foreign diplomats informing them that he accepted France's new constitution. The Portuguese government declined to receive the text of the constitution and, after cautiously seeking a shared response with Spain's Bourbon King, Carlos IV, only replied to the letter a year later, on 23 May 1792. By then, new ideas were flowering, the blade of the guillotine falling, Napoleon Bonaparte was only seven years from declaring himself First Consul and Queen Maria of Portugal was hopelessly mad. The letter was signed by her son, Dom João.

The reign of Queen Maria had begun happily. She was described by the Spanish ambassador as prudent and enlightened. She chose sound ministers, respected her father's wishes, founded an academy of science and a marine academy; she sought to conserve the best of Pombal's ventures, to discard the failures and to appease his enemies. It had been said of the Marquis of Pombal that he tried to follow an impossible policy. Poor Queen Maria, lacking his fierce regalism, soon gave way to doubt, a terrible sense of guilt and profound melancholy.

Her first torments arose over the protestations of innocence of the surviving members of the Távora family who had been released from prison. Among them was the son of the Duke of Aveiro, locked away as a boy and grown to gaunt manhood. Dona Maria appointed judges to consider the claims, then demanded in a frenzy that they settle the case overnight. Aveiro was found guilty, the others innocent. Pressure for rehabilitation and compensation, her pious concern to protect her father's memory, to bury the scandal of his affair with the young Marchioness of Távora, preyed on her mind and left her deeply disturbed.

In 1786 the queen lost a fond husband and affectionate uncle with the death of the king-consort Dom Pedro III. Two years later their eldest son, José, the twenty-seven-year-old heir and prince of Brazil, whose close interest in Voltaire and liberal inclinations alarmed the conservative court, died of smallpox; the queen, from religious scruples – though there were hints of a nastier purpose – had forbidden vaccination. In the same year the odious disease killed Queen Maria's sister, other relatives and her confessor. From guilt, grief and despair, she slid into the abyss of madness.

When William Beckford, in 1794, was received at Queluz palace by Dom João, he heard 'the most terrible, the most agonizing shrieks . . . inflicting upon me a sensation of horror such as I never felt before'. The queen, he learned, suffered from dreadful hallucinations of her father's image, visions that haunted her night and day. Mentally insane, physically sound, Queen Maria survived the storms and upheavals of war that ravaged Iberia in the first years of the nineteenth century. She died in 1816.

Beckford himself was looking back on a world about to end, the last decadent years of absolute monarchy in which he had participated joyfully – and emulated, in elaborate luxury, with his own bizarre court of retainers, musicians, cooks, blacks, dwarfs. England's wealthiest, wittiest, most brilliantly unconventional traveller – driven abroad at the age of twenty-six to escape scandal in England over a homosexual affair – had gone to some trouble and vast expense in three long visits to Portugal, between March 1787 and July 1799, to ensure that his own life, in Rose Macaulay's words, consisted of 'gorgeous, exotic scenes of beauty, levity, passion, romance and travel on the grand scale'. The unrestrained journal he kept of his first nine-month stay is rich in comment on Portuguese social life (the puritanical English snubbed him) as well as self-mockery of his own aesthetic tastes, whether for long church masses or beautiful girls or boys. And if the banquets of quail, salad and strawberries with his aristocratic friends, the Marialvas, are recorded, so are the shoals of beggars in Lisbon streets. The day the queen remitted the tax on *bacalhau*, he wrote dryly, she 'of course received much acclamation'.

In 1835, at the age of seventy-four, he produced his *Recollections of an Excursion to the Monasteries of Alcobaça and Batalha*. In it is a glimpse of the court of 1794: Queluz palace and its gardens bright with birds and flowers sent from Brazil, the opulent life of Dom João's Spanish wife, Carlota Joaquina, who – 'surrounded by thirty or forty young women, every one far superior in loveliness of feature and fascination of smile to their august mistress' – amused herself by making him run and dance a bolero amidst 'odoriferous thickets'. He was impressed by Dom João, the acting prince regent even though he was 'certainly the reverse of handsome'. He liked his shrewdness and thought him singularly pleasing despite the 'baneful influence of his despotic consort'. Dom João, for his part, expressed interest in Beckford's visit to Alcobaça, discussed the entertainment offered by the fathers and courteously asked the question on which every traveller has animated views: 'How did you find the roads?' (The Lord Abbot, on this occasion, had seen to it that the reverend fathers and all their numerous dependants had mended them.)

Troubling the prince more even than his deranged mother or his shrewish wife was the 'frightful intelligence' from France – 'every country in Europe is labouring under a heavy torment – God alone can tell upon what shore we shall be all drifting!' Beckford, in his lively 1835 flashback, already knew the shore, Brazil, where the royal family, court and government fled from the reach of Junot's advancing army in November 1807. He knew of the military genius of the Peninsular War, Sir Arthur Wellesley, later Duke of Wellington, and the consequences of the war for Portugal – among them a liberal constitution, a disastrous civil war between two royal brothers, the loss of independent Brazil, anticlerical suppression of the monasteries, a new young queen.

The grandiose ambitions of Napoleon Bonaparte, who had himself crowned emperor in 1804, were confounded not only by Nelson at Trafalgar a year later, and by the brilliant tactics of Wellington, but by quite ordinary people of spirit who wanted none of him. To the Portuguese, revolutionary ideas from France – widespread despite zealous attempts to suppress them – were one thing, rule by France another.

Napoleon's forces invaded Portugal not once but three times without achieving a firm grasp of the prize. General Junot, boasting of conquest, was the first of Napoleon's leaders to be forced to swallow his words. On 6 June 1808 the angry citizens of Oporto locked up the French governor, reiterated their loyalty to the absent prince regent and sparked a movement that quickly reached the Algarve, freeing all but Lisbon, the fortresses of Peniche and Setúbal and four garrison towns of French command. From Brazil, a proud Dom João – given the news by doughty fishermen from Olhão who had sailed their tiny craft without charts across the Atlantic – declared war on France.

Portugal and Spain, also engaged in a similar struggle, needed help, and England – who else? – responded. In the first days of August Sir Arthur Wellesley landed a sturdy English force of some 9,000 troops close to the Mondego river mouth. Soon joined by another 13,000, they provided muscle to a force of 8,000 Portuguese in defeating the French at Roliça and Vimeiro, to the north of Torres Vedras. Negotiations that followed their defeat concluded with the astonishing Convention of Sintra, by which the French were carried home in British ships with all their arms and booty. Never satisfactorily explained, the convention enraged the Portuguese and disgusted the British public. (Both Byron and Wordsworth, believing their beloved Sintra despoiled, though the convention was probably signed in Lisbon, purged anger with passionate words.)

The second invasion of Portugal was planned by Napoleon himself. It began in 1809 with the arrival in the northern town of Chaves of Marshal Nicholas Soult who left an occupying force and moved on to Oporto, once again ready, its citizens believed, to hold high the flag of Portugal. But Soult was strong, the old grey city unable to withstand the attack. Faltering defenders retreated to the River Douro's southern bank across a fragile bridge of boats, a frail lifeline that broke apart under the weight of the fleeing populace. Hundreds fell into the fast-flowing water; many drowned – a tragedy mourned to this day.

Once again it was Wellesley to the rescue. He arrived in Lisbon, the forces at his disposal now including as well as some 17,000

English troops a disciplined army of 7,000 Portuguese, many of them trained by William Carr Beresford, a stern English officer whom the distant, desperate prince regent had made marshal and commander-in-chief. Soult's Oporto-based forces, pushed north into Galicia, were no longer the main threat; another French army was advancing west from Spain. With Abrantes, on the River Tejo, as his headquarters, Wellesley led his army eastward along the line of the river and defeated the French at Talavera – the victory won him the title of Viscount Wellington. Short on supplies, the route to Madrid blocked by massed armies, Wellington returned to Portugal. The enemy still threatened, but he had a formidable plan in mind for a defensive arc around Lisbon that would resist the force of the mightiest army.

The lines of Torres Vedras, as the system of fortifications was called – work began there – consisted, when complete, of 152 redoubts, strong masonry forts with 600 guns, across two lines of defences stretching from the sea to the Tejo, the first extending twenty-nine miles from the mouth of the Sizandro river to Alhandra, the second – a few miles behind the first – twenty-four miles long, with a third line to cover any forced embarkation. Hills were restructured, rivers dammed and diverted, ravines walled with stone, great earthworks raised and homes destroyed – 'We have spared neither house, garden, vineyard, olive trees, woods or private property of any description,' Major John Jones, one of the eighteen English and Portuguese engineers, wrote later. The entire massive project, constructed, like Mafra, with underpaid and conscripted Portuguese labour, was near completion in a year – astonishingly in total secrecy.

In May 1810 Napoleon ordered a third invasion of Portugal. An army of 65,000 men under the command of Marshal Masséna marched from Valladolid to Viseu. In September, heading for Coimbra, Masséna found his way blocked by Wellington and, though allied troops held a strong position on the hills of Buçaco, decided to attack. In the battle on 27 September – all the palpitating turbulence of war is vividly depicted in tile panels across the walls at Buçaco – the French came off poorly, losing nearly 5,000 men. (A

French officer, counting scores years later, wrote that 200,000 Frenchmen were lost in the peninsula alone.)

Now came the moment, the colossal conjuring trick, Wellington was waiting for. The Lines looked secure, 126 forts ready and garrisoned with 29,000 militia, 247 guns in place. (More artillery was installed later, in case.) Judiciously pulling back his field army, some 60,000 men, before the main French force, he at last – on 9 October – ordered them into position behind the Lines. Masséna appeared, riding over a hill, and saw with utter amazement, instead of open terrain leading to Lisbon, an altered landscape of fortifications and field works, a gigantic barrier he knew at once he could not cross. After this shock, there was a shot or two, an attempt by increasingly hungry French troops at blockade, but on 15 November, leaving only straw-stuffed sentinels to delay the chase, the French army was gone for ever.

Torres Vedras is a busy commercial town today, its castle walls standing on a hilltop above a church crammed with the faithful on Sundays and clusters of matchbox houses. Within the castle walls are medieval graves, across a narrow valley the restored fort of São Vicente and, all around, a landscape with its secrets hidden beneath phlegmatic modern building, industry, roads, farms and fields. Persistence and a handy booklet with maps, *The Lines of Torres Vedras*, produced by the British Historical Society of Portugal, will reveal some of those secrets to anyone hoping to stand in the footsteps of Wellington, trace the principal forts and walk the long miles of earthworks. But a conjuror's magic is for the passing moment; the Portuguese who built the defences also took them down, time and weather blur lines, soften edges and bury stone.

The bogey of Napoleon was banished but the picture in Portugal in the following years was bleak. The country was ruled like a colony from Brazil, humiliatingly governed by the English officer Marshal Beresford and desperately impoverished. France failed to pay the agreed compensation and the British, through another Anglo-Portuguese treaty, traded directly with Brazil. Yet again, as Oliveira Martins, the historian, says, the Braganças sold the kingdom as Esau sold his birthright. Brazil, delighted in its raised status, with a royal court and enhanced economy, became a kingdom in 1815. The Braganças' domains were now the United Kingdom of Portugal, Brazil and the Algarve, suggesting a unity which was belied by the diversity of opinion in Portugal and within the royal family itself.

Dom João VI, who at last became king on his mother's death in 1816, had a genuine concern for his people but an undeniably ungainly appearance – Beckford barely hinted at the bloated body, huge hands, puffy lips. He suffered from piles, and was weak, inept and indecisive. His calculating wife, Carlota Joaquina, sister of Spain's King Fernando VII and herself no beauty, choosing to see his mother's madness in her husband's poor health and perfectly understandable fits of melancholy, tried more than once to have him declared incapable. Maritally, it appears, Dom João functioned successfully: before moving to Brazil, the royal couple produced nine children, three sons – the first died in childhood – and six daughters. In Rio de Janeiro, they lived apart, dividing their children like a pack of cards. Dom João kept his heir, Pedro, born in 1798; Miguel, four years younger, was brought up by his mother. Pedro grew up with liberal ideas; Miguel inherited his mother's ambitions for absolute power. From boyhood they were inexorably bound for disaster – programmed, as in some dreadful computer war-game, on a course that could lead only to grief and trauma in Portugal and continue to involve the unshakeable, unloved British ally.

Passing through Lisbon, in September 1817, an English barrister, Henry Matthews, unwell and in low spirits, disliked everything he saw. 'The gay and glittering city proves to be a painted sepulchre,' he wrote in his diary. 'Filth and beastliness assault you at every turn.' Nor could he understand why the Portuguese were less than welcoming.

There is no doubt of the fact that neither the generosity and good faith of the English, nor the blood profusely shed in defence of this country, have endeared us to our Portuguese allies. They dislike us mortally. How is this to be explained? Is it that malicious sentiment of envy, which seems to have overspread the whole continent, at the prodigious elevation to which England has arisen; or is it the repulsive unaccommodating manners which an Englishman is too apt to carry with him into all countries?

The Portuguese were used to English manners, to the English in trade, in peace and in war. But they had not always fought shoulder to shoulder. Sir Francis Drake had sacked Prince Henry's Vila do Infante at Cape St Vincent in 1597. A year earlier forces under the Earl of Essex had looted and burned Faro, carrying away among the booty 200 volumes of theological works, a treasure of the Algarve diocese. (Essex gave the books to his friend Sir Thomas Bodley who promptly added them to his newly founded Bodleian Library in Oxford.) But neither Drake nor Essex nor any other Englishman had dominated Portugal with Beresford's heavy hand – and now he had gone too far.

Liberal ideas had spread in Portugal largely through the *Maçonaria* (the Masonic Order) – Lisbon alone had thirteen groups by 1812 – whose Grand Master, in 1817, was Lt-General Gomes Freire de Andrade. Bitterly resentful of English control of the army and the regency council, determined on national self-respect, desiring constitutional monarchy, he and eleven others plotted to rid Portugal of Beresford and the British. The plot was discovered, the plotters charged with conspiracy against the government, its institutions, the life of Marshal Beresford. Following a brief trial and summary judgement, all twelve were executed on 17 October 1817. The bloodstained place of execution, called the Campo do Curral and used as a cattle pen, for bullfights and fairs, was renamed, in 1880, the Campo dos Martires da Pátria and today, an island in Lisbon surrounded by a stream of traffic, it is a green and pleasant tree-shaded garden.

In 1820 Beresford, alarmed at liberal success in Spain and planning to request increased powers, went to Brazil. Portuguese liberals saw their chance, and with army officers in Oporto leading a revolt, successfully expelled the Lisbon regency council and set up a provisional junta nominally headed by a relative of the executed conspirator of 1817, Gomes Freire de Andrade. The leading ideological reformer of the 1820 revolution in fact was a jurist from

Figueira da Foz, Manuel Fernandes Tomás; the enlightened constitution that he and colleagues had secretly drafted, affirming the sovereignty of the nation instead of the king, establishment of a liberal Cortes – a true parliament of the people – broad voting rights, freedom of speech and the press, the end of feudal and clerical privilege and the abolition of the Inquisition, was the basis of the document that became law in 1822. He died the same year from illness, and so avoided learning that the time had not yet come for liberal ideas to take firm root in Portuguese soil.

King João, after fourteen years in Brazil, reluctantly returned to Portugal in 1821, to an ecstatic welcome from a population faithful to monarchy and Church, and little interested in Jacobin notions. Dom João, pragmatic as well as tolerant, agreed to swear his support of a regime in which his own powers were sharply reduced – he could, for instance, suspend laws but not dissolve the Cortes. His termagant wife, predictably, refused to swear the appropriate oath, used patently false declarations of ill health to avoid threats of exile, and merely moved out of Queluz to a mansion in Sintra to set up her own campaign of intrigue for the anti-liberals.

Pedro stayed in Brazil which, fired by events in Portugal and the radicals' rude indifference to its affairs, declared its independence in 1822 and acclaimed Pedro as constitutional emperor. Miguel joined a band of young nobles already conspiring to restore absolute monarchy; only the authority of the monarch himself ended the revolt. But Miguel had also won himself a new, triumphal title – *generalissimo* – and, as support for absolutism intensified, hot-headed supporters hailed him as king. For a moment, the kingdom rocked. Once before, Dom João had fled from attack; this time he went no further than a British ship in Lisbon harbour, the *Windsor Castle*, and had the recalcitrant Miguel brought aboard. Sadly observing that he had failed Miguel as a father and knew only how to punish him as a king, Dom João sent his son into exile.

Yet the anti-liberals had won a victory: the constitution was suspended, the new Cortes was disbanded and the king once again became an absolute monarch. And if he was counselled by eminent Portuguese like the Duke of Palmela, the British were there, too, as mediators. Even Beresford, whom the radicals believed they had

1 The Belém tower, Lisbon

2 Lisbon: alongside elegance there is a build up of human pressure, an endless preoccupation with housing

3 *Casa do Povo* (House of the People), a social centre that is a feature of virtually every town and village

4 In the Beira town of Idanha-a-Velha (once the Roman Egitania) a travelling salesman displays his wares on the steps of the *pelourinho*, town pillory

5 Between the boulders is the home of an elderly resident of Monsanto. The Misericórdia charity organization is delivering a hot lunch

6 The northern town of Amarante

7 Alentejo homestead

8 Slate rooftops in Piódão

9 *Espigueiros*, corn stores, at Soajo

10 Faro: the future looms in building styles

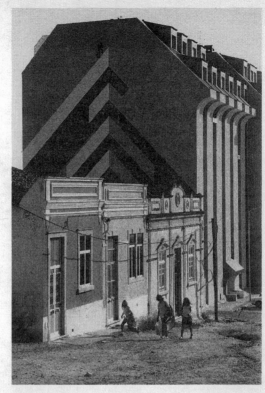

11 In an Algarve village: a meeting of the ways

12 *Moliceiro* regatta (once they gathered weed for fertilizer) in the Aveiro lagoon

13 Folk art and humour ('Living alone sets me to thinking') on the swan's neck prows of the *moliceiros*

14 *Dia dos Rapazes*, 'day of the boys', a wintertime *festa* in Trás-os-Montes villages when boys don masks and devilish disguise

15 Rite of passage: masked boys in robes of rags 'terrorize' village girls in the far north

16 Art in *azulejos*: the ornamental façade of the tile-making Viúva Lamego factory in Lisbon

17 A sculptured Fernando Pessoa, poet, sits among the crowd outside a Chiado coffee-house

seen the last of, was back in Lisbon. But the circumstances were different now: peace had to be made with an offended Pedro in a slighted Brazil.

In May 1825, hurt feelings were soothed. Dom João declared his 'beloved and esteemed son Pedro' the rightful successor to two crowns, imperial and royal, and conceded him effective sovereignty in Brazil. By treaty, in August 1825, Brazil was recognized as an independent empire, the title of emperor to be held by Dom João for the rest of his life. Any hope of peaceful recovery for Portugal, still scarred from Napoleon's aggression and the simmering fires of political strife, ended when poor, obese, ugly and unlucky King João VI died in March 1826. His widow, malignant to the end, ignored the funeral.

Pedro, Emperor of Brazil, had the best of intentions for a constitutional monarchy in Portugal, which he had not seen since childhood, and wanted to make peace with the brother he barely knew. He wrote a new, less democratic, constitution which, among other changes, allowed for an upper house of hereditary peers. At the end of April, as soon as his *Carta Constitucional* was signed, he abdicated in favour of his seven-year-old daughter, Maria da Glória – on condition that in time she marry his brother, her uncle Miguel, now in Vienna, who in turn must accept the new constitution.

Miguel meekly agreed and, arriving in Portugal in February 1828, swore to uphold the 1826 constitutional *Carta* of King Pedro IV. Slightly modified, the charter became the basis of government until the end of monarchy in 1910; Miguel's oath of loyalty evaporated within the week. Absolutists surged from all directions: anti-liberals blamed Chartists for the loss of Brazil, ordinary folk, endlessly dreaming of a new Sebastião, saw their Messiah in Miguel; his awful mother reappeared to whack her enemies with the broomstick of her son's authority. Moderates as well as radicals fled; the traditional Cortes, the old parliament of three estates, was called; on 11 July 1828, Miguel was crowned king.

The little princess, Maria da Glória, was, as it happened, sailing from Brazil towards Portugal. Her ship, pausing at Gibraltar, caught wind of events and sailed on to England, where the little girl was received as a queen. However, hard as it was for the liberals to accept, Dom Miguel was a popular king and by 1830, when the fanatical Carlota Joaquina at last died, he was no longer a compliant mother's boy.

All Portugal, it seemed, stood strongly with Miguel. Yet out in the blue Atlantic, the Açores, as they had before, held different views from the tradition-bound mainland and in 1830 grandly proclaimed Pedro regent in the name of his daughter. The tiny island group seemed an unlikely power base for the emperor of all Brazil yet Dom Pedro abdicated his empire, as he had his kingdom, for one of his children – his youngest son, who became Pedro V – and sailed eastwards determined to win his daughter her throne in an open, liberal society.

On Terceira island Dom Pedro set up, in March 1832, an undeniably odd government-in-exile. It included cautious moderates like the Duke of Palmela and radical thinkers like José Xavier Mouzinho da Silveira, a reformer credited with establishing the structure of modern Portugal. Many of the exiles, like Mouzinho da Silveira who came from the Alentejo town of Castelo de Vide, had been caught between the shrill demands of Jacobin liberalism and the rigidity of Miguelist absolutism. Many had been imprisoned, many died – and all of Portugal was to suffer from the sad, wasteful War of the Two Brothers.

In July, Dom Pedro invaded Portugal, arriving with a modest support force in Oporto without difficulty, but was able to hold the city only in conditions of siege and starvation; he was entirely unable to make headway into the conservative countryside. The stalemate broke dramatically a year later: on 24 June 1833 the Duke of Terceira secretly landed a liberal army of 2,500 men on the Algarve coast between Monte Gordo and Cacela Velha. (This peaceful hamlet overlooking a quiet lagoon was the setting in a later age, it was whispered, for secret meetings between the two Iberian dictators, Franco and Salazar.) The liberals quickly occupied Tavira, Olhão and Faro and turned inland. On 20 July they occupied the ancient town of Alcácer do Sal. On the morning of 24 July the garrison at Almada surrendered without resisting and on the same day the liberals crossed the Tejo and entered Lisbon in triumph.

Dom Pedro sailed swiftly from Oporto to Lisbon – which he

was seeing for the first time as an adult. He congratulated the joyful liberal army, bestowed the title of Visconde Cabo de São Vicente on his dynamic English admiral, Charles Napier, for disposing of Miguel's fleet off the Cape on 5 July – a battle in which sail, with twice as many guns, gave way to steam – and restored his constitution in the name of his daughter, now fourteen.

But the civil war was not yet over. Miguel's troops still held much of the country, and it took nearly another year of tragic battling between forces of the *Libertador* versus those of the *Usurpador*, of Portuguese against Portuguese, and the might of the grandly named Quadruple Alliance – of Spain, France, England and Pedro's liberal forces commanded by Terceira and Saldanha – to defeat the Miguelistas. Demanding guarantees for his officers and amnesty for political offences, Miguel finally capitulated at Évora Monte on 26 May 1834, and went, more or less quietly, back to Austria and exile.

Liberal government under a constitutional monarchy was in this way imposed on Portugal against the majority will. In the spirit of revolution, Mouzinho da Silveira, a common man's Pombal, as reforming chief minister, swept away tangled systems of tax and feudal privilege, separated judicial from administrative functions, reorganized the courts, education and the laws on lands and monopolies. Religious orders were abolished, too, by the unsparing axe of the fiercely anticlerical minister of justice, Joaquim António de Aguiar, and all monasteries and convents were seized. (The 12,000 monks and nuns were promised pensions.) The 1834 revolution marked a great turning-point in Portugal's history. All the same, there were huge war debts to settle and the sale of confiscated property to pay them off brought the already wealthy landowners and the merchant bourgeoisie to the top of the heap.

Dom Pedro, deserted by liberals who charged him with being too soft on his brother, too domineering and – the unkindest cut of all – politically undaring, died of consumption in September 1834, aged only thirty-six, a bare three months after the liberals' victory. He had been emperor of Brazil, king of Portugal. His body was eventually taken to Brazil. His heart he bequeathed in eternal appreciation to the 'most Noble, Heroic, forever Loyal and Unconquerable City of Oporto'. It was taken there by steamship and ceremonially placed, in a silver urn of conserving liquid within a mahogany box, in the chancel of the church of Nossa Senhora da Lapa. Once in a while city authorities take down the box from behind a locked grille, open it up and take a look. The heart has always been found in a perfect state of preservation.

Oporto, a tumultuous city rising from the great, grey Douro, inspires grand gestures, passionate prose, tender poetry, lyrical painting, political dreaming and revolutionary action. Brilliant figures of Portuguese culture were born in Oporto, and lived, died and left their hearts there, if not in so visceral a sense as King Pedro IV. Nineteenth-century activist writers like Almeida Garrett and the journalist Ramalho Ortigão profoundly altered the cultural scene in Portugal. Their contemporary, Camilo Castelo Branco, among the greatest – and most prolific – of Portuguese writers, lies buried in Oporto's Lapa churchyard. Portugal was witnessing a literary as well as a political explosion: for modern readers, Portuguese history is brought to life by the nineteenth-century writer Alexandre Herculano and in the vivid, dramatic, and often humorous novels, stories and articles of the time, which live on through the unmystical embalming fluid of printer's ink.

Maria da Glória, Queen Maria II, had grown to womanhood in the swirling world of constitutional crisis. She was well prepared for a reign of grim challenge and contest between supporters of her father's charter, those who believed in government more radical than the charter and those who wanted, like most of rural Portugal – divided in 1833 into seventeen, then eighteen, districts – to live by traditional patterns.

The cautious Palmela led her first government, the Duke of Saldanha – Pombal's grandson – her second. A radical election win in Oporto turned into a popular uprising in September 1836, from which emerged the Septembrists of extreme or temperate opinion. Politicians changed sides, agitation simmered, debts grew. Anti-clerical attitudes faded and peace was made with the Church – the queen was awarded a Golden Rose from the pope as a token of esteem. The 1826 constitution quivered, shook, and was modified and restored. There were elections, eloquent debates, sharp divisions and genuine social reforms, notably by the idealistic Manuel da Silva Passos, from Oporto, and a clear-thinking friend of his, who became – for his bravery in combat, where he lost an arm – Baron, Viscount and Marquis Sá da Bandeira. Their concerns ranged from health to prisons, from the abolition of slavery to a new liberal approach to the African territories. A strong-minded Beira lawyer, António Bernardo da Costa Cabral, improved trade, established granaries, reformed the tax system and national and municipal administration. But in a worthy programme of public works, a minor sanitary regulation proved his undoing.

Costa Cabral decided that, for sanitary reasons, burials inside village churches should stop. The order, in September 1846, struck at the spiritual and emotional core of village customs. The righteous indignation of devout women in the north was stirred to active protest in Fonte Arcada, east of Braga. Personifying the protest, one name lives on: Maria da Fonte, symbol of the people's wrath. (A statue of her, one of the few representing women, adorns public gardens in the Lisbon neighbourhood of Campo de Ourique.) Soon, large groups of country folk armed with pitchforks were demonstrating volubly in several towns, joined by anyone with a grievance. The anger, fanned by enemies of Costa Cabral, grew to a national rebellion so threatening that he fled in disguise to Spain.

Queen Maria looked again to the familiar presence of the three dukes, Palmela, Terceira and Saldanha. By 1851, Saldanha – who had many of the skills of his grandfather, Pombal – brought Portugal a period of stability by electoral reform acceptable to the old Chartists, reborn as Regenerators, and the old Septembrists, remoulded as Historicals.

The reign of the young queen of Portugal coincided, by historical chance, with young queens inheriting the thrones of Spain and England too. Crisis-ridden Portugal suffered many of the same problems as Spain, but while poor Isabella II experienced a disastrous civil war and ignominious flight as the Spanish crown collapsed, Dona Maria da Glória's ship of state rode the tides without sinking. Nor was she lacking as wife and mother.

At sixteen she had married her father's second wife's brother, the Duke of Leuchtenberg, who died soon after his arrival in Lisbon. A year later, in 1836, she married Ferdinand of Saxe-Coburg-Gotha, a cousin of Queen Victoria's beloved consort, Prince Albert. Their first child, Pedro, was born the following year. The naval hero Charles Napier was among the forty guests invited after the birth into the royal bedroom – 'where, lo and behold, seated in a chair was the Queen of Portugal, looking as if nothing had happened!' The marriage was happy although there was a moment, early in 1850, when the queen's honour was impugned by grave insinuations in London's *Morning Post* concerning her relations with the Count of Tomar. All the bastards born to kings across the centuries were clearly quite a different matter from this calumny, ascribed to Miguelist malice. Ferdinand, her consort, Portugal's King Fernando II, created the oddest monument of his wife's reign – the Gothic Pena palace on the crags of Sintra. A cultured man, he is also credited with rehabilitating national treasures damaged in anticlerical fervour, like the Mafra monastery and Alcobaça, restoring the Bragança tombs and rescuing the exquisite gold monstrance attributed to Gil Vicente from a molten fate in the national mint. The queen produced eleven children until, in 1853, her strength gone in giving birth to the last, Eugénio, she and the baby died. She was thirty-four years old.

Queen Maria II was succeeded by her eldest son who became, at sixteen, King Pedro V. A dutiful and serious boy, he was encouraged to travel for two years while his father acted as regent. In 1858 he married Stephanie de Hohenzollern-Sigmaringen – whose brother, Prince Leopoldo, married Dom Pedro's oldest sister Antónia. Leopoldo and Antónia lived on into the twentieth century; their granddaughter married Portugal's last king. Stephanie died of diphtheria a year after her marriage, and Pedro and two of his brothers fell ill with typhoid fever following an autumn hunting trip to the royal estates at Vila Viçosa. Three of the Bragança brothers, including the king, were dead by Christmas 1861. The young king had been well liked. Suggestions of poisoning circulated – anonymous pamphlets shouted regicide! Crowds were dispersed by the cavalry and the rumours faded.

In the brief reign of Dom Pedro V, an ageing Saldanha had

reluctantly returned to diplomacy, and his place as leader of the Regenerators was taken by a constructive and determined engineer, António Fontes Pereira de Melo – whose energetic efforts in transforming Portugal from a moribund to a mobile society went into the language as *fontismo*. Telegraph lines were installed. A section of railway between Lisbon and Oporto was inaugurated at Carregado in 1856. Alexandre Herculano worried that easy rail connections with Europe and – worst of all – Spain would lead directly to a diminished spirit of national pride. Others noted with concern that Portugal's railway was thirty-one years behind England's. Portugal not only was a late entrant to the industrial age but still had a heavy public debt, the irreducible heritage, it seemed, of Napoleon and civil war. Poverty remained widespread and emigration, the visible index of the country's health, was always an issue.

Queen Maria da Glória's blue-eyed, fair-haired second son Luís, who became king at twenty-three, considered a career at sea – and has the odd distinction of being the only king of this sea-starred nation ever to have commanded a ship. Hermenegildo Capelo, the renowned African explorer, sailed, at nineteen, under his command to Angola. Dom Luís continued to take a close interest in naval matters (he founded the Museu da Marinha, the maritime museum in Lisbon), but enthusiastically encouraged the arts and sciences as well. He himself was a proficient cello player and translator of Shakespeare. He was affable and accessible, and left politics to the politicians – which, unsurprisingly, led to his being judged a model constitutional monarch.

He was Dom Luís, *o Popular*, married to a woman who was widely liked – Maria Pia, daughter of Victor Emmanuel of Savoy (later king of Italy); they had two boys, Carlos and Afonso. He was admired outside Portugal: there was a thought, when Spain's Queen Isabella II was deposed, that Dom Luís could abdicate in favour of his son and ascend the Spanish throne. He politely declined. 'I was born Portuguese,' he replied, 'and Portuguese I want to die.' (His father, Ferdinand, was also, to his surprise, invited to be king by the Spaniards.)

The reign of King Luís (1861–89) was productive and peaceful. In government, Regenerators rotated with Historicals who, with Reformists, became Progressists. In the Civil Code of 1867, the abolition of primogeniture was intended to promote land reforms, but it created lasting problems with fragmented properties – to this day clear title is by no means common. The code also allowed civil marriage and, in an act of daring enlightenment, abolished the death penalty for civil crimes, a stance from which the Portuguese have never retreated. In Vienna, in 1989, at a conference on security, the Portuguese delegation stated that Portugal, on principle, would not consider extradition to countries with the death penalty.

Through *fontismo*, industry grew and trade expanded in textiles, tobacco, cork, canning. As ever, the British were prominent. In the literary world, bursting with brilliant poets, novelists, historians, philosophers, it surprised nobody when the enormously popular Oporto author, Júlio Dinis, published a novel in 1868 called *Uma Família Inglesa*. His English family, Mr Richard Whitestone and his two children, Jenny and Carlos, were familiar characters to many northern, urban Portuguese.

The passions and predicaments of the Whitestones, Mr Whitestone's English idioms and mutilated Portuguese grammar entertained the book's readers. Yet as King Luís's reign eased to a close, imperious English attitudes were about to impose a profound and deeply mortifying humiliation on Portugal. The context was the greedy scramble for Africa which had surged in the 1870s and intensified in the early 1880s, the catalyst the 1885 conference in Berlin which accepted German and Belgian claims in Africa, although they were justified neither by historical association nor by the new condition of effective occupation.

In previous African territorial disputes with Britain, Portugal's stand had been supported – in one instance by no less an arbiter than the United States's President Grant. Portuguese explorers in Africa, to their countrymen's frustration, had never achieved the universal fame of Livingstone (who bumped into an experienced Portuguese merchant traveller, António Ferreira da Silva Porto, during his celebrated trans-African journey) or the bold American-hired Stanley. Now Portugal, indignant at the entry of the brash imperialist bullies, Bismarck and the Belgian King Leopold, into regions Portuguese discoverers had explored and mapped long before, ambitiously drew up a brand new map of its own in which Portuguese territory stretched like a broad belt across the continent from Moçambique in the east to Angola in the west. Because of its colour, the map was called *Mapa Cor-de-Rosa* ('the Pink Map'). Cartographers in Lisbon's relatively new (1875) Sociedade de Geografia who took into account Portugal's historical prerogatives failed to consider the most formidable imperialist of them all, Cecil Rhodes, with his own dreams of British dominion from the Cape to Cairo.

Dom Luís died in October 1889 and was succeeded by his son, Carlos, a plump young man of twenty-six, intelligent, energetic, keen on sport – football became popular during his reign – and a talented painter. He was married to the tall, devout Amélia of Orleans, daughter of the French Pretender, the Comte de Paris. That their birthday fell on the same day, 28 September, was thought on the occasion of their grand marriage in 1886 to augur well. It did not. Dona Amélia involved herself in good works, joined battle against tuberculosis, produced two fine sons as well as a daughter who died at birth, but was never popular. King Carlos came to the throne in a crisis, was caught in the mesh of economic disaster and militant republicanism and came to an unhappy end.

In January 1890, Britain's Lord Salisbury issued an ultimatum: Portugal was to renounce and withdraw from the vast territory – including today's Zambia and Zimbabwe – between Angola and Moçambique. There was no compromise, no arbitration; the old alliance was at stake. Portugal had no choice but to concede. The ultimatum provoked a wave of fury across the country. The government, Progressist, fell. The government of Regenerators that replaced it fell. A coalition government was formed, and failed. A second included the eloquent historian Oliveira Martins, in charge of finance. He too gave up in disgust, and died shortly afterwards. The monarchy in the person of newly installed King Carlos I was blamed for not upholding the interests and the dignity of the nation. Public subscription for a navy able to defend Portugal's honour – and still vast territory – contributed to the acquisition of a cruiser symbolically named *Adamastor*, the terrifying giant who personifies the stormy cape in Camões's epic *Os Lusíadas* and threatens vengeance on those who dare to trespass. In Oporto, dauntless *cidade invicta*, republicans revolted – a spark, quickly extinguished, of the raging fire to come.

Crisis followed crisis. Portugal was broke. A generous flow of emigrants' money from Brazil helped a little – Alexandre Herculano observed that Brazil had never been so lucrative for Portugal as when it was no longer a colony. But in 1892 the government was forced to declare itself bankrupt. The rotating system of government, *rotativismo*, functional in quieter times, collapsed under pressure – social, economic and personal. Elections for the Chamber of Deputies were rigged, majorities created for the House of Peers by *fornada*, literally a baking, like a batch of buns, by the king as constitutional moderator.

Country folk were excluded from events, their puzzled helplessness portrayed in wickedly precise cartoons by Rafael Bordalo Pinheiro around the character of Zé Povinho, a downtrodden, bumbling, loutish Little Joe. Urbane writers, notably Eça de Queiroz, most cuttingly brilliant of all Portuguese novelists, depicted the follies and tragedies of a crumbling society. Several intellectuals sank into a depression so severe they committed suicide – the shock to the Portuguese intensified when a vastly popular hero of African campaigns, Mouzinho de Albuquerque, killed himself in 1902. The Spanish philosoper Miguel de Unamuno, in 1908, viewed the despairing Portuguese as a suicidal people. Thousands – across the country, across society, across generations – emigrated to Brazil, the colonies, America, anywhere. By 1907 the yearly total of emigrants exceeded 40,000. The land emptied of people. Moderate thinkers offered solutions, which were ignored. Republicans dreamed of reform, radicals insulted the king and extremists conspired. The system, it seemed, was damaged beyond repair.

King Carlos, fully aware of the politically charged climate, in May 1906 appointed a strong-minded reformist, João Franco, as premier. Unable to pursue his reforms against heated opposition, Franco dismissed the Cortes, jailed his opponents and ruled by decree. Demonstrations against his dictatorship frequently ended in violence. In January 1908 the police arrested a large group of leading Republicans, including a promising young doctor, Egas Moniz (who became a Nobel prizewinner in 1949). All were deported and, on 31 January King Carlos, in the peaceful setting of his palace in Vila Viçosa, unhappily signed the decree presented to him by João Franco.

The next day the king, his queen and his two sons returned to Lisbon. As their open landau drove through the Terreiro do Paço two shots struck the king, killing him instantly. A second assassin fired at the heir, Luís Filipe, mortally wounding him. In the tumult that followed, guards quickly killed the two assassins. The Republicans denied involvement, insisting that they sought change by legitimate means. Yet a service had been done for them and they were quick to support subscriptions in aid of the assassins' children. The murder was perpetrated, it appeared, by members of the secret society, Carbonária, whose intended target had been the hated João Franco. They still had not found Franco when the king's carriage drove through Lisbon.

After the first blood-spattering regicide in Portugal's long history, its last king, Manuel II – at eighteen diffident, bookish and entirely different from his father – ascended the throne. King Manuel I had been the Fortunate, an empire and wealth at his feet. Every omen for his namesake presaged ill fortune: on the very day he was born, 15 November 1889, Brazil had declared itself a republic and dispensed with their own last Bragança, the Emperor Pedro II. By another coincidence, noted later, Salazar was also born in 1889, as was Adolf Hitler.

For all the Republican fervour, the excitement and sense of inevitability, the young King Manuel, marked by the horror of his experience, was sympathetically received wherever he went. Day-to-day politics, for which he had no taste, superficially continued much as before the dictatorship of João Franco, who had vanished into exile. Dom Manuel himself tried to set up an inquiry on the conditions of life of working people but faced the familiar frustration of rapidly changing governments – in his twenty-month reign there were six. Yet Republican urges were not to be contained. Dr Bernardino Machado, moderate leader of the Republican Party, was pushed aside by activists and the secretive Carbonária grew rapidly. Revolution was in the air, and everyone knew it. The question, as it would be again and again, was what the armed forces would do. In the end, it was the murder, on 3 October 1910, of Miguel Bombarda, a respected Republican doctor specializing in psychiatry (his doctoral thesis was *Delírio das Perseguicões*), by a patient – mad, not monarchist – that precipitated action.

The revolution began hours before dawn on 4 October. Military operations were organized by captains and lieutenants. The Republicans had also won to their cause a rear-admiral, Cândido dos Reis, who was to command ships in the Tejo. Disrupted plans and meagre support led him to believe that all was lost. As the sun rose over the broad river, he shot himself. Many officers, shaken at the news, gave up. Others, led by second-lieutenant António Machado Santos, a purposeful Carbonária rebel – stuck to the strategy. Rebel naval and infantry troops and determined throngs of civilians (*populares*) occupied and held the Rotunda, today the Praça do Marquês de Pombal, as two warships bombarded the Paço das Necessidades, the young king's residence. By early morning the Republican flag flew above the Avenida da Liberdade and, at two o'clock, King Manuel was persuaded to leave by car for Mafra.

The next day, as the republic was formally proclaimed in Lisbon's city hall, the boats of fishermen ferried the king, his mother, his grandmother and a small retinue from the Ericeira beach to the royal yacht, the *Dona Amélia*. Before the ship sailed – for Gibraltar – the young king wrote a letter. 'I am Portuguese and will be always. I believe I have done my duty as king in all circumstances ... *Viva Portugal*.' Portugal's last king, Manuel the Unfortunate – *o Desventuroso* – lived out his exile in England. His mother, Dona Amélia, lived with him until 1913 when he married a relative in Germany, Augusta Victoria of Sigmaringen, when she returned to France to live in Versailles. Only once did she return to Portugal, in 1945. She died aged eighty-six in 1951.

Dom Manuel never returned. He devoted himself to researching, collecting and cataloguing old and rare books on Portugal, creating the immensely valuable library kept today, at his wish, in the ducal palace at Vila Viçosa. He died on 2 July 1932, aged only forty-two, at his home in Fulwell Park, Twickenham, of a sudden asphyxiation arising from inflamed tonsils. Only the day before he had been watching tennis at Wimbledon, by chance with the ex-king of Spain. King George V and Queen Mary, informed in the royal box of ex-King Manuel's death, arranged for the club flag to be flown at half-mast. Manuel was buried after a resplendent state funeral in the Royal Pantheon of the Braganças in the church of São Vincente de Fora in Lisbon. The last king left no children. His widow remarried – to the distress of monarchists who clearly felt she should have preserved her royal widowhood inviolate – and died, a widow once more, in 1966.

The ties that bind Portugal and England stayed firm. The Foreign Office in London in 1910 had discreetly informed two Republican delegates that the British would not intervene to save the monarchy – the alliance, after all, was between nations, not regimes. English monarchs would continue to do the honours. It was remembered that King Edward VII had enjoyed Portugal – he had visited it both as prince and, a mere twelve years after the anguish and rancour of Lord Salisbury's ultimatum, as king. Queen Elizabeth II visited Portugal twice and, in the wet and windy February of 1987, Prince Charles and Princess Diana came on a brief royal tour in which they flattered the Portuguese, were mobbed by the resident English, promoted British trade and industry, and attended a Te Deum in Oporto's cathedral celebrating, to the day, the six hundredth wedding anniversary of King João I and his English bride, Philippa.

Portugal's own royal pageantry is long gone, yet neither the leaders of the First Republic, the interposing armed forces, the unconscionably durable Salazar, nor the volatile governments of the Second Republic – launched in 1974 – ever entirely disposed of the idea of monarchy. The conspiracies and vigorous attempts to restore the monarchy in the years after its collapse faded in time to sighs and yearnings. In Italy, the younger brother of King Carlos, Afonso, a bluff, genial Duke of Oporto, found ample consolation in exile and eventually married a rich American widow, Nevada Stoody Hayes Chapman, twenty years younger than he was; she was his sole beneficiary when he died, in Naples, in 1920. The decision a generation later of Spain's Generalissimo Franco to designate as his heir Prince Juan Carlos, son of the Count of Barcelona, grandson of King Alfonso XIII, raised wild hopes in Portugal (the exiled count lived in Estoril) that Salazar would follow a similar path, but he did not.

Dom Duarte, Duke of Bragança, born in 1945, and his two younger brothers, Miguel and Henrique, are descended through both parents in a direct line from Dom João VI; they live modestly in Portugal and on occasion are addressed as Royal Highness. Royal drama and not a little comedy arise now and again through insistent claims to the Bragança titles and properties by Dona Maria Pia, born in 1907 the illegitimate daughter of King Carlos. Argument on her origins is only exceeded by wonderment at her sometimes bizarre antics – her marriage to an Italian, a second marriage to a Portuguese by the name of Amado Noivo (whose name means a well-loved bridegroom) and, at an advanced age, abdicating her pretender's claim, to a Sicilian-born accountant in exchange for a pension and the gift of a car. Yet monarchists, Catholic, traditional and politically few in number, are not so easily mocked. In the long shadow of an ancient monarchy with its old lustre and glory, it does not seem unreasonable to dream that Portugal will once again – come restoration – be great.

It is axiomatic that the Portuguese nation aspires to greatness – it is proclaimed, in praise, hope and despair, from every other page of the history books, from the benches of Parliament, on television, in the newspapers, in every open space. Reality demands that it must settle for less. The monarchy, constitutional since 1834, was abolished by bold-spirited Republicans – frustrated poor and middle-class townspeople, some intellectuals, even landowners – who desired a new society, 'an era of peace, of prosperity and of justice', as the Republican paper, *O Mundo*, declared. Fine, flowery phrases contrasted, as so often, with ordinary human needs and failings. The republic joyfully proclaimed on 5 October 1910 was ended by military *pronunciamento*, a coup, on 28 May 1926. In under sixteen years the Portuguese had suffered forty-five governments.

The crisis-scarred era of the First Republic began with a provisional government headed by Dr Teófilo Braga, a positivist philosopher and multi-talented writer of verse, prose, history, law and literary criticism. The cultivated Brazilian-born Coimbra professor, Bernardino Machado, assumed responsibility for foreign affairs. A lawyer, the fanatically anticlerical Afonso Costa, was minister of justice, and António José de Almeida, a doctor with innovative ideas, took on education. Tearing into action, they abolished noble titles, legalized the right to strike, created a bicameral parliament with a president who had no power to dissolve it, founded new universities in Lisbon and Oporto (at last ending Coimbra's monopoly), changed the national hymn, banished the *real* ('royal') coinage and brought in the *escudo* ('shield'), suppressed religious teaching and, once again, the Jesuit and other orders. In a move deplored by the hard-working poor, they also ended public holidays on saints' days.

An objecting bishop of Oporto was dismissed, the rector of Coimbra University was replaced by the gentle, respected Dr Manuel de Arriaga and, most controversial of all, in April 1911 a Law of Separation ended Catholicism as the state religion and put church matters and financial control into lay hands. And although other laws radically improved the status of women, children, old folk and tenants, justice was soon being perceived as persecution and, just as quickly, factions began to form.

On 24 August 1911, a newly constituted National Assembly elected the seventy-one-year-old Dr Manuel de Arriaga as first President of the Republic of Portugal, a position he held like a dignified juggler through several strident governments until his eighth premier, an army general, Joaquim Pimenta de Castro, was overthrown on 14 May 1915. Arriaga's first choice as premier had been João Chagas, a journalist and diplomat – still a rare combination – who, unable to survive fast-growing dissension, had lasted a full two months. On the second occasion Chagas was invited to form a government, on 15 May 1915, with Lisbon in a revolutionary rage as sharp as – and more damaging than – that of the headier 5 October 1910, an angry politician shot at him and he lost his right eye.

From the original single party of Republicans grew other groups – Democrats led by the aggressive Afonso Costa, Unionists, Evolutionists and more. The First World War briefly led them to create a 'sacred union'. Portugal, as in the days of the kings of old, sought no quarrel in Europe but worried about German activity in Africa and, perhaps even more, its poor image and inferior status abroad. The British, in turn, short of maritime transport, promised appropriate defence – providing Portugal requisitioned the dozens of German ships sheltering in Portuguese ports.

Portugal, on 24 February 1916, promptly seized the ships and on 9 March Germany declared war. In nine months, an expeditionary force was prepared, and on 26 January 1917 the first contingent of twenty-four battalions embarked for France – and if they were not the best in combat, wrote historian Oliveira Marques, they were no discredit to their flag. Flanders, for the Portuguese troops and for the uncomprehending citizenry at home, was a shattering experience. Portugal's two divisions, beaten in the battle of the Lys in April 1918, lost 7,300 men. Nearly 100,000 Portuguese men fought in the Great War and there were other grievous losses, in Africa as well as in Europe. The cost of intervention, morally, financially and in lives – thousands of Africans died, too – was cruelly high. The dead are honoured and mourned in countless town monuments and in the symbol of the perpetually guarded tomb of two Unknown Soldiers, killed in Europe and Africa and buried in Batalha Abbey. Portugal's participation in the war caused bitter argument for decades.

The 'sacred union' sundered even before the war was over. The Democrats took a turn at ruling, with Afonso Costa as prime minister for the third time. Food was short, workers dissatisfied. There were strikes, protests, clamorous dissension. In yet another armed revolt the government, in December 1917, was roughly toppled. The new leader, Major Sidónio Pais, with wide military, administrative, even academic experience – as a mathematics professor at Coimbra – was effusively welcomed across the country as the man of the hour to lead a shining 'New Republic'. He was the first president elected, in April 1918, by universal suffrage (universal for men; women did not begin to vote until 1931, and universally only after 1968). His ideas for resolving Portugal's hideous problems centred on the United States system of executive president with strong powers – he himself was also prime minister. (He liked

Americans: an American base in the Açores, leading ultimately to the NATO alliance, dates to his regime.) He offered conciliation, promised tolerance.

But events – the war, eroding economic crises and fierce social agitation – were against him. Plots arose on all sides, among Republicans, monarchists, anarchists, syndicalists, secret societies. Intending to visit Oporto on the night of 14 December 1918, he was shot and killed in Lisbon's Rossio railway station. His assassin turned out to be from none of the likely groupings but a twenty-four-year-old Alentejano radical with lofty ideals of freedom and martyrdom – which, since Portugal had no death penalty, he was denied.

The republic was born – and reborn – in the surge of lofty ideals. Portugal, like other new republics, could not escape the acute pangs and wrenching pain of a difficult birth. Hope blossomed and faded in an hour. The dilemmas in the system seemed insoluble. Ideas formed, were shaped by brilliant thinkers and admirable leaders, and were chopped to pieces by the ruthless axe of opposing opinion. There seemed to be no urge to compromise. There seemed to be, in endless plotting and conspiracy, only discord and blood.

The naval hero of the Rotunda, Machado Santos, with a singular gift for the grand gesture, in one dramatic crisis handed the president the sword he had worn in the founding of the republic. Disliking all factions, he set up his own. He was honoured, had risen to admiral, yet was cut down in the deep hatreds poisoning the young republic. On 19 October 1921, he was murdered with four other leading politicians, including the premier. The government that followed, the republic's thirty-second, lasted sixteen days.

The last years of this frail republic were fraught by instability, horrendous inflation, fraud and confusion, conspiracies and military insurrection. There were positive aspects – António José de Almeida, the first republican minister of education, who became president on 5 October 1919, managed to complete a full four years in office, a record. Far more dazzling to the Portuguese, desperate for esteem and self-respect, was the audacious flight in a tiny hydroplane, *Santa Cruz*, across the southern Atlantic to Brazil by two daring pilots, Sacadura Cabral and Gago Coutinho. The year of this first historic crossing of the south Atlantic was 1922; Charles Lindbergh made his famous transatlantic solo crossing in 1927.

On 28 May 1926 an army general in Braga, Manuel Gomes da Costa, stated firmly: 'The nation wants a military government, surrounded by the best talents, in order to bring to the state administration the discipline and honour lost long ago.' Whether the nation wanted a military government or not it had one – and by 9 July it had had three. 'Portugal, the week I was in Madrid,' Will Rogers wrote home to the United States, 'had three revolutions and four changes of government in one day, and they haven't got daylight saving either, or else they could have squeezed in another revolution.'

By the *pronunciamento* of 28 May a Democratic government was overthrown, the National Assembly dismissed and the president, Bernardino Machado, aged seventy-five, forced from office by military coup for the second time. (With other eminent Republicans he went into exile in Paris.) Military dictatorship, headed by General Óscar Carmona, initially as acting president, lasted until 1933, when Salazar's Estado Novo – New State – was established. Carmona was elected president in 1928, and three times re-elected for a seven-year term. He died in office in 1951. By the 1933 constitution, he held the right to name his own premier. Throughout his life, and for many years after it, there was only one name: Dr António de Oliveira Salazar.

6 Decorous despot, gentle revolution

Portugal's First Republic, western Europe's most turbulent parliamentary system, ended bloodlessly but in grief for what might have been. With the highest of ideals, its leaders had failed to establish a secure and progressive society. Salazar, a bleak landmark across decades of Portugal's recent history, crafted a stable authoritarian system in a rigid, unprogressive, widely despised police state. When at last it was ended bloodlessly by military coup, on 25 April 1974, grief for the wasted years and opportunity and lives evaporated in the explosion of joy and hope. Only as democracy grew to health could the Portuguese consider calmly how they had endured the twentieth century's longest dictatorship.

Salazar was born in Vimieiro, a hamlet close to the Beira village of Santa Comba Dão, on 28 April 1889, eight days after Adolf Hitler (whose ideology he greatly admired). He was the only son, after four daughters, of middle-aged parents – his mother was forty-three when he was born. His father, about fifty, owned a little property and tended other property for absentee landlords; his caution earned him the neighbourhood nickname *o Manholas* ('crafty'). Young António's parents, conservative and deeply religious, saw their son's future in the Church. Frail and timid, doted on by his mother whom he adored, António took extra lessons and won a place in the seminary of Viseu at the age of eleven. He was studious, obedient, clever. At nineteen, in 1908, he astonished his superiors and his family by announcing he would not be entering the priesthood. In 1908 King Carlos was assassinated and the dictatorship of his premier, João Franco, abolished, events which undoubtedly had an impact on the shrewd young Salazar.

In 1910, as the monarchy collapsed under republican fervour, Salazar entered the University of Coimbra. Steering clear of revolutionary politics, he joined an élitist Catholic group strongly opposed to the contemporary egalitarianism, wrote pieces for its magazine – whose editor, Manuel Gonçalves Cerejeira, would be the Cardinal Patriarch of Lisbon during Salazar's rule – and got on with his studies. When the two of them visited Paris, for a Congress of Catholic youth, Cerejeira went sightseeing and Salazar immersed himself in work. This was the only trip which he made abroad in his life, apart from brief encounters in Spain with General Franco. He graduated with high marks in law in 1914 and by 1918, already lecturing in political economy and attracting attention, he had his doctorate.

From the university setting, too, came the woman who was the domestic mainstay of his life. Maria de Jesus Caetano Freire was a maid who cleaned the flat he shared with Cerejeira and another student, Mário de Figueiredo (who Salazar later brought into his government). When Salazar moved to Lisbon, Maria de Jesus became his housekeeper, brought up two little girls, nieces of hers, whom he adopted, and – a famous Dona Maria – fiercely protected his privacy from the outside world for the rest of his life. Yet he was, it was said, attractive to women. When he was in his fifties, a French journalist, Christine Garnier, blonde and graceful, with high cheekbones and fine ankles, spent weeks at Salazar's invitation holidaying with him in the Beira countryside, where he was born and where he frequently retreated. She wrote a book about her holidays; he returned to his austere existence; speculation on their friendship was discouraged.

In 1926, when the First Republic was overthrown, General Carmona as head of a military triumvirate invited the well-known economics professor from Coimbra to become finance minister. Salazar had already had a taste of politics. In 1921, he had been elected to Parliament and entered the Chamber of Deputies; appalled by its turbulent factionalism, he hastily retreated to his serene academe. But when he was asked to handle finance again in 1926, he accepted. A photograph shows a tall, stiff man, long nose on a clean-shaven face, intense, dark, almond-shaped eyes, dark suit and the high laced ankle boots he always wore. A few days afterwards he resigned, his conditions of acceptance unfulfilled. In 1928, with the country's finances in even greater disarray, he was again offered the job – on any terms he set.

On 27 April 1928 Dr Salazar was at last installed as finance minister. The photograph now shows a distinguished figure with an aura of confidence – the inelegant boots are not in the picture. (Later, to correct a foot defect, they were custom made.) The terms he had demanded and won included complete control of government and departmental expenditure; nothing was to be spent without his approval. It was, as he himself said, a rigid code. 'I know very well what I want and where I am going,' he stated, adding that no one should expect him to complete his task in a few months. Yet his first budget, published on 1 August, showed no deficit and from 1929 onwards there appeared the even greater marvel of healthy surpluses.

Salazar very quickly appeared to be indispensable. His accounting skills, a rising escudo and amortized debt had earned him prestige. His sharp mind sliced through governmental waffle, national and overseas administration, international issues. Backed by General Carmona, he held the crucial support of the military. (He saved on butter, not guns.) No orator, he spoke from carefully prepared texts of suffering and sacrifice; usually, he meant his own in the heavy cross of duty bravely borne. No charismatic leader, he had the introvert's gift of cunning. In 1932 he was appointed President of the Council of Ministers – prime minister; the total authority he had demanded in finance now was his over every aspect of Portuguese life.

Fascism, in the 1930s, was fouling the air. Hitler, Mussolini, the durable Franco came, saw and conquered. Shrill, gaudy, terrifying, murderous, their poison spread across the earth. Salazar, while sedately spurning their rhetoric, the ostentatious parading and glossy plumage, was deeply influenced by their ideology and inquisitorial methods. He established a rigorous and all-encompassing censorship. A special police force of Social Vigilance and Defence, which later became the much-feared PIDE (Polícia Internacional e de Defesa do Estado, International and State Defence Police) was modelled on and trained, in the beginning, by the Gestapo.

At the outbreak of civil war in Spain in 1936 Salazar created the paramilitary Legião Portuguesa to defend, he said, the 'spiritual heritage' of the nation from Bolsheviks. A military-styled youth group, Mocidade Portuguesa, was formed in the image of the Hitler Youth; it became compulsory for children between eleven and fourteen. Both organizations (which survived until 1974) adopted the Nazi salute.

Additionally, a network of informers was built, its strands reaching to the far corners of the Portuguese territories and deep into the fabric of Portuguese society. At the close of the Second World War, when Hitler and Mussolini were dead, Iberia still lay in the shadow of fascism; in Spain it lasted until the death of Franco in 1975, a year after Salazar's baneful dictatorship, uneasily inherited by another professor, Marcelo Caetano in 1968, had been swept away.

Salazar was a wise chancellor according to the panegyrists who admired his financial wizardry, which was based on standard pruning of expenditure and the imposition of taxes. He was admired for his modesty and sanctity by many more, their backs stiff with righteous pride as he endlessly repeated his theme of 'Deus, Pátria, Familia'. That the political and moral order he imposed sprang from the illegitimacy of a military coup was not a matter for open discussion. The Church, for its part, nominally separate from the state, was reinvigorated by the Concordat of 1940. With a strong distaste for party politics but anxious for the appearance of legality, Salazar sought to channel political rumbling within a non-party União Nacional (National Union), the foundation of his New State, a 'unitary, corporative' republic. In 1935, a rubber-stamp National Assembly reopened in pomp and ceremony but to little purpose. Restricted and artificial elections excluded genuine opposition. Polls were blatantly rigged. Salazar rarely called his ministers to a council meeting, never argued in open debate nor faced a matching opponent. In the small room in which he worked in his official São Bento residence, he was a solitary, omniscient father to the nation.

During Salazar's long rule there was much construction and economic growth. His minister of works, Duarte Pacheco, was vigorous, energetic and imaginative; his death in a car accident in

1943, at the age of forty-four, profoundly affected Salazar (and Loulé, his home town, where a broken pillar is his poignant if contrived memorial). He was, perhaps, the heir that Salazar never named. Dams were built; bridges were constructed to span the Tejo, the Douro and other important waterways; airports and sea ports grew or were improved; roads were cut, extended, tarred, and lined with bright shrubs and shading trees. Massive hospital blocks rose. Legal humbug transmogrified colonies into provinces; the great home-based monopolies still took the profits, Portuguese emigrants to the colonies prospered. A few Africans became *assimilados*, or *civilizados*, with the status of Portuguese citizens — a difficult choice, for it meant the loss of community rights. Most Africans were *indígenas*, natives, compelled to work by a subtlety of the law; massive forced labour was a continuing commonplace.

In agriculture, Salazar's plans for self-sufficiency in wheat from the Alentejo included subsidies and guarantees of purchase. He had written, while at Coimbra, an ambitious paper on the problems of wheat and had outlined solutions. Unfortunately, his ignorance of land-use factors led to increased soil erosion and his politician's caution with the latifundists, the reactionary owners of the great estates, led to further exploitation, continuing illiteracy and more emigration. Portugal, despite its rustic image, has never thrived from its agriculture. The problems of the extreme fragmentation in the densely populated north and the vast feudal estates in the south, so scenically splendid, so enchanting to the eye, stayed as they were.

Salazar was at his most astute and diplomatic in confronting the awful choices of the Second World War. In March 1939, six months before the outbreak of war, and as the Spanish Civil War was ending, he signed a treaty of friendship with General Franco, the mutually protective Iberian pact. Salazar not only succeeded in keeping Portugal neutral but, with Hitler's troops in 1940 threatening non-belligerent Spain from the Pyrenees, won further assurances from Franco that the two nations would consult to safeguard their independence.

His ministers and the army included admirers of Germany like himself; but most Portuguese rooted for the allied forces and, since taking sides was forbidden, showed it in their own way. In Lisbon, boots drummed the cinema floor as Hitler appeared in newsreels. Mussolini was routed in fits of coughing. At a glimpse of King George VI or Winston Churchill voices would shout '*Viva . . . Benfica*', Benfica being the name of one of Lisbon's own doughty football clubs; there was no greater or more unambiguous compliment.

Refugees came to neutral Portugal in their thousands, among them, less desperate than most and of immeasurable benefit to Portugal, the oil millionaire Calouste Gulbenkian. Jobless royalty found sanctuary in pleasant villas, the rich partied with the famous, and spies flourished in Lisbon and Estoril – the Germans from the Hotel Parque, the British from the grander Hotel Palácio. Graham Greene and Malcolm Muggeridge added literary lustre to the British secret service in Lisbon. The Duke of Windsor was there, a guest of the rich, a pawn in wartime plots. The German Legation frequently complained that its messages were censored. More serious threats forced Salazar to sell wolfram to Germany, a concession he balanced by allowing British forces in 1943 use of the Açores.

At the end of the war Portuguese across the land celebrated the allied victory and Salazar announced free elections, artfully describing his regime as an organic democracy. In October 1945 liberals formed the first legal opposition party, the Movement of Democratic Unity (Movimento de Unidade Democrática, or MUD). The democratic hopes of the party's members quickly faded, however, and the police used the membership lists for reprisals.

At the war's end President Truman had coolly declined an invitation to visit either Portugal or the Açores. But in 1949 Portugal entered NATO, and joined the United Nations six years later. President Eisenhower beamed approval at Salazar over warm handshakes at Queluz. At the war's end Britain owed Portugal some £76m, an astonishing turnabout in the old alliance. The historian António José Saraiva wryly observes that *salazarismo* put an end to British tutelage for the first time since Pombal. Spain accepted the United States' Marshall Plan for reconstruction; Salazar prevaricated over the 1948 grant. His fixation over borrowing, his generally anti-capital stance, left Portugal virtually free of foreign debt but was, in the long term, to be regretted.

*

Salazar's brand of home-grown, élitist economics brought enormous wealth to a lucky few. When the Portuguese magnate Alfredo da Silva died in 1942 – he was owner of the CUF (Companhia União Fabril) conglomerate of more than a hundred companies – *Time* magazine put his personal fortune as the world's sixth largest. The Portuguese spoke enviously of 'the twenty families', their stupendous affluence built on Salazar favouritism. Small businesses struggled in a choking system of licences and permits. Workers, in closely regulated national syndicates, were forbidden to strike, paid abysmally and penalized for the slightest infringement. They could be dismissed, or the entire union dissolved, without explanation.

In 1961 an exploding Angola was the catalyst to war across all Portugal's African territories. At the end of the year India took possession of Goa. Salazar had demanded his small garrison to 'conquer or die' and when, in the face of an Indian invasion force of 30,000, it sensibly did neither, he ordered a court-martial of the governor-general. (Through military discretion, it was dropped.) To Salazar, for the rest of his life, Goa was 'occupied territory'. Only in 1990, when there was still a matter of a bank hoard of jewels to resolve, did an Indian president officially visit Portugal. The year 1961 was among the most dramatic and eventful in the era of the Estado Novo, yet much of the outside world still saw only the illusion of a stable nation, financial order and Portugal's sunny face. Supervised by António Ferro, Salazar's industrious promoter of propaganda, tourism had taken off after the tasteful conversion and refurbishing of castles and mansions into national *pousadas*. (With the accent on tourism, the propaganda secretariat became overnight the information secretariat.)

After 28 April 1965, Salazar's seventy-sixth birthday, foreign investment was allowed. There was gold in the bank and all his purse-clutching instincts were against a foreign presence in national industry. But now there were African wars to pay for; soon they would absorb up to half the budget. Salazar still doggedly pursued his autocratic, increasingly isolationist, path. Portugal was 'proudly alone', the rest of the world out of step. Blindly, Salazar was determined to crush his enemies with an iron fist. Portugal's destiny depended on him. There was no one else.

This was not a conviction shared by all Portuguese. Certainly Salazar is the landmark figure on the route from Pombal's rescued nation in the eighteenth century to revolution in the twentieth, and his long dictatorship strongly suggests that the Portuguese, still sighing for a lost Sebastião, are amenable to firm leadership and a steady hand at the helm. Yet, for all the stifling censorship and the large number – perhaps 20,000 – of secret police, there were frequent manifestations of opposition and consistent resistance to Salazar's rule.

The first, best organized, most continuous threat to the tidy, sanitized New State came from Communism; for Salazar, defender of a Christian, western civilization, Communism was an obsession. Founded in 1921, the Partido Comunista Português (PCP), grew to a disciplined national movement, adapting its jargon and tactics to the circumstances and the times. For decades, Communists operated the only concerted resistance to Salazar's dictatorship. Mário Soares, who founded Portugal's Socialist Party, Partido Socialista, in 1973 and was its redoubtable leader until he was elected president in 1986, was himself briefly a Communist.

A department of PIDE was devoted solely to catching Communists, and did so with energy, skill and dedication. All resistance was harshly suppressed, but Communists were arrested, interrogated, tortured, imprisoned and deported with especial zeal. The party's first secretary-general in Portugal, Bento Gonçalves, was among thirty-two political prisoners – Communists, anarchists, militants – who died in the concentration camp of Tarrafal set up by PIDE in 1936 on the island of Santiago in Cape Verde. Not many? Salazar's Portugal had no blood-stained killing fields. His tyranny was forged on subtler terrors and the loss of liberty, not mass slaughter. PIDE filled other prisons: Aljube with its fearsome *curros*, literally 'bull pens'; the Peniche fortress – from where Álvaro Cunhal, the Communist leader for half a century, and nine comrades made a stunning escape on 3 January 1960; and Caxias – where, in another famous exploit, seven men got away in an armoured Mercedes Hitler had given to Salazar. But the relentless dust, blazing heat and horror of Tarrafal and its blackly dubbed *frigideiras* ('frying pans'), are a grim memory for survivors.

Salazar's repressive legislation expanded in 1949 to allow PIDE powers to detain any person without charge and on a renewable basis for 180 days (copied by South Africa only in 1965). Those detained could be locked away in Portugal or dispatched to the Açores, Cape Verde, Guinea, São Tomé, Angola or even as far as Timor. When the dictatorship ended, the twenty-two members of the PCP central committee had served a total of 308 years in prison.

Opposition to the Salazar regime came from across Portuguese society and political opinion. Blanketing censorship created an image of a country sunk in apathy – 'as tidy and quiet as a cemetery', as Mário Soares put it. In reality, anger rose among eminent conservatives as well as liberal professors, among disciplined military officers and unbridled anarchists. It was expressed variously, at times provocatively and violently, and to no effect whatsoever for very many years.

Emídio Santana, who called himself a *militante anarcosindicalista*, tossed a bomb at Salazar on 4 July 1937. It failed to detonate. Santana spent sixteen years in prison, emerged to edit an anarchic paper, *A Batalha*, and lived to witness the revolution explode in 1974. Aiming to restore democracy, Captain Fernando Queiroga marched south from Oporto on 10 October 1946 at the head of the Sixth Cavalry Regiment. Key units failed to join him. He surrendered at Mealhada, near Coimbra. He was jailed for three years, and then went gloomily to Brazil. In April of 1947 Hermínio da Palma Inácio and Gabriel Gomes, both mechanics, sabotaged twenty or so military aircraft at the Sintra base, their action the only success in a conspiracy to install a Junta Militar de Libertação Nacional. Officers were dismissed and brought to trial; the two mechanics went into hiding. Palma Inácio surfaced in 1961 in the hijack of a TAP airliner and again in 1967 at the head of an ill-defined revolutionary group. He was often imprisoned, and often escaped – but not always. When the doors of Caxias were opened wide in the first joy of revolution, Palma Inácio was among the scores who emerged.

University professors and other intellectuals protested, were dismissed and went into exile or struggled in oblivion. They were not surprised; many of Portugal's finest writers and thinkers had been similarly silenced when they supported attempts to restore the republic. When the eminent administrator, General José Norton de Matos, a distinguished governor of Angola, the man who had prepared Portugal's forces for the Great War, presented himself, at the age of eighty-two, as a liberal Republican candidate in the 1949 presidential elections, the impact was considerable, but nothing was changed: without guarantees of a fair election, he withdrew. General Carmona was returned unopposed. On Carmona's death in 1951, attempts to present candidates opposed to Salazar's choice, General Craveiro Lopes, were forcibly crushed. It was little comfort that the general, later marshal, showing signs of wanting to moderate the dictatorship, was himself replaced by the diehard Admiral Américo Tomás seven years later in a notoriously fraudulent election.

The opposition candidate (two others retired) for the 1958 presidential elections was General Humberto Delgado, dynamic, out-spoken, confident and bold. In active service, and as director-general of civil aviation, he had veered from being a stout defender of all things Salazarist to voluble dissidence. His reply to a question at a crowded press conference that, if he won, he would promptly dismiss Salazar – '*Obviamente, demito-o*' – set the scene for a dramatic campaign: he was the general *sem medo* ('without fear'). In Oporto a crowd of 200,000 thronged to hear him speak. Back in Lisbon, hundreds of police and mounted guards of the Guarda Nacional Republicana (GNR) were unable to restrain the crowds eager to see and hear him; Delgado himself was prevented from speaking. His campaign was hindered at every step, his supporters and campaign committees arrested, yet it was clear he had vast popular support – and he, unlike Norton de Matos, would not withdraw.

Polling took place on 8 June 1958. The official results gave Admiral Tomás 758,998 votes and General Delgado 236,528 votes; the reverse would have been likelier. Abroad, the patent electoral fraud was ridiculed. In Portugal, protests were presented promptly and uselessly. Many people wore mourning. There were strikes, quickly suppressed. Delgado, failing to find support at the upper reaches of military command, involved himself in clumsy plots, sought asylum in the Brazilian Embassy and went into exile, joining other notable dissidents, like Henrique Galvão, organizer of the TAP aircraft hijack, in colourful and widely reported exploits. The spectacular seizure on 22 January 1961 of the Portuguese cruise liner, *Santa Maria*, off Venezuela, a gaudy adventure on the high seas to which they gave the irresistible code name Operação Dulcineia, won enormous publicity for the exiles' cause. In 1965 General Delgado's name made headlines again. He and his secretary were murdered near Badajoz in Spain on 13 February by four PIDE agents. Their crudely buried bodies were discovered on 24 April. Twenty-five years later, on 5 October 1990, the eightieth anniversary of the republic, Delgado's remains were ceremonially transferred from a Lisbon graveyard to the national pantheon.

Humberto Delgado, the symbol of resistance, more than anyone opened the eyes of the world to the vicious injustice and hypocrisy of the Salazar regime. An open letter directed at Salazar in 1958 struck with the same resolute force: the bishop of Oporto, Dom António Ferreira Gomes, wrote to protest about the inequities in society and the misery in which the poorest labourers languished. His letter was not well received. Church officials, and Cardinal Cerejeira himself, were dismayed at any controversy. The liberal bishop was sent abroad to rest and meditate, and was prevented by PIDE from re-entering the country. His letter and his exile became for Catholic dissenters caught in a Catholic dictatorship their badge of courage and honour. In a cry of rage from Brazil some time later Henrique Galvão also wrote a celebrated open letter: 'Your Excellency has intimidated and beaten into submission eight million Portuguese whom you have turned into the wretched morons who wander around to the tune of *Fado*, Fátima and Football.' Here is Zé Povinho, the nineteenth century's Little Joe cartoon character, updated.

And still dissension grew. In 1961 the defence minister, General Botelho Moniz, an asp in the bosom of the council, tried to force Salazar's resignation, and failed. On the eve of New Year's Day, 1962, liberal officers, supporters of Delgado, tried to invade the barracks at Beja, and failed. Workers struck in a rising tide of conflict, ending in pitched battles with police. Some died, hundreds were injured, hundreds more arrested. University students began to express dissent. Their annual celebrations became a public stage for satire. Banning fed student anger, spontaneous outbursts, further heavy-handed repression. In the spring of 1962, police invaded Lisbon University; the rector, Marcelo Caetano – with Salazar an architect of the New State – resigned in protest. The universities in Oporto and Coimbra declared solidarity with Lisbon. Fires smouldered; invariably agitation met with a harsh response. The university crisis (preceding the more famous May 1968 student battles in France) proved to be a preliminary for dramatic confrontations in 1969 with the weak leadership of Salazar's successor – Marcelo Caetano.

On 3 August 1968, in the Santo António fort beside the sea in Estoril, which had become his summer sanctuary, Salazar fell. His regular chiropodist, washing his hands before tending to the great man's feet, heard a crash. Salazar had fallen heavily from a canvas director's chair and banged his head on the tiled floor. He appeared to suffer no ill effects but on 27 August he experienced headaches. On 6 September a neuro-surgeon diagnosed a haematoma of the brain; an operation was needed to extract it. Salazar was taken by his doctors to hospital. By 3 a.m. the next morning President Tomás and the council ministers had gathered like a flock of crows outside the room where Salazar lay. There was no heir, no political testament. Only one thing was clear: intrigue over the succession had begun.

At 4 a.m. doctors operated. The diagnosis was confirmed. Salazar had a chronic intracranial haematoma causing immense pressure on the brain. The operation was a success, the pressure relieved. Ministers' wives who had waited beside their husbands hurried to the hospital chapel to praise God. A bland public statement was issued. On 16 September Salazar screamed with pain: a heavy haemorrhage had occurred in the right side of the brain, the opposite side to the haematoma. Salazar's lifelong friend Cardinal Cerejeira arrived at the hospital. Deeply shocked, he gave Salazar the last rites. That evening President Tomás invited Marcelo Caetano to take office as premier.

Salazar did not die until 27 July 1970, almost two years later. He was not toppled by dissidents. He held normal conversations with occasional visitors – his ministers, even journalists. He was never told that Caetano had taken his place. It seems a last cruel joke on the Portuguese that the man whose dictatorship brutally atrophied their spirit of enterprise, who deprived his country of its basic freedoms and the opportunity to seek the benefits of post-war expansion, should believe to the end that he held its fate in his hands.

Salazar was often called *bota-de-elástico*, not because of his lace-up boots but for his inflexible stick-in-the-mud attitude. Caetano's first speeches were directed at the ultraconservative *botas-de-elástico* who had sustained Salazar's regime. 'Life must go on . . . This country has been accustomed for a long time to being governed by a man of genius; today it must adapt to government by common men.' A far more open personality than Salazar, a brilliant teacher and expert in constitutional and administrative law, he had contacts everywhere from the Church, the military and big business to students; his wide-ranging connections had got him the job.

Caetano's theme was renewal within continuity, an unhappy compromise, but he also quickly corrected some of the most obvious injustices. The bishop of Oporto and other notable exiles were invited home. A deportation order on Mário Soares was rescinded. Soares, the son of a spirited liberal Republican imprisoned and deported for his views, was a ceaseless irritant to the Salazar regime. He was born in 1924, and had been a youthful organizer of the MUD party and lawyer to the family of General Delgado. Several times imprisoned, he was banished to São Tomé in 1968 without trial and for an indefinite term. When Marcelo Caetano allowed him to leave in 1970 the conditions he imposed drove Soares to continued exile.

Caetano tried hard to satisfy left, right and centre. PIDE changed its name – to Direcção-Geral da Segurança (DGS, the Directorate-General of Security) – but not its face or its direction. The single party, União Nacional, became Acção Nacional Popular (Popular National Action) and in 1969 Caetano insisted there was nothing to impede democrats from being elected. Among those elected – in still restricted procedures – were Francisco de Sá Carneiro and Francisco Pinto Balsemão. Both would become post-revolution premiers; in Caetano's interregnum they both resigned. In his cabinet, Caetano included liberal ministers and, as under-secretary for health and welfare, the first woman ever appointed to a Portuguese government.

For the African territories there was vague talk of federal, or autonomous, association – many years after other colonial systems had been swept away by the wind of change in Africa. 'Night and day this problem is in my mind,' sighed Caetano in 1972. 'Constantly I seek ways to relieve the sacrifices of the Portuguese people.' But there was no attempt at dialogue; no concessions were made. In 1972, an aged President Tomás had himself re-elected. (After the Delgado turmoils of 1958 an electoral college, not the electorate, voted the president to office.) A state of emergency was declared and more young men were shipped off unwillingly (some deserted, many emigrated) to fight in the futile, costly, demoralizing colonial wars in distant Angola, Guinea-Bissau and Moçambique. In thirteen years of war, over 100,000 men were under arms; 8,290 lost their lives and 26,223 were maimed and injured.

The disappearance of Salazar had been for many Portuguese a joyful release. Soon, the joy faded into disillusion. Caetano belonged to the superannuated corporate past. A decent man pushed by modern forces and pulled by diehard intransigence sank into the safe cushion of immobility. His bright spring was short. Spring passed into an arid summer. His few reforms for a peaceful transition of Portugal from the grim obscurity of *salazarismo* were overtaken by events. Caetano had the chance, the goodwill, to seize his inheritance and make of Portugal an honest, open, modern nation – and fluffed it. The key to the transformation of Portugal, as it had been for Prince Henry the Navigator, for the kings Dom João II and Dom Manuel I and for the great discoverers, even for the foolish, tragic Sebastião, lay in Africa.

It seemed typical of Portugal's acceptance of authority that the man who lit the spark of revolution was no youthful firebrand but a sixty-four-year-old monocled general, António de Spínola, who had fought in the Spanish Civil War on Franco's side and had received training from the Wehrmacht in Nazi Germany – it was when he was in Berlin that he had acquired the habit of wearing a monocle. He had also seen the Russian Front, in the Second World War, as an observer for the Germans. Yet if he looked like a character from a German melodrama, he was a tough fighter who never held back from combat and was respected by his troops. As governor-general in Guinea-Bissau from 1968 to 1973 he had attempted to counter insurgency with social reform and a range of community projects. Concluding that Portugal could never win the war by military means, he wrote a book setting out his ideas for federation. Called *Portugal e o Futuro* ('Portugal and the Future'), it was published in Lisbon on 22 February 1974.

Caetano read a pre-publication copy – it had 'a kind dedication from the author' – and wrote later: '. . . when I closed the book I had understood that the military coup which I could sense had been coming was now inevitable'. On 14 March he sacked General Spínola from his new job as deputy chief of staff of the armed forces along with the chief of staff, General Costa Gomes; both had refused to declare loyalty for current African policies. On 16 March officers loyal to Spínola began to move troops to Lisbon from Caldas da Rainha and were quickly intercepted. The pattern was familiar: another military coup had failed; the old order, immutable, barely quivered. Caetano, President Tomás, the entire establishment, blinked and relaxed.

On 25 April 1974, the regime collapsed. Forty-eight years of Salazar oppression were swept away in a smooth military operation without a shot being fired. The old general had gripped attention centre stage; some two hundred junior officers, their script outlined months before on an Alentejo farm, were waiting in the wings. And like the good-humoured performance it was, it began with a song. At 22.55 the night before, the radio programme *Limite* played the plaintive '*E depois do adeus*' ('And after the farewells'), a warning for attentive listeners that the countdown had begun. At twenty-nine minutes past midnight came the song '*Grândola, vila morena*' . . . 'Grândola, dusky town, land of brotherhood: it is the people who hold sway within your walls . . .' The singer, and composer, was José (Zeca) Afonso, a true folk hero of the revolution. His moving song was the signal to proceed.

By 3 a.m. troops were in command of the vital points and life-lines of Lisbon. The radio continued to broadcast popular songs, many formerly banned. At 8.30 a.m. the first announcement of the Armed Forces Movement (Movimento das Forças Armadas, MFA) was broadcast, followed by appeals to keep calm and stay at home. The Terreiro do Paço, bordered by arcaded ministries, filled with troops. Soon excited *lisboetas*, far from staying at home, filled the streets. Some headed for the PIDE headquarters – where, that night, trying to get away, PIDE agents shot into the streets, the last violent act of the regime. Four died, several were injured. Crowds grew in the Largo do Carmo: the prime minister, Caetano, President Tomás and several ministers had taken refuge in the Carmo barracks of the Guarda Nacional Republicana. Captain Salgueiro Maia, commanding the area, demanded their surrender. Fearful that '*o poder caísse na rua*' ('power would fall to the mob'), Caetano convinced Captain Maia that as a matter of etiquette he should surrender only to a general. He telephoned General Spínola who, pointing out it was not a revolution of his making, agreed to accept the unconditional surrender of Caetano and his government. Early next morning Marcelo Caetano and the deposed president, Américo Tomás, were flown to Madeira and, ultimately, Brazil.

Spínola did not take part in the coup but he had read the MFA programme – essentially, the overthrow of *salazarismo*, decolonization, restoration of democracy and the honour of the armed forces. He at least knew what was up and was elated to be called upon to act so soon. For Lisbon, all Portugal and the rest of the world, the revolution – in fact, only just beginning – came as a total surprise. Nobody, in 1926, had foreseen the rise of tyranny; nobody, in 1974, anticipated the events of 25 April or had the slightest idea who was in charge. When it emerged that the Moçambique-born Major Otelo Saraiva de Carvalho was the principal strategist and operational commander in a committee of three, with Major Vítor Alves and Captain Vasco Lourenço, and that the MFA programme was the work mainly of Major Ernesto Melo Antunes, few people were much the wiser. Of them all, it was Otelo, the improvident radical idealist – known, unusually, by his uncommon first name – whose fame endured.

The diplomatic networks, the CIA, were caught short. There had been plenty of rumours, including the distinct possibility of a coup from the right under the Moçambican commander, General Kaúlza de Arriaga. The American ambassador, new and without diplomatic experience, for whom Portugal was a gift of an assignment, was in the Açores. His deputy was telephoned at 4.20 a.m. by the house guard, a former PIDE/DGS man, who said insistently: '*Perigo, perigo*' ('Danger, danger'). The diplomat did not understand. His wife, half awake, murmured: 'That's the name of the guard,' and both went back to sleep. At 6.30 a.m. a call from an aide told him there were tanks in the street.

The euphoria of the crowds, the incredible relief that a long nightmare was over, a myth overcome, is a powerful memory for many Portuguese. Soldiers, the mostly anonymous Young Captains, as they were called, whose anger had been fed by iniquities in Africa, low pay and an inequitable promotion system, were conquering heroes whose peaceful mission was reinforced when bright red carnations, an Otelo inspiration, sprouted from rifle barrels and spread across Lisbon, a symbol of the revolution forever after. Across the country, as well as in the capital, rapturous crowds celebrated the revolution of the flowers in the forgotten thrill of liberty, equality and fraternity.

Caetano's portrait was torn down, municipalities dismissed, PIDE offices wrecked. In New York the exchange rate of the escudo rose. On 26 April Spínola announced a Junta of National Salvation consisting of seven military officers, coordinating committees and a council of state. Censorship was abolished, elections promised. Street names changed. Graffiti, vibrant in colour and expression, appeared overnight. A mother named her newborn son António Spínola. To a huge welcome, Mário Soares returned from France and Álvaro Cunhal, in exile for fourteen years, from Czechoslovakia. On 1 May, Labour Day, thousands came to Lisbon to cheer them, the two men united then as they never would be again. Within days, as parties formed, Communist activists moved into buildings owned by the Salazarist regime, into municipal offices and influential positions in the media and management.

On 15 May Spínola was inaugurated as president and a provisional government formed. Spínola chose a liberal lawyer, Adelino da Palma Carlos, as prime minister and appointed civilian ministers, except to the ministry of defence. All shades of political opinion were represented – Mário Soares, one of three socialists, was foreign minister, his prime responsibility to end 'that worst of our afflictions', the colonial wars; the social-democrat Francisco Sá Carneiro was a minister without portfolio – as was the Communist Álvaro Cunhal. Henry Kissinger, whose interest in Portugal until then had been slight – before 1974 Mário Soares was never received by any American official above third secretary – promptly ordained that Portugal, a NATO member, be excluded from NATO's innermost secrets.

Portugal in revolution seethed and fumed. Before May was out strikes erupted – workers wanting more money, better conditions, managements purged of Salazar bosses. The infant government was charged with 'betrayal of the working class'; the PCP – the Communist Party – was as helpless as Canute in restraining the great waves of strikers. Prostitutes published a manifesto requesting legal status within a union; declaring support for the MFA, they offered a 50 per cent discount to all ranks below lieutenant. There was a shortage of bread, transport was in disarray, administration in a shambles. Portugal, high on hope, was quivering in a fever. To lower the heat, a militia was formed – COPCON (Operational Command for the Continent), an élite force commanded by Otelo Saraiva de Carvalho, a brigadier now and military governor of Lisbon.

Disagreements arose. In July, the prime minister, Palma Carlos, resigned. From the MFA candidates, Spínola chose Colonel Vasco Gonçalves, whose high rank and financial substance he believed would be a guarantee against radical sympathies. Gonçalves instead proved to be a dedicated Marxist and a strong supporter of the PCP. He remained prime minister until September 1975, through four short and turbulent provisional governments. Spínola himself was forced aside and resigned in September 1974. Opposed as he was to early decolonization, reluctant above all to hand Angola to the most radical of the liberation groups, his tenure was in doubt from the beginning. Succeeded by the army commander, General

Costa Gomes, he continued to involve himself in complex power play and was tricked – it seemed – into attempting a coup early in March 1975. It failed, and he escaped to Spain. The Junta of National Salvation was extinguished and a Supreme Revolutionary Council (CRS) created, with full legislative powers. All leading MFA radicals were members of the council. The tempo of revolution quickened.

Invisible barricades rose as grand structures fell. In March, private banks and insurance companies were nationalized and the giant monopolies were taken over by their employees; CUF, the largest of all, by now a conglomerate of 186 companies, went to the state. In small and medium businesses workers demanded the keys, the cash, the ownership; often, when offered the books, the overdraft and the organizing, they had second thoughts. In the Alentejo, farm labourers, Portugal's wretched of the earth, seized from absentee landlords the great estates, millions of acres that became overnight collective, or cooperative, farms.

The MFA headed the power structure. Communists, long-established, forced the pace in the name of the MFA and revolution. They had the backing of the prime minister Gonçalves. What they did not have was strong popular support. The MFA had promised elections and, despite social tumult, fulfilled their promise. On 25 April 1975, the first anniversary of the day of the carnations, 91.7 per cent of all registered voters went to the polls.

For Mário Soares the result was vindication of his years of struggle, a triumph for his republican convictions, his eloquence, his shrewd political skills. The Socialist Party (PS) won 37.9 of the total vote, followed by the right-of-centre Popular Democrats (PPD), with 26.4 per cent; the Communist Party (PCP), achieved only 12.5 per cent. Small parties, to the right as well as to the left, won smaller fractions. Conservatives were strongest in the north, Communists in the Alentejo, Socialists in Lisbon and the south. The elections were for a constituent assembly, not yet a national parliament. A sulking Álvaro Cunhal made it clear he believed votes were no measure of a party's influence. In June, repudiating the soft-edged stance of Eurocommunism, he told a journalist that Portugal would never be a country with democratic freedoms. The radical left continued to squeeze, to exhort, to militate with hardened determination.

The seizure by its printers of a distinguished pro-Socialist newspaper, *República*, the only major paper to survive Communist takeover, provided Mário Soares with a stick to brandish at Communist aggression and, for their inaction, the MFA themselves. Newly precious civil liberties were under attack from the militant left. The Socialists resigned; another provisional government was formed – the fifth. It survived barely three weeks. Tempers frayed. The conservative north, seeing its traditions, town councils, property and values in jeopardy, raged at Communism as a Bolshevik menace and leftist radicals as unholy devils. Cunhal was rescued by troops in Alcobaça. Otelo was spat upon in Oporto. Sá Carneiro joined Soares in tongue-lashing the lame and disunited MFA. To head the sixth and, as it turned out, the last provisional government President Costa Gomes appointed the navy commander, Admiral José Pinheiro de Azevedo. Thought to be radical, he emerged uncertainly to the right.

But all authority had evaporated. Transient movements materialized and as quickly faded. In November, striking construction workers laid siege to the constituent assembly in São Bento palace. Otelo refused to let the COPCON forces intervene. The humiliated government was forced to accede to the workers' demands. Then the government itself went on strike. President Costa Gomes called in the army to restore order and replaced Otelo as military governor of Lisbon with Vasco Lourenço, from a new grouping of MFA officers urging moderation, the Group of Nine. The radical left was allegedly readying its communes, the enraged northern conservatives preparing an almighty showdown. Contingency plans were prepared to transfer the seat of government from Lisbon to Oporto. The crunch came on 24 November when, at Rio Maior, for ever after a historic frontier, northern farmers raised barricades and cut the road.

On 25 November the tempest passed, the revolution sputtered and stopped as suddenly as it had begun. Left-wing paratroop units rebelled in the expectation of wide support, but found themselves alone, abandoned by the PCP and rejected even by the MFA radicals. The MFA revolution had been made in peace. Nobody wanted bloodshed. The action, in which commandos swiftly neutralized the rebels, cost them two deaths and was the only military confrontation of the revolution.

Portugal's passionate nature, it is frequently said, is expressed more in word than in deed. They are often thought to be people filleted of backbone, weakened by a crushing burden of unenlightened dictatorship, undesirable wars in Africa and unremitting poverty at home. The familiar image shows inertia, ineptitude, an innate reluctance to do that which can be left undone. Criticism flows in a steady stream, from foreigners, from the Portuguese themselves. Yet the Portuguese, it is clear, have many rare and wonderful qualities. If they choose, they are capable of anything. The leap from impotent inaction to revolutionary fervour is an example, the sequence of events since the revolution ran its course another.

The coordinator of the smooth commando operation on that memorable 25 November was a dour lieutenant-colonel, António Ramalho Eanes. Promoted to general, he was appointed commander-in-chief of the army. Radical opinion faded, elated reactionaries were icily ignored, moderate pragmatists were the new heroes. The MFA in February 1976 agreed to give up governing power, keeping only a guardian role. A constitution aiming to set Portugal on the path to socialism, phrased in revolutionary language, was ratified on 2 April 1976.

On 25 April, a day rich in symbols, elections for the National Assembly and the first constitutional government were held, the winners – as they had been a year ago for the constituent assembly – Mário Soares and the Socialists, their vote down slightly to 34.9 per cent. In second place, with 24.3 per cent, was Sá Carneiro's PPD, the Popular Democrats, followed by the right-wing Centre Social Democrats (CDS), a party Christian Democrat in spirit led by a clever professor of law, Diogo Freitas do Amaral, who had been a university colleague of Caetano. From 7.6 per cent in 1975, the CDS now had 16 per cent. The Communist vote was 14.4 per cent. Despite the shocks and fears of transition, the broad picture was little changed. But who would be president of the new, democratic Portugal? The choice, for Socialists, Popular Democrats and CDS alike, was easy: the sad-faced soldier, Ramalho Eanes.

The campaign showed all the contrasts in Portugal's cautiously mutating society: Eanes, trying hard to look comfortable in shirtsleeves in public, had the stout support of parties of the centreright and left. Rural Portugal liked his solid moderation, his country accent, his caution. Was he too stiff, his undertaker look depressing? Not with Manuel Alegre beside him, Socialist orator and poet, who added colour and sophistication to the campaign. There was opposition: the outgoing prime minister, Pinheiro de Azevedo; a Communist, Octávio Pato; and at the extreme left, Otelo. When the votes were counted on 27 June 1976, General Eanes, with 61 per cent, had won by a landslide. Otelo's small comfort was that he came second with 16.5 per cent, more than double the Communist vote.

President Eanes was barely installed before challenges arose. He appointed as prime minister the Socialist leader Mário Soares, but the Socialists did not have an overall majority and the opposition nagged Eanes for a coalition. Until July 1987 no single party achieved an overall majority. In the two years after revolution the Portuguese had six governments; between July 1976 and July 1987 they elected ten. These were long, hard years, a dispiriting mirror of the stormy First Republic. Patiently, again and again – for general elections to the 250-seat National Assembly, for municipal elections, for two further presidential elections, for, most baffling of all, the twenty-four seats allotted to Portugal in 1986 in the European Parliament – the Portuguese went to the polls.

In the catalogue of winners and losers, left switched with right and centre in hops, skips and jumps. There were odd deals and strange marriages of convenience. Mário Soares took office as prime minister three times and holds the record for durability (just over two years) in that politically troubled period. Several governments lasted only months, one a mere two weeks. In 1979 Portugal had a woman prime minister, Maria de Lourdes Pintasilgo, a radical Catholic, appointed caretaker until the next elections.

Personalities are remembered with emotions that range from affection and admiration to loathing and despair. For many present-day Social Democrats, the guiding star was Francisco de Sá Carneiro. His election success at the end of December 1979, in a 'Democratic Alliance' with Freitas do Amaral's CDS and the small Monarchist party, was the first overall majority in post-revolution Portuguese politics. His death on 4 December 1980, when his aircraft crashed on take-off from Lisbon airport, was a profound shock for his party, the alliance and the nation. With him died his Danish companion, Snu Bonnier, for whom he had left his wife, and his defence minister, Adelino Amaro da Costa. Inevitably, suspicion persists that the aircraft was sabotaged. Sá Carneiro was a vivid and dynamic politician and forceful speaker. His long-time colleague and successor, Pinto Balsemão, whose publishing company owns *Expresso*, the foremost weekly newspaper in Portugal, lacked the sparkle of Sá Carneiro or his great rival, Mário Soares.

Soares's third term of office as prime minister, from June 1983 to July 1985, lasted longer than any other non-majority government but, like most, ended ungracefully. At the time, a period of grim austerity, Soares had reached a coalition accord with Carlos Mota Pinto, leader of the Social Democrats. When the party – now transmuted from PPD to PSD – elected a new leader, a tight-lipped young economist, Aníbal Cavaco Silva, finance minister to Sá Carneiro, the agreement shattered and Soares's government fell.

By the ingenious mechanism of the electoral process wonderful plots are woven. Here was Soares overcome and the canny Cavaco Silva, in November 1985, the new prime minister, although his party, the PSD, like all the others before it, lacked a majority. But the mood was different; austerity had eased to a growing prosperity, inflation was down, money was beginning to flow in from the EEC. Portugal was fed up with endlessly tottering governments. So when, in April 1987, the government was brought down on a vote of censure, the rage and frustration among the Portuguese people, who were yearning for stability, was fierce. Back at the polls, on 19 July, 5.6 million voters from across every party line gave Cavaco Silva an unprecedented mandate – 50.15 per cent of the vote, 146 seats and a fat majority – to solve their problems and transform their society. In Cavaco Silva, they had voted for a free-market economist who was all for Europe, NATO, the United States and Mrs Thatcher.

But here was the twist: the censure motion that had shortened the life of Cavaco Silva's first government was organized by none other than Ramalho Eanes. By 1986 Eanes had been president for ten years, his re-election in 1980 (against a Democratic Alliance candidate, General Soares Carneiro, and the determinedly battling Major Otelo) outright confirmation from voters that they valued his prudence and judgement – enough, it seemed, when his term as president was coming to an end, to support a new centre-left Democratic Renewal Party (PRD), which was to be his vehicle to the National Assembly. Here again, for the Portuguese, was a father-figure, dedicated and austere. Yet in the cut and thrust of day-to-day politics Eanes proved painfully awkward and inept. Voters made their view cruelly clear: Eanes won a seat in 1987 if only because he headed the party list (the Portuguese system puts parties before candidates); the PRD sank swiftly from 18 per cent and forty-five seats to 5 per cent and seven seats. In August 1989, without ever occupying his seat, Eanes resigned as head of the party.

The Socialists in those momentous elections were not at all disgraced. They won 22 per cent of the vote and fifty-nine seats. The party leader now was Vítor Constâncio, a solid, teddy-bearish figure, formerly governor of the Bank of Portugal. Mário Soares, who had never missed an election, was not a candidate. He had succeeded Eanes as the first civilian president since 1926, his election in March 1986 a narrow win, on a second round, over the Christian Democrat Freitas do Amaral, who was backed by Cavaco Silva and the PSD. Communists, detesting both CSD and PSD, gave their vote, crucial in the final count, to Soares.

In the 1987 electoral earthquake the Christian Democrats, like Eanes's PRD, slipped, from 10 per cent and twenty-two seats in 1985 to 4.3 per cent and only four seats. But if the right was down, so were the Communists, from 15.5 per cent and thirty-eight seats to 12 per cent and thirty seats. Cavaco Silva, the man in the centre, the modern-minded technocrat of modest origins – his father runs a service station in the Algarve – appeared to be the man for the future.

If it was not a cloudless Utopia, the scene in Portugal in July 1987 looked bright: a workable blend of right-of-centre government with the seasoned Socialist trouper, Mário Soares, in the prestigious balancing role of president – who would be, as he put it, a non-party president of all the Portuguese. (So successful was he that five years later he won re-election by a landslide.) There were outstanding men and women in the front ranks of government, in the major and minuscule parties and as determined and articulate independents. They knew each other well. In the older generation many had walked the same path, suffered pain, prison and exile. They had fought a common enemy, shared campaigns, differed and, at times, quarrelled. Ageing Republicans shared the benches of Parliament with young progressives who had learned their politics in student confrontations. Conspicuous were the brainy professionals, the young economists. All of them, in a way, were the heirs of the Young Captains of 1974 – whose last hold on power was broken when a constitutional amendment in 1982, with military agreement, subordinated military power to civil and placed the appointment of military chiefs in government hands.

In 1989, on 25 April, the Portuguese celebrated fifteen years of liberty in a democratic, open and tolerant society. In the Senate Room of the National Assembly Agostinho da Silva, a twinkling philosopher in his eighties, a dauntless survivor from the First Republic, told youngsters to cherish the dream of glory. In the great hemisphere of the main chamber Mário Soares paid tribute to the brave captains of that other April in Portugal and reviewed the successes of those fifteen years – among them the end of Portugal's international isolation and its restored prestige. He spoke of what troubled him, of inequality and poverty. Listening in the public gallery were several ageing Young Captains. Some were serving officers, others in the reserve forces, or private life – Melo Antunes worked for UNESCO. Also present were Mário Soares's clear-headed and capable wife, Maria Barroso, the Cardinal Patriarch of Lisbon, Dom António Ribeiro, and beside the Cardinal, the familiar figure of an unchanged, still monocled Marshal Spínola. Only the title of Marshal, also bestowed on the Second Republic's second president, Costa Gomes, was new.

Spínola had returned quietly to Portugal years before. Américo Tomás, too, had come back from Brazil; he died in Portugal, aged ninety-three, in 1987. Marcelo Caetano, unwilling to return, taught law in Brazil and died there in 1980. He is remembered by many students, who sigh for the lost years of his regime, for his brilliance as a teacher. Salazar, whom he succeeded, is remembered, but not by everyone: an *Expresso* poll early in 1989, the hundredth anniversary of his birth, showed that 24.7 per cent of young people between fifteen and twenty-four had no idea who he was. A boy interviewed in Santa Comba Dão thought vaguely that he owned a house near by.

By tidy chance, the fifteenth anniversary of the revolution fell three days before the hundredth anniversary of Salazar's birth. In tolerant, pluralistic Portugal there exists an ultra-right element, a small corps of young fascists and a few old Salazarists who habitually lunch together on 28 May to mark the 1926 military dictatorship that brought Salazar to power. A newspaper photographer is there to capture the chilling moment of their Nazi salute, but no paper gives much prominence to it. When, on the hundredth anniversary, an ultra-right group sang the national anthem over Salazar's tomb in Vimieiro, arms extended in salute, commentators expressed disgust. But the tears and cheers of that ugly day were not of much interest to most Portuguese. After all, one of the liberties that 25 April signified was freedom of expression, an irony that escaped the fascists at the tomb.

Communists, in that April of 1989, did not have much to celebrate. They had influence, especially in the unions, but their popular support was sliding. Álvaro Cunhal, the lionheart of the movement, his mane of white hair still impressive, the smile relaxed, was seventy-five. He had his Order of Lenin, and he had at last recognized that Stalin was imperfect and perestroika the force for the future; he had shaken the hand of Gorbachev. But the Communist day of justice in Portugal, the vision to which he had devoted his life, would never come. The party, which could still present to the television cameras teeming congresses and bumper festivals of the hard-line faithful, had obvious rifts. No discipline could restrain the urge of several of the younger members for a new look in Portugal's oldest party. Dissidence was a more vital issue, for the moment, than the succession. The challenge of the articulate thirty-nine-year-old woman, Zita Seabra, who had been a member since she was fifteen and had been expelled in 1988 from both the party's political commission and its central committee (and from the party itself in the first days of 1990), was watched by the Portuguese with fascination. The older generation within the party had little to console them except, perhaps, the announcement, early in 1989, by the Cape Verde government that the Tarrafal concentration camp, 'the camp of slow death', was to be restored as a monument to their anti-fascist, anti-colonial fight. The collapse of Communism in eastern Europe, the tumbling of the Berlin Wall, left Portuguese Communism out on a limb. During a party congress in May 1990 Carlos Carvalhas, youthful and articulate, was elected Cunhal's heir. But, in an outdated party, resignations multiplied.

The Socialists, without the adept Mário Soares at the helm, seemed to lack force. Political commentators delighted in comparing the merits of Vítor Constâncio, the Socialist, and Cavaco Silva – the two shy economists who led the two main parties. Then in October 1988, troubled by opposition from factions within the party, Constâncio suddenly resigned. A new leader, Jorge Sampaio, quiet-spoken and with a benign, ruffled look, was elected. The party paid a united tribute to President Soares. Sampaio, a political activist since the election campaign of Humberto Delgado, stood for greater deregulation of the economy and more privatization. It was a policy that closely resembled Cavaco Silva's. The two men, both born in 1939, also had in common an English education. The *estrangeirados*, if they had ever left, were back in force. Any easy compatibility between the two men evaporated when municipal elections in December 1989 showed a heavy swing to the Socialists, who won control of more that half the *Câmaras*, the municipal councils, including the largest cities. Sampaio, in a risky political partnership with the Communists, stood for mayor of Lisbon – and won. Immediately, Socialists began looking hopefully to the general elections of 1991; Sampaio optimistically declared he would switch from being mayor of Lisbon to leading the government as prime minister.

Small parties, including Monarchists and independents, make their presence felt, Gulliver voices in Lilliputian bodies. For the more substantial Christian Democrats, the pudgy, suave Freitas do Amaral remained an eloquent critic of Cavaco Silva's government, his displeasure sharpened by chagrin: the PSD, who had backed his try against Mário Soares for the presidency, declined to settle his campaign debts, still outstanding years later. The bright light in the CDS was the black-bearded and stylish Francisco Lucas Pires, whose main arena in recent years was the European Parliament. Basílio Horta volubly but vainly challenged Mário Soares for the presidency in 1991. Now and again, the party's grey eminence materialized from the shadows – Adriano Moreira, who had been minister, and rebel, in the Salazar years.

It did not take long for the holy glow of the Social Democrats to dim after their spectacular election success in July 1987; the sharp lesson of Socialist success in the municipal elections in 1989 forced Cavaco Silva to an instant remodelling of his government. Concentrating on the major economic reforms he had been elected to achieve, he had ignored the sniping of the opposition, the sharp focus of a merciless press, on the failings, real and supposed, of his ministers and of himself. Arrogance was a common charge; he had once said he never had doubts and was seldom wrong. The timidity had gone. His boundless confidence was irritating – to the opposition. The hottest issue of these years was the revision of the 1976 constitution. The new free-market Portugal had no place for Marxist ideals or terminology.

The revolution faded in different ways for different people. Manuel and Margarida Ramires Fernandes are successful professionals working in an increasingly materialistic Algarve which has small regard for the radical politics of their youth. Yet they cannot bring themselves to throw out the first newspapers of the free-spoken era that began on 25 April 1974: 'To us the graffiti that burst out on the walls was not just emotional and gaudy street art, but the joyful expression of a newly free people.' In April 1989 the Lisbon city council, in a commendable clean-up campaign, decided to regularize the superabundant posters forever blooming on city walls. For Manuel and Margarida, for many Portuguese of their generation, this was not another milestone on the road from revolution but the end of the road.

For Otelo, too, the past was little more than memory. He was the magic man of the revolution and also its odd man out. His broad grin, his brown-eyed charm and lavish personality bewitched Portuguese and foreigners alike. But his politics slid leftwards of Robin Hood and the romantic revolutionary to – a criminal court found – terrorism. Although he consistently denied a connection between his FUP party, Forces of Popular Unity, established to back his 1980 try for the presidency, and the clandestine terrorist organization, FP-25, Popular Forces of 25 April, responsible for bombings, bank raids and political killings, he was found guilty of leading the FP-25 and sentenced in 1987 to fifteen years' prison, later extended to eighteen years.

The case provoked a storm of controversy. Otelo the liberator of Portugal, his defenders and many concerned democrats believed, should not be allowed to fade away in prison. In May 1989, the Supreme Court freed him on legal technicalities, notably that he had been submitted to excessive preventive detention. Twenty-eight other defendants in the FUP/FP-25 case were also released on the same grounds. (But not everyone. The case lingered on and some of the defendants embarked on hunger strikes to keep themselves in the public eye.) In December 1990, the sentences were confirmed and reimposed; for many, amnesty was the solution. Few truly cared if Otelo was guilty or not guilty. He was an individualist with a puckish allure for whom revolution had become revelation. As one newspaper put it, ruminating on the matter, he would always be different. After his release he quickly faded from the limelight.

In these years there was, above all, a transformation not just in governments and policies and structures of a newly free society but in the entire Portuguese people. Raul Brandão, a traveller and writer in the early twentieth century, observed how 'the great inert mass adapts itself to all regimes'. And so it had appeared for centuries. But not any more. On that emotional Labour Day of 1974, Mário Soares, with Álvaro Cunhal beside him, gazed at the huge throng and exclaimed: 'It was today, it was here, that we destroyed fascism.' The Young Captains had opened the way with their gentle revolution to a democratic Portugal. It is the Portuguese people, for the first time in their ancient country, who have chosen their leaders and fixed their direction, and who are resolutely confronting the future. It is a new tradition where traditions are strong and custom a haven. But nothing lasts in politics, neither the politicians, nor the enthusiasm of the voters – by the end of the 1980s, abstention was already an issue. But, the patient Portuguese believe, things could be worse. For youngsters, too: at the very least, since that revolutionary April they may kiss in public.

7 The poor relation

Gone from the currency is the tostão, the smallest coin in the system. Yet the word is still in the language, used daily to express a mean tip – or nothing; low pay – or none. A bureaucrat declares that Portugal is using 'to the last tostão' grants provided to modernize agriculture. A sixty-seven-year-old *campino*, a retired Ribatejo herdsman, remembers that when he started work, at seven years old, for the ducal house of Cadaval, he earned twenty-five tostões a week. When the tostão was withdrawn in 1979, its value was a trifling ten centavos, one tenth of an escudo, yet this was no ordinary coin. The tostão which entered the currency and idiom in copper in 1915 was first minted, in gold, in the reign of King Manuel the Fortunate, who came to the throne in 1495. Its value was 1,200 réis, a fortune. The real itself went out with the monarchy, although there are still old folk who say 'réis' when they mean modern money, the modest escudo.

In mid-1989, a Portuguese columnist, calculator in hand, worked out that if he left Portugal with 10,000 escudos in his wallet and travelled in turn to Germany, Denmark, Switzerland and Greece, changing cash for cash as he went, he would return to Portugal with 5,120 escudos – 'without having spent a tostão'. The golden glow of coinage in the day of Dom Manuel I, when Portugal ruled over a vast empire, is cold comfort to the constrained Portuguese explorer of today. The currency shifts and slides in perpetual motion, new issues meet new needs, 10,000 escudos will not buy as much this week as last, and few Portuguese – a minuscule 3 per cent – go abroad on holiday. But turning the picture of the evanescent escudo the other way up shows it buoyant and smiling: foreign money rolls in from investment and, as it has for decades, from sun-seeking tourists and industrious emigrants, a vital, sustaining, hard-currency cushion.

The exigencies of basic economics in a competitive and over-crowded world seem at first remote from the horrors of slavery, from the forceful commerce of a vigorous empire, from the mys-terious silent trade of the north African desert. Here, in this south-western, sea-edged corner of Europe, the link is palpable. As EEC pamphlets, charts and directives pile up on paper-filled desks and the sun, slanting through the window, intensifies their blue covers with the circular emblem of stars, the image grows of a dark-robed Prince Henry the Navigator, his eyes fixed on a blue horizon, dreaming of discovery, of converting the heathen, of trade in a new community of peoples. Portugal's visionary prince preceded Jean Monnet, founding father of the EEC, by five centuries, yet the thought arises that they had much in common.

Prince Henry was in Ceuta, pressing for information on the mysteries of Africa, when he learned of the 'silent trade'. Merchants told him of caravans, laden with salt, coral beads and cheap market products, that set off from southern Morocco across the Atlas mountains for Senegal. Near the Senegal river, the Moroccans beat drums to announce their arrival, laid out their goods on the river bank and retreated to a distance. After an interval they returned to the river. Beside their own goods were small heaps of gold, placed there by tribesmen who lived near by in opencast mines. If the Moroccan traders considered the gold insufficient, they reduced their own pile of goods, and withdrew. Whoever first took the other's pile concluded the bargaining. Drumming signified the close of business, the departure of the Moroccans. Perhaps from the gold miners' caution, perhaps from lack of a common language, the barterers never met. Puzzling and bizarre, the silent trade was of long standing – Herodotus wrote that it was controlled by the kings of Timbuktu.

Prince Henry's stout efforts were not rewarded by gold, but some seventy years later, Dom João II, concentrating on his multi-directional discovery masterplan and with his São Jorge da Mina fortress – Fort Elmina – established on the west coast, remembered the silent trade when he dispatched Bartolomeu Dias on the momentous first voyage around Africa's southern cape. A secondary mission for Dias was the dumping at points along the coast of six well-dressed Africans, four of them women, each with a message for the unknown Prester John and a sample bag of gold and other desirables that the Portuguese king hoped would lead to new trade. As it was, the countries of the Gulf of Guinea would be known for centuries by the names the Portuguese gave them: the Grain Coast – from the pepper-like *malagueta* called 'grains of paradise'; the Ivory Coast; the Gold Coast – now Ghana; the Slave Coast – Benin.

The Portuguese took with them to Africa new plants for food, new skills like reading and carpentry, their fine horses, their powerful religion, their sibylline language. They took away, above all else, slaves. Where the Portuguese went, others followed. Slaving grew to such monstrous levels that, in the eighteenth century alone, the most conservative figures suggest that between seven and ten million slaves were taken out of Africa and transported – by the British, Dutch, French, Swedes, Danes, Portuguese and Arabs – to Portugal and Spain, to the West Indies and to the east, to the Americas, north and south. And if Portugal was still the major trader of the Congo river basin and busily shipping slaves to Brazil, by far the greater maritime power and slave-trader now was England – from where in time surged the outrage and concern that fired the anti-slavery movement.

Denmark was the first to declare abolition of the slave trade in 1804 and England – where slaves became free in 1772 – ended trading in 1807. The United States followed in 1808, the Dutch, Swedes and French by 1818, Spain by 1820 and Portugal, which under Pombal had emancipated slaves in the home country in 1773, stopped traffic within its empire in 1815 and, with Queen Maria da Glória freshly enthroned, prohibited all slave-trading in 1836. It took another fifty years to enforce the legislation. No nation emerged from this gross saga of inhumanity with its honour intact.

In Portugal, in 1555, an enlightened Padre Fernando Oliveira wrote a passionate denunciation of the slave trade. There was no 'just war' against Muslims, Jews or heathens prepared to trade peacefully. To enslave them was tyranny; there would be no African sellers without European buyers. He railed against traders claiming spiritual merit in saving souls even as they cruelly abused suffering bodies. 'We were the inventors of such a vile trade, never previously used or heard of among human beings,' he wrote with sorrow. But no one was listening except the Inquisition, who quickly locked him up.

In the sixteenth century, when the far-sighted padre was paying the penalty for his unusual opinions, the Portuguese were busily engaged in consolidating their empire. They had invented not only 'the vile trade' of slavery but – advanced as they were in astronomy, geography, nautical and natural sciences – superior firearms. Theirs were the first ships with heavy artillery. The warships of King Manuel I were equipped with heavy-calibre cannon with a breech-loading system designed for astonishingly rapid reloading and firing. Their flintlocks and muskets were ahead of their time. In the east the Portuguese sought trade; their offers were hard to refuse.

In Japan – Marco Polo's noble island of Cipangu – the Portuguese, the first Europeans there, landed in 1543 at the island of Tanegashima, an event commemorated annually with a lively festival. What is being celebrated is not just the appearance in Japan of the Portuguese – whom the Japanese called 'barbarians of the south' and viewed as strange-looking creatures with round eyes and fleshy noses – but the introduction of firearms. For the Japanese the arrival of the Portuguese, and their muskets, is linked with unification of their faction-ridden country by a powerful feudal lord, Toyotomi Hideyoshi, armed with the new fire-power.

Trade, based largely on Japan's desirable silver, became an immediate binding force. Religion closely followed trade, both imperatives of Portugal's maritime expansion. Padre António Vieira later observed: 'If there were no merchants going to seek earthly treasures in the East and West Indies, who would transport thither the preachers who take heavenly treasures? The preachers take the Gospel and the merchants take the preachers.' For the nation that was the most powerful in the seas of the Orient, the takings, in the end, were few. But among them were the Japanese Namban screens now in Lisbon's Museum of Ancient Art. Made in Kyoto around 1620, they show, with exquisite art and gentle mockery of the 'barbarians', the arrival of the Portuguese in Japan.

Now it is the arrival of Japanese business in Portugal which is desired. Delegations come and go – 'Portugal rediscovers Japan,' the papers say. Mitsubishi has invested in acrylics in a joint venture. Telecommunications stirs the field. The Aoki corporation has bought property in Lisbon, Cascais and, in Sintra, two architecturally celebrated *quintas*, Penha Longa and the odd neo-Manueline Regaleira with its weird grottoes. The Portuguese would have preferred a nice big electronics or automobile plant and were much comforted when the Nissho Iwai group, in 1989, invested both in paints and in a factory that would build 40,000 Daihatsu jeeps and commercial vehicles a year. Days after the announcement, news came that the giant American company, Ford, was to build a car audio components factory that would provide 1,700 jobs. It was the biggest private foreign investment in years.

Salvador Caetano's tightly run group, among a wide range of activities, produces and exports Toyota four-wheel-drive and light commercial vehicles and buses. Spain is a good market, England another. But his ventures in Portugal are a minuscule proportion of Japanese interests in Europe. For most Japanese, focusing on the faster-beating business heart of Europe, Portugal's highly rated workmanship and low labour costs are outweighed by a simple fact of geography: Portugal is too far away.

Distance never troubled the Portuguese. More than anyone, the Portuguese were everywhere, enticed by the promise of discovery and the lure of gold, in the service of king, God and empire, for the thrill of adventure and hope of reward. The discovery of gold in Brazil at the end of the seventeenth century sparked off the first great gold rush of modern times. The gold built Mafra for King João V and some of the most beautiful *solares* in northern Portugal. It intensified the slave trade, expanded British exports of woollen and worsted textiles to Portugal and, to Portugal's rage and frustration, British smuggling of gold out of Portugal. Gold fever and then diamond frenzy ravaged Portugal; thousands of young men, whole families, emigrated year after year after year.

They left from congested Lisbon, the overcrowded Açores, the overpopulated Minho. At first the emigration was untroubling, an easing of social pressure. The scandal of the angrily determined Portuguese 'boat people' destroyed complacency. In a boat designed for a maximum of eighty passengers, 428 people sailed illegally in 1854 from São Miguel in the Açores to Pernambuco in Brazil. Once the tap had opened, the flow of emigrants became a flood. Between 1886 and 1926, some 1,300,000 people left Portugal. The driving force was no longer lust for gold but desperation and hunger.

The reasons were plain enough. Resistance to the French invasions, then the tragic and costly War of the Two Brothers had left Portugal profoundly exhausted. Recovery was slow. The industrial revolution, igniting the torch of modern societies, passed Portugal by. City people suffered from lack of work; industrialization failed to keep pace with improving transportation and where industry was developing conditions were wretched. *Camponeses* were afflicted by the distortions of land ownership, oppressive landlords, eighteen-hour working days and, after 1870, a new and terrible crisis, the desolation of vineyards across the land by the dreadful phylloxera, a plant louse that had sneaked in from America. A prolific breeder, it lives off the root of the vine, which then sickens and dies. Years passed before growers' woes were over and the disease conquered by grafting Portuguese vines on to resistant American stock, still the practice today.

Emigration itself was a sickness. Oliveira Martins called emigration 'the barometer of national life'; never was it set at 'Fair'. The *partidas* – the word that once had signified sailing away to empire and glory – seemed unstoppable. Government attempts to halt the flow by reforms were ended by resentful landowners and employers. And then there was a new reason to emigrate: conscription.

The first republican governments wanted to form a new national militia, an unpopular notion echoed more than fifty years later when Salazar sent conscripts to fight in Africa. The evasion of recruitment, desertion and clandestine emigration became sadly commonplace and this, as the men left behind wives, mothers and children, profoundly affected family life and the demographic balance of the nation. Salazar, in his first years of power, believed he could stop the flood of emigrants, that he could even reverse it.

wave in the stands. Wherever Olympic gold medallists Rosa Mota and Carlos Lopes have run, emigrant enthusiasm sustained them through the marathon. The one place emigrants are often strangely ill at ease is in Portugal, when they have returned for good. Suddenly too many, it seems, have changed too much. Their houses are sharp-edged and showy on the muted landscape. Their ways, their expectations, are often out of place. A flood of returning migrants is a prospect many Portuguese view with alarm. A sudden influx, they know from experience, creates turmoil.

In 1974 revolution shook the structure of Portugal to its bones. Many of the rich vanished abroad. All was confusion and uncertainty. The economy was in chaos, funds disappeared, several foreign-owned companies fired their workers and closed their doors. In Africa, the revolution, with decolonization as one of its prime goals, triggered immediate collapse of an economic system that favoured settlers. Hundreds of thousands, most from Angola, were forced to flee to Portugal – rich industrialists, wealthy plantation owners and managers, small shopkeepers, civil servants, teachers and road-builders and their entire families – many of whom had never seen Portugal.

For these *retornados* adjustment was hard. In time, rage softened to nostalgia but for the present most felt only bitterness for Angola, unprepared and riven by nationalist differences, and for Moçambique, lacking an entire managerial and technical class and soon under assault from South-African-supported right-wing rebels. For Portugal, struggling with its own numerous problems, the appearance on its doorstep of over 700,000 penniless, bewildered and homeless refugees was devastating. Yet, somehow, the Portuguese coped. There are stories of broken lives, of loss and woe, of animosity in poor northern communities to the revolutionaries' decolonization policy and the new pressures it imposed on them. Thousands of distressed families took to Portugal's new migration routes. But many of the *retornados*, with the same enterprise that had won them success, status or wealth in Africa, were soon energetically rebuilding their careers in Portugal.

Portugal's first commissioner to the EEC, António Cardoso e Cunha, is a *retornado* from Angola. From a family who had been in

Population rose in the forty years between 1926 and 1966 from 6 to 8.5 million – but a further despairing 1,300,000 Portuguese emigrated.

The goal, for many generations, was Brazil. A few emigrants went to Africa – by 1945 Portuguese settlers in Angola and Moçambique numbered about 100,000. After the Second World War the flow changed direction: booming industry and new development in northern Europe were an irresistible lure for vast numbers of Portuguese who left without passports and smuggled themselves across frontiers and over the Pyrenees, seeking work and a decent life far away from Portugal. Some went permanently, others temporarily or seasonally – and then they came home.

When I first came to Portugal, struggling to make myself understood, I was surprised how many people in isolated villages and languishing towns spoke French. Or a little American-accented English. Or a few words of German. Today, there is a little joke that Europe is the continent the Portuguese discovered last. Some 780,000 Portuguese emigrants live in France, 80,000 in Germany, about 70,000 in Switzerland, 35,000 in England (and more in the Channel Islands). Sometimes it seems as if they all come back at once.

At Christmas and in the heat of summer, the Portuguese burst across frontiers in family-crammed cars and rumbling buses – at Vilar Formoso one summer the Guarda Fiscal counted 861,000 emigrant arrivals, nothing exceptional. They come by air. They brush aside the miseries of the long journey in the bleakly uncomfortable special emigrants' trains from the Gare d'Austerlitz in Paris to Lisbon's Santa Apolónia or Oporto's Campanhã. They come laden with bags and bundles and gifts and foreign cash. They are here to *matar saudades*, for good cheer, a breath of home, for home news and home cooking. They buy land, dream of the big stucco-and-tile house they will build. And then, for the work and the wages that Portugal could never match, they go back. As a sturdy Portuguese who worked for twenty-six years in a French transport company put it: '*Eu adoro muito mais os francos que lá recebo*' (Yes, I love Portugal – but I love even more the francs that I get in France.) The pleasures of reunion disguise the deep scars of emigration on the inland areas. The remoter villages sink back into silent impassivity after the emigrants have gone. Even in new times, with the rush of emigration eased, youngsters head for the cities. Only the old are left.

Saudade is an emotional, fathomless yearning. In *fado*, the plangent music that luxuriantly expresses Portugal's profoundest passions and sorrows, *saudade* is the ache in the singer's vibrant voice above the mellow guitars. But *saudade* reaches beyond *fado*, beyond frontiers, to the very edge of Portuguese experience. It is in a late-night telephone call to a Lisbon house. The caller, Luís Francisco relates, confirms he has the right number. 'Do you know my father?' he asks, giving the name. 'You don't know him. Oh, well, it doesn't matter. You sound so young. I have a son younger than you who knows nothing of Portugal though he plays football here in Germany.' Germany! He is calling Lisbon from Germany. The one-sided conversation rambles on. 'I hope I'm not bothering you, but I had such *saudades*, such longings, to hear a voice from home and I knew no other number.'

It has been calculated that there are nearly four million Portuguese emigrants. Figures differ. Officialdom excludes blurred status and the migrants who live in what is loosely called an irregular situation. There are some 50,000 Portuguese in Australia, an extensive South African population of 650,000 – which includes 90,000 or so who left Moçambique after its independence in 1975. There are around 160,000 Portuguese in Venezuela and, in brotherly familiarity, well over a million in Brazil. More than 400,000 Portuguese are settled in Canada. In the United States, the Portuguese – like so many other immigrant nations – became a major presence.

For close on two centuries it was the dream of every Portuguese boy to seek his fortune in America. Thousands upon thousands embarked from continental Portugal and, in a deluge that still trickles on, from the Açores. They were whalermen, they mined for gold, they fought the Indians and, red-blooded Luso-Americans, took part in all America's modern battles. In California they farmed, on the east coast they fished. They grew into large communities: over 320,000 in California, 270,000 in Massachusetts; in Fall River and New Bedford more than half the inhabitants are of Portuguese,

mainly Açorian, decent. They are numerous in little Rh[o]
in America's own islands of Hawaii. In New Jersey there[...]
large population – some say 160,000 – in Newark and [...]
With the Americans of Portuguese origin who live in [...]
and Florida and Pennsylvania and elsewhere, the total [...]
1,200,000.

Not everyone made a fortune. Few have been touche[d]
fame. Some are still hesitantly discovering America or [...]
their education. But they are united by a bond stronger [...]
a Luso-link based on language and culture that ties the[m]
other and to Portugal. Individual successes are the succe[sses]
Luso-Americans and of all Portugal. The writer John D[...]
(for Jean-Paul Sartre, 'the greatest writer of our time'),
Chicago in 1896 of a Portuguese family, researched *Th[e]
Story* in Portuguese and wrote it with love. John Phili[p]
bandmaster and eminent composer, is still 'João Filipe' [...]
name of the urban architect William L. Pereira, famou[s]
designs at Cape Canaveral, in Houston and Los An[...]
honoured across America – and in Portugal. When Op[...]
António Borges made the cover of *Fortune* magazine as r[...]
business institute, Portugal's press noted it with pride. P[...]
writers illuminate American culture, scholars add lustre [...]
of American universities, Portuguese skills are in bankin[g]
in journalism and radio, on the stage and in films. Ne[w]
rave reviews for Maria de Medeiros's performance in *Hen[...]*
were hailed in the Portuguese press. Portugal was amuse[d]
emigrant from Aveiro was elected president of an asso[...]
magicians in Boston, unsurprised when an emigrant, [...]
revealed that, as a limousine driver, she earned more than [...]
in Portugal's government. Portugal is unhappily accus[ed]
being poorer than most, the poorest country in western [...]
poor relation to its own emigrants.

Emigrants are generous. They send money to the[ir]
church, to their local fire brigade, to their families – [...]
invaluable in paying off the foreign debt. They are patri[otic]
Benfica or any top football team plays in a world football [...]
ship, fans fly in from far places and hundreds of Portu[...]

west Africa for three generations, he had been a wealthy entrepreneur with interests in land, cattle-breeding, diamond mining, a brewery, a fishing fleet. In Portugal he began again with nothing 'but my brains and skill'. With a government loan he bought a farm. Other *retornados* were his partners. They grew fruit, vegetables and, for the first time in Portugal, mushrooms in quantity – 900 tons a year. For a period Cardoso e Cunha was minister of agriculture. With Portugal's accession to the EEC he was appointed commissioner.

Retornados became doctors, lawyers, farmers, town council officials, politicians. António Almeida Santos, who had been a lawyer in Moçambique for twenty-one years, was soon in the upper ranks of the Socialist Party and a minister of state. Gilberto de Sá Pessoa spent forty-six years in Moçambique. Starting out as a delivery boy at fourteen, at sixty he was a property tycoon – and overnight a *retornado* with nothing. In Lisbon, with a loan, he opened a steakhouse, then another. Much younger men and women set up businesses in Lisbon, in the Oporto area and across the country with the help of a government resettlement scheme. Not everyone succeeded; to this day thousands of old colonials bemoan the lack of compensation for their losses overseas. Of all the *retornado* stories I know the oddest – and happiest – is that of Armando Pereira de Almeida. A cattle farmer for twenty-two years in Angola, he lost everything he owned. In Portugal, with a few borrowed escudos, he bought a lottery ticket – and won. With his winnings he purchased a stately *quinta* and twenty hectares of vineyards overlooking the Douro river. The view is dazzling, his life agreeable, his luck extraordinary.

Most reality is less romantic. In 1999, Macau reverts to Chinese rule and an uncertain future. Its 100,000 Portuguese citizens, with EEC passports, are free to go where they choose in the Community – including England, an intolerable irony for despairing millions in Hong Kong where British rule ends in 1997. Macau is used to the Portuguese; many might come to Portugal.

The Portuguese also have a heavy conscience over the atrocities perpetrated in their old colony of East Timor by the Indonesians, who invaded in 1975 just as the Portuguese were preparing to grant independence. Resistance was vigorous, the price high: over 100,000 Timorese people were killed or died of disease and starvation, 40,000 children maimed or orphaned. Many hundreds have been detained or are missing. Portugal, supported by the United Nations and the European Parliament, argues for East Timor's right to freedom on every diplomatic front and provides for over 2,000 refugees who have escaped to Portugal. It is a haven, but cruelly far from the wild sweet island which Captain Bligh of the *Bounty* made famous in 1789 after his epic forty-one-day journey across the Pacific ocean. For the Timorese, hopes are no longer pinned on Timor or Portugal but on Australia.

Portugal also lives easily with thousands of African and mixed-race immigrants, most of whom arrived after the revolution. Among them are cultured men and women and professionals with skills and talents – Portugal's most famous footballer, Eusébio, is from Moçambique. The great majority, about 60,000 from the Cape Verde islands, work in construction and live in squalid *barracas* and *bairros de lata* – shacks and tin-roofed slums – on the outskirts of Lisbon. Intensive construction has drawn a number to the Algarve. History repeats itself, social philosophers say. Africans were numerous in Lisbon in the sixteenth century. And if these are still rough times for too many blacks, one thing has changed. Nobody throws their dead bodies, as they did in the heyday of empire, to the dogs.

Horrors fade, others take their place. Scandals roll on. In normal modern society it is assumed that honest work is met with honest pay. Work, wrote Voltaire, banishes those three great evils, boredom, vice and poverty. In Portugal, that is not quite true. Thousands of honest Portuguese workers used to go to work each day without knowing when they would be paid. *Salários em atraso* – wages in arrears – was one of the ugliest, most unjust after-effects not so much of the 1974 revolution but of the oil-price crisis and the international recession that followed it.

In March 1975 more than half the economy, including all national banks and insurance companies, went from private to public ownership. Of the great monopolies CUF, the biggest of seven giants, owned several great shipyards including Lisnave in the Tejo estuary. It had extensive interests in the chemical industry. It owned the TAP airline, several insurance companies, copper mines and a leading bank. No sorcery could have transformed overnight vast family-owned enterprises to sound state management ready to counter the hazard of international commerce and slumps of world recession. For Mário Soares and the Socialists, elected to power in 1976, hope for the future lay in Europe. But in the ten years before accession to the EEC in 1986 the economy was not a pretty sight. An IMF agreement meant tight fiscal policies, austerity, higher taxes, lower public spending. The IMF targets were reached and passed but at brutal cost. Across scores of state-owned companies and debt-burdened private companies wages stopped.

In 1972 Fernando Deodato, aged twenty-five, got a job as a roller operator in a porcelain factory in the industrial town of Setúbal. He earned 1,800 escudos a month. He was married. He and his wife, Silvina, who worked as a finisher at the factory, rented a room in the nearby village of Gambia. When the Young Captains occupied Lisbon on 25 April 1974, the factory workers, more than 1,500 men and women, downed tools to celebrate.

'The factory owner was not pleased,' recalls Deodato. 'He was a decent man, an *antifascista*, but we had our disagreements. He didn't like me, thought I was a trouble-maker, and fired me. Then came the news of the revolution. On 28 April the workers met and demanded I should be reinstated, and I was. It was the boss who was forced out, not by us but by the banks to whom he owed money.'

On 24 May, a month after the revolution, the Council of Ministers decreed a national minimum monthly salary of 3,300 escudos. Wages in the first year after the revolution actually rose by an average 35 per cent, and even stayed well above rising consumer prices. But when financial problems became severe – inflation rose to over 29 per cent in 1984 – the Setúbal porcelain factory was one of hundreds of companies across huge sections of industry in trouble. Competition, stagnation and heavy debts forced one company after another to fire workers. Disputes occurred, bankruptcy threatened, bargains were made. Workers, despite the efforts of the predominant trade-union federation, the Communist-led

CGTP-Intersindical (General Confederation of Portuguese Workers) or the moderate, mainly white-collar UGT (General Union of Workers) were unable to exact cheering terms. Wages in arrears seemed better than the sack.

There was a time in the mid-1980s when more than 150,000 workers suffered the awful insecurity of not knowing when, or if, they would get paid. Glass-workers in the town of Marinha Grande laboured for more than a year without pay to help keep their bottle-making factory alive. In ship-repair yards, workers waited months for the sight of a pay packet. In the Setúbal porcelain factory, Fernando Deodato and his workmates persevered in the face of dreadful uncertainty that became a way of life. 'Families and friends helped out with food. There was weekend work on farms. We survived.' The tragic absurdity of it was that the factory was respected, its production high quality and easily saleable – its export order books full. But outstanding debts, and interest, to two banks had never, in over fifteen years, been cleared. Solutions were offered, discussed, rejected. The factory closed. New managements appeared, disappeared. In mid-1990 workers were still awaiting back pay and real solutions. '*Falta de vontade* [a lack of will]' says a disgusted Deodato.

But things elsewhere were looking up. In January 1989 the Lisnave ship-repair yards, among the worst cases and now the world's biggest repair yards in terms of ship numbers and tonnage, paid the last of the *salários em atraso* to its patient workers as part of a no-strike deal. By the end of 1989, the number of late-paying companies was down to ninety-four; the numbers of workers still waiting for delayed wages was down, officially, to 12,000. The question now was when, not if, they would be paid. Deodato's monthly wages, when he got them, before an $11\frac{1}{2}$ per cent social-security contribution, were 55,000 escudos (55 contos, the Portuguese might say – about $365 or £220) – and 1 per cent of the take-home pay went to his union, CGTP-Intersindical. In those fifteen years he had even built himself a small home. Setúbal, for years a crisis-torn industrial town, had scores of new business projects, a handsome new training centre, an unheard of optimism that stretched across the nation. Despite inflation and other curses, unemployment had fallen to levels government economists began to boast about, talking of 'maintaining' unemployment at 6 per cent, the lowest unemployment rate, except for Luxembourg's, in the EEC.

Figures, like photographs, can lie. Images are selected that reflect a point of view and may exclude the full reality. Healthy balance sheets can hide human misery. Portugal's impressive leap forward, its heady economic achievements (inflation in 1988 went below 10 per cent although it was up again, to 12.7, a year later), the creation of many thousands of new jobs, encouragingly low unemployment and fast economic growth, veil the shattering difficulties of daily life even for those not among the 300,000 or so registered unemployed.

The unions insistently contradict government figures. Low unemployment? Government statistics include short-term training programmes, say the unions. The prime minister, Cavaco Silva, reviewed with some pride the rising per capita annual income of the Portuguese – $1,200 in 1974, it rose from $2,100 in 1985 to over $5,000 by 1990. The World Bank praises Portugal for its rate of growth, the International Monetary Fund describes Portugal as industrialized, no longer developing. But Portugal is still at the bottom of the heap in the European Community – and the unions point out that though workers represent some 62 per cent of the active population, their wages – when they get them – only total around 42 per cent of national earnings. Cavaco Silva could insist that, despite inflation – his government's most irritating economic problem – real wages stayed ahead of rising prices. But in agriculture, construction and industry they did not; unions, opposition politicians and many angry voices cried foul.

Few are greedy or unrealistic. Many manage by moonlighting. Some, like Deodato, get spare-time farm work. Cultured multilingual junior civil servants, sorely underpaid, may take on translation and similar private commissions. Most Portuguese know that their cheap labour is a persuasive lure for foreign investors and that they earn less than any other EEC country, *five times* less than, say, Germany. But when the buying power of a pay packet is down, when government proposals are unsatisfactory, when work hours are too long – 48 hours a week is common; only in 1990 was the legal maximum reduced to 44, with 40 hours as a target for 1993 – the Portuguese go on strike.

In 1988 there were 188 strikes, involving more than 173,000 workers and calculated at 198,000 lost work days. In transportation alone – trains, the Metro, buses, Tejo ferries – there were ninety-six strikes affecting 60,000 employees and thousands of commuters. The strikers' frustration was scarcely appeased when, the day before Parliament's summer recess, politicians voted themselves a 24 per cent wage increase. None were consoled that by EEC standards Portugal's strike rate was low. In 1989, with few disputes resolved and some intensified, the strikes, largely in the public sector, continued. No wage rises matched the 56 per cent increase politicians awarded themselves this time. As 1990 began, with professionals alarmed at reforms and with workers' unrealistic expectations unfulfilled, strikes were already being marked on the calendar.

Strikes were mostly brief, the strikers multifarious: civil servants and schoolteachers, their salaries pegged to a cumbersome and unjust ranking system, employees in banks and the gas and electricity service, doctors and health workers, dockers, journalists, employees of the national airline and the state-run *pousadas*, tourist guides, swimming-pool lifeguards, farm-workers, metalworkers, stoneworkers, cork cutters, the technicians, electricians and painters of the Tejo river bridge, staff in embassies, the treasury and tax offices, the attorney-general's office and the national lottery. Courts closed as magistrates went on strike. Frontiers jammed as customs officers went on strike. Driving examiners struck, surprising many of us who had doubted their existence. Musicians expressed protest with a concert outside Parliament. Quick to learn, secondary-school students went on strike over access to universities – whose disgruntled professors went on strike. On a cold winter's day in Bragança schoolchildren went on strike for classroom heating.

Government relations with the unions, and the unions with each other – the two national umbrella organizations or the small independent trade unions – slide between fair and acrimonious. CGTP-Intersindical has been the stronger, and is six years older, with just over half the total trade-union membership, divided among some three hundred unions. It has the support, too, of most of the seventy or so independents. Unions operate in familiar ways by challenge, indignation, negotiation, working to rule, strike. The government lists successes, reminds the nation of the programme it was voted in on, and ploughs on. A remark by Cavaco Silva that failing the challenge of 1992 would be more serious than a teachers' strike promptly set off another strike but left his priorities crystal clear.

General strikes are fortunately rare, agitation voluble but peaceable. Determined picketing is not a Portuguese habit, though other habits are changing. When the national police force, Polícia de Segurança Pública (PSP), demonstrated in Lisbon's Praça do Comércio in April 1989, in support of a union of its own – which the law forbids – helmeted shock troops with dogs were called in and the ardour of the demonstrating policemen cooled by crowd-control hoses. It was a disturbing confrontation of police *versus* police that could, some suggested, have turned into a blood-bath. But it did not. The confrontation, though dramatic and soggily emotional, remained peaceful. One policeman, weeping convulsively, was soothed by UGT secretary-general José Torres Couto, who complained later that he had been struck by a police superintendent and called a *filho de puta* (son of a whore). No one was surprised at the insult or the tears, both common enough – Otelo himself was seen to weep over Salazar's coffin – but the angry scene was an uncommon event to be discussed for weeks. The police, for their part, were coldly reminded that they already had perfectly legal avenues for protest. Later, by a legal compromise, they were allowed, not unions, but professional associations.

The wave of strikes reflected many people's concern that they were being left behind on the road to prosperity. The principal issues on which these justifiable fears were focused were a *pacote* (package) of labour reforms and land reforms within a proposed law, *Lei de Bases da Reforma Agrária*. The post-revolutionary 1976 Constitution had incorporated the extensive land expropriations in the Alentejo (a spontaneous snatching of over a million hectares rose to over 3 million hectares) through cooperatives and delegating cultivation rights of small and medium-sized farms. The Constitution had

also severely restricted employers' powers to fire workers. Cavaco
Silva had campaigned on a platform of liberalizing these laws. For
Portugal to be competitive in the European common market, rigid
restrictions would have to go.

For many long and bitter months the *pacote laboral* was a rally-
ing cry in the cause of social justice, the catalyst for a general
strike, the crux of constitutional reform; battle lines were drawn
up, with the unions and apprehensive workers on one side and
employers and energetic pragmatists, their sights fixed on
Europe, on the other. Even as the first industrial robots made in
Portugal were ominously stretching their tireless arms, stormy ac-
cusations, declarations and denials rent the air. Workers from
across the country, seeing their post-revolution gains in jeopardy,
gathered to denounce the *pacote*. Banners went up across city
streets and ancient town squares: '*Não! ao Pacote Laboral.*' Hundreds of cloth-capped protesters made a dramatic, dusty, three-day
march to pack the public galleries of the National Assembly and
demonstrate outside it.

Both the agrarian and labour reform laws were finally passed.
Changes were significant. Land returned to former owners by
mid-1990 totalled over 750,000 hectares. Pessimistic farm workers
continued to fear the old latifundist menace in the restoration of
private ownership. Agricultural cooperatives had already declined
in number (from 1,408 in 1985 to just over 300 in 1988). In
1990 argument raged over the government's plans for land
farmed under contract. In industry, in 1988, though jobs were
still protected, employers were freer to make collective dismissals
and lay-offs; the grounds for firing individuals were marginally
extended. Revolving short-term contracts, through which thousands of employers had circumvented the labour laws, could still
be used – but only for genuine short-term jobs. Foreign companies had developed early retirement and voluntary redundancy
schemes and would maintain them; among Portuguese companies,
Salvador Caetano was one of few to have started a pension
scheme. Social security, by 1989, provided some 70 per cent of
Portuguese pensioners with 14,600 escudos a month – pathetic,
but up 135 per cent from what it had been three years earlier.

In December 1990 the minimum pension rose to 20,000 escudos. There were still many points of friction. Portugal would clearly have to proceed at a slow pace in narrowing the immense gap that separated the levels of social security for Portuguese workers from those of other EEC countries. For now, the feeling was that the labour law would have to do.

When it came to revising the Constitution itself, there was never any doubt that the pragmatists would win in the end. The vital question was on what terms. Changing the Constitution required a two-thirds majority in Parliament. Cavaco Silva's PSD needed Socialist Party votes and got them – too easily in the opinion of some Socialists (and, it was hinted, Mário Soares), who believed that both principle and bargaining counters were at stake.

The 1976 Constitution, written with post-revolutionary fervour and Marxist in its ideology and language, was clearly out of step with the times. The 1989 Constitution was approved by a large parliamentary majority on 1 June. 'Socialism died at dawn,' the left wept as collectivization, the irreversibility of nationalization and the ponderous weight of state controls vanished. Most Socialists, who had negotiated each clause with the Social Democrats, believed that the new document was, as Almeida Santos said, 'the most generous in the Western world in recognizing and guaranteeing workers' rights'. But the word 'worker' was no longer used in an ideological sense.

The transformed Constitution protected the fundamental rights and liberties of Portuguese citizens in Portugal and abroad. It opened the way for privatization – of the companies nationalized in 1975, of television and the press, of the post office and telephones, of transportation and health services. Now land reform was targeted upon relentless EEC imperatives. The economy was unblocked, an honourable social philosophy maintained. The prime minister, Cavaco Silva, a believer in the free market, had fulfilled a 1987 campaign promise. And soon, forestalling a fresh flow of criticism that the poor were excluded from the benefits of the expanding affluence, he announced programmes aimed to eradicate poverty and drugs, and to establish a practical home-loans mortgage system, a topic as stinging and fraught for the urban Portuguese as land ownership is down on the farm.

A new and economically liberalizing Constitution was an immensely significant step in Portuguese progress. But money pouring in in abundance from EEC structural funds had already started to have an extraordinary effect on the face of Portugal. In 1986, the first year of membership, Portugal received Esc.49.5bn ($320m); between 1986 and 1989 the figure was Esc.380bn. It was spent on roads and railways and airports, dams and irrigation, telephones, agriculture, investment incentives and job training. In addition, unlimited low-interest investment loans were available from the European Investment Bank. The tap was open, cash flowed through programmes of such bewildering diversity and assorted acronyms – like PEDIP (industry), FEDER (regional development), FEOGA (agriculture) – that the secretary of state for planning and regional development, Isabel Mota, never went to a meeting without a handy glossary. As for the money, projects by the thousand were waiting for it.

Portugal has a few conglomerates, groups with tentacles reaching across Portugal, to the former Portuguese territories and, increasingly, across Europe. They are listed on the stock exchange in Lisbon or Oporto. Foreign involvement is strong. Yet the large majority of companies, over 106,000 of them in 1989, are small and medium-sized businesses (*pequenas e médias empresas*, PMEs). Three quarters employ fewer than ten people, a high proportion fewer than four – and, more than the giant multinationals, these companies generate jobs. A whole new area of development, funded by the EEC, is in *formação profissional* (job-training courses).

Some independent entrepreneurs run spacious plants in new industrial zones. Others are in packed and poky workshops in congested industrial areas around Lisbon and the northern commercial capital of Oporto. Thousands have started, or expanded, a business with EEC money. They are in textiles, a major industry that employs over 200,000 people (but pays far less than any other European country). They are in shoes – a thousand or more factories employ over 40,000 people and, in 1989, exported over sixty million pairs of shoes. They own metallurgical and electrical works. They are in granite and marble, timber and furniture and cork and chemicals. They own shops and hotels and tourist enterprises. They are in agriculture, in fishing and fish canning.

Computers are routine – not just in banking and business – though their setting is sometimes bizarre. In the grand former monastery of São Bento that is today's Parliament, Natália Correia, MP and poet, took one look at the newly installed electronic controllers of MPs' speaking time and condemned them as an unaesthetic technological dictatorship. In Braga, which in August 1989 celebrated the nine-hundredth anniversary of the consecration of the cathedral's high altar, the ancient city archives have been computerized. Some small town councils across the land still use the heavy handwritten ledgers, described with a little smile as old technology; the majority have moved on to computers.

Informática (computerization) reigns in many otherwise antiquated town halls, and strategies are being elaborated and incentives devised for Portugal to develop its own scientific parks and Silicon Valleys. Dynamism and innovation are the buzz words, stagnation a thing of the past. Tourist brochures promise dozing villages, elevating landscapes, empty beaches, perfect ease and leisure, but although the Portuguese approach to life often seems relaxed, if – to paraphrase Milton – in conversing they forget all time, sloth is not a Portuguese characteristic. Entrepreneurial enterprise is tenacious and persistent both in high finance and in the ancient traditional skills and crafts: in the classical *azulejos*, hand-painted tiles, made by Viúva Lamego and Sant'Anna, in the renowned Vista Alegre porcelain, in the sparkle of Atlantis crystal.

The carpets hand-stitched by generations of women and girls in the Alentejo town of Arraiolos used to adorn the castles and grand houses of Portugal; now they are an export product snatched up by eager foreigners. The vivid, boldly geometric patchwork quilts of Ermelinda Cargaleiro, born in 1899 near the Tejo river town of Vila Velha de Ródão, are radiant showpieces which have been displayed in Lisbon's Museu do Traje (Costume Museum) among others – seeing one on the bed of her artist son, Manuel Cargaleiro, a dazzled Frenchwoman promptly organized an exhibition in France. In the north the filigree skills of the goldsmiths and silversmiths of Gondomar are celebrated; whole villages of women and bright, smiling girls are employed part time to do much of the eye-straining preliminary twisting of the fine wire. In Jovim, a rickety hamlet of small houses with small dark rooms, I watched a young woman called Olga work, head down, tweezers in hand. 'Every one of us can do it,' she said. But too soon, eyesight weakens. Elsewhere in the industrial north, the cash paid for part-time work fosters the shabby and illegal use of child labour.

Rosa Ramalho, a spirited countrywoman born in 1888, charmed and tantalized the art world with her strange, simple clay figures. She lived in Galegos de São Martinho, a village close to Barcelos whose business, in daunting bulk, is pottery and ceramics. Rosa's original pieces are collector's items; relatives continue her work. Close by, thin women with delicate hands are doomed by the inescapable legend of the cock of Barcelos to paint it on vases and pots hour after hour, day after day. (A man sentenced to death for some paltry crime pleaded his innocence to a judge about to dine on roast cockerel. 'If you are innocent,' said the disbelieving judge, 'let the cock crow.' It did, and does, and undoubtedly will go on doing so for ever.) Near Mafra, it is the artistry in clay of Zé Franco that is famous.

In the Alentejo wine town of Redondo, entire families paint plates in a humorous folk-art style of considerable charm. Estremoz potters, close by, are renowned for their engaging glazed figurines. How delicate are the flowers and leaves that pattern the plain, painted Alentejo furniture. There are nimble-fingered women who still – bobbins flying over a fat bolster – make lace. Doll-making is a lively craft, gaudily painted wooden carts and carved ox yokes are happily surviving cottage industries. Craftsmen still work imaginatively with cork.

In Lorvão, near Coimbra, they make hand-whittled toothpicks, an enterprise with its origins in the turmoil that followed the closing of the convents. Portugal, its lead in the race long ago lost, still produces firearms and other weaponry in well-guarded factories – and also fireworks in tiny, family-owned workshops down leafy lanes near Ponte de Lima. The *fogueteiros* of the Minho contribute to crackling, dazzling firework displays at fairs and festivals, to the Portuguese habit of letting off celebratory rocket cannonades at the slightest excuse and, as PMEs, to the economy. Theirs is a more hazardous occupation than most. A missing finger is not uncommon and, once in a while, nasty accidents occur. 'Not so long ago,' the owner of a small firm in Santa Cruz told me sadly, 'six people died in an explosion in the valley.'

Loulé in the Algarve, with its coppersmiths, leatherworkers and weavers of strips of palm, esparto grass and rushes, presents itself as the crafts capital of the south. The old market town, it is true, is hard-working and still retains much of its down-to-earth rural practicality and grace, yet there is a touch of guile in the image. To me, the crafts (*artesenato*), unassuming mirrors of old skills, are the pretty face of a major, ever-expanding, highly visible, brash and bountiful industry, tourism.

Portugal is not lacking in natural resources and there are other valuable industries – the gold mine at Jales to the north produces more than 250 kg of gold a year as well as silver and, in 1990, fifteen companies were prospecting. At Neves Corvo in the Alentejo there are rich deposits – some 35 million tonnes – of high-grade copper, as well as tin. In 1989, the first year of actual production, the Somincor company exported over 400,000 tonnes of copper concentrates to West Germany, Spain, Canada and Japan. Close by, at Aljustrel, is a pyrites mine. Portugal still produces, in the Western world's biggest mine, the tungsten that Hitler desperately desired in the Second World War, and a little coal. Portugal is the world's second biggest exporter of marble, granite and slate – even Italy, the biggest producer, buys the handsome Portuguese white, pink and cream marble. There is uranium at one end of the scale, with large, untouched reserves in the Alto Alentejo, and salt at the other – and not just from evaporation in ancient coastal pans of seawater; a rock-salt mine under Loulé has been quietly and profitably worked since 1962.

Above ground, there are extensive if environmentally controversial eucalyptus plantations feeding the profitable paper pulp and cellulose industry and – never let it be forgotten – well-tended vineyards producing Portugal's most famous product, port, as well as other exalting wines in profusion. Not overlooked by canny foreign buyers jockeying for position – spurred on, you might say, by EEC rulings on the ABC of H_2O – is Portugal's healthy supply of natural mineral water. The multinationals and foreign-owned firms, heavy investors in the major industries, operate briskly run organizations, companies, banks. The British, as always, are prominent even if new EEC relationships have bumped and jarred the old alliance.

Textiles, the prime industry, bringing in about a third of foreign earnings, has EEC guarantees of protection against dirty dealing. Advanced systems are in use for mechanical cutting and automated looms. New technologies are closely studied in university research projects. The Portuguese have waited years for a telephone, spent hours reporting it out of order, waited days, even weeks, for a repair. Now they export them to China. Foreign markets expand. The Instituto do Comércio Externo de Portugal, with wide regional as well as overseas representation, replaced the old Foreign Investment Institute. Industry hustles with a new urgency. The finance scene is broad. Flopped across it, like restive sunbathers on a summer beach, are the alluring money-bags of mass tourism.

Summer arrives and so have the tourists, a newspaper headline shouts. It's June, more than half a million visitors are frolicking in the Algarve, the sun is shining, the skies are blue, the sea is a comfortable 19°C. Lower down the column is a brief mention of 'negative aspects'. Among them is the reaction of the English, who dominate Portuguese tourism, to the disorganized growth of resort areas. 'Developers have paved the old paradise,' English newspapers grieve; '. . . one of the most impressive building sites in tourism history . . .', 'uncontrolled development', '. . . road to ruin'. Many Portuguese, for whom the Algarve is a holiday Utopia, add their criticisms of mushrooming construction, dust and disorder. The minister of commerce and tourism, it was reported, is considered establishing penalties on the industries and constructors mainly responsible for the continuing *porcaria* (filth), though by-laws banning roadside rubbish dumping have been ignored for years.

The response from tourism promoters is vehement and various: hurt denial; accusation – 'a malicious campaign'; rejection – 'tourists here are the most *reles* [worthless] in Europe'; and an effort, not always practical, to respond to the problems of leaping construc-

tion. Among the more agreeably earnest and most futile exercises
in a campaign asserting that the Algarve 'is quality' was a mailing
to *algarvios* of a brightly illustrated anti-noise leaflet. The words
whisper silence is golden. The pictures show people – in a car,
with a big radio, on a motor-bike – making a gratifyingly loud
noise. All of them look happy. Anti-litter leaflets merely added to
the litter. Yet such is the appeal of the Algarve, such the magic of
a villa in the sun, that the contradictions and complaints, shifting
policies and restraints, seem to scare away few investors; some
development owners endured far worse with the revolution and its
aftermath. Too few developments are triumphs of architecture.
Too many bear the marks of speculation and indifference to the
shape, the feel, the colour of the land – the worst kind of vandalism.
Yet with EEC money and foreign investment, with retirement
savings, the incentive of post-1992 and the Universal Exposition,
Expo '92, in Seville, the Algarve, in its way, flourishes. There are
timeshare hard sells, hoardings, new hotels – 'beating every challenge', one boasted when it was built, fitted and furnished within
two years. Some claim concern for the environment, a secondary
consideration; with nature in contest with bed nights, money is the
arbiter. Yet there is justified rejoicing that Portugal wins well over
a hundred Blue Flags for its stunningly clean beaches – over thirty
in the Algarve. With more roads, a larger airport and a more
efficient water supply from new dams, the bustling coastal resorts
of the Algarve – a small proportion of the region, but much the
most conspicuous – are growing a new image. Not of quality, by
which tourism promoters mean more heavy spenders and fewer
lager louts and cheapo packages, but of an unaffected cheerfulness,
a diverting leisure zone for all tastes in all seasons.

Investment in tourism, as travellers know, is not concentrated
solely on the Algarve. Wild slopes with craggy trees and scented
herbs, fields enclosed by weathered stone walls, are crudely metamorphosed into plots and sites. Reptilian waterslide parks with their
corkscrews and kamikazes and rapids surfaced in the Algarve and,
an instant success, soon erupted further north. The north won
beguiling labels long ago – the green Costa Verde and the silver
coast, Costa da Prata. The region south of Lisbon promotes itself

now as the Costa Azul – the blue coast. The coves and beaches of the Alentejo are suddenly the Costa Dourada, golden coast. The Costa del Sol is no longer a Spanish prerogative. As well as the established tourist information offices there are burgeoning regional tourism centres with a sharp competitive instinct. On the coast, new marinas are mapped. New projects bloom by the day, breaking new ground, following the motorways and new expressways that bring Spain and all of Europe within quick and easy range. On the Douro, for more than three centuries a daunting challenge and wild haven for port-wine makers, cruises have begun and a costly hotel and marina complex is planned on the newly open, navigable river. In 1990, twenty-one courses were enjoyed by golfers – with thirty-six more projected. Stately old hotels are brushing themselves up to meet new times. Trendy health and fitness clubs are springing up smartly in fashionable resorts and top-rank hotels to tone the muscles and cleanse the spirit.

Councils blandly claim no projects proceed without close study, yet overnight building, the get-rich-quick urge and angry grumbling are not confined to the Algarve. The lure of tourism is strong, Portugal a splendid 'product'. Tourism is a vital source of income – one third of 1988's foreign investment of Esc.138bn ($900m) went into tourism. (Investment in 1989 was more than twice that and doubled again in 1990.) It is the largest growing industry – an industry that, unrestrained, could irrevocably change the face of Portugal. I like to believe that Portuguese pride in their own resounding history and affection for their cultural *patrimônio* is enough to provide a sturdy safeguard against excess. And if it is not, the certainty remains that in the soaring hills, the quilted plains and cork forests of the Alentejo, in a thousand and one green dreaming valleys and tranquil villages, Portugal will be recognizably Portugal for a while to come.

It is the Portuguese who are changing, rather than Portugal. *'Quer ser um yuppie?'* an ad for a foreign bank asked – 'Do you want to be a yuppy?' The job requirements included a degree in economics or business management. Chances were that whoever got the job was already a yuppy. Never before have the young and upwardly mobile had it so good. Managerial posts are among the professional jobs most advertised in the weekend paper, *Expresso*. Universities and business schools cannot turn out graduates fast enough. One institute puts it, with rare brevity, *'Quem sabe, sobe'* – literally, 'Who knows, rises.' Belmiro de Azevedo, head of Sonae, one of the largest and fastest-growing groups in Portugal, regularly invites the best management finalists to lunch; head-hunting is not only common but a tough new profession.

The traditional professions are faltering by the wayside. Economic fever has toppled law, which from the First Republic on led the professions, from its supreme seat of influence. Mário Soares, the Socialist leader Jorge Sampaio, the centre-right Freitas do Amaral, the Social Democrat Sá Carneiro and the dogged old Communist Álvaro Cunhal, whose degree papers written in prison won high marks from none other than Marcelo Caetano, all based their political careers on law. The Social Democrat Cavaco Silva, with his finance and economics degrees from Lisbon and doctorate in economics from York University in England, leaped to the heights of politics from a radically different springboard. If the social problems of a poor country are a daily challenge, the prime focus of government policy, with a competitive European Common Market to consider, is money management.

Or was it always? Prince Henry the Navigator, commerce among his complex motives for reaching out into the Sea of Darkness, held numerous titles and privileges. Among monopolies awarded him by his older brother, King Duarte, was the economically useful manufacture and sale of soap. Dom João II, in one matter at least a less than perfect prince, resolved an embarrassing problem to financial advantage by shipping a group of Jewish children off to São Tomé to colonize the island and work the new sugar fields alongside black slaves and *degredados*. Ordinary folk had craft guilds to watch their interests – the *doze de povo* (twelve representatives), or for Lisbon and Oporto the Casa dos Vinte e Quatro ('House of Twenty-Four'). Lisbon's *Câmara* begged Dom João III to marry his father's widow in order to avoid having to return her dowry. (He did not. The money was reluctantly returned.) The Marquis of Pombal, among many unusual measures to improve the economy,

raised the social status of merchants – and enraged the nobility –
by permitting them to wear swords.

'The age of chivalry is gone. That of sophisters, economists, and
calculators, has succeeded,' wrote Edmund Burke in the eighteenth
century, 'and the glory of Europe is extinguished for ever.' In a
different context, *'Cada coisa a seu tempo'* ('Everything in its own
time') say the Portuguese, for whom true glory lies in the past.

Portugal's money managers, determined to achieve harmonious
integration with Europe, glorious or otherwise, are changing not
only old links and patterns of trade but also the burdensome effects
of revolution. High on their list is the privatization of the companies that were dramatically and hastily nationalized in 1975, some
eight hundred firms that ended up as sixty-eight state-owned
enterprises and more than a hundred companies in which the state
had a share. In careful manoeuvres intended to avoid rocking the
boat – only 49 per cent of the shares were initially offered for sale –
and aimed at persuading Portugal's mistrustful and conservative
savers to enter the market, privatization began in April 1989 with
a popular choice, a northern-based brewery, Unicer.

What a success it was: in a half-hour, three-times-oversubscribed
sale under the glass dome of Oporto's Palácio da Bolsa (stock
exchange), its nineteenth-century grandiloquence a stage set for the
sharply suited businessmen slotted in rows of chairs facing a computer display screen, 11,866 stockholders snapped up 3,185,000
shares with a base price of 2,500 escudos. Twenty per cent had
been reserved, at a lower fixed price and with a two-year resale
ban, for company workers, emigrants and small investors. Foreigners were restricted to an easily evaded limit of 10 per cent; most
of these shares were speedily acquired by a Colombian company.

The Unicer sale was a smooth re-entry into the free-market world
with, in its aftermath, all the snap and snarl of serious money, as
Portuguese companies fought off the Colombians – and each other
– and inquiries began on the alleged illegal instant resale, at a handy
profit, of workers' shares to an Oporto family – suggesting, if
nothing else, that the humblest of investors were not averse to a
quick buck.

Other partial privatizations followed, the rules modified here and there as time passed. A bank, Totta e Açores, encouragingly oversubscribed, was second, succeeded by an insurance company, a newspaper, a shipping line, more beer, companies involved in chemicals, cement, glass, fuel and mining. The first 100 per cent privatization was the direct sale of EPSI, a polymers company at Sines, to the Finnish company, Neste Oy, already linked to Portugal in an oil-exploration contract. Companies passed from public to joint stock – with private-sector management. Winners were matched with lossmakers as incentives in parleying management contracts. The policy was to privatize cautiously down the line, postponing only areas like armaments, airports and the railways. Plans included selling by private negotiation, and limits higher than 10 per cent for foreign buyers. Free-market economists and employers' associations, dismissing anxiety over Portugal's insufficient savings, pressed for a speed-up. The government's nationalist concerns in multinational economics were tossed off as distinctly old-fashioned.

Calculations of treasury proceeds for the first year alone were Esc.54bn, about \$360m, from the part privatizations and another Esc.45bn from the sale of EPSI. Eighty per cent went towards redeeming the bloated public debt – at the time of the Unicer sale \$32bn. But as capital markets braced themselves for continuing privatization, many thousands of voices were raised in anger. Monstrous discrimination, they cried. Justice, they demanded.

The clamour came from the dispossessed – over 120,000 ex-shareholders and owners of the nationalized companies who, in fifteen years, had received only trifling compensation for their losses – bonds of up to twenty-eight years with low, sliding interest and based on miserly valuations ten times less than estimated 1980s values. Cavaco Silva had kept his distance: his government was not responsible for the nationalizations, and therefore, he felt, not obliged to be generous. He was cautious, too, on those *retornados* who, he said, had paid a high price for decolonization. He himself had only brief colonial experience and no complex. The path he trod was painfully narrow: on one side, land-eager Alentejo farmers persistently raged over government conservatism; on the other, conservatives in the business community vociferously protested perfidy – joined by Margaret Thatcher, speaking on behalf of the British whose property had been expropriated (with eight-year bonds, most were better off than the Portuguese). Where, in the end, did he stand? 'If Cavaco Silva is anything, he is a leftist,' said the president of the Portuguese Confederation of Industry. But this viewpoint was from the right.

'*Quem rouba pouco é ladrão, miserável, infamado; quem rouba muito é barão, muito honrado e celebrado*' ('A poor, wretched thief steals a little, the celebrated baron steals a lot'): the aphorism dates to the turn of the century when the chiefs of industry were lambasted in the press as *despóticos* and *tirânicos* who were always obese, lascivious, avaricious and crapulous. Bankers grew richer, Zé Povinho poorer. Salazar's monopolists were their natural heirs. In the transition to a modern Portugal attuned to the European market – though still with an ocean between haves and have-nots – a new image is forming of the impresario as an innovative leader, imaginative, tenacious, daring and successful. They are young or look younger than they are, they are self-made men, some graduated in – even taught – economics, they have broad administrative or banking experience. They speak of sprints and takeovers, of cash flow, joint ventures, performance and global strategy. Most emerged, shining like newly minted coins, in the late 1980s. But the image needs only the turn of a silicon chip to fit quite a few athletic survivors of revolution and dispossession: old names with skills in new money figure prominently in the upper ranks of business.

The financial press watches with absorbed fascination the doings of Belmiro de Azevedo, born in 1938 (in Marco de Canaveses, where Carmen Miranda came from), who in a few years built his Sonae group from negligible beginnings to a money-pumping machine embracing some sixty companies in agro-industry and biotechnology, property and tourism, timber, stores and supermarkets, communications and banking. Galloping beside him is Américo Amorim, born in 1934, his group of more than thirty companies and his fortune built up from cork. High in the lists of the rich and canny are Ilídio Pinho, his wealth derived from packaging and transport, Macedo Silva in sugar, Manuel Gonçalves in textiles, Fernando Guedes in wine – exporting to 125 countries the renowned Mateus Rosé, port from the house of Ferreira and a wide range of other wines within the ambit of his company, Sogrape. All of these *barões* (barons of industry) are *nortenhos* (northerners), with a long tradition of leaving the south standing – though it is not irrelevant that the north escaped the worst assaults of nationalization. All of them are thought of as new rich.

There is also the old money élite: Jorge de Mello and, back at the helm of Lisnave, his brother José Manuel, grandsons of the billionaire Alfredo da Silva and owners until 1975 of the mighty CUF group – the first bank privatized in 1989 had once been a star in their empire; António Champalimaud, a contentious fighter who married into and sought to rival the de Mellos. In the forefront, shrewd and determined, is the Espírito Santo family. Stripped of its assets in 1975, the family, with a financial base in Luxembourg and banks and finance companies in Switzerland, the United States and elsewhere, sprang back with an investment company and a private bank, the Banco Internacional de Crédito, one of twenty-six commercial banks operating profitably in Portugal in 1989. In that year, the bank which had once been theirs, still nationalized, was Portugal's second biggest: the Banco Espírito Santo e Comercial de Lisboa. 'Holy Spirit and Commerce': God and Mammon in efficient and profitable partnership. It was the Espírito Santo family who won an undeclared prestige race: their holding company, with the considerable advantage over any Portuguese concern in the free movement of money, beat all opposition to the quotation lists of the London Stock Exchange and, in 1989, began buying back their former companies. The first Portuguese bank to be listed on a foreign exchange was the private Banco Comercial Português, in 1990 Portugal's most profitable bank.

Merchant banking and high finance used to mean marble halls and soft-spoken, discreet bankers. Not any more. The Espírito Santos, formerly hosts to royalty, are back and running in the fiercely complex, risky and predatory international money race. Foreign banks are multiplying. Spain has moved conspicuously into Portuguese banking. Glowing profits are certain in the looming privatization of the remaining nationalized banks. The postal service, with its 1,040 branches and outposts, has shifted rapidly

from an outdated network of dismal warrens and rude service to a
smart, modern financial giant. In the suddenly flourishing, newly
liberalized money markets, all the voracious and diverse operations
of aggressive finance and money management are assiduously
hustled from direct and intermediary financing and factoring to
leasing and dealing, to an assortment of investment groups and
funds, the sole focus of them all, the name of one of them, multi-
money. The megathrill of the 1990s: money games, in which the
Portuguese are recognized as international players.

The cold eye of an accountant balances success against failure, solid
growth against inflation, profit against loss. (Stern alarms sounded,
as well as a rare sigh for Salazar, when the Bank of Portugal
dropped gold, nearly nine tons of it, in the lap of Drexel Burnham
Lambert, the mammoth American junk-bond traders who sank
into bankruptcy.) The lost decades of war and nationalized, traum-
atized companies, are not forgotten. Nor has Portugal outgrown
its bureaucracy-riddled past. Banks and business groan at ministerial
inflexibility. The stock exchanges in Lisbon and Oporto are increasingly unified, modernized, growing (in 1990 there were thirty-odd
brokers and over 150 companies). They had taken off with a boom
and a sparkle after the crisis and enforced closure of revolution.
The crash of '87 sent them into a sudden deep spin – a 70 per cent
fall. But if foreign buyers soon came back with hungry energy –
'*Bolsa nas mãos dos estrangeiros*' ('the exchange in foreign hands')
became a familiar headline – Zé Povinho and the small investors,
the pleasures of speculation soured, stayed away.

Comparisons, for Portugal, are often odious: Portugal's biggest
company, Petrogal – petroleum products – has only a quarter the sales
of, say, Belgium's Petrofina. No Portuguese bank appears in the
world's top hundred – in 1989 a survey in the *Financial Times*
publication *The Banker* placed Portugal's main savings bank, Caixa
Geral de Depósitos, as 135th in a list of a thousand. No other bank
showed up until the 500s. No Portuguese company appears in *Fortune*
magazine's celebrated lists. In a ranking of the five hundred largest
European companies in *Eurobusiness* magazine, Petrogal came in at 366
and EDP, the electricity company, at 476. Hopes for the escudo to

enter the European Monetary System looked thin when, in June 1989, Spain made the leap with its stronger peseta and freer economy.

The EEC gave Portugal until 1995 to take state weight off the economy and remove the last restrictions on banking, credit and capital flow. New economists who have been taught grasp and greed look critically at Portugal's struggle to deregulate smoothly. When credit limits began to be removed in April 1990 it was not, for them, soon enough. Cavaco Silva pointedly remarked: 'Portugal needs to do in ten or twenty years what other countries achieved in a century.' Incessantly urging on the Portuguese people to greater effort, he also knew there were limits. On the very eve of a crucial trip to Brussels he signed a dispatch, published in the legal *Diário da República*, guaranteeing all workers the day off to celebrate Carnival. It was most reassuring. I had begun to believe, in the mad frenzy for money, the fun had gone.

The yuppies are here, women as well as men, with degrees and diplomas and bursting ambition, with business English and discreet and impeccable clothes. They are leaping fully-fledged, and in rapidly increasing numbers, from universities, institutes and business schools – management courses exceed economics courses by some twenty-seven to ten. Even as students their talents are on display. Soon, they become administrators, directors, brokers, analysts, overnight market-makers. Specialized courses aid older executives to survive the onslaught and stay ahead. Age and treachery, they are reminded, will overcome youth and skill. (The American magnate Malcolm Forbes had the aphorism embroidered on a cushion on his yacht.) The confident faces, their estimable achievements, appear in the financial pages of the daily press, in the glossy business magazine, *Exame*. So what, I often ask myself, will happen to the business Portugal I am used to?

I have learned that *amanhã* and *próxima semana* do not mean tomorrow or next week. I endlessly await the second coming of Jesus, the plumber. I know that courteous protest is like punching cottonwool. I have learned never to take yes for an answer. In my travels I meet people in business whose aggression I never see. I have observed the long day's labour of country folk, of exhausted women and forbearing men. I think of pale children at work in northern factories, and stitching and sewing at home for a few miserly escudos.

In the tourist-rich south my telephone is a frail and faltering instrument. I stand in line recording sagas of hope or hopelessness in the *finanças* section of the town hall or in the newly glossy post office, where impatient supplicants cannot win. My electricity lurches, sways and, sick at heart, stops, and I am not comforted when the power company, EDP, boasts that, in one year, the country is powerless for only 86 minutes. For the first time, in a neighbourhood family restaurant, I feel cheated. Insurance treats me with imperious injustice. I wonder about the aspirations of the 800,000 or so youngsters who will be seeking work over the next four years and if the whizz kids and *Wunderkinde* will prevail. I conclude that in this promised land of Dom Afonso Henriques's battlefield vision, this land of hope, glory and infinite promise, no Common Market agenda will instantly transform a country calendar which still has Carnival as a highlight. The rush to money? What's new about that?

8 Family affairs

People who abide by a country calendar are, it is said, slow to adapt. By 1 February, an old lady worries, her potatoes must be in and, by the end of April, dug out. By the end of June the Alentejo plains are stripped, much of the straw baled. Already, the cork-cutters, the cork oak's trunk shrunk by the heat, are beginning the delicate task of stripping the cork. As August begins I hear a tap-tap-tapping across the sun-baked Algarve fields and know the almond harvest has begun. I see my neighbour, José, tapping the trees with a long wooden pole to shake off the opening husks, some still green velvet, most already gritty and hard. His wife, Fernanda, uncomplaining in the intense heat, stoops to collect the fallen nuts. It is the tiny, tickling insects that land on her by surprise that she dislikes most of all.

Across the country, the grape harvest (*vindima*) is an exuberant annual event; port-wine shippers especially, vast sums pinned to the Douro vineyards, only relax when it is all over in October. And like the crops, Carnival in February and the summer *festas* in every town and village are time signals as fixed, crucial, interlocked and invariable as the sun and the moon, day and night, the calendar itself. And yet everyone is adapting.

José and Fernanda, with a household family economy like many thousands of other small farmers, adapt not only to the annual ritual of supply and demand that sets the buyer's price, but to the knowledge that the traditional almond crop is diminishing as exotic fruit or the land itself leaps in value. For them, perhaps, it doesn't matter: their daughter, granddaughter and, now, great-granddaughter live in America – city lives that leave the hands soft, painted nails unchipped. The farmers with larger commercial crops and the wine-makers are adapting to EEC regulations and the challenge of a Common Market. The cork-cutters – no machine has yet been devised that can replace them – adapt to the new trends that have raised demand for the ancient product.

Patterns were set centuries ago. Romans built roads. Swabians devised the smallholdings of the Minho. The Moors shaped the south. Dom Dinis established the rhythm of country fairs. Dom João I established the House of Avis and, with his English queen Philippa and their five remarkably individualistic sons and one daughter, took Portugal from the Middle Ages into the Renaissance, planted the seeds of discovery and demonstrated across Europe the power of a strong, united family. Even now historians argue that it was Pedro, the European traveller, not Henry, staring out to sea, who was the clever one.

The Portuguese have long experience in adapting – to the whims and eccentricities of kings, to empire, war, frustration and poverty. Through the centuries the singular essence of Portugal stayed pure. Eyes look at you that are the clear blue of the Celts and the dark brown of the Moors: from diverse origins the Portuguese became one intensely nationalistic people, with local rivalries but without linguistic, racial or religious minorities. The medieval Cortes reflected the social divisions: nobility, clergy, the *povo*. Only the nineteenth-century republican spirit and the force of twentieth-century revolution blurred the lines. Even so, conservative tendencies and the urge to family respectability prevail over radical attitudes.

From the nobility came leaders. In Portugal's expansion after the discoveries, Oliveira Marques notes that half of the forty offices of governor or viceroy of India between 1550 and 1671 came from five families – the Meneses, Mascarenhas, Noronhas, Castros and Coutinhos. John Dos Passos includes the da Gamas, the Albuquerques and Sousas among the great patriarchal clans of the era. Some hundred years later the Marquis of Pombal forcibly married his second son to a Coutinho, the fourteen-year-old Isabel; the family, deeply angered by his upstart ways, had the marriage annulled. (The poor girl was then confined by Pombal to a convent though she married happily after his fall.) The Noronhas were so wealthy and powerful that Dom José warned Pombal, in his vengeful campaign of humiliation and destruction of the noble class, not to upset them. Among the most renowned Noronhas was William Beckford's friend, the Marquis of Marialva. Today these are common family names that do not necessarily signify grandeur. I know an Albuquerque who is a waiter.

In modern Portugal, there are still a few dukes, marquises and counts. Nobility has not been recognized since the fall of the monarchy in 1910, but the old families are still there – and social snobbery. I can gawp at the partying, if I want to, in the weekly *Semanário*'s magazine, *Olá*, which concentrates on the rich at play, their plush homes and glossy life-styles. Old families do not welcome the new rich to their clubs; there are no grandees among the northern industrialists. Wealth and power have shifted drastically. Yet despite the shock of revolution, the sudden development of a new class of money-market technocrats and impresarios, divisions are not just between old and new, rich and poor, success and failure. The aristocracy and landowning classes, feudal by history and rich by inheritance, have adapted, too.

The nobility sneered at Dom Dinis as *o Rei Lavrador*, 'the Farmer King', for his passion for the earth and his determined land reforms. The farm properties of the current Duke of Palmela, still vast, are configured to the rules of the EEC. In the Minho, in Ponte de Lima, Francisco de Calheiros, the Count of Calheiros, youthful and Byronically dashing, is frequently found in work-worn sweater and wellies. An energetic man, an *engenheiro* qualified in electrotechnology, he farms, tends vineyards, promotes his wife's family textile business, is involved in local administration and presides over the area's manor-house *turismo de habitação* organization, Turihab. His own family home, Paço de Calheiros, a fine, handsomely proportioned mansion dating from the sixteenth century, with coronet-embroidered pillowslips and a view across to the river, is one of many architecturally graceful *casas antigas* in the scheme.

Filipe Graciosa is a veterinarian, horses his speciality and passion. Everyone – every tiny child, if you ask them – has a long full name. Filipe's is Dr João Filipe Giraldes Pereira de Figueiredo; he is a son of the Marquis of Graciosa, whose dulcet title comes from one of the Açores' nine emerald islands. I have encountered Filipe in white coat examining horses at the national horse fair held each November in Golegã and driving teams of national stud horses with easy flair. The director of the national stud stables, at the animal research station of Fonte Boa, near Santarém, he has displayed for my camera the flowing lines and elegant mobility of the lovely light grey Lusitanian horses bred there. I have seen him, too, as *equitador*, dressed in courtly crimson coat and tricorne hat, one of the small group of master horsemen who ride the beribboned Alter Real horses of the Escola Portuguesa de Arte Equestre, the school of horsemanship that displays the classic dressage movements in exquisite art form. (The relaxed, seemingly effortless Portuguese style is known as the art of Marialva after the Marquis of Marialva who was head steward to the royal court from 1770 to 1799.)

Sons and daughters of the old families take little for granted. They go to university, marry correctly, enter the professions, participate actively in the modernizing of Portugal – outside the cut and thrust of party politics. These families have experienced and survived the shattering effects of revolution; the challenges of 1992 could never be as fearful as the shocks of 1974.

At Golegã, seven years after the revolution, beside the sandy track of the Largo do Arneiro, where horse events are held, I saw a small, two-storey building, stables below and hospitality rooms above, with a large painted sign across the front declaring it to be the property of the Agricultural Association of the Ribatejo. All the breeders and many grand families had come to the fair. Magnificent horses whinnied and pranced, many restrained by *campinos*, grooms and herdsmen, in gaudy red waistcoats, green stocking caps, tight breeches and white stockings. Downfield, gypsies and horse dealers touted sad nags, donkeys and mules. Yet the structure had changed. The old families now were renting what once had been theirs.

It is a system that operates, in various modifications, for other grand properties – the famous *solar* pictured on the bottles of Mateus *rosé* belongs not to Fernando de Albuquerque, Count of Mangualde, but to a foundation which he heads. His cousin, Fernando Mascarenhas, the Marquis of Fronteira, no longer owns his splendid family palace but maintains it – and welcomes visitors there – through another foundation which also encompasses the Alorna stately home. Family inheritance is not quite what it was.

To say that most Portuguese do not find bullfighting offensive is, to say the least, an absurd understatement. For daring with glamour, for the sight of blood and certainty of drama, the Portuguese go to a bullfight. It is, moreover, not sport but art: a *corrida* – or *tourada* – to the Portuguese, uniting beauty with cruelty without a blink, is a cultural event.

The Portuguese *corrida*, in a long season starting officially on Easter Sunday, is markedly different from Spain's. Star of the spectacle here is the *cavaleiro*, a horseman splendidly clothed in embroidered satin coat, ruffles and tricorne hat in the style of an eighteenth-century grandee and skilled in classical dressage; the horns of the bull he faces are ball-capped and sheathed in leather. Critical judgement is based on artistry in combination with skill and valour, on the grace and style of man in partnership with horse in close counterpoint with the bull.

The *cavaleiro* and his back-up team of *peões de brega*, ready with cape to distract, play and prepare the bull, are succeeded in the arena by a troupe of volunteer *forcados* who face the bull barehanded – a single file of eight young men in tight breeches, white stockings, scarlet cummerbund and short, patterned coat. The reckless audacity of the unpaid *forcados* gives the spectators the old-fashioned thrills of man tangling with and dominating beast. In this arresting, uniquely Portuguese, contest the lead man, with swaggering step, challenges the bleeding and bewildered bull to charge him. '*Toiro, eh toiro*,' he shouts, pressing closer – 'Bull, come on, bull.' If all goes as planned, he grips the onrushing bull around its neck and is held there by his seven stalwart supporters. Often, the front man and those behind him are tossed like matchsticks to right and left. Their *pega*, too, like the *cavaleiro*'s performance, is judged on style as well as valour.

At the end, the exhausted bull is not publicly stabbed to death but herded away in the soothing company of farm steers to the music of their softly clanging bells. But, as in Spain, trumpets sound the sequences of courtesies and encounter, the bull's upper back is repeatedly pierced by *bandarilhas* and blood flows darkly down his sides. And though there is no mortal thrust, no public slaughter (prohibited since 1799 when the Count of Arcos, son of the Marquis of Marialva, was gored to death before king and court), the bleeding bull suffers again later as the barbs are withdrawn; shortly afterwards he is butchered.

For the successful *cavaleiro*, the rewards include lasting fame and profitable contracts abroad. For the *forcados*, there is neither money nor prizes nor even a fund to cover their considerable medical costs, only enhanced masculine pride, the respect of their fellows and prestige for their group.

To the small articulate minority in Portugal who vigorously oppose bullfighting, all this energy and dedication is sadly misplaced. But the opinions of those in favour are strong, and at times loudly expressed.

For many Portuguese the Ribeiro Telles family of *cavaleiros* are brilliant exponents of a national culture, their horsemanship heroic, their artistry superb. There are other skilful *cavaleiros*; the Telles's extra magical ingredient is family tradition. In July 1988, David Ribeiro Telles, a genial, bald country gentleman aged sixty, celebrated the thirtieth anniversary of his *alternativa*, first professional bullfight, with a *corrida* that included all three of his *cavaleiro* sons – João and António, both admired and with several years' experience, and the fledgling Manuel. (David has eight other children, all girls.) It was not a farewell; the proceeds went to an anti-cancer charity. As David noted: 'There is no contest tonight, only the desire that together we do our best and give the public total satisfaction.'

Tradition, thrills, professionalism, family: a combination guaranteed to give most Portuguese a warm glow. I find the inherent cruelty of bullfighting disenchanting but must add that from a day spent with the family at their ranch near Coruche for a magazine story, I found the Telles family to be modest, courteous and infinitely hard-working. The land slopes gently across 400 or so hectares – David is a *ganadero* (bullbreeder) too. The family house is old, white, large and sprawling. David's wife, a smiling matriarch, was engaging and energetic. I watched David and his sons work out in their practice arena – testing horse, rider and, among undamaged opponents, the spirit of a sprightly heifer. Some of the girls watched, too, from a small gallery. On its wall was a small tile with the words: '*Tu podes assim tu queiras*' ('You can be what you want').

What Francisco Olazabal, aged fifteen, wanted to be was an enologist and he didn't even like wine then. He had no doubts. He is the great-great-great-grandson of Dona Antónia Adelaide Ferreira who, in the nineteenth century, owned vineyards across the Douro and founded the House of Ferreira, the port-wine company popularly known by its friendly diminutive, Ferreirinha. His father and an uncle are *administradores*, his grandfather, Fernando Nicolau de Almeida, a renowned taster. He grew up – like generations of English port-wine makers – between Oporto, the wine-storage lodges of Vila Nova de Gaia and the family *quintas* up the Douro.

A first *vindima* is something of an initiation – I remember meeting Nicholas Delaforce, eighteen years old, straight from school and learning the business. I had talked port, Oporto and the Douro traditions with managing director David, the sales director Richard, Nicholas's lively retired grandfather John – and, it seemed, a tribe of decisive Delaforces. Nicholas is the sixth generation in port – but other port-wine families have blood lines as long. On the green slopes of the Douro vineyards time passes quickly.

Some families might have a common thread, like the clans in port or the Espírito Santos in finance. Cupertino de Miranda, not a name to forget, was prominent in banking and the prime mover of Lusotur, the developer of Vilamoura, 4,000 acres planned in 1966 as a self-sustaining tourism city, the largest privately owned development in Europe; descendants appear in the social pages and, as the fortunate heirs, in the financial press. Early this century Norton de Matos was a distinguished colonial governor and statesman; in 1988 an *engenheiro* Norton de Matos was in charge of Petroquímica e Gás de Portugal. Family names ring across history and continents, yet it is no longer simple in the gusts and eruptions of new times – despite an astonishingly large and informative press – even for knowledgeable and socially aware Portuguese to be sure who is who.

For one thing, many Portuguese come from truly gigantic

families. In Sintra, in the summer of 1982, Fernando d'Orey, a forty-seven-year-old geology professor at the University of Lisbon, took me round the theatrically elaborate Quinta da Torre da Regaleira, its exotic gardens and alarming sunken wells and grottoes. He was born in the house, had been married in its chapel and was conservator on behalf of his brothers and sisters who had inherited the bizarre property from their father, Waldemar. Of eighteen children he was the seventeenth. It was, he said, 'a marvellous sensation living among the romantic fantasies of the last century'. Yet he found it more practical and more comfortable to live with his English wife and four children in the *quinta*'s converted coach-house. A large family gets around – three of them have been members of Cavaco Silva's government. At a family reunion held in Lisbon's Estufa Fria greenhouse-park, 1,200 d'Oreys showed up.

In the house which had been her family's for three generations Maria Eugénia Sá da Bandeira – another historic and distinguished name – spoke of her large family to *Olá* magazine. 'Imagine what it's like,' she said, 'buying shoes for fifteen, or toothbrushes.' Another matriarch, Maria Simões de Almeida, has seventeen children, a family that, with husbands and wives and their children, adds up to close on a hundred. In north Portugal's *vinho verde* country I have met many people for whom, for reasons that are as much custom as religion, anything but a large family would be unusual.

In Geraz do Lima the Casa dos Cunhas has belonged for centuries to the Sottomayor Correia de Oliveira family. One of the family is a lawyer, António Correia de Oliveira, one of six children and, in his thirties, a father of six. 'Not a lot,' he said; 'my grandparents had fifteen.' I met dashing young Miguel Reymão, an agronomist who works for a bank. He is one of ten brothers and sisters whose family owns the Quinta de Luou, a member of the Association of Bottlers and Producers of Vinho Verde which aspires to a high quality and more individual wine. No Reymão lives on the estate, a flourishing twenty-one-hectare farm near Ponte de Lima which is run in the manner of many such properties by a *caseiro* (manager). The future of the family's pleasant country house? Tourism, perhaps.

On 1 July 1824, José Ferreira Pinto (who added Basto to his name), the founder of the Vista Alegre porcelain factory, brought all fifteen of his children into the firm. Since then the company has changed, sunk a little, risen to new heights and become a shining commercial success much ogled and lusted after and finally infiltrated by foreign companies. As for the Pinto Bastos they are, as one member of the family says, not so much a family as an epidemic. Family interests sprawled into shipping and industry and machinery, into holding companies and the dangerous seas of high finance. Quite the most popular member of the tribe is Évora-born António Pinto Basto, a trained mechanical *engenheiro* with an appealing light tenor voice who became a professional *fadista*, his '*Rosa Branca*' a golden hit.

Transforming old family concerns into EEC-conscious holding companies capable of strong competition became a business priority as the 1980s ended. Jerónimo Martins, a family grocery founded in 1792 and in the same family until about 1920, created a new group in 1989, built on a supermarket empire and a Unilever association, and a new image which left family considerations behind. But no proud Portuguese company would ignore its history. Bold publicity reminded everyone that Jerónimo Martins had outlasted five political regimes, the French invasions, two world wars, four revolutions and the Chiado fire that, in August 1988, burned its most distinguished shop to cinders.

Families fought for first place in the new, open, free-market Portugal. In the sale by the government of EPSI, the Sines polymers company, to the Finnish Neste Oy, the wealthy Portuguese family companies, Quintas & Quintas (seven of them led by older brother Nelson) and the Violas, through their Cotesi company, won a 10 per cent share. In the winning team of six young economists in an annual international management game were three brothers from one family, two from another. In *Exame* magazine's analysis of 199 stock-exchange members in September 1989, families owned and operated 75 companies, far exceeding in number the powerful groups (34) or state companies (27). Disliking inquiry into their affairs, many only joined the stock exchange for reasons of prestige or financial advantage. Not all families are lovingly united: cork magnate Américo Amorim, one of eight, overcame family opposition in the disposition of his inheritance. Ilídio Pinho from Aveiro split away from his family, though he stayed in his home territory to become a successful entrepreneur. In Portugal's biggest construction company, Soares da Costa, it was the oldest brother who was forced out.

Women in Portugal traditionally left business and important decisions to men. In family life, mother was rarely a professional woman. When the respected republican fighter and resistance leader of the Salazar era, António Macedo, died in his eighties in 1989, among the notable men and women at his funeral was the elderly Virginia Moura, another fighter for democracy. She was also the first woman engineer in Portugal. Within a surprisingly short time – with the 1974 revolution leading, in 1979, to absolute legal equality with men – women active in professions and politics as well as in family life surprise nobody. Except, of course, by what they say and do.

Of the Costa Salema family, Helena Roseta – one of eight brothers and sisters – is the most forthright and conspicuous. Born in 1947, she is a qualified architect, has been *Presidente da Câmara* (mayor) of Cascais, a Member of Parliament within the PSD party and an independent deputy on the Socialists' bench outside it. She is not the only achiever. Her husband, Pedro Roseta, a PSD deputy, has been ambassador to the Organization for Economic Cooperation and Development, OECD. Each of her brothers and sisters is a professional success, their husbands and wives often public figures – one sister is married to António Capucho, a PSD minister, one of the d'Orey clan and elected to the European Parliament in 1989. Another sister, Margarida Salema, a lawyer, was selected by Cavaco Silva for the PSD list and also won a seat at Strasbourg. In a profile on the family the newspaper, *O Independente*, found not a dud among them – even the upcoming generation showed every sign of intellectual brilliance in fields as diverse as architecture and maritime biology. The family's modest explanation for its strong public presence: 'The family is big, the country small.'

Other family names are conspicuous because of common cultural links. Saraiva is a name that leaps to mind – but which one? António José Saraiva, a lecturer in literature adored by his students at the University of Lisbon's Faculdade de Letras, whose books on Portuguese literature and the Middle Ages are considered classic reading. Or his brother, José Hermano Saraiva, a noted historian whose career ranges from education minister in Salazar's last cabinet, ambassador to Brazil, writing and editing history books, to television presenter and newspaper editor? António José's son, journalist José António Saraiva, won national attention as the highly accomplished director of *Expresso*, his own columns pungent, thoughtful and eminently readable.

Not all Serrãos are historians, though students might at times think so as they read Joaquim Veríssimo or Joel Serrão – or Vítor Serrão, born in 1952, whose books include a study of mannerist painting in Portugal and a portrait of Sintra more evocative and thorough than most.

Serrão is a respected name to inherit and on which to build a reputation. A cultivated family like this and thousands of others produces cultivated children. But, proportionally, the cultural world is small. Many a shrewd businessman has sprung from rural roots and an illiterate background to a secure financial position and new social status. Yet despite intensive efforts to improve education in recent years the heritage of wide illiteracy is not yet overcome: only 42 to 45 in a thousand Portuguese read a newspaper, far fewer a book. It is, of course, sport, not culture, that excites the crowds. As to family ties, far better known than any eminent historians are distance runners Domingos and Dionísio Castro – not only brothers but twins – who entered on married life with an exuberant double wedding.

With its deep roots and long blood lines, traditions and kinsfolk and, increasingly, professional success and the money that goes with it, the classic Portuguese family is a rock of ages. The family might appear to have sundered where sons and daughters have left villages and farms to study, to work or to emigrate. But the glue holds. Wealth, class and life-style affect only the degree of sophistication of joyous, loud reunions.

In the pleasant *quintas* of the Douro river valley the clan gatherings of the port-wine families are legendary, as is their hospitality: there is much to be said for sitting on a shady terrace overlooking the river on a cool evening with a glass of excellent tawny in hand. But downriver near Cinfães one bright day, I saw a pale, thin man accompanying a young girl up a steep, wooded hill. She was all in white, her long dress gathered in one hand, a candlestick in the other. They were father and daughter returning from her first Holy Communion to their home, a small, starkly simple cabin. Well-dressed Oporto relatives, a married couple and their chubby son, had come to the celebratory lunch of casseroled fish and chicken and much wine – and I, too, a nosy stranger, was invited. The girl, her white gown exchanged for a ragged dress, stayed shyly apart. The girl's mother and older sisters who prepared the meal over charcoal fires in the earth-floor kitchen were, I noticed, all pregnant and all barefoot. But for this celebration at least it was family feeling, not rural poverty, that prevailed.

It is not uncommon to see family groups of twenty or thirty in country restaurants: chatty old ladies in Sunday best and shining shoes, the overweight *pai de família* red-faced and contented, the young marrieds – women sitting with women and men with men – and the children, small girls twirling their demure, calf-length skirts and already keeping an eye on the younger ones.

Children, whether from aristocratic families, the bourgeoisie, or smallholdings and farms, love and respect their parents, visit them frequently when they are away from home, very often marry into their own community – and occasionally never break away at all. In the rural setting in which I live, a young man quite often stays at home until he is married. He is doted on and spoiled. If he is talented he may start a small business, like many a local plumber or electrician. Edelberto Estrelo in Areeiro turned a teenage knack with wiring into a successful enterprise. His living-room, packed with refrigerators, television sets, washing machines and other *electrodomésticos*, grew to a spacious showroom – an extension of the family home. He does installations and repairs; his mother runs the shop. When he marries, his wife – if she has no profession or job of her own – will help out.

Young couples frequently live with one or other set of parents – separate housing is too often prohibitively costly. When babies arrive, grandmothers are instant babysitters. And when there is no handy mother-in-law, grandmother, older sister, cousin or other relative, then babies fit in with daily activity – tucked into the corner of a *minimercado* (a modernized village store), or among the laundry in a *lavandaria*. Family life can sometimes be too close: mother-in-law may be a useful baby minder but she may be as interfering and troublesome as the mother-in-law jokes suggest. Mental breakdowns are not uncommon; family pressures are the prime cause.

In such a convinced family-based society it is often assumed that everyone has someone. None of the 10,000 or so blind people in Portugal has a trained guide-dog and, though there are specialized education programmes and social aids – the leading blind association is run by an energetic blind professor of philosophy – there is a strong dependence on family. For the elderly, who have grown up knowing only the church-linked Misericórdia charity, social security, a national welfare system, remains a phenomenon. Frozen foods, increasingly varied and popular, cater to a whole new society on the move, to working mothers, to overworked housewives and, as a lasagne packet phrases it, to men who are 'temporarily' on their own.

Until recently, when emigration patterns changed and wives accompanied their husbands to France, the United States and elsewhere, there were in Portugal, particularly in the north, hundreds of thousands of women living temporarily, or permanently, without men. Women tilled the fields and harvested the crops, managed family affairs, and were very often listed as heads of three-generation families. Sometimes these women were *viúvas de vivos* (widows of the living), who might not have seen or heard from their husbands for years on end. Caroline B. Brettell, in *Natural History* magazine, describes the case of a woman from near Viana do Castelo who married in 1927. Her husband, leaving her with a baby son, took off for Brazil and only returned, to die in his own village, in 1978. Single women in this context were often more fortunate. A proverb says: 'When I married and was trapped, I exchanged silver for

copper. I bartered my freedom for money which does not flow.'
Even now it can seem as if whole families consist only of women,
harvesting olives, shucking corn, making the millions of paper
flowers that brighten almost every village *festa*. The menfolk may
be working abroad or in some other area, or merely taking refuge
in the male territory of the village *taberna*.

Among rural women, God-fearing and with an ear to the gossip of
neighbours, the black of mourning predominates. In large families
it seems as if mourning never ceases. In 1988, 98,236 deaths were
registered in Portugal, 52.4 per cent of them males. Widows, well
over 400,000 of them over sixty, outnumber widowers by five to
one. Custom dictates two years' mourning for a father, at least a
year for any other relative. A widow traditionally wears black for
the rest of her life and, in rural communities at least, is considered
sexually provocative if she does not.

In my neighbourhood, a gentle countrywoman in her forties with
three grown daughters was quite modern and daring when, on her
husband's death in a road accident, she chose not to wear the
mandatory black headscarf and – at the height of summer – black
stockings. Yet the most withered and ancient women, shawl-
wrapped even in hot sunshine, unconcernedly expose bare flesh as
they bend to work in the fields or hurtle along on the pillion of a
grandson's motorbike. Knee-high pop socks, along with a pension,
help to ease even a widow's pain. And if baptisms and marriages
are obviously happy occasions, Portuguese couples bringing in
close relatives and friend as *padrinhos* (witnesses), funerals too can
be less gloomy than one might think – after, that is, the doleful
tolling of the church bell and the grim moment when the coffin is
opened at the graveside for loved ones to verify that the corpse is
who it should be. Friends of mine who live near a village cemetery
lightly considered offering funeral teas to all the people who linger
at the graveyard – the tables to be shaded, perhaps, by striped
black umbrellas.

From birth to death, in a traditional rural family, links bind
tightly even across oceans where sons, daughters, cousins have
settled and extended the family further. In marriages abroad Por-

tuguese will most likely marry Portuguese. Beldora, the lissom and beautiful American-born granddaughter of my hardworking neighbours, married a young American whose Portuguese parents come from the same *freguesia* (parish). Love bloomed from a casual encounter and a comfortable convention made for a good marriage – and, a year later, a bonny baby daughter. But I know too – as does the whole neighbourhood – of the young girl who, with her family's acceptance and understanding, moved in with her boyfriend, and of the odd affair of the eldest daughter of shopkeepers who ran away to marry a divorced man nearly twenty years older. What was odd was that not even the arrival of a baby granddaughter healed the breach. To the Portuguese, small children, no matter how noisy and ill-behaved, are angels to be adored and worshipped, overdressed and underdisciplined. A childless woman is pitied. It is not unusual for her to bring up a child or two from a hard-up relative's brood.

National statistics on birth, marriage, divorce and death indicate that the Portuguese are marrying more but having fewer children, a trend common in Europe but not yet alarming in Portugal. In 1989, in a total population of 10,410,000, there were 73,195 marriages, in percentage terms a slight increase over 1988 but well below 1975, a record year with 103,125 marriages. Over 2,800 couples already had children. Nearly three quarters of the total, 72.3 per cent, were celebrated in a Catholic church. But also, in 1989, 9,657 marriages ended in divorce, 7 per cent more than the year before. Significantly, over 35 per cent of all divorces occurred in Lisbon. In the same year, birth figures, maintaining a slide over recent years, fell from 16.2 in 1980 to 11.5 per 1,000 inhabitants. Of the nearly 120,000 babies born, 14.5 per cent, an upward tendency, were born *fora do casamento*, outside marriage. The flamboyant listing of royal bastards in the past was one thing, today's officially benign and open attitude another. Infant mortality, though improving, was still the worst in Europe: 12.1 deaths in every 1,000 live births; in every 1,000 children born seventeen die before the age of five, fourteen in the first year of life.

Modern attitudes encompass, through the civil code, mutual parental responsibility for all babies. In sophisticated Lisbon society, changing relationships, unwedded bliss and divorced couples who take to the freedoms of single life, are common. Unmarried couples who live as *companheiros* have legal rights and a social place. An open attitude, though, depends on background and education.

It is not so long since the marathon champion Rosa Mota faced challenges during her daily training runs in her home town of Foz do Douro, close to Oporto – not from experienced runners but from a male-oriented social attitude to a woman in shorts. In Athens in 1982, when she was twenty-four, she won the first-ever championship event held for women; in 1987 in the steam heat of August in Rome she become world champion and, in 1988 at Seoul, Olympic gold medallist. In 1990, at Split, she won the European marathon championship for the third time in a row. Her triumphs on the track made her Portugal's *rosa imperial*; her victories were *brilhantíssima*. Yet as she ran in the streets at home, she was called names rather less laudatory. 'Slut, they used to shout at me,' she recalls. 'A woman's place is in the home. Go and cook, go and wash the dishes. *Vergonha* . . . shame on you!' Portuguese women active in sports were new. There was no track (nor was there, in Oporto, until 1989) but the streets; and distance running in Portugal, the marathon above all, means street training and a will of iron.

Economists snap that this is no longer a horse-and-cart society. It is an unfortunate choice of words. They mean, I think, that Portugal has rid itself of its backward, rustic image in the restructuring of the economy, in the building boom, expanding education and numerous development programmes. Yet even as yuppies struggle to decide which of five offered jobs they should accept and white-gowned teenagers dance in a rite of passage at Oporto's annual debutantes' ball, the gulf widens between rich and poor, knowledgeable and ignorant. In the cities, the cars of the young professionals crowd the roads; in the countryside, tractors and combine harvesters spread and multiply. But in 1988 the unfortunate twelve-year-old António Teixeira died in the Alto Minho, run over by his parents' oxcart, and a year later an elderly couple and their mule drowned as they tried to cross a river with a laden cart. The horse and cart, both as necessary transportation and as a symbol of poverty, is still with us.

In the cities, Lisbon and Oporto above all, dreadful poverty persists and hundreds of thousands of people live in appalling social conditions. 'The mass of men,' said Thoreau, 'lead lives of quiet desperation.' It is rarely quiet in, say, Fontainhas, an Oporto neighbourhood where families are crammed into minuscule homes, tiny, terraced boxes with other families packed close on either side, and communal lavatories and washhouses at the end of the row. Nor is it quiet in the *bairros de lata* of Lisbon, tin-and-cardboard townships where some 50,000 people battle to survive in conditions even more degrading and wretched. Take a wrong turning on the old tram routes of Lisbon and you can end up, all too literally, at the end of the line, among grubby shacks, stinking rubbish, scrawny women, howling infants and skinny girls in high heels and mini-skirts who hover hopefully at the sound of a car.

Because of the sheer hopelessness of overcoming bureaucracy, many houses, including solid houses of brick and tile, are illegally built *casas clandestinas* – a vast, continuing and seemingly ineradicable problem in Portugal. There are about 200,000 in greater Lisbon alone and 700,000 or so across the country, some with running water, most not. When, as happens all too often, there is a fire, or the city council demolishes illegal constructions, amid the tears and lamentations emerge disturbing stories of elderly couples who have lived all their lives in these homes, bearing and raising large families. Not all inadequate homes are illegal: a family I met when the oldest son, sixteen-year-old Francisco, rescued two infant brothers from a fire that devoured their cramped, wooden house had lived in a street whose name you could never forget: Rua dos Ácidos Sulfúricos.

In Lisbon, older, finer houses, costly to maintain, seem always to be falling down. In the five years to 1988, twenty-one houses collapsed in Lisbon, and loss of life was averted only because most gave painfully clear warnings of imminent caving in. Hundreds more houses are dangerously precarious. Almost every day, there are newspaper stories of the miserable lives led by large numbers of *lisboetas*, often elderly, in decayed rented premises with leaking roofs, stopped plumbing, blocked drains. 'They sleep on the floor, cook in the street, and wash at the neighbours',' was a headline in the tabloid daily, *Correio da Manhã*. Rough calculation shows that nearly half a million Portuguese houses are in need of restoration or repair, the widescale dilapidation largely due to frozen rents between 1948 and 1985. By 1989, the rent law reclassified categories and allowed rents to be raised on an approved scale. But neither *senhorios* (landlords) nor tenants are happy. As for the ramshackle buildings, though there are government-operated conservation programmes, for the most part landlords only begin refurbishing when the protected tenants die. Few new buildings cater to people who seek to rent rather than buy, although in 1990 an ambitious 'leasing' plan, leading to ownership, brought new hope. For most people, finding decent premises for rent at a price they can afford is hopeless.

Cavaco Silva's government claimed in 1989 that in three years its housing programme had supplied 150,000 families with a decent home and, through credit subsidies, helped 26,000 young couples acquire their own home. It was not enough. Only about 40 per cent of the Portuguese live in their own home – about two in every five and, in Lisbon and Oporto, one in five. The Associação de Empresas de Construção e Obras Públicas do Sul (AECOPS), the leading construction association, calculated a shortage of 800,000 *fogos*, or hearths, the formal definition of a new home even if it is a small heartless apartment. To catch up and keep up with demand they figured on an annual construction of 130,000 *fogos*. The National Habitation Institute, for the 1990s, planned on an annual 70,000.

Housing is a fraught subject, a national nightmare riddled with frustration. Government incentives to save for loans calculated against savings are paltry, although the massive new headquarters in Lisbon of the Caixa Geral de Depósitos, the country's prime, vastly prosperous savings bank, is evidence of the Portuguese savings habit – in early 1989 Esc.3,000bn was on deposit. But applicants for credit are too often unable to meet the conditions for obtaining a loan in a system that fails to match earnings to the cost of housing. Terms vary and interest rates shift, but credit is generally available for about 80 per cent of a property's value at an interest rate of about 17.5 per cent for a maximum loan-period of twenty-five years. And if this is acceptable to young professionals established in careers, it excludes large numbers of people barely able to cope with the awful dilemmas of day-to-day living. In Lisbon, some 2,500 derelicts and drop-outs live and sleep in the city streets.

Below the heights of São Jorge castle in Lisbon lie the shimmering neighbourhoods of Alfama and Mouraria, so full of bustling life, so photogenic. For the 12,000 people who live in them, life is not always rosy. Their picturesque homes, too, behind the banners of laundry and the pretty flowerpots, are in a desperate state, and at least half have no bathroom. A dozen *balneários públicos*, announced the Lisbon municipality, promising at the end of 1988 to improve these antique bathhouses, provide some 184,000 baths a year. Another telling statistic from the Instituto Nacional de Habitação revealed that only 58 per cent of Portuguese homes have a fixed bath or shower and only 78.5 a private lavatory. Four million Portuguese, not much under half the entire population, manage without publicly supplied water in their homes. (By contrast, travellers in Portugal will have discovered that all Portugal's licensed catering establishments not only have a toilet but a bidet – a legal requirement due, apparently, to a fixation of Salazar's.)

More than three million Portuguese live below the EEC's poverty line. Their life is stark, demanding, with little dignity and rife with intractable problems. Those with jobs can spend hours getting to and from them. Buses are insufficient. Seventy thousand people commute to Lisbon each day from the south bank of the Tejo. When strike action stops public transport, as it often does, commuting is even more gruelling. Basic costs rise regularly, as does the rat population. Lisbon's periodic anti-rat campaigns are the source of black and bitter jokes. The quality of Lisbon garbage was rising, someone observed, when a car chassis was found one morning in a builder's skip. When the minister of works proudly announced that the new Estoril motorway was the first in Portugal to be constructed according to EEC environmental protection rules with fifteen ecological passageways for the local fauna, a good many people – certainly the hundred or so families dislodged by the new road – were sure they knew which was the dominant species.

Yet family life has its comforts. Very few Portuguese go away on holiday – in 1988 of the 32 per cent of the population over fifteen who took holidays at all (mainly from greater Lisbon and Oporto), only 22 per cent left home, a third to stay with friends and 11 per cent to go camping. But an astonishing one in seven homes has a video, nearly half of them in greater Lisbon, and far more a television set; one in ten, surprisingly, has a dishwasher. Over 92 per cent have a refrigerator and 57 per cent a washing-machine and vacuum cleaner (Lisbon again with the mightier share, 86 per cent, over the northern interior's 28 per cent). Hi-fi owner-ship nowhere exceeds 28.7 per cent. Then again not all homes have electricity (99.1 per cent) although for sure the most remote family in its humble dwelling has worldly hankerings. An apt cartoon during an election campaign showed two black-clad countrywomen in front of a crude stone house. One is saying to the other: 'If I vote for Senhor Capucho, the Senhor President of the junta has said that next week I will have electric light, running water, a flush lavatory and a parabolic antenna.'

Those who do not complain are never pitied, wrote Jane Austen. Here they say '*Pobreza não é vileza*' ('poverty is not a crime'). Yet it is clear that as the poor become more desperate and the well-off more avaricious, more Portuguese are turning to crime – pathetic and distressing backstreet abortions at one end of the social scale, tax evasion at the other. *Expresso* in 1988 printed a list from government fiscal sources showing that 289 taxpayers admitted earning Esc.10–12m a year (a million was then worth about £4,000 or $6,500), thirty-four between Esc.20–50m and just two over Esc.50m. Robbery, fraud, corruption and drug dealing – Portugal is conveniently situated on international supply routes – occupy a vast middle ground.

Portuguese law permits family planning, there is free contracep-tion to youngsters under eighteen, and legal abortion, since 1984, in cases of danger to a mother's health, malformation of the foetus or rape. The law also recognizes doctors' rights to refuse an abortion. Yet the number of adolescent mothers has tended to rise each year even as illegal abortion thrives. (In Lisbon, only two hospitals cope with post-abortion complications.) Nearly half the child mothers in one study had never heard of family planning. Abortion becomes a heated issue when police raid an illegal clinic, usually on an anonymous tip-off, when it is suggested that class and money can procure a legal abortion, when it is argued that women have rights to abortion beyond the present law.

Social and Catholic services assist young mothers, many of whom, after initial doubts, keep and raise their babies, at times among the swarming families they were yearning to escape. Yet, inevitably, in society's darkest corners, ignorance, fear, stunted intelligence and terrible despair lead to dreadful acts of rejection, of newborn babies dumped in rubbish containers, of small children as well as babies being abandoned. Each year, in gentle Portugal, which worships its little darlings, some 30,000 unfortunate children are maltreated, neglected or sexually abused. A few homes and refuges exist; the wives of the former president, Ramalho Eanes, and of Mário Soares are active in focusing attention on their needs. In Faro, foreign residents consistently support a model, well-run refuge. Helplines have also been introduced although, with an expanding telephone system still so fallible, I wonder at times how any hapless child can get through.

Children are not always the victims, however; innocence soon vanishes in cities under pressure. Lisbon and Oporto watch with alarm the growing prevalence of youthful thugs, as mean and nasty as the rats that plague the *barracas* in which they grew up.

Drugs, especially, have brought a grim new intensity to law-breaking in Portugal, but in a society long constrained by poverty, thieving follows a standard pattern. Banks are occasionally robbed, and jewellery and watch shops broken into with regular ease by thieves whose motivation goes no further than personal enrichment. A small-time Portuguese burglar's character and upbringing, as well as the national habits, are revealed by a distinguishing feature of every household robbery: the first place any burglar looks for cash and gold, his true desire, is under the mattress. Perhaps it is a sign of changing times that a jittery assailant recently tried to force the victim of a street stick-up, a journalist with nothing in his wallet but his Multibanco cash card, to march to the nearest cash-point.

Robberies are pathetic, imaginative, greedy, bold. A man of twenty told a court that he had stolen some cakes because he was hungry, and was provisionally released with a caution by a judge who murmured a phrase from Camões on the wretchedness of poverty. A man seen tenderly holding a baby became known as a practised robber of car radios. Car break-ins and theft is common – parents who momentarily left their sleeping baby in their car saw car and baby disappearing down the street, though happily soon recovered both. Cattle rustling, and smuggling, have a long history. It made the papers, though, when, on a peaceful Sunday night, someone stole thirty pigs from a *quinta* near Palmela. Near Oporto police thought it odd to see a man leading a handsome horse through a built-up area; questioning revealed he had stolen it from a circus.

Thieves' loot has included 1,700 kilos of sugar, 28 tonnes of salt, 400 kilos of lobsters, mounds of mountain cheeses, diesel compressors and a minister's Mercedes. Thieves have filched from a lottery, a radio station, a hospital, a prison and, selectively, from museums and churches. Timid burglars at times have ignored cameras and radios, taking tape cassettes instead – inexplicably, Portugal leads Europe in the illegal copying of tapes: a considerable proportion of all tapes sold in Portugal are illegal, or bootleg, reproductions.

Football victories distract fans from pickpockets; newspaper photographers had cameras snatched during Carnival; six thousand chickens vanished in a lunar eclipse. A phony priest accepted offerings in Setúbal; a fake repairman fooled owners of videos; gypsies regularly con the gullible into parting with items of gold 'to be blessed', a false police inspector confounded real ones and a road-sweeper who fiddled his lottery ticket admitted fraud.

Deplorable and petty as all this is, it is a matter of some pride in Portugal that the world's greatest ever fraud (listed in *The Guinness Book of Records*) was committed by a Portuguese. In the 1920s, the likeable Alves Reis, swindled his way from Angola to vast wealth and power in Lisbon and the glamorous capitals of Europe by ordering, on Bank of Portugal notepaper, the English firm of Waterlow to print 580,000 five-hundred-escudo notes. The 'Portuguese Bank-Note Case' had enormous repercussions: the Bank of Portugal sued Waterlow and won. The vast scale of the currency swindle added to Portugal's instability and provoked the military coup which led to the appearance in politics of Dr António de Oliveira Salazar. Reis's sumptuous home in Lisbon is now the British Institute and library. His family was left with nothing but his extraordinary reputation. Today his grandson works as a computer programmer.

The arrangement that the white-haired Maria Branca dos Santos had with thousands of investors, to whom she paid interest of 10 per cent per month, worked well for twenty years. She was religious and grandmotherly, barely literate but good with figures. Lack of confidence in Portugal's post-revolution governments and the nationalized banks led more and more people to invest with her. The bubble only burst after a weekly newspaper, *Tal & Qual*, published an interview that led to a brief surge of deposits, the close attention of press and television, and finally panic. Her doors closed. She was unable to pay. Documents showed that 'the people's banker' had handled more than Esc.17.5m contos (about £72m). Hundreds of naïve investors had entrusted her with their life savings. She was arrested in October 1984. The case against Dona Branca, for issuing cheques without cover, aggravated fraud and criminal organization, opened in Lisbon's Boa Hora court in February 1988. At its conclusion in 1990, the sentence for Dona Branca, aged seventy-eight and ill with Parkinson's disease, was ten years.

The winsome old lady who paid out large interest until the money ran out became an international celebrity. She was not, however, the phenomenon she was made out to be. Imitators quickly moved in, offering even higher interest. Fraud, one way or another, has edged vigorously into public life.

Building constructors celebrate rapidly expanding tourism and a bursting building boom with casually illegal construction, double contracts and quite open law-breaking. Tax avoidance is one motive, but a part of this apparent nonchalance is due to the complexities of a paper-ridden bureaucracy inherited from the long rule of Salazar. Permits are slow to appear, so constructors go ahead without them, preferring the possibility of a fine to endless delay. A small gift (*lembrança*), gracefully presented, can at times oil the wheels of bureaucracy. Corruption seemed too strong a word – until, with the dizzying flood of EEC funds and heavy foreign investment, the rake-off increased.

In 1989 a government inquiry found irregularities in a third of all municipalities irrespective of political party and, in several cases, abuse of powers and gross corruption at the highest level. In the sixteenth century, when municipalities assumed more or less the form they have today, the men of highest influence were worthy community leaders known as *homens bons* (good men). Clearly, times have changed. Although newspapers itemized charges, ranging from pronounced misuse of Community funds to a mayor's profiting from the sale in a bar of rissoles made at home by his wife, no mayor stepped down in shame and none was deprived of his mandate. Nevertheless, anti-corruption measures are being intensified: in 1988 the Polícia Judiciária in Lisbon were investigating 192 cases of possible mishandling of money from just one European fund; in 1990 investigators were probing the affairs of senior administrators within Portuguese ministries and as far away as Macau.

Violent crime is far outside the lives of most Portuguese. A tabloid newspaper quite surprised itself when it reported three murders in a week, one at least involving drugs. Reported murders often seem to stem from drunken quarrels. Sometimes, vengeance is the motive. Disputes over land or water have often led to violence. In rare instances there is a *crime passional*. Occasionally, fear of witchcraft is the catalyst, or *loucura* (madness).

Psychiatrists were brought into the case of Vítor Jorge, aged thirty-eight, who, on the night of 1 March 1987, massacred seven people, including his wife and eldest daughter. Multiple murder was unknown in Portugal. Straightforward murder cases are resolved with a prison sentence from about ten to fifteen years, and compensation for the victim's family. The trial in Leiria of Vítor Jorge proved high courtroom drama. Defence and prosecution argued the question of responsibility. In a concluding irony, the prosecutor requested a sentence of twenty years, the maximum in Portuguese law (except for terrorism which gets twenty-five years) and the defence appealed for the impossible: life imprisonment. Vítor Jorge was sentenced to twenty years in prison with an additional six months for illegal possession of a weapon.

Political assassination since the expiry of PIDE and the Salazar era is happily very rare. With the exception of the FP-25 post-revolution terrorist organization formed in 1980 and more or less contained by 1985, the year in which the group tried to shell – the shots missed – a NATO fleet in the Tejo river, the few political killings of recent years have tended to reflect someone else's quarrel, the Basques', for example, or Moçambique's. The most memorable was when a young Arab assassinated another Arab in the crowded lobby of a large tourist hotel during a conference, and escaped. His broadcast description – a short, dark-haired man with a moustache – fitted several million Portuguese men but a young Arab who took a taxi all the way from the south coast, where the murder was perpetrated, to Lisbon, was promptly arrested. A trial found him guilty only of carrying a false passport.

The law is not an ass in Portugal but, through the Constitution, an expression of the sovereign will. An odd compliment came Portugal's way during the French bicentennial celebrations in July 1989: a French daily observed that Portugal was the only one of the thirty-three official representatives that was innocent of abuses against human rights. But Portugal itself suffers. The coast from which brave men sailed to adventure, discovery and empire is now the open door to Europe for drug traffickers. The pressures of a society in dramatic transition, with crushing urban poverty, the debilitating scourge of drugs and the rising addiction of young people, unceasingly push the deprived, the feckless and the greedy to the windy side of the law.

Is justice too gentle? Are the police efficient, sufficient and properly paid? In 1989 there were 18,751 men in the peace-keeping force, the Polícia da Segurança Pública, a third of them in Lisbon; the salary of the anti-drug force of the Polícia Judiciária was around $500 a month, a fraction above the average Portuguese salary of

67,000 escudos (about $450) in September 1990, but a pathetically small salary compared with the street values of drugs. The wonder of it is, perhaps, that no Mafia rules nor, outside areas of Lisbon or Oporto, does menace lurk in even the darkest streets. Where crime pays is predictable: in the dark corners of the drug world and under the bright sun of beach-bag tourism.

The Portuguese family is undergoing new challenges and trials every day. There is no enemy to fight, no cause to defend, no dastardly regime to overcome or escape; their concerns are closer to home, in the hopes, successes and failures of children, in relationships between wife and husband. The post-revolution generation faces the acute problems of a developing country – in education, in housing, in jobs, in acquiring a suitably supercharged EEC mentality. Suddenly, small Portugal is like an erupting volcano. Are families suffering? Many, yes. But there have been worse upheavals – emigration, Salazar's policies and repression, the revolution itself. The family, close and united, the frame on which this new society is taking shape, on the whole stays strong.

9 The lovely land

'Few understood our sky, our meadows, our houses, our rivers and our boats, our windmills, our trees, our things as well as he.' The words were written by Luís de Pina in a biographical tribute to the Portuguese film director and cinematographer Aquilino Mendes, who began a sixty-year career of filming in the 1930s. Implicit in the compliment is the conviction, shared by all Portuguese, that Portugal is unique not for its distinguishing characteristics, its historical and artistic triumphs, but for a special glow, a kindly light, that shines upon the land down to the last blade of grass. Whether that light has the cut-diamond brilliance of Lisbon, the Alentejo and the Algarve, or the grey granite mistiness so dear to Oporto poets scarcely matters. Portuguese nostalgia for this lovely land is simultaneously passionate and tender and justified.

Judged on physical beauty, Portugal is perfection. In a tally of natural features are unsullied sandy beaches and steep rocky cliffs along five hundred miles of Atlantic coastline; rivers as dramatic and grand as the Douro, as peaceable and clean as the Lima; valleys that are serenely green and fertile. Like a titanic collar shaping the far north are the mountain ranges of the Peneda-Gerês in a 270-square mile (70,000-hectare) national park; the Serra da Estrela, mountains of the stars, a sturdy backbone, is the snowy setting for gentle skiing in winter and a herb-scented pasture for shepherds' flocks in spring and summer. Lousã, Açor and other *serras* form the ribs, smoothly rounded and open to the skies or thickly forested. Driving on the twisting secondary roads of north central Portugal is like being on a slow, refreshing and estimably bucolic rollercoaster. Further south lie the tumbled hills of the Caldeirão ('the cauldron') separating the great undulating Alentejo plain, a third of the country, from the Algarve.

Portugal dazzles with its beauty. Here is glorious space, exuberant variety, designer landscaping in an infinity of unfolding vistas painted by sunlight and passing clouds, coloured in seasonal patterns by tapestries of wild flowers, a charmed, unreasoning world in which birds sing sweetly and grief is forgotten. Byron only had to lean against a rock at Seteais to write a poem. There are added beauties and mysteries in the islands – the green patchwork quilts, the deep craters, the dramatic outline of Pico in the Açores, and the exotic flowers and rich wine of mountainous Madeira, the sun-lovers' cluster of desert-island retreats with their long idyllic beaches off the Algarve's balmy Sotavento shore. South of Sines tiny Pessegueira has the lure of a romantic ruined castle. An hour's boat-ride from Peniche, among the craggy and formidable Berlengas group, looms the bird sanctuary of Grande Berlenga. In Portugal, absorbed by colour and form, seduced by nature, the sublime decorator, it is easy to be lyrical. Except, that is, where the curtain of tranquillity is parted and the vision erased.

The demands of an expanding population, a modern country, are changing the look of the land. Areas of woodland are being bulldozed to make way for new factories and urbanization projects. Villages grow as emigrants return and settle. Each development inevitably threatens, among other things, the flowers of the earth. In this time of radical change the great issue is whether to count the gains and mourn the losses or to conserve – the flowers, the landscape, its wild creatures, the lovely, familiar Portugal.

There has always been change, of course, but now the dimensions are different. The past lives on, discovered and rediscovered by archaeologists, professional and amateur, who have found numerous great *antas* (megalithic dolmens), like those in the Peneda-Gerês, at Gouveia, Zambujeiro and Baião, who have tenderly scraped the surface of half of Portugal – it seems – to reveal enthralling glimpses of prehistoric man, the Iron Age *castros*, the widespread and powerful presence of Romans, of Visigoths and Moors.

The remains of old civilizations are coming to light in every neighbourhood. Few have the impact of the Roman settlement of Conímbriga, near Coimbra, the magic of the temple to Diana in Évora, the interest of Milreu in Estói, Cetóbriga on the Tróia peninsula and Miróbriga at Santiago do Cacém, but no tourist leaflet is now complete without its local *castro* – fortified town, archaeological site or necropolis.

In the Baixo Alentejo two Portuguese archaeologists, Manuel and Maria Maia, have discovered evidence of civilizations from the Bronze Age to the Romans close to the Neves Corvo copper and pyrite mines near Castro Verde (*castro* in the south is more likely to mean a Roman camp). About 500 BC, when the Celtic Lusitanians were established in the rugged Beiras, this southern area of Portugal and all Andalusia belonged to a farming and mining people, the Tartessians. One school of thought pronounces the Tartessians to be the same as the Turdetanians, a name with an undeniable ring to it. A highlight of the Maias' many discoveries is a stone inscribed with the Turdetanian alphabet, or numbers, the first found in the Iberian peninsula. Turdetania was also where Portugal's national hero, Viriato, in about 147 BC first found renown as a warrior, beating the forces of the Roman governor, Vetilius.

War, invasion, and the fear of it changed the land. Each king, even the Spanish kings of Portugal, gave much thought to the nation's defences, and built. Wellington's Lines of Torres Vedras are there, too, already hard to discern – not nearly as visible, in the end, as the *minifúndios*, the small farms of the Minho, carved out by Swabians, the Moors' heritage in the Algarve or the great estates, the *latifúndios*, that were the rewards of Reconquest in the Alentejo. Not every change or renovation was felicitous. In the small Alentejo town of Pavia, one of the largest dolmens in Portugal was metamorphosed in medieval times by the determinedly devout into a rock chapel, the Capela de São Dinis, possibly by Italians who lived there in the thirteenth century and gave the town its name. Inside – the key is kept in the café in the square – on an altar faced with blue seventeenth-century *azulejos* stands a blank-faced madonna figurine in a wine-red robe. It is a curiosity, no more, an odd-looking symbol of contrasting convictions, the source – perhaps – of the common Portuguese saying: '*Roma e Pavia não se fizeram num dia*' ('Rome and Pavia were not built in a day').

Passing time softens the crude and obtrusive, enhances the graceful and adds the pleasing patina of history. The churches and monasteries which withstood the Great Earthquake of 1755 and those that were built in its ashes stood firm even when Pombal expelled the Jesuits and the anticlericals of 1834 banished all Church authority, dissolved the monastic orders and seized their property. Many convents and monasteries are still in use – as barracks, schools, colleges, *pousadas* and elegant business establishments. A Douro monastery passed from Benedictine monks to Cistercians, was closed by Pombal, reopened by Queen Maria I, closed again and sold by the Liberals to a wine-maker; it now belongs to a French champagne firm.

Among the most substantial of recent restorations and conversions is the Mosteiro de Refoios, close to Ponte de Lima. The twelfth-century monastery, remodelled in the sixteenth century – the 1581 plan still exists – and later renovated, is to be an agricultural college, the Escola Superior Agrária, totally modern in its science, entirely in harmony with its setting. The architect, Fernando Távora, a professor at the University of Oporto, also designed the conversion to a splendid *pousada* on a Guimarães hillside of the vast Santa Marinha da Costa monastery.

The skilful adaptation of classical structures should, ideally, be linked to a close control of all construction and to sound land use. In Portugal, nearly everywhere, this is no more than an ideal. In 1989, Nuno Teotónio Pereira, an architect and president of the Associação dos Arquitectos Portugueses (AAP), stated that urban anarchy was reaching catastrophic levels – degraded building, clandestine *bairros*, haphazard construction on city outskirts. The solution, he suggested, lay in improved legislation. Or, of course, in a greater respect for existing legislation. Portugal had no lack of qualified architects – the AAP has 4,000 members, several of international eminence – but there is a fierce conflict between the struggle for survival of ordinary people and the need for imaginative solutions to the problems of sudden growth, balancing the merits of the past with the requirements of the future. The Tavira *Câmara* in the Algarve, concerned for the singular architecture of its historic centre, published a *Guia do Construtor* ('A Builder's Guide'), but around 180 *Câmaras*, the AAP noted, did not employ an architect and many more followed no plan. Developers' greed, the promises of tourism and rapidly expanding industry magnify a national dilemma.

A greater dilemma would be no growth at all. Now the money is flowing and the banks themselves have commissioned some of the most conspicuous new buildings. Several have won prizes for their architects, notably Álvaro Siza Vieira, who is responsible for the reshaping of the burned Chiado area of Lisbon. But too many new buildings are intrusive elements in ancient city centres. A more assiduous watchdog than the institute which is charged with protecting Portugal's heritage is the Duke of Bragança; well before Prince Charles began to speak out against aggressive architecture in England, the duke, a mere pretender who will inherit no throne, his aim narrowed on buildings that disfigure the culture of ages, was fiercely attacking Portugal's *monstruosidades*.

The Algarve, since so many tourists holiday here, is the focus of much criticism. Foreign travel writers, among others, become querulous over the excessive building, even as they cheerfully promote the slicker developments that got in first. Concerned Portuguese are ruder still about the errors made and the lack of foresight. The beanstalk towns – Quarteira, Portimão and Praia da Rocha, Armação de Pera and Albufeira – are, in the terminology of the government, with the infrastructure and the eggs of the golden goose in mind, 'zones of controlled growth'. By 1990 the Algarve had a plan (PROTAL), itself a fresh issue.

I can still, in this changing Algarve, become rapturous – over the olives, soaked in brine and herbs, and the delectable dried figs my neighbours give me, over the outburst of almond blossom in January, the pink cistus blooms and shimmering bee orchids in March, the honeysuckle and wild irises of April, the blooms and subtle grasses of the hot, dry summer, the sprawling, scented garden that I have made, the great old olive tree that tickles the roof tiles with its laden branches in October, the roses that bloom in December, the view – emblazoned by heavenly sunsets – across farm fields to the Atlantic.

Behind me are the rugged boulders and thickets of wild shrubs of the *barrocal*, the limestone hills that separate the *litoral* of the

coast from the high *serras*; on either side orchards of almonds and
figs, purple-black and leafy green, guarded by gnarled evergreen
carobs, each so obligingly fruitful and so astonishingly dissimilar.
The blossoming almond tree inspires poets with its vision of massed
flowers – but try and find a flower on the fig. And Adam and Eve
notwithstanding, it is the carob that is 'the tree of life'. From its
tiny yellow pistils grow long dark pods, wizened beans that were
the biblical 'husks the swines did eat' and which sustained John the
Baptist in his forty days and nights in the desert; to the Portuguese
the carob is the *pão de São João*, St John's bread. It is slow-growing
and resistant to drought, and yields a greater harvest of food than
any other wild tree; it has well over thirty uses. From the tiny
seeds, so consistent in size that they were the original *qirats* or
carats still used as a measure of weight, come stabilizing oils. The
chocolate-cum-date-flavoured bean, rich in vitamins, minerals and
proteins, low in fat, is widely used in modern health foods. A
traditional nourishing feed for livestock, it also fed Wellington's
cavalry in the Peninsular War.

Where I live, history is no more than an arm's length away: the
walls of this house, half a metre thick, were built from hand-hewn
stone two hundred years ago. And although there is a giant cement
factory a few miles away, there are still people in the neighbourhood
with archaic skills, artisans who craft the Algarve's vivid country
carts and others who make the gaudy trappings for the mules and
donkeys that draw them, farmers who work their land in the
ancient ways. I know the sheep must be here when I hear a certain
rustle, a steady munching across – and on – the drystone walls.
The shepherd nods and smiles to me, whistles and grunts to his
sheep, and ambles on, stick in hand, a cotton bag over his shoulder.
Only his shaggy dog, Pirata, pauses for a greeting. But I can hear
the strident buzz of a mini-tractor across the land, and the impatient
blasting of the baker's van on his early morning rounds has driven
out the musical fluting of our local knifegrinder; new buildings dot
the hills.

The Algarve has always been at variance with itself, more Mediterranean than Atlantic, as much African as European, its Islamic
heritage visible in a Christian society. It is altogether, in its 5,000

square kilometres, a contradictory cosmos. In the east, the leeward
Sotavento, between the Guadiana river, frontier with Spain, and
Faro, lies a land of salt-flats and marsh, of lagoons and islands and
beguiling, glowing beaches, the bird-rich area contained within
the Parque Natural da Ria Formosa. Near Portimão – the Romans'
Portus Hannibalis and now a major port – the land curves, rises,
flows, the long beaches rimmed with red sandstone cliffs alternating
with pirates' coves. Further west, after Lagos and Sagres, on a wild
and exhilarating coast – protected by law – the Atlantic overpowers
the land, allowing a scattering of trees in hidden valleys tucked
between high windswept cliffs. Inland from those three Algarves is
a fourth: a hardy area of chilly mountains where moonshiners
distill *medronho*, of small farms, pine forest, terraced plantations of
eucalyptus. Up at Monchique, on the peaks of Foia and Picota, the
view reaches across a boundless sky to the Alentejo, condemned, in
the words of traveller Antero de Figueiredo, 'by the retreating
gods of Islam to be a hell of burning thirst', and down to
'the cobalt sea lapping African sands'. The Moors were here,
and medieval armies, but not yet the mightier armies of mass
tourism.

Life is becoming faster – some say richer. The standard of living
is rising, along with expectations, but not every *algarvio* wants to
live in the fast lane – or have one in his backyard. In the planning
of the Via Infante de Sagres linking the new bridge across the
Guadiana to the western Algarve, farmers' concern over the ex-
propriation of good agricultural land was largely ignored, as were
environmental considerations. New roads stretch down and across
the map; congested pressure points are relieved like Mafeking.
New expressways slice through mountains. But when the prime
minister, Cavaco Silva, made a visit to the north-eastern Trás-
os-Montes judiciously timed to coincide with the opening of a new
stretch of highway, journalists remarked on the absence of rejoicing.
Few of the region's farmers had benefited from EEC funds.
'Ministers, prime ministers, have been here before,' remarked a
transmontano, 'and the people have work to do.'

Travellers who venture into the Trás-os-Montes and explore its
broad plateaux and deep river valleys often emerge as if from a

mystical experience, from a journey over the rainbow into magic lands or the Middle Ages. They are bemused in a time warp, lost to reality, intimidated by the wild splendour of nature, charmed by the down-to-earth and hospitable people. Journey over, they return (with a little reluctance) to the twentieth century. It is, in truth, a place of marvels and social oddities. A system of communal life was once common in pastoral hamlets. One of them, Rio de Onor, survives, with a foot in Portugal and another in Spain, its own unanimity more crucial than any law of Lisbon or Madrid; it is the home of forty or so families who live peacefully by ancient rules of collective ownership, which existed long before Communism and look fair to outlive it.

Close to the granite canyon of the international Douro – here the river is a daunting frontier with Spain and supports eighty species of birds, half of them migratory – I have seen griffon and Egyptian vultures, rare black storks and golden eagles. In a Trás- os- Montes town I met a man with a pet wolf called Diana. Wolves are no longer numerous – 'but we hear them from time to time,' I was told. 'They are out there.'

In that isolated north-east corner of Portugal towns are few, communications poor, and the villages, tucked above an unseen river, are little changed by time. In one of them, Lagoaça, I met Júlia and António Rodrigues. Their children grown up and gone to the cities and skilled jobs, they run a small café-bar in a street of ancient stone houses, where mules are stabled downstairs and families live in small, neat rooms above, an entirely practical *transmontano* custom. 'Our central-heating,' a woman said, patting her placid mule. The Rodrigues grow most of their own food. Almonds, olives and figs do well in the microclimate of the valley; on the plateaux, winter is cold and hostile. Júlia makes cheeses, even her own soap. She crochets beautiful bedspreads, a celebrated local industry, but does not sell them. Her husband simply says: 'We don't need the money. We have all we need.'

The terrain is stark, the villages remote. People live off scraps of land. They have every right to be miserable. Instead, they are stoutly independent. I asked about a local medical service – and, sitting by Júlia's fire on a cold, wet May day, I met her neighbour,

Dona Amélia, a bent, eighty-two-year-old widow with a low, lilting voice and a memory for poetry. Like many such women, Júlia had said, she was skilled in herbal remedies – but *orações* (orations, or prayers) were part of the cure. Dona Amélia told me her recipe for repelling bad spirits: nine grains each of rye and salt, nine drops of olive oil, a pinch of incense – and an *oração*. For the common cold at least five herbs help. Sick with love? Softly, the old lady recited a poem on the five senses that would move any heart.

'They call me a *bruxa*,' she said. A witch. It is an honoured occupation in rural Portugal and Dona Amélia herself – whom others might call a *curandeira*, a healer – was an esteemed lady from a large and respectable family. One day I met other members of the family harvesting their wheat. Everyone who can takes part; even the aged Dona Amélia was there. The small farms and fragmented ownership are a historical problem that impedes mechanization. I watched more than a dozen people working non-stop to load a modern thresher, bag the grain, and sift the chaff from the straw. The wheat had been cut by hand and brought to the hired machine.

Yet the isolated Trás-os-Montes is changing, too. A first phase of investments in the *sector agrícola* involving more than Esc.13bn was completed in 1989; a second, seven-year phase, supported by the World Bank, began in 1990: rural development to a value of Esc.90bn, about £360m. Long overdue in terms of social progress, it is sure to be bad for magic.

Huge sums of money are being ploughed into the land but what this transforming fertilizer will actually achieve is the big question. Reform, to historians, is nothing new and is often damaging. By the Civil Code of 1867, by which two thirds of a property had to be shared equally among heirs, farms were divided into even smaller pieces. A Bill of Rural Development was proposed by none other than the liberal historian Oliveira Martins, and ignored. In a later era, Salazar applied inappropriate measures, supported the *latifúndios* and ignored the aspirations and needs of the small farmer. Through the years, agriculture tottered and the poor stayed poor – close on 50 per cent of all farm holdings are less than one hectare. Equally, the rich get richer. A study made in 1954 showed that of the tiny 0.3 per cent of holdings larger than 200 hectares were the estates of four landowners who, between them, owned 235,000 acres. Two were the Duke of Palmela and the Duke of Cadaval – still listed, long after the 1974 revolution, in the top cluster of wealthy landowners. In 1990, a survey of the flat, fertile Tejo valley of Lezíria, one of three subzones of the Ribatejo, showed that a minuscule 3.2 per cent of farm properties covered 49.5 per cent of the total area. The largest, the state-owned Companhia das Lezírias, once a royal gift, was heading for privatization and, in association with private investors, a mixed-farm development that would include *turismo rural* – hunting, golf and other leisure activities, perhaps a safari park.

As the 1980s ended, agriculture, together with forestry and fishing, was still contributing under 10 per cent to the gross domestic product. Almost a quarter of Portuguese workers were farmers, more than half of them over fifty-five years old, over a third illiterate. Just over 51 per cent of the territory is agricultural land. Portugal, as well as importing 70 per cent of all its energy, was importing close on half its food, and much of what Portuguese did grow, because of poor soil, quirks of climate and outdated methods, cost far more than EEC prices and gave far lower yields. Yet not all was gloom.

With accession to the EEC in 1986, Portugal won, as well as huge development funds, a special grant of 700 ecus (some $850m) to restructure agriculture, and a ten-year leeway on tariffs and prices on most agricultural products. (Wine and olive oil were among products allotted less time to meet EEC obligations.) Within three years, investment in agriculture shot up 700 per cent, much of it in the fertile Ribatejo and Estremadura in the west. Projects by the thousand were proposed to finance institutes and funds and were accepted. Attitudes were suddenly positive, farmers, and their better-educated children, alert to possibilities. In sixteen municipalities of the Alto Alentejo, among them Elvas, Estremoz, Borba and Vila Viçosa, 450 olive cultivators formed an association to replant 12,000 hectares of olive trees, which meant hauling out old olives, two million of them, installing irrigation systems, and replanting to EEC higher-density strictures. The target: 2,000 kg a hectare in the third year, 4,000 kg in the fifth year, against 800 to 900 kg for the traditional plantations. But for each 2.6 hectares cleared, only one hectare of new olives would be planted, leaving land free for other uses while maintaining the same level of olive production.

Portugal produces 40,000 tonnes of olive oil a year – of which the Portuguese themselves consume all but a fraction in their cooking and in the canning of sardines and tuna. The calculations are sound, reality less tidy. Trees are generous in some years, unfruitful in others. The green and tasty oil that I use, for example, comes mainly from one large, fickle tree. The olives are pressed in November in the local factory – which charges nothing but keeps a proportion of the oil. The first pressing is virgin, pure, fine, light-weight. From the second pressing comes the smooth, slightly heavier, oil that most Portuguese use for cooking.

Ripping out ancient groves of benign, silvery olive trees as if they were so many matchsticks was a wrenching prospect. The dynamics of EEC membership, the radical changes demanded in the name of agribusiness, competition and intensification were daunting. It seemed to me that this lovely land was being vandalized. Yet urged on, advised and educated by government – on the television, in the press, in educational courses, in fairs, in workshops and seminars – many thousands of Portuguese farmers and technicians have accepted the EEC conditions, subsidies and challenge.

They are examining the soil and selecting crops with a new eye to market needs and prices. They are heeding the call for quality as well as quantity. They follow advice, not the ways of the past, on pesticides and nutrients, and are dutifully watchful of hygiene, the proper care of livestock, the niceties, the regulations. They are acquiring advanced machinery, erecting greenhouses, experimenting with seeds and new biological techniques, switching crops, organizing, reorganizing, planting, harvesting, marketing. And all of it, at times, for nothing. The Portuguese climate is fickle: a sudden tempest, an unforgiving rain, weeks of blistering sun, are enemies no farmer can fight.

Consolation comes with a record year – in 1989 the yield per hectare of wheat, in all 600,000 tonnes, was up by 28 per cent. (The eastern Alentejo was still the prime bread basket; Beja – where temperatures are the highest in Portugal in summer – produces around a third of the national crop.) Oats, rye and barley were up, too – and in Canada, a variety of barley developed by the Estação Nacional de Melhoramento de Plantas, a plant improvement station in Elvas, won an international contest. Although Portugal expects to be importing cereals and vegetable oils for some time yet, there are new sights to be seen on the land – broad swathes of sunflowers and, for years a profitable import for re-export, the soya bean. How different the Alentejo looks now from when the nineteen-year-old Fernando Pessoa, the poet, just returned from South Africa and writing in English, saw it from a train in 1907:

> Nothing with nothing around it
> And a few trees in between
> None of which are very clearly green,
> Where no river or flower pays a visit.
> If there be a hell, I've found it,
> For if it ain't here, where the Devil is it?

Revolution, usually equated in Portugal with the Captains' coup of 1974, has new meanings. What is happening on agricultural land is revolutionary. Methods and mentalities have been revolutionized. Suddenly farmers are younger, technically educated, ambitious and growing in number. By 1990 there were, as well as agricultural schools and colleges, over forty education centres providing agricultural training (*formação profissional*) to 17,000 youngsters at a time, women as well as men. The women you usually see in the fields are stooped and bulky in brimmed hats and overalls over long sleeves and trousers. The winner of the Young Farmer of the Year contest in 1989 was a woman, twenty-four-year-old Maria João Festas. Where not long ago foreigners were startling their Alentejo neighbours with crops of Iceberg lettuces, no Portuguese farmer is now surprised at anything.

Reconversion programmes do not mean overnight transformation. Bureaucracy remains cumbersome and the harsh realities of marketing provoke simmering resentment and, again and again, explosions of anger. The fruit-growers of the west, bitter that imported fruit is distributed where theirs rots on the trees because prices will not cover the labour of picking, have blocked the roads with their tractors. Rice growers from the Baixo Mondego and the Sado estuary have demanded in vain that rice imports be suspended; Portugal is the third biggest producer of rice in Europe – at costs ten times as high. On the 300 or so cooperatives farming, with variable success, some 360,000 hectares, the days of absentee landlords are long gone but polemic continues and farmers worry over reform laws and the effects of returned expropriated land, as well as the standard farmers' grumbles over weather, slow credits, long hours, low income.

> *Vi tantas águas, vi tanta verdura,*
> *As aves todas cantavam d'amores . . .*
>
> I saw such waters, such greenery,
> All the birds were singing of love.

The words, from a sixteenth-century sonnet by the Portuguese poet, Francisco Sá de Miranda, are as true now of the far north as they were on that distant day when he wrote them. In the cool, well-watered valleys of Portugal's oldest and most intensively cultivated lands of the vine, the region of *vinho verde*, narrow roads become avenues lined with green curtains where tree supports are still in use. Small fields are edged with vines in other traditional ways. In numberless smallholdings is squeezed a large population of some two million, the densest level in Portugal. For over 150,000, viticulture, making wine, is business as well as pleasure. For some of them, the old ways of granite fermentation tanks in ancient timbered cellars are not yet over. But *vinho verde*, too, is changing, from an inconsequential summer drink (a disparaging friend of mine calls it cabbage water with needles) to, at its best, an all-year-round ambrosia.

The name *vinho verde* comes, it is believed, from the ever-green landscape – even wine producers are not certain. It is known that the Romans made wine here. In 1509, the chronicler João de

Barros wrote the two magic words together, but gives no clue to his meaning. That the region, just under 10 per cent of continental Portugal, is green and beautiful is due to the natural laws of geography and climate – the rainfall, between 1,500 and 2,000 mm a year, is the most abundant in Portugal.

Vinho verde, a light and refreshing drink, is not green wine but white or red – *verde branco* or *verde tinto*. The grapes which make it are fully matured. The taste is dry, with infinite shadings. That famous fizz, the cheeky piquancy, is not added, but already there – wine buffs call it *pétillance*, Portuguese wine-makers *agulha*. The name *vinho verde*, the region demarcated in 1908, is a registered Denomination of Origin; a rare collective, and protective, description. Production is carefully regulated. And though, in the verdant north, it seems as if tall vines adorn every cottage, surround every field, line every road and byway, *vinho verde* does not, as an appealing promotion had it, grow on trees. Modern techniques mean low vine supports – and a whole new generation of quality wine.

On the smallholdings, every inch of granite-based soil is valued and well manured – the brown-eyed oxen of the north with their beautiful carved yokes have uses that go beyond ploughing the land and pulling carts. Around each house, in tidy rows and patches, grow homely vegetables – beans, cabbages, corn, onions, potatoes. Almost every house has its chickens and chained dogs, its pots of cheerful flowers. Framing all is the *ramada*, the bower of vines which provides shade in summer and *vinho verde* at the day's end. All growers value the cool and pretty bower – but new times demand new methods. In vineyards across the region vines stretch along wires from cordon posts and *cruzetas*, church-like crosses some six feet high. In the spaces between and underneath a tractor can pass with ease. Ladders are no longer needed for pruning, spraying, training, tying or harvesting.

Among the expanding range, *vinho verde* made by single-*quinta* producers – estate-made wine – is notable. Members of the Association of Producers and Bottlers of Vinho Verde may produce wine only from grapes of their own production. They cannot buy from anyone else, as bulk producers do. And they must bottle their own – meaning they must have their own winery. The result is that each makes limited quantities with individual characteristics pleasing to the connoisseur.

Scintillating with character, too, are the growers and their estates. They include white-haired Dona Hermínia Paes, owner of the neo-classical nineteenth-century Palácio da Brejoeira at Monção, set in forested parkland with a hidden grotto, well-tended gardens and exemplary vineyards. Near the shining tanks of her modern winery, bottles with Brejoeira's renowned *vinho verde* were being filled as I watched. The wine Dona Hermínia produces from a single grape variety, Alvarinho, is the classiest and most costly of all *vinho verdes*. But if the Brejoeira label is exclusive, the grape is not. Alvarinho is also made by other wine-makers like the Adega Cooperativa Regional de Monção – whose city charter, conceded by King Afonso III in 1261, specifically mentions nobly made wine. International fame came early: Minho wine initiated Portugal's centuries-old wine trade with England.

Members of the association are concentrating on their white *vinho verde*, looking to export markets and the potential of a wide-open and competitive Europe. The labels on the slender bottles show their origin – elegant manor-houses, ancient ancestral homes, some open to paying guests. One of these is the Paço d'Anha, close to Viana do Castelo, which has been in the same family since 1503; as in many such houses built around, beside or over their wineries, its living-rooms are up a stairway, the winery at ground level – and the family chapel beside the driveway. Among other outstanding country houses is the Casa de Sezim with its majestic gateway and remarkable wallpapers gaily painted (by J. Zuber of Alsace) with nineteenth-century views of America. The property dates to 1375 and is the home of the former ambassador António Pinto de Mesquita and his wife Maria Francisca; he is the twenty-second owner in a direct family line. Their son, José Paulo, is *administrador* of the vineyard, the wine among those highly praised at tastings.

Wine-making techniques vary from *quinta* to *quinta* – in the gleaming winery at the Solar das Bouças in Amares, 500 litres are pumped from one tank to another in two minutes; the sophisticated cooling system goes to $-25°$ centigrade (fermentation temperature should never exceed $18–20°$ C) and uses more electricity than the rest of the village put together. Elsewhere, the tanks are kept cool by the naturally cold water from *quinta* wells.

Red *vinho verde* is also produced – in the past well over half the annual production was red – and arouses a good deal of curiosity. A leading enologist, Bento de Carvalho, attended a tasting with foreign enologists which included red *vinho verdes*. 'They couldn't understand it at all,' he laughed, 'but after the tasting I took them to a hearty dinner. Over the food, they tried it again. No, I can't say they instantly liked it but now they understood it. Unlike a good white, the *tinto* cannot be tasted in isolation. But in our business we are very lucky: we can talk about wine over wine.'

Across the country on St Martin's day, 11 November, the year's new wines are tasted and, if pleasing, tasted again and again. At Golegã, Portuguese enthusiasm for fine horses and for wine – from classy flavours to the rough *agua pé*, literally foot water, traditionally accompanied by roasted chestnuts – is spectacularly blended at the annual horse fair.

Up in the north the joy of wine never fades. In the Alto Minho they say: 'I want in my house all that will fit into it, as much land as I can see, and as much wine as I can drink.' The Portuguese, who are close to the head of the list in world per capita consumption, rarely touch any wine but their own. That still leaves a lot of wine: Portugal, through its wine-making skills, had become by 1988 the seventh biggest producer in the world. As well as the familiar classics, new names, not all of them from an established *região demarcada*, were catching world attention. Wine fanciers familiar with Bairrada and Dão were looking with new enthusiasm at the table wines from the Douro, the *zonas vitícolas* like Cartaxo and Tomar in the Ribatejo, and the quality Alentejo wines from Reguengos, Borba, Redondo, Vidigueira and Portalegre. Portugal's wines, made largely from indigenous grape varieties, have always been distinctive. Suddenly the awkward initials VQPRD mattered dreadfully: they stood for *Vinhos de Qualidade Produzidos em Regiões Determinadas* (quality wines produced in demarcated regions), twenty-eight of them areas newly 'determined', the new prestige word, by EEC regulations, operating through the Instituto da Vinha e do Vinho, which controls grape variety, vineyards and the wine produced.

On Portugal's 350,000 or so hectares of vineyards, providing one fifth of the gross agricultural national product and on which a quarter of all active agriculturalists work, great changes are taking place. First, up to 10,000 hectares are being taken out of production, mainly fertile land in the Ribatejo and the west, the compensation so enticing that a number of *camponeses* had to be restrained from heedlessly hauling out quality vines. Another 30,000 hectares, 20,000 of them in demarcated regions, are being restructured in a nine-year conversion and renewal programme ending in 1996 (when the EEC transition period for Portugal's agriculture ends). This means not only that new selected vines are being planted, in areas where new plantings have been forbidden for many years, but that whole Douro valley hillsides are changing shape. The Portuguese are undergoing a fiercely competitive reordering of an ancient commerce. The latest technologies are being applied. Port-wine makers, with centuries of experience, have something of a head start.

After a port-wine tasting, a wine writer, Oz Clarke, wrote in lavish praise of a Graham 1955 vintage: 'Wonderful year, wonderful wine – it was as dark and chewy as Harrogate toffee, as sweet as brown sugar, perfumed with mint and roughened up by pepper. That's what vintage port is all about.' To me, vintage port is about sturdy vines adorning the great steps of the terraces on the dizzyingly high banks of the River Douro, about the renowned *quintas* – graceful, comfortable, inescapably romantic – about the generations of people who have shaped the hills, who harvest the grapes, who apply knowledge and experience and nose in the blending, and who nurture the wine to maturity in dark, humid warehouses, the lodges of Vila Nova de Gaia. Vintage port is schistose soil and a contrary climate that can switch from hot, intense sun to chilling rain. I have seen snow on the high lands and I have sweated in the valleys: the Douro valley, experts say, is a zone with a Mediterranean ecology. Port is about the River Douro, born in Spain, forming a 37,000 square-mile basin that is Iberia's largest, a quick-silver waterway winding and thrusting its way down to Oporto and the Atlantic.

Port can be the noble vintages that appear perhaps three times in a decade, 'wood' ports aged in casks, tawnies, rubies, an aperitif white. The quantity made, stored and sold, as well as quality, is regulated by the Port Wine Institute in Oporto. No wine is more strictly controlled. Portugal's 1988 exports exceeded 70m litres (in port shippers' parlance this was close on 135,000 pipes, each pipe 534 litres) and earned nearly Esc.35,000m, about $230bn.

Life in the lodges seems leisurely, a matter of waiting, watching, tasting and blending. But in the vineyards each year at harvest-time – *vindima* – the calm breaks. Grape-pickers, mainly women and girls, dot the slopes. Stocky young men, proud of their strength, carry the 50 kg (110 lb) baskets of grapes along the steep terraces.

Inside the cool winery at Taylor's upriver *quinta*, Vargellas – which has its own riverside railway station – barefoot men tread the grapes in *lagares* (open tanks). There is a holding of breath, a drama, at the *corta*, the first cut, or crushing of the grapes. The men, their thighs ghostly white in contrast with brown faces and arms and the rich purple of the must, raise knees high in rhythm. Gradually, they speed their pace. An accordionist eases the task. After dark grape-pickers come to watch and to dance, usually with each other. Vargellas is an eminent *quinta*, maker of famous vintages. The scene is echoed at Ferreira's Quinta do Porto at Pinhão and other illustrious *quintas*. But up in the hills in ancient wineries the treaders tread without music or female company, carefully supervised by each buying company's technician. Obliged by law, the *Lei do Terço*, to hold in stock twice the quantity of wine that they actually sell, the major firms buy from small wine-cellars. Fortunes depend on this three-week *vindima*.

All shippers aim for wine with concentration and body; each has a different technique for achieving it. Alistair Robertson of Taylor's believes the foot cannot be beaten for extracting vital colour, but his company has also been experimenting with fermentation vats. At the large and impressive winery of Seagram-owned Sandeman near Régua, gleaming auto-vinificators process every grape; Sandeman, with other large wineries, handles a considerable share of the harvest.

Multinationals, since the 1970s, are a powerful presence in port, but the regulations since EEC entry permit qualified individual enterprise. Small family firms, like the Bergqvists of Quinta de la Rosa who used to sell their grapes to Sandeman, now market a single-*quinta* port under their own label in the manner of French châteaux. Controls remain rigid. In 1990 the state, contrary to EEC regulations, still held its profitable monopoly on *aguardente*, the grape brandy used in the making of port to arrest fermentation. Liberalization began only in 1991.

The story of port began in the late seventeenth century when the first British wine buyers explored the Douro, staying in inns that were vile and full of fleas. Stretching across time, it continues to unfold. In Vila Nova de Gaia, in the dusty cellars of Ferreira's lodge, I had the honour of tasting a full-bodied port wine bottled in 1863, a century before the arrival of gleaming metal tanks, high-tech temperature controls or the EEC.

'We used to give the pickers straw to sleep on,' a retired shipper in his eighties told me, describing the changes he had seen. The changes are coming faster now, in social conditions, wine-making techniques and in the River Douro itself. Once dangerous and fierce, the Douro, now tamed by dams, is the greatest single provider to Portugal of hydroelectric energy. In the waters of the 136 km (75 mile) gorge dividing Spain from Portugal I have seen fishermen in wooden boats rowing, long oars crossed, facing forwards from old fears and from habit. Downriver, sailing-boats and windsurfers skim the water like flocks of birds. Near Vargellas, Alistair Robertson and his vivacious wife, Gilly, are adept water-skiers. But the river, now navigable to its full length in Portugal, is opening up to new traffic.

Navigability of the Douro is not a new idea. Philip II of Spain, when he grabbed Portugal in 1580, had his eye on the Atlantic. The notion faded when the Portuguese snatched their country back in 1640. In modern times navigability became an issue, furiously debated by one government after another. Finally, a decision was made: there would be a navigable Douro up to the frontier with Spain. Daniel Pinto da Silva, a Douro man born in Régua, a hydraulics engineer for Electricidade de Portugal (EDP), knows the river from childhood, before any dams had been built, and he has devoted his life to it, in the last few years bearing the title of project coordinator. EDP wanted energy and there are eight dams, three of them at the frontier, to provide it. But more than thirty years ago EDP engineers had a dream, a vision of an open waterway. Each of the five dams in Portugal has a lock, with hydraulics designed by Pinto da Silva, to lift and lower Europe's standard barges along the Douro's length. The lock he designed at Carrapatelo, 35 m (114 ft) high, is the tallest in the Western world. Between Oporto and Barca de Alva 210 km (130 miles) of waterway are open. In the Trás-os-Montes are buried sizeable deposits of iron ore. Coal, granite and timber lie close to the river. Dredgers are at work, clearing the shallows. River ports and piers are under construction; some are complete. At Oporto, whose main port for decades has been north of the city at increasingly saturated Leixões, surgery is restraining the shifting mass of the huge sand bar at the Douro's mouth that was a hazard even before Crusaders sailed into the river in 1147. Other solutions for safe passage and the harbouring of ships are under study. Spain, building a river port at Véga de Terrón, watches closely, as the dream of a waterway to the west becomes reality.

Spanning the Douro at Oporto a new rail bridge will replace Eiffel's sturdy lace structure and new high speed trains will run on it. In Aveiro, in the estuary of the River Vouga south of the misty lagoon of the swan-necked sailing *moliceiros*, the port is expanding: a new dock, a container terminal, longer quays, are transforming a trading post used by the Phoenicians into Portugal's third largest port (after Lisbon and Oporto). New dams provide energy in the north, irrigation projects multiply in the Beira interior and Alentejo – only about one seventh of the agricultural land is irrigated – and water-supply systems surge. In the south, new dams will help resolve a perennial water shortage: where I live, a colossal drill, with my neighbour Fernanda fervently praying on her knees beside it, thunderously bored 168 metres – over 500 feet – before striking water. And I was lucky; many holes are dry. Algarve tourism consumes torrents of water. Vale do Lobo has boasted, as an 'interesting fact' about its golf course – one of nine along the coast, with more to come – that it 'takes two million gallons of water daily to keep the greens green'. Fernanda and her husband José and many thousands of rural and scattered houses like theirs exist on the rainwater that fills their cisterns, only calling on the fire brigade to deliver extra water in dire emergency.

Natural gas, from a terminal at Setúbal, will flow to Lisbon (in 1990 the only city with piped gas) and in a network of ducts to eight 'strategic zones' up to Braga and across Portugal. In Lisbon, besides a reconstructed Chiado, a dozen new hotels and vast commercial complexes, architects have plans for a second bridge over the Tejo, for a south-bank mole and artificial islands that will narrow the river mouth; they intend to restore the midriver Bugio tower, a thumb in a ring of stone, to its seventeenth-century setting as guardian of the southern shore – Outra Banda, as the *lisboetas* say, 'the other side' – and create a new south-bank city and port.

Some projects are virtually complete. Others await further studies and financing. Not every grand scheme will see the light of day, despite lavish investment and the outpourings of EEC money – at the end of 1989, tripling the amounts received, another 1300m contos of Community structural funds, around £5bn, was guaranteed over the next four years. Not since the gold of Brazil has Portugal seen such riches.

Unprecedented spending on public works is one thing, but the Portuguese are quick to mock grandiloquent failures, including their own – some of their lordliest buildings have never been finished: Batalha's elaborate exterior chapels stand open to the sky; miss the main entry to Ajuda palace above Belém and the next gap shows stark severed edges directly beside the classical courtyard. Parliament is among many imposing buildings that are permanently under construction or repair. So was the Memória church, in the Rua do Jardim Botânico below Ajuda palace, when I went there. Two workmen were eating their lunch in the empty nave. One unlocked the door to a side chapel which contained the tomb I had come to see. In a surprisingly small wooden box with iron claw feet on a carved marble base were the mortal remains of the Marquis of Pombal.

Pombal, in the eighteenth century, represented racing change. Since then there has been nothing quite like it in Portugal until now. The cautious conservatism of a God-fearing people whose daily life and food are bound to the land and the sea is as easily dismissed as that of the venerable old man in Camões's *Lusíadas* who stood on the shore crying doom as Vasco da Gama's ships prepared to sail. But as in that greatest of Portuguese endeavours, not everyone reaps the rewards of glory, some 40,000 Portuguese fishermen least of all.

So much sea, so few fish, is a refrain constantly repeated. With a coastline 840 km (522 miles) long and two archipelagos, the Açores and Madeira, Portugal has an exclusive economic zone twenty times larger than its national territory. But its 40,000 fishermen were handicapped by old, small boats – a few years ago half the 18,000 boats were twenty years or older and 85 per cent of them were 5-tonners or less. A decline in the catch that started in the sixties reached its nadir when the Portuguese in 1986 were virtually forced out of their historic north Atlantic cod-fishing ground. From then on, the only way the fishing graph could go was up.

The EEC agreed a transition period to 1996 and provided funds (800m ecus in the initial five years) for a programme of renovation, for new boats and new equipment designed to exploit the vast tract of the economic zone. New EEC agreements, notably those with Morocco and Mauritania, allowed rights in further waters, a rigorous system that Portuguese concerns stretched – as Spain's had done – by independently forming binational companies or bilateral accords. In the nature of intense competition, disputes arose – including a particularly bitter one with Canada, over cod. Community politics do not always coincide with Portuguese interests; the Portuguese will fight fiercely for their historic rights, for justice – and also for *bacalhau*. An increased cod quota in 1991 generated wide rejoicing.

The seaports and traditional ways of Portugal's ancient mariners are changing fast. The taciturn clam-diggers and oystermen of the Algarve Sotavento are very probably nurturing bivalves bred in a laboratory, the large and succulent oyster a flourishing descendant of the robust Portuguese oyster, which was renowned, before a decline in the 1970s, in France and England. Now, bypassing the mumble of the harbour auctioneer, fish auctions are computerized. Ports are being modernized. (Fishermen at Portimão no longer juggle nervelessly with full baskets of sardines, nor toss them to the quay.) There are new training courses in the ten seaport schools of the Escola Portuguesa de Pesca – the students, grumbling at all the theory they must learn, are no longer only the sons of fishermen but come from inland towns as well. Coincidence? A survey showed that over 80 per cent of Algarve fishermen, many of whom had started work at ten, hoped their own sons would take up other, more rewarding work.

The fishing industry, revived by heavy investment, is, however, facing the future with new confidence. By 1990 the secretary of state for fishing, counting up the new boats and completed projects, was proudly affirming Portugal as a fishing power in the Community. Traditionally, around 350,000 tonnes of fish are needed to supply the Portuguese alone, who consume considerable quantities not only of their beloved *bacalhau*, but also of the cheaper fish from a choice of over seventy other varieties. This means cheap shellfish like cockles and whelks, squid, sardines and horse mackerel, sea bream and bass, tunny from the Açores, scabbard fish from Madeira – fish charcoal-grilled, boiled, fried and stewed in steaming *caldeiradas*. The Portuguese are also still in the forefront of sardine canning. Sardines, twice the length you would imagine from the size of the standard tin, amount to about a third of the entire catch and are a conspicuous and valuable export.

How lovely the boats look as they turn to face the gentle breezes in a sunny harbour, or motor smoothly in and out of port. The fishermen in their woollen caps and sea rig are so rugged, so picturesque. Once, I went to sea with them, setting off late in the afternoon across the sand bar of the Douro aboard a sardine trawler from the fishing village of Afurada on the Gaia side of the river. It was no pleasure – the Atlantic mist chilled my bones, diesel fumes stirred my stomach, and the night-long blaring of the radio provoked a thumping headache. The great fishing-net went out again and again, rowed into a great circle by a single oarsman in his tiny boat across a black and heaving sea. Winching it back was a slow process and the catch poor – few, and measly, sardines. Oporto in the morning was a welcome sight.

Fishermen live with discomfort and danger each day of their lives. I watched the wives of the Afurada fishermen bring the men their dinner boxes and wait, quite still and in silence, as the boats set out. I knew why. In the ethnology museum in Oporto a verse in displayed on a wall:

> *Tudo que no mar embarca*
> *Tudo a barra do Porto vem*
> *Tudo vejo vira barra*
> *So o meu amor não vem.*
>
> Everyone who goes to sea
> Must cross the Oporto bar.
> I see them all returning;
> Only my love does not come.

Back in 1982 how we all laughed when the Ministry of Agriculture ordered that every cow and ox be issued with an identity card. It was, though, the beginning of a consistent attempt to regulate cattle sales, slaughter and milk production, never very high. It took the Dutch, mainly, to show what could be done. Encouraged by the initial absence of milk quotas in Portugal, Dutch farmers set up dairy herds in the Alentejo and Ribatejo. On their farms they keep fifty or more cows, usually Friesian. They produce annually upwards of 9,000 kg of milk per cow. The Portuguese have been producing an average of 3,500 kg. Altogether the amount of milk produced each year by cows in Portugal is around 1,300 million litres, about 1 per cent of EEC production. To the Portuguese it seemed quite enough: the per capita consumption of milk in Portugal is 60 per cent less than the European average. Only recently have children, and not all of them, been provided with milk at school. An older custom still prevails in the chilly north: sending them off to school warmed by a tot of strongly alcoholic *bagaceira*. There are well-managed Portuguese dairy farms – a Benavente couple called Barão Gomes, with four farmhands and an eye to genetics, health and feed, manage 300 generously productive cows. In the north, a group of some thirty dairy cooperatives supply the biggest milk-products cooperative, Agros. Four of the five largest cooperatives are built on dairy produce. By 1989 there were twelve cattle-auction areas, corrals in the centre and north of the country; the number of cattle auctioned had tripled over three years. Yet in 1990, when European Community dairy farmers owned an average of seventeen cows each, the average for Portuguese farmers was 3.88, a figure that patently lacked scope for dynamism.

Pigs, in Portugal, are big business. The Feira Nacional do Porco at Montijo on the south bank of the Tejo attracts some 130 exhibitors each September and about 50,000 visitors, who buy and eat the numerous assorted spicy sausages, suckling pig, various cuts of pork and – an Alentejo favourite – *pézinhos de coentrada*, coriander-flavoured trotters. The national pig and sausage fair, it is the biggest gathering in Iberia concentrating on pig breeding. The proper care of pigs and the hygienic disposal of their waste are much discussed basic issues. Regulations are rigid, sometimes broken. No festive slaughter, for instance, is permitted without government supervision; when one is approved, the joy is great. Guests are invited to watch the butchery, the draining of blood, singeing of the carcass and evisceration, a gory spectacle I have seen described on one occasion at least as a ritual with cultural objectives.

How soothing it is, driving through the midday heat of the Alentejo, to see flocks of sheep the colour of old piano keys dozing as still as boulders in the shade of the cork trees. Under another tree, a tousled dog beside him, the shepherd also snoozes. In winter, he is more conspicuous, more watchful, much more dashing in a sheepskin *pelico*; lacking only a white tie, it is an Alentejo rendering of a formal tailcoat. You are, though, rather more likely to see him in blue jeans and windcheater; perhaps even, on a wet day, in yellow oilskins. Near Serpa or Nisa he is involved in the making of an esteemed cheese. Or he works, perhaps, for an estate or in a cooperative able to adjust to circumstance; his life is uncomplicated. In the clouds of the Serra da Estrela, for all the saleability of the *serra* cheese, tending the family flocks makes no one rich. On the slopes of Arrábida, above the industrial town of Setúbal, the flocks survive thanks only to the dedication of a small number of traditionalists rallied around Quinta do Anjo in Palmela. Like the luscious rounds of Azeitão cheese of which they are the source, they are an endangered species. The pastoral life, it is clear, has fading appeal.

In the north the shepherds see themselves under siege – from wolves (predators are often, in fact, feral dogs), from the rigours of the climate and, an entirely modern threat, from the encroaching eucalyptus. Victory was theirs when the Constitutional Court in 1989 vetoed a controversial law, the *Lei dos Baldios*, which, by attempting to pass management of uncultivated land to local authorities, infringed the communal rights of ownership crucial to a humble shepherd and his flocks. Of all the possible uses for wasteland, plantations of the profitable, quick-growing eucalyptus were by far the likeliest.

Four paper-pulp companies, as the 1990s began, were producing 1.5m tonnes of short-fibre pulp, worth over $2bn to Portugal and much desired by makers of quality paper. State-controlled Portucel, with exports of 800 tonnes, headed the list of Portuguese exporters. Soporcel, the British Wiggins Teape group then its major shareholder, was the most highly capitalized company on the stock exchange and owned the largest pulp mill in Europe. Both were moving intensively into paper production. All four companies, including the much smaller Swedish-owned Celbi and British Caima, despite charges of pollution and the horrible stink emitted by the massive production plants, were considered a shining industrial success, earning Portugal around $2bn a year, or about 5 per cent of the gross domestic product. The minister for industry, Luís Mira Amaral, happily called the eucalyptus Portugal's 'green petroleum'. A drawback to the companies' continued growth is their overwhelming need for the basic material. Planting their own groves of eucalyptus, tall enough for felling in ten years, half the maturing time of a pine, seemed the long-term answer; Soporcel alone planned to expand its 30,000 ha of afforestation to 55,000 ha before 1992. Portucel's need is more than twice as big. The eucalyptus invasion, fiercely challenged by ecologists and Greens, has led to violent confrontation between GNR mounted troopers protecting newly planted saplings and angry villagers trying to haul them out.

The eucalyptus war, as the press called it, was as much about changing values as the changing landscape, the demands of aggressive economic growth against the kind of life, the look of the land, that the Portuguese desire. EEC subsidies for razed olive groves were an undoubted spur to rural rupture, but what will happen to the family, the question is asked, with its traditional *caseiro* economy, if farms with their patches of wheat, their olive, fig and cork trees, are swept away? 'Must we eat eucalyptus leaves?' demanded a *camponês* from Valpaços in the Trás-os-Montes, as hundreds of villagers marched towards the new plantation on its bleak hillside and the waiting GNR.

The eucalyptus, the tall Australian blue gum with its flaky bark, is accused of excessive consumption of water and soil nutrients, of the destruction of bird and wildlife habitats, of desertification of the terrain. Many of the rampaging fires that blacken and destroy enormous areas of the country each summer – in 1990 an astounding 32,354, according to the national fire brigade – are attributed to arson not unconnected with the cellulose companies' insatiable hunger for land (extending to the tiny Açores islands and more recently to the vastness of Angola). Put on the defensive, the companies argue that they are as concerned to prevent and to fight fires as anyone, that only poor soils are planted with eucalyptus and that good agricultural land is put to other uses like corn or wine. An ecologist, Fernando Pessoa, battling for the preservation of cultural roots, argues that the cellulose companies are reconstructing *latifúndios*. Soporcel owns more sheep than any shepherd and, like many other large landowning companies or cooperatives, is developing hunting schemes.

Emotions rise, tempers become heated, arguments over land use rage. President Mário Soares worried aloud about the rampaging eucalyptus. At the beginning of the 1990s, Portugal's forest area occupied over three million hectares, 34 per cent of the land, as compared with just over 50 per cent for agricultural use. (Technical studies suggested that, in terms of soil use, agriculture should be markedly reduced and forestry doubled.) The word *inculto*, or uncultivated, is used to describe 15 per cent of the land and includes 5.6 per cent for specified conservation zones – the Peneda-Gerês national park, sixteen mainland natural parks and reserves, and some half-dozen protected areas. The minute percentage left is listed as 'social'. Dismissing unease, the minister for agriculture, fisheries and food said in 1989, when the eucalyptus ranged over 14 per cent of forest land and 4 per cent of all Portugal, that the eucalyptus would never exceed 20 per cent of the forest area. This meant that it would remain at about half of the pine-forest figure – 43 per cent, mostly in some 1,200,000 ha along the Beira littoral and into the northern heart of Portugal – and soon catch up with the cork oak's 668,000 ha, a 22 per cent share. The acorn-rich holm oak, common in the Alentejo and Algarve, also grows, in wide sunny spaces, on nearly a fifth of forestry land.

An abundance of tall shade trees adorn Portugal, the parks of Lisbon, the northern roads where, far from the evergreens that patch my view, great chestnuts offer a true seasonal autumn. There is still wild woodland, even once-royal *tapadas* (hunting preserves), guarded by modern foresters, much of it what the Portuguese call *mata* or *matagal* (thicket). True forests are the old, bosky, richly variegated ones like the 'glorious Eden' of the Sintra hills and the Carmelite-planted Buçaco slopes, with tales to tell of hermits and hermitages, monks and monasteries, kings and war, adventure and passion – at Buçaco, before his banishment and exile, Portugal's last king, Dom Manuel II, knew the joys of young love (and the embarrassment of scandal) in the arms of a music-hall songstress. Rather more prosaically, forest officials look at forestry issues, figures, problems. And problems loom, they say, for the cork oak, among them the advanced age of many of the trees and also of the cork workers themselves.

In the roll of merit, the brash, lucrative eucalyptus has nothing on cork. Egyptians 3,000 years ago buoyed up their fishing nets with cork. The external fuel tank of *Columbia*, the United States' first successful space shuttle, was insulated with cork – cut, it was reported, from 225 Alentejo cork oaks. Marcel Proust lined with cork the room where he wrote in the Boulevard Haussmann in Paris. Jane Austen went to a school whose headmistress had an artificial cork leg. Corking baseball bats – it made them lighter – is part of American baseball lore. Many of the virtues of the evergreen cork oak were understood by ancient European communities who stripped its bark for the soles of sandals and for stoppers for their wine and water flasks. No synthetic product yet invented beats cork for versatility. Radioactive isotopes are transported in cork-lined capsules which can withstand heat of 800°C – and accidental drops of thirty feet. Cork is used in aircraft, for gaskets in the automobile industry, in the girders of buildings. It is in ventilation ducts and the air-conditioning systems of nuclear submarines. Sports enthusiasts use it for dartboards and decoy ducks, table-tennis bats and fishing-rod handles, in all sorts of balls. It is widely used in footwear and, treated and dyed, as a practical and handsome covering for walls and floors.

Cork is an insulator, against sound as well as heat. It is also watertight and non-toxic, and has no odour or taste – it is an unmatchable stopper for long-lived wines. Portugal turns out 30 million bottle corks a day, 500 million a year especially for champagne, which needs so perfect and poreless a cork that they are made from a quality called 'extra first' in the business.

Portugal produces about half the world's cork (around 130,000 tons) in some 700 factories, but also controls, largely through the group headed by Américo Amorim, 80 per cent of the world commerce – neighbouring Spain is the second largest producer. In an industry that is itself buoyant, supply cannot keep up with demand. Above all, cork production needs patience: a cork oak, though it lives for 150 years or more, needs twenty years to mature before the first 'virgin' bark can be cut; after the first cutting, the tree will give five or six increasingly bounteous harvests in the first fifty years, each better than the last as long as it is carefully cut. Cork stripping is a skill which was traditionally passed from father to son. A bad gash permanently affects the tree and future growths of cork. A skilled cutter with his axe strives to leave the bare trunk as smooth as a baby's bottom.

The tree looks strangely naked – a pale, brick red – when the cork is stripped. With time, the red dims to grey as the bark slowly grows back. Not until nine or ten years later is the cork bark fully restored and ready once more for cutting. It is a pace that suited the old Portugal but deeply irks the new impresarios busily promoting their wonder product from the cork-oak forests of Portugal.

*

In these lands of the naked trees, the passing of the years shown on every tinted trunk, pigs devour acorns, sheep graze, turkeys gobble – and hunters shoot. 'All of us know,' wrote a dedicated hunter in *Diário de Notícias*, 'that the weakness of a vast legion of Portuguese hunters is a rabbit.' Not to mention partridge, quail, a variety of fauna and fowl, even tiny songbirds. Hunting in Portugal, the royal right and grand passion of many of its kings, shifted in 1988 from a potshot pastime, often unlicensed and illegal, over some 1,200 hunting reserves, to a major, controlled, club and tourist activity in newly defined hunting zones. Municipalities, investors and Portuguese landowners, big and small, rapidly turned huge areas of marginal land, agricultural as well as forest, over to organized hunting – of numerous species of birds, of rabbit and hare, of fox and deer. On 15 August 1989, when the hunting season opened, some 250,000 licensed hunters went out shooting over 90,000 hectares of land, and a starling fell dead in my garden. By December 1990 hunting zones extended over 577,172 ha, or 6.5 per cent of all Portugal.

Hunting laws, based on limited seasons and quotas – and a proper distance from residential areas – are rigorous but hard to enforce. Penalties are low, game guards few and underpaid. Years of too many hunters left too few targets. The birds were vanishing. Few in Portugal cared that millions of migratory birds were being shot, trapped, netted and glued in a heedless slaughter. Newspapers reported hunters' acute disappointment and their howls of frustration and rage when the shooting season opened late and closed early. Now, breeding game for shooting parties, though costly, is profitable and fashionable. Foreigners find Portugal's climate agreeable, bird-shooting a well-managed sport. Clubs and *quintas* with dog-training facilities hold pheasant shoots and private hunts or organized drives of wild boar. Licences were issued to Portuguese hunters only after they took a test. Yet undisciplined, trigger-happy or merely careless hunters still shoot wolves, lynx, stray cats, their own dogs, an occasional wife, and each other.

The blood lust of the hunter in a generally equable and unmalicious society seems odd. Explanations vary from a natural urge to escape day-to-day frustration to a deep-seated desire to reconquer an empire – certainly, platoons of hunters *vestidos a rigor* in camouflage jackets and caps look little different from photos of the African wars. Only the guns, sold by some 600 gunshops across the land, are better. And for those who do not care to shoot there is, in Santo Estevão, near Benavente, from October to March, the *Equipagem de Santo Huberto*, the St Hubert Hunt – horses, scarlet coats, hounds and huntsmen, unlucky fox, ritual blooding of bouncing maidens and all. The procedures are still English, many horses Lusitano, the members multinational. The ritual which opens the season is entirely Portuguese: a mass and the blessing of the hounds by the local priest.

The image of the poor Portuguese *camponês* is surprisingly closely linked to the costly business of hunting. Like the designer of fashion furs who blindly maintained that animals are there to be made into furs, Portuguese tradition holds that animals exist only for human use and pleasure. No law protects animals from cruelty. In my neighbourhood you might see a small boy in the hardware store buying handfuls of cheap mousetraps. They are intended, not for mice, but for songbirds. His mother will stew some; the rest he will sell for a few escudos to the local *tasca*. His father is probably a respectable man and keen hunter who will give his son a licensed rifle when he grows up.

Greyhound coursing is also popular. The rules and conditions vary: at their most barbaric, live hares are chased and torn to pieces in front of a large and appreciative crowd. How the men roar and the children laugh when the hare zigzags in a desperate and inevitably futile attempt to escape the dogs.

The Portuguese feel close to animals and nature. Most have simply not considered the idea that there is pleasure and relaxation in nature which simply can be enjoyed without the massacre of birds and beasts. There are, of course, exceptions. António Teixeira directed a bird protection society for years before moving to new fields in the National Department of Parks, Reserves and the Conservation of Nature. The architect, monarchist and Lisbon city councillor Gonçalo Ribeiro Teles, the first environment secretary in post-revolution provisional governments and then minister for quality of life, struggled against the people's total incomprehension of laws aimed to protect the soil, the environment, and parks and natural reserves. Luís Palma lives in Lisbon and is employed by the national hunting service, which comes under the forestry service, which is part of the Ministry of Agriculture, Fisheries and Food. Palma dedicated all his spare time to bird study, especially birds of prey. He won a solid reputation and wide respect for his work. Environmental protection for the Cape St Vincent coast, among other successes, is largely due to the studies and arguments of Palma and his colleagues.

Hunters, out and about every Sunday, Thursday and holiday in the season (and, illegally, outside it) still outnumber birdwatchers by a disheartening 3,000 to one, yet things are looking up. The numbers of Greens, especially among young people, are growing. Conservationist groups like the activist Quercus, the ecological association Amigos da Terra (Friends of the Earth) and the Liga para a Protecção da Natureza are newly conspicuous. The specific campaign of Grupo Lobo to save the last of the wolves has won legal backing, though the law is ineffectual. In the Alentejo Fapas established a successful vulture-feeding programme where colonies of great griffon vultures are threatened. An animal-rights league campaigns against continuous thoughtless cruelty. No longer a trend, conservation has arrived. It was therefore pure malice when a gossip columnist slyly wrote that the favourite dish of the prime minister, Cavaco Silva, was the delicacy of his traditional Algarve boyhood: a platter of *passarinhos*, fried songbirds. The slur was an easy way of ridiculing the ever-correct Cavaco, skilled at brushing off the stings of the press. To Cavaco Silva's government, which by 1990 included an environment ministry, and to all environmentalists, education was the key.

The tide turned in 1987 when Carlos Pimenta, as secretary of state for the environment, energetically promoted tough anti-pollution laws and won funds to back them. He began the process of controlling industrial fumes and effluent, toxic waste, solid waste and noise – cheered on by ordinary folk whose protests over foul smells and contaminated water had been ignored for years. He had clandestine holiday homes in beauty spots demolished, sponsored educational projects in schools and, above all, raised national consciousness on conservation issues. Under his successor, José Macário Correia, new pollution laws filled some gaps, defined permissible levels of discharge from the cellulose companies, increased fines for environmental damage and generally tightened the rules – a landowner, a woman who had failed to stop a woodcutter destroying trees supporting twenty-seven storks' nests, was taken to court and found guilty. Standards in some instances, to the dismay of cost-conscious industrialists, are even higher than those set by the EEC.

There are countless controversies and anomalies. Toxic waste became an issue as the Portuguese, whose rubbish is all too often dumped at roadsides, rushed to stop offshore waters from becoming a dumping ground. Oil tankers heedlessly fouled the pristine shorelines of Madeira and Porto Santo; with no preventive measures, Portugal needed international assistance to eradicate the black tide. The small Green party, Os Verdes, joined with Communists to stand in the European elections, nailed their placards to roadside trees – and left them there. (The Greens, divided, broke up first.) In the quiet Reserva Natural da Serra da Malcata, whose Mediterranean woodland is the habitat of a few remaining lynx, the air force and army, with their vehicles, nonchalantly engaged in manoeuvres – only low-key escape tactics, they insisted. At Alcochete, on the south bank of the Tejo close to a crucial estuary bird reserve, environmentalists fought a government decision to expand a military shooting range. Ecologists worried over the impact on Almodôvar in the Alentejo of a projected United States tracking station.

In this lovely land, where the rural Lima, the Mira and other quiet rivers are clean, extraction of sand from rivers and lakes causes alarm. Worse, intensive industry and the refuse and ordure of the densely populated northern areas have fouled, to varying degrees, the Aveiro lagoon and the Vouga, Mondego, Leça, Cávado and Ave rivers; with 1,300 mainly textile factories on its banks the little Ave (it means 'bird') is one of the most polluted rivers in Europe. Other small rivers, as well as the vital Tejo and Sado, also suffer high levels of pollution. Again and again there are reports of fish killed by pollution; a few small rivers are at their last gasp. But a clean-up is under way and, in the pellucid Sado estuary, dolphins swim. EEC legislation threatens abusers of the environment, EEC funds aid the slow cleansing process.

The impact of the EEC on Portugal and the Portuguese is immeasurable. Changes are taking place every day – forced by family pressure, national institutions and individual zeal – but the EEC, with its rules and standards and money, is a catalyst more powerful than any. Inevitably, there are doubts and fears: industry worries over the price of anti-pollution measures; agriculture worries that farmers will be unprepared for the hot competition after 1996, when the transition period and catching-up concessions end and the party is over; conservationists worry that fast change will damage the shape of the land for ever. On the slopes of the Serra da Estrela cheese-makers worry about laboratory checks and constraints. The most important factor, pre-EEC, in the making of the classic cheese, was the temperature of the women's hands.

As the money flows, every farmer, every businessman and every minor branch of government, often aching from years of frustration and poverty, dreams of the funding that will transform paper plans to reality. Already, vast sums have been spent. The effects are vividly apparent in economic progress, in low unemployment, in the concrete invasion of the coast, the altered landscapes, the modernizing of Portugal. Often, it is hard to keep down the aggressive thrust of business and builders. Environment protection laws exist to do just that.

But Portugal is small, hungry, vulnerable. All Portugal, it seems at times, is up for sale. Human, social and environmental issues count for little before the powerful engine of free-market wheeling and dealing, the urge for a quick buck. With the best will in the world things can go wrong and, in Portugal, often do. A little self-mismanagement – the EEC's mammoth agricultural surpluses are a memorable example – can at times usefully slow the pace, allow time for rethinking, and produce hidden benefits. Here in Portugal scientists studying the rare great bustard, a large bird with an extraordinary mating display, which requires wide open space for its habitat, were heartened by talk of a more restrained farm policy. Total extinction for the bustard in western Europe seemed certain if the initial EEC decrees for expanding traditional farmland were put into practice.

Bustard lovers are few and the issue of bustard survival is not central to any account of the state of the land. All the same, there was a moral in the seismic miscalculations that made food mountains grow and in the stubborn confrontation over world trade and subsidies. If the immense structure of the European Economic Community, with its Council and Commission and Parliament and currency, can admit to misjudgement, mismanagement and other human failings, there is hope that the fundamental Portugal will survive its impact, as well as the fierce challenge from the west and the east, and that the Portuguese, their traditions, their ravishing countryside and, among other natural splendours, the rare great bustards, will not be swept away by the ruthless meteor of change.

10 Hearts and minds

In Portugal, a nation of surpassing ability in discovering, defending and colonizing a worldwide empire, there are no easy standards for measuring achievement. Statistics are cruelly bald. Merely to declare that two million in a population of over ten million are illiterate or that Portugal has won but one Nobel Prize gives no idea of Portugal's true state of heart and mind. A little elaboration makes the picture clearer: of the twelve EEC countries Portugal has by far the lowest proportion of city-dwelling citizens – and only two cities, Lisbon and Oporto, with more than 100,000 inhabitants. Fully 70 per cent of all Portuguese live a rural life; in the other countries of the EEC more than half are city-dwellers. A basically rural population has considerably different preoccupations, values and attitudes from those who live a faster, more competitive and crowded life.

Portugal's position on most charts is low, but a recent comparison of per capita consumption of wine put the Portuguese in the top five, at just over 100 litres a year. The polite Portuguese are also – the statistics show – among the world's most murderous drivers. The annual mortality rate from road accidents in Portugal is 27 per 100,000 people, the highest in Europe. Yet it is not to be presumed from this conjunction of appalling facts that excess drink is the main cause of the high road-accident rate. It is not. In this society transport and roads are changing fast. As I write, mule carts, motor bikes, cars, vans and lorries are all out there on the road at the same time, the mule plodding along, the car-driver showing his fine Portuguese explorer's instinct by bursting up blind hills and overtaking on bends. You would be safer in the

Alentejo: the statistics show 76 per cent of families there have no car.

The challenger instinct tends to collapse when it comes to commercial activity – Portugal appeared twenty-first on a list of twenty-two countries rated for their industrial competitivity. (The United States was top, only Greece was lower than Portugal.) By contrast, Portugal's growth rate is high. Statistics state certain facts – inarguable on the face of it. But there are so many shadings, so many impressions, so many imprecise, soft-edged qualifications. Take an enduring theme: a woman's place.

An illiterate builder's labourer could not bring himself to vote for a highly qualified woman in a recent political election. He approved her policies, he said, but she – a mere woman, he implied – could never make them work. He ultimately voted for another candidate, a man whose achievements passing time has shown to be modest. Nevertheless, despite such attitudes, the status of women is rising. Even if earthier rating systems undeniably predominate, a modest regiment of women is admired and respected for their professional capability.

There would be many more – no law discriminates against women – if Portuguese women did not continue to think of themselves as socially subordinate. Sincere women as well as men at times ask the *Comissão da Condição Feminina*, Commission on the Status of Women, founded in 1977 to defend women's rights, why – if the laws are at last just – it exists. The Commission, educating and advising, campaigns above all to transform the outlook of men and women in the full knowledge that most Portuguese women still acquiesce in the inferior status accorded to them by history.

In a system based on Roman law and influenced by centuries of Muslim rule, men dominate. From the sixteenth to the nineteenth century, the compilations of laws, or *Ordenações*, confirmed the total authority of men as heads of families. A father had power over his children (to the age of twenty-five), full right to manage his wife's property (though not to sell it without her consent), to beat his wife when he chose, to kill her for adultery. Married and single women suffered through centuries of emigration. Single women could at least sell, buy and travel freely – right up to 1969 a husband could refuse permission for his wife to obtain a passport and travel abroad. (After 1958, with numerous professional women needing to travel, permits were granted by an official department.) Across the centuries the law, and custom, has favoured men, demeaned and subjugated women.

From earliest times the records tell of a few exceptional women. The melodious name of Countess Mumadona, who governed the first true Portuguese territory in the tenth century, rings down the ages as that of a fiercely defensive amazon – the wooden castle she built at Guimarães preceded the castle which is there today. She was wealthy, too: bequests in her will extended from the Minho to Aveiro. Of the Portuguese queens, the shrewd, strong-minded Leonor, wife of Dom João II, set up a welfare system that still survives in the Santa Casa de Misericórdia ('Holy House of Mercy'), a charitable institution to be found in every municipal town in Portugal (its endowments liberally bolstered these days by the national lottery).

An unusually thoughtful chaplain to poor mad Queen Maria I republished, with her approval, a 1577 work by Rui Gonçalves, a Coimbra university professor, in praise of women's abilities. But women's abilities, even as mothers, were not officially endorsed until the Civil Code of 1867 gave a wife shared parental control with her husband over their children; if he died, the children were no longer held to be orphans. The code came into force fourteen years after the death in childbirth – her eleventh child – of thirty-four-year-old Queen Maria II. Like her good friend Queen Victoria, her convictions centred on family, duty and female domesticity.

As the republican spirit grew, the pace of women's social progress quickened. In 1889 Portugal had its first woman doctor, Elisa de Andrade, soon followed by others. In 1910, within months of the declaration of the First Republic, divorce was permitted for the first time in Portugal – and on equal terms; adultery was also to be viewed in an equal light; and a family law pronounced marriage to be based on equality. Some things being more equal than others, a wife no longer owed obedience to her husband, nor could she be brought back by force if she left, yet he still had the right to manage her property.

Women began to work in the civil service, to attain an all-round education. In 1911 Carolina Michaelis de Vasconcelas, a philologist, became the first woman university professor. Women soon distinguished themselves in letters, the arts, in law. But political rights were non-existent. Carolina Ângelo, a doctor, a widow and mother, struck a blow for feminism when she demanded to vote in an election as a head of family, as allowed by law. She voted. The law was quickly amended to exclude women. In 1931 the right to vote was conceded to women with the minimum of secondary-school diplomas. Men only had to know how to read and write.

The status of women, all the same, had risen startlingly in the 1920s. 'All seemed plain sailing for Portuguese women,' remembers Elina Guimarães, a distinguished feminist and one of Portugal's first women lawyers, 'but a political event set women back for almost half a century.' She was referring to the military coup of May 1926, which mutated into the dictatorial regime of António Salazar and his Estado Novo.

Salazar did not dislike women, only independent women. 'The great nations should set an example by confining women to their homes,' he once wrote to his French friend Christine Garnier. 'Convinced as I am that a wife who has in mind the care of her home cannot do good work outside, I shall always fight against the independence of married women.'

The 1933 Constitution of the Estado Novo declared that everyone was equal before the law 'except for women, the differences resulting from their nature and for the good of the family'. By 1939 a husband could once again force his wife to return. The Concordat of 1940, agreed between Portugal and the Vatican, prevented Portuguese who had celebrated a Catholic marriage from obtaining a civil divorce. The feminist National Council for Portuguese Women was compulsorily closed. Censorship stopped criticism.

As late as 1966 a new Civil Code stated that the husband 'is head of the family and, as such, is to decide on and direct all matters concerning marital life'. The sudden passing from power of Salazar in 1968 and his replacement by Marcelo Caetano brought a false dawn for women as for other sections of society. Women were granted the vote on the same basic literacy qualifications as men –

except in local elections where only male heads of families could vote. The principle of equal pay for equal work was written into the laws. Then in 1972 three women, Maria Teresa Horta, Maria Isabel Barreno and Maria Velho da Costa, jointly published a book, *Novas Cartas Portuguesas* ('The New Portuguese Letters'), which dealt openly with women's sexuality. The book was impounded, the authors charged with offences against public morality. The case of 'the three Marias', as it was quickly dubbed, was widely reported in the world press.

With the Young Captains' revolution of 25 April 1974 everything changed. The restoration of democracy brought with it enlightened attitudes to women. Adelino da Palma Carlos, a wealthy anti-Salazarist lawyer nominated prime minister in the first provisional government, was the husband of the feminist Elina Guimarães. The three Marias were acquitted. Women were appointed to top posts in government – a woman was a minister. Careers as magistrates, in diplomacy, in local administration, were thrown open. Discrimination in the civil service was abolished. Job descriptions changed – household help was no longer *criada* (servant or maid), but *mulher-a-dias* (daily) or *empregada doméstica* (domestic employee). A rewritten clause in the Concordat allowed Catholics a civil divorce. Family planning entered the health services. Above all, every man and woman over eighteen years of age was eligible to vote in the 1975 election for the new Constitution.

Subsequent legislation embodied the brightest ideals of a democratic society. In marriage, the male family figurehead vanished; husband and wife equally share responsibility. A wife no longer needs her husband's consent in business matters. No child may be branded illegitimate. Jobs and promotion are not limited by sex. Portugal's modern leaders crafted, and recrafted, a Constitution to be proud of, laws founded on total equality. They envision a land of equal opportunity, a paragon of liberty and justice. In dismal reality profound inequalities persist across society.

In 1979, Maria de Lourdes Pintasilgo, a chemical engineer, was appointed prime minister. That hers was a six-month caretaker role did not diminish the significance of the appointment. In 1980 a woman for the first time became a regional civil governor: Mariana

Calhau Perdigão in Évora. Seven years later the number of women in the top strata of politics had shifted marginally. Cavaco Silva's government of forty-six included four women, but there were no women at all in the Council of State; of eighteen civil governors three were women. Over half the national electorate, 52 per cent, were women; of 250 members elected to Parliament, nineteen were women.

In the municipal elections of 17 December 1989, fewer than five women were elected to head the 305 *Câmaras*. In the reshuffle that followed it, government posts rose to sixty; the number of women holding them went down. In that year a woman, Assunção Esteves, was elected one of ten new judges to the Constitutional Court. Perhaps it was due to her youth – she was thirty-two – that she obtained fewer favourable votes than any of her male colleagues. But as one deputy is said to have put it: 'How can a woman who wears her skirts so short be a judge?' Others have also confused feminine with feminist; to most men and women in Portugal, it is not an issue. In the 1989 election campaign for the European Parliament PSD candidate António Capucho blithely handed out to patently delighted women hundreds of party-sloganed plastic aprons. He was one of twenty-two men, and two women, who won seats.

At the bottom of the scale, violent men uninhibitedly and brutally beat their wives – the police, as in many societies, turning a blind eye. Refuges for battered wives or victims of rape, or statistics on the extent of the problem, are virtually non-existent. Unemployment unfailingly hits women more than men. Women are often paid, no matter what the laws state, less than men. Far fewer women than men have access to job training. Women decorate church altars, teach the catechism, mutter the mass, populate the churches. You will see women as beasts of burden, great bundles on their heads – cabbages, sometimes, like a bizarre parody of an Ascot hat. In rural life, women's status is little altered by constitutional rights.

A Portuguese ambassador to England in the seventeenth century, Francisco Manuel de Melo, a literary man, wrote his thoughts on marriage around a simple conviction: *Do homem a praça, da mulher a casa* ('man out and about, woman at home'). For the majority of Portuguese men and women, the sentiment is as valid now as then. Old saws and tragicomic tales on the masculine sense of superiority persist – like the one about the man riding a donkey while his wife walks behind. Asked why, he says the donkey is too small to carry them both. Mutual consideration is the missing key, not sexual role, responsibility or rhetoric.

Well over half of university graduates are women. Women have won conspicuous success in the large, professional mid-section of society – in education and law, as economists and administrators, in pharmacology, science, medicine – 37 per cent of all doctors, totalling over 27,000, are women. But success is far from prosperity and egalitarianism has its ironies. Salaries paid to government-employed teachers and doctors are so low – a hospital specialist in orthopaedics, as the 1990s began, earned a basic 108 contos a month, about £5,200 a year – they feel deprived, exploited and oppressed.

Brilliant Portuguese women shine in music and the arts. The pianist Maria João Pires, who seems so fragile, but plays with such power and intensity, is idolized in Portugal, acclaimed abroad. The ballet dancer Maria Almeida reached the summit of her career as prima ballerina in London's Royal Ballet. Maria Helena Vieira da Silva, born in Lisbon in 1908, and the much younger Paula Rego, with the dark-eyed composure of many of her mysterious creations, are among the greatest contemporary painters. All of them, by no coincidence, studied, worked and found fulfilment abroad. These Portuguese women have a distinguished artistic reputation and an admiring following. Are they celebrities? Even in Portugal their names are less well known than those of the top club footballers. The numerous talented and clever women living and working in Portugal today are little known outside their own professional circles. Honours are rarely heaped upon them. When the élite Academia de Ciências de Lisboa elevated Isabel Magalhães Colaço, a Lisbon professor of law and the first Portuguese woman to obtain a doctorate, and the writer Agustina Bessa-Luís, from associate to full membership, they were the first women to gain the distinction in the Academy's 210 years of existence. But suddenly the newspapers seemed full of stories on 'the first woman who . . .'

In 1989 the first women were admitted to the Escola Superior de Polícia, a police college. Women pilots have been around since nineteen-year-old Maria de Lourdes Sá Teixeira won her wings at Sintra in 1928. Now, commercial airlines are opening their doors to women pilots – the first, Eva Vaz, joined the regional airline, *Linhas Aéreas Regionais* (LAR) in 1988. Soon afterwards, Teresa Carvalho became the first woman to win her wings in a TAP Air Portugal training course. Legislation opened the armed forces to women. Among a group of uniformed future aviators pictured in 1989 at the Academia da Força Aérea was the smiling, nineteen-year-old Paula Costa – the only woman and, in her second year, top of the class. As it happened, just as the air force was letting young women in, over thirty qualified male pilots, lured by civil aviation salaries far above their own, were trying to leave.

Finance had its first women, too – among them Judite Correia, one of a select band of stockbrokers officially accredited to the stock exchange; in 1991 she launched her own finance company. In the week that Maria de Jesus Serra Lopes was elected the first woman dean of the Ordem dos Advogados, a legal society, Manuela Morgado, a banker, was elected – for the second time – to head the Associação Portuguesa de Economistas. A number of women are directors, executives in investment companies, in advertising. Few have power; all major enterprises are governed by men. But at a time when famous-name merchandizers were hectically opening branches in the main streets of Portugal, three friends, Teresa Catarino, Carmo Franco and Leonor Lobato, who had opened a shop with their own line of children's clothes called Cenoura – the word means carrot – saw their small business become the first notable franchise operator abroad.

Glossy women's magazines – *Marie Claire, Máxima, Elle*, Portuguese mirrors of French style – appeared at the end of the 1980s to show us the new, snappier, stylish woman, to portray the personalities of public life. I learned from them that the articulate Communist rebel, Zita Seabra, had considered a career in ballet. She was pictured in a tutu. Vera Calado – whose surname means quiet – is a motorcycle-rally champion. Her career was not stopped by accidents but by the long hours of her hospital job. Horsewoman

Luísa Maurício beats all comers in endurance events. And there was television's Channel 2 newsreader, Manuela Moura Guedes of the velvet voice, a svelte, accomplished presenter and interviewer, revealing that when she left her country home to attend university in Lisbon her no-nonsense parents lodged her with nuns.

Portuguese women are still crossing a great divide. In the tremors and turbulence of a shifting society the Portuguese male seems more sharply defined. Often, he wears a moustache (47 per cent of all Portuguese males – one of the least vital of EEC statistics). Often, he seems cut from a standard drinking, smoking, womanizing pattern. Fact or fancy, a friend of mine claims that idle Portuguese men habitually clutch their crotch – *tomates* is the slang word – as if to confirm, like women checking a purse, that nothing is missing. The popular tabloid, *Correio da Manhã*, referring to a report on its inside pages on the troubles of fruit and vegetable growers, bannered the front page with a bold headline: *Afinal temos tomates* (After all, we have tomatoes). It was true: Portugal is the second largest producer in Europe and among the top five in the world. But only the pure in mind in a readership with a bawdy sense of humour would miss the joke.

Sex, since Salazar, has burst out of the closet with rollicking, bare-assed exuberance. Bouncing nubile girls compete in Miss Wet T-Shirt and Miss Kiss Top Less disco contests. The popular press presents for family entertainment a succession of cheerful, slightly dated pin-ups. Bosoms bulge, buttocks are extravagantly rounded, the lingerie discreet, the smiles wholesome. Portuguese women do not apparently feel demeaned by the eye-popping female voluptuousness. A group of factory women wrote to one paper asking only for more photos of muscular men. In publicity, the law forbidding the use of the female image as object is not conspicuously effective. A survey of television viewers showed they regarded advertising as part of the entertainment.

The cruder images of imported pornography are also available. In a free society, those who seek assorted sexual stimulation will find it. Lisbon has about 1,200 registered prostitutes, some from the provinces, some from the islands, some from Spain, Brazil, France and elsewhere – a listing I saw included a 'Prussian'. Prostitu-

tion is not a crime – although pimping and procuring are. White
slavery is a vicious fact of life – girls who have run away or been
tempted to leave home are caught in a trap that often ends in a *casa
de passe* (brothel) in Portugal or across the border in Spain. The
Church, the police, the O Ninho aid group which works to re-
integrate prostitutes into society, have expressed alarm over the
rising numbers of very young girls who have surfaced in countryside brothels. And, whatever they were promised, some of them
work in establishments that, like much of rural Portugal, lack
electricity and running water.

Portuguese culture avidly embraces the eternal themes of love,
sex, suffering and death. Throw in a measure of money, power,
violent crime, a touch of incest, and you have the basic ingredients
of classical dramatic literature, theatre, films and art. Journalism,
its main thrust world or local news, economy and sport, leaps
lightly across the field: history at its most thrilling mixes with the
advice of agony aunts on pimples and unreciprocated passion. The
sharp-edged opinions of lucid commentators appear beside the eloquence of the finest creative writers. When the fervent romantic,
Natália Correia – an *Antologia Erótica* written in Salazar's era earned
her a three-year suspended prison sentence – and the mordant
novelist José Cardoso Pires were asked by *Expresso* to discuss
libertines in the Portuguese context, it made for diverting reading.
For Cardoso Pires, an impish interpreter of *machismo*, the masterful
Portuguese masculine type he calls *marialva*, prominent in his
novels, is solidly anti-libertine.

Definitions of love and sex, how the arrival of the contraceptive
pill altered relationships and other such stimulating topics are freely
discussed. Yet in a fast-expanding, lively press the coming of true
sleaze was a certainty. Mere scandal is nothing new. Portugal,
lacking in so much else, may be without memorably depraved and
conniving libertines but the Portuguese can look back across a
broad counterpane of history to misdoings of royalty, aristocracy
and ministers, to the open maintenance of mistresses, lovers and
bastards. Gossip marvellously elaborates more recent affairs closer
to home. But as the 1980s ended there fell into the lap of Lisbon *o
caso Taveira*, the Taveira case.

A brand new scandal sheet printed scenes from a videocassette that showed the well-known architect, Tomás Taveira, taking his pleasure with two unidentified women. Never in Portugal had there been so public an intrusion into private sexual habits. In an enraged counterattack, Taveira sued for 255,000 contos, over £1m. Sexual morality was not an issue, nor the sexual acts performed, nor even that the women (so it was reported) had been filmed without their knowledge or consent. What was new was the public exposure of the private life of a Portuguese celebrity solely for money. In pornographic scandal Portugal had come of age. For the rest, encounters of post-feminist woman with the macho mentality, if not fought in teeth-gritting silence – silence is not the Portuguese way – will only be resolved with time and true social development.

Right now, most Portuguese have more urgent preoccupations. Work. The cost of living. Food. The fear or reality of sickness. Education, a perturbed area. A 1989 study found that 21 per cent of the population over fifteen was illiterate, twice the level of illiteracy in Greece, three times Spain's, four times that of France. In Portugal the appalling figure encompassed 1,600,000 adults, many of them elderly, rural women who had never gone to school, but also a large proportion of youngsters who had dropped out. Five million adults had had less than six years of schooling. Current school failure rates were put at 33 per cent; in the EEC the average for drop-outs and failures was 10 per cent. Most schoolchildren have to repeat at least one year. Only 40 per cent of children attend secondary school and attain nine years of schooling – the EEC average is 70 per cent – and only 11 per cent of school-leavers carry on to higher education. Entrance to university is itself an issue.

That so many older people are illiterate can be blamed on Salazar's rigidly patriarchal view on the merits of social order above those of a broad-based education. In 1930 seventy out of a hundred could not read but, as he put it, 'I consider more urgent the creation of élites than the necessity of teaching people how to read.' His intellectual and economic élites were extremely narrow. Many of the finest scholars and educators of his era, among them

Jaime Cortesão, António Sérgio and, later, Vitorino Magalhães Godinho – a teacher, in 1942, of the seventeen-year-old Mário Soares – were sacked as dangerous liberals. For the depressing statistics on the post-Salazar generation the causes lie elsewhere.

The 1974 revolution, taking off from the ideas for educational reform of Marcelo Caetano's education minister, the scientist Veiga Simão, made education universally available. School heads were booted out by exulting students and replaced by a *conselho diretivo* – a committee. Four years of compulsory education soon became six – now the objective is nine. Struggling parents eagerly sent their children, scrubbed clean and well-dressed, to school (though, as families grew, they too often pulled out older children to tend younger ones). Middle-class parents grumbled that schools were not what they used to be – but what they used to be was élitist.

The days of heady excitement dimmed to frustration as the new-born system, built on high hopes and a liberal philosophy but desperately low on funds and efficient organization, began to crack. Many buildings are old and decrepit, newer ones shabby, even dangerous, from lack of maintenance. An Almada secondary school, alarmed at a perilous electric installation, posted exam times on its noticeboard with the qualification – '. . . *se não chover*' ('if it doesn't rain'). Most schools are forced to crowd classes – and too often dismiss them when the teacher fails to appear. Some have day and night shifts. The start of the school year at the end of September is inevitably marked with delays and uncertainty – for children, their parents, the teachers.

The number of teachers leapt in ten years from around 40,000 to 140,000 but as a body they are underpaid and, in many instances, demoralized. 'One school can be well run,' says a teacher in Loulé, 'another a horror, incompetently directed. And after my last rise, so much went in taxes I actually earned less.' Teacher absenteeism became chronic. Teachers in the first years of their career are often posted by the Ministry of Education to schools far from where they live. They are obliged to find accommodation, transport and solutions to the separation of professional from private life. Primary schools, particularly, are often isolated. One in every four married teachers – more than 60 per cent are married – is married to another teacher. They can spend years posted apart without hope of setting up home together. The problems of couples with children are even worse. Unsurprisingly, many marriages founder.

The daily crises in education, the inadequacies and complaints, the disturbing illiteracy figures, suggest a dismal backwardness in a dispirited society. In fact, they are the dilemmas, not at all intractable, of fast expansion and of rising aspirations. The initial obstacle is a dispersed population. The average population density is 110 per square kilometre; in places it is as low as twenty.

For the high rate of failures and drop-outs social inequalities are seen as the root cause, the industrial north a notorious example. In the districts of Braga, Oporto and Aveiro, ignorant and desperate parents encourage under-age, ill-fed children to work in factories, or at home, for employers who often compound their unscrupulous use of child labour by paying pittances below the minimum wage. It is a blight – Mário Soares called it *uma vergonha nacional*, 'a national disgrace' – that can only be eradicated as social conditions improve and parents are persuaded to keep their children at school. Socialists announced plans to introduce a law setting the minimum working age at sixteen but, as the 1990s began, Portugal was the only EEC country which allowed fourteen-year-olds to work. A habit of history was not yet discarded: across the centuries fourteen marked the coming of age for royal succession to the throne.

Their history lavished on the Portuguese a cornucopia of culture, imperishable traditions, their very soul. Not all the grandeur, the pervasive accomplishments of a more glorious age, sprang from books – a particularly reactionary deputy in Salazar's Estado Novo argued the merits of an illiterate, uncorrupted *povo*, on the grounds that Portugal's grandest achievements had been deeds of uneducated men. Specious phrases flew. Education is a rousing theme to which few politicians, or thoughtful parents, are indifferent.

The Portuguese have had an illustrious university since the year 1290. The founding of the University of Coimbra by King Dinis – it opened in Lisbon and moved to Coimbra in 1308 – is usually dated to a letter Dom Dinis wrote on 1 March 1290. Later that year, on 9 August, Pope Nicholas IV issued a Bull approving its establishment. But that the university was intended to serve the whole of

Portugal is clear from an earlier document, a petition for an *Estudo Geral de Ciências* (a general study of the sciences), drawn up by twenty-seven churchmen who met on 11 November 1288, in Montemor-o-Novo. They came from across Portugal – the abbot of Alcobaça was there; so were priors from Coimbra and Lisbon, from Guimarães and Santarém. And how absurdly pleased I was to see, in the brief list of clerics who came from as far north as Mogadouro, from Estremoz in the east and Torres Vedras in the west, the rector of my own small southern parish, São Clemente of Loulé.

In the long roll of students who went to Coimbra across the centuries is Portugal's epic poet, Luís de Camões, a saint – Lisbon's cherished António, whom we call St Antony of Padua – the novelist Eça de Queiroz, his friend the philosopher Antero de Quental, the brilliant and multifaceted brain specialist Egas Moniz, who won a Nobel Prize for medicine. Salazar himself studied here, as did his successor, Marcelo Caetano. Among government ministers, between 25 April 1974 and 1990, there were eight Coimbra law graduates. But things have radically altered. Lisbon University predominates. Many Portuguese, men and women, now study and earn degrees abroad. Coimbra, though still the hallowed queen of academe, has been forced off her pedestal, obliged, above all, to be one of a crowd.

In 1970 Portugal had four public universities and one private university – the Universidade Católica Portuguesa, founded by Cardinal Cerejeira. By 1990 there were five private universities and fourteen autonomous public universities, now including – as well as Lisbon, Oporto and Coimbra – Évora, Aveiro, Minho, Trás-os-Montes and the Alto Douro, Beira Interior, Açores and the minuscule, often malcontent University of the Algarve. An Open University had just been launched. Public institutions of higher learning included fourteen polytechnics and several widely ranging specialized institutes. Private institutes numbered about a dozen. Some 156,000 students in 1990 were receiving the benefits of advanced education – at the state institutions virtually for free. Calculations set a figure of 230,000 within five or six years.

Education was exploding across the country. Évora had back its majestic university building and cloisters where the Jesuits had taught until their expulsion in 1759. The Catholic University, a yuppy cradle, its faculties spread across several cities, went imaginatively modern with the geometric forms of a new, pink Escola Superior de Biotecnologia in Oporto. The University of Porto itself grew, with new faculties of architecture and letters. Beira Interior, starting in 1986 with 300 students, was finding space for over 2,000 by 1990. Congestion, in Lisbon University, had been a fact of life. It was hard to find who or what you wanted. Scientists in the department of zoology and anthropology worked in antiquated labs and offices in the great, echoing Colégio dos Nobres built by the Jesuits, with its vast corridors and *azulejos*-panelled walls, telephones a long march away. As the 1980s ended, they moved, along with other faculties, to the still raw Cidade Universitária, a whole new city-state Lisbon campus. But there is no ignoring the Jesuits, nor are their solid buildings wasted; soon afterwards, the economics faculty of Lisbon's Universidade Nova moved into the former Jesuit college at Campolide, rescued from the army, expensively restored, refurbished and modernized.

There were, of course, innumerable problems. Entry to university became increasingly competitive as candidates far outnumbered the available places; in 1990 there were 95,000 candidates for 40,000 places. Students denounced as élitist the controversial new entrance exams, a *prova geral* (generalized test), that failed to allow for twelve years of specialized study. Since education was cheap, few scholarships were available (though the average cost to the state was 330,000 escudos per student per year). Accommodation was a problem – no new student residences were built for years and, when funds became available, they were still insufficient. Libraries fell behind student needs, or closed too early. Canteens here and there closed at weekends. What did the future hold? Were there jobs? Universities established protocols of cooperation with business and industry – the provinces especially pleased to have handy, on-the-spot technological research. But in the great race for qualifications and success many students did not complete the course.

In Portugal's 1990 budget, education had the top slot with close on 390m contos (about £2,600m). In actual investment and expenditure only public works had fatter accounts. Roberto Carneiro, the boyish-looking education minister, had his plans ready. They began by improving facilities for children under six – over 400 kindergartens were opened in a year – and closing 200 tiny primary schools (600 more were listed) attended by less than ten children, who were transported to other, larger schools. New schools – primary and secondary – are rising fast. To keep the children there and halt the failure rate, Carneiro expanded the school-milk programme, built gymnasiums, supplied computer systems – mainly through an inter-university scheme called Project Minerva – and improved teacher training. Teacher salaries were raised, promotions accelerated. The curriculum itself was reformed.

Private schools and colleges got a better deal and, through state subsidies and contracts, were able to assume a wider role. Special education was on the list although nobody actually knew, existing institutions apart, how many handicapped there were. (Suddenly, for the first time, I saw a reference to guide dogs for the blind.) Developing the concept of restoring and recreating fine furniture and antique pieces, practised and taught in the workshops of the Fundação Ricardo Espírito Santo Silva in Lisbon (the Foundation's Alfama mansion also has a Museum of Decorative Art), schooling in archaic arts and trades was given a boost. Adult education was intensified: the first programmes had proud successes as elderly women and men hunched painfully over large writing books, but the total figures were nothing to boast of. You would see courses advertised for gardening, for *calceteiros* – the artistic laying of cobbles – for ceramics and decorative tiles, for a host of cultural activities. There is even a circus school.

In industrial Barreiro a sixteen-year-old boy was telling me once of his ambition to be a mechanic. 'Of racing cars?' I asked without thinking. 'No, just cars, any cars.' The modest aspiration to him seemed a wild dream; I thought there was hope. The keenest, the most concentrated, efforts were made, richly fuelled by EEC funding, in *formação profissional* (technical training). It was, in mass education, the nearest thing to a sure bet: 80 per cent of all youngsters who took courses got a job. Professionals who added to their capabilities enhanced status, potential and income. The swelling economy, the appeal to investors of armies of young, robust, hard-working – and cheap – Portuguese was a catalyst. The huge technical gap was one of the more unfortunate results of revolution. The distinguished Instituto Superior Técnico, founded in 1911, boasts that around half of Portugal's engineers are IST alumni – and twenty of the ministers in post-revolutionary governments – but in the ardent leftist spirit of the 1970s much technical education had been abolished as élitist.

Élitist was not the word to apply to Cavaco Silva's education minister. Roberto Carneiro, an only child, part Chinese, who grew up in the Açores – his father a musician who could play fourteen instruments – was a brilliant student who took his degree in chemical engineering. Tempted into politics by a friend, whose sister he married, he remains a romantic speaking effortlessly of Portugal's greatest writers and philosophers, of his projects, of destiny. To Carneiro, eradicating inequities in the system and bringing education and culture to all children in the nation is the 'great challenge of the last years of the century'. He and his wife, Maria do Rosário, adore children. At only forty-one, he was father to nine. Naturally, they go to state schools.

A Portuguese friend of mine twisted his ankle studying birds in the Trás-os-Montes. The nearest doctor was some distance away. No problem, said a man leaning on the bar of a hamlet *taberna*, and sent a child to fetch the village specialist. My friend was soon walking comfortably, his ankle healed under the expert care of a woman whose skill in fixing the broken bones of goats was well known.

Traditional healers, *bruxas* and *curandeiras* – witches and traditional healers – are not even now uncommon. Superstition is strong, the saints revered, the power of prayer never underestimated. When fifty-four-year-old Eva Pinto received a new heart through the skills of heart surgeon Queiroz e Melo in 1986 – the first transplant in Portugal – her thanks went first to God. She was going strong three years later, and praising God, when Queiroz e Melo had done twenty-seven transplants. To sophisticates, to the educated younger generation, rural superstition and the more intense expressions of

18 Ploughing and sowing in the Algarve

19 In the glassworks of Stephens, oldest in the land

20 Roving blacksmith, Algarve   21 Haymaking in the Minho

22 Minho farmer

23 Alentejo shepherd

24 The 'faithful friend', *bacalhau*, on the menu at a Faro restaurant

25 Shopkeeping in Redondo

26 From a giant dolmen in Pavia
faith made a small, stout chapel

27 Braga: the Bom Jesus sanctuary
and its celebrated stairway

28 Megalithic stones: the cromlech of Almendres near Évora

29 Countrywomen in Estói

30 Ribatejo *campinos* in a steer-herding contest

31 The long approach of the faithful to the shrine of Fátima

32 Prayers for the dead on All Saints' Day

33 *Fado* in the informal style of a bar in the Bairro Alto, Lisbon

34 Football: fans watch from the comfort of a Loulé cafe, the Louletano. There was no celebration; this time, Benfica lost

35 And another Fátima: young, professional Maria de Fátima and her husband Carlos, son Tiago and daughter Andrea. No longer is every female an obligatory Maria

36 Business is bright in the decorous, three-table Lisbon Stock Exchange

37 Dr Judite Correia, who heads a finance company, in her elegant office. She was the first woman stockbroker in Portugal

religious faith seem quaint. More extraordinary, to most Portuguese, is the increasing access to modern medicine through new district hospitals and proliferating health centres.

Since social and medical matters are often at odds, it is not surprising that the health service has also been the sector of government most fraught with conflict and crisis. Some of the conflict appeared as much personal as professional: hostility between Cavaco Silva's initial health minister, Leonor Beleza, a tough-minded woman whose name means beauty, and the suave surgeon, Machado Macedo, who led the Medical Association, simmered close to a state of war. Doctors disputed her appointment of non-medical hospital management. Not all doctors agreed with her decision that blood donation must be non-commercial – despite the efforts of a donors' association and the national Blood Institute, and imports of blood, shortages were often acute. Outrage was expressed at her plans to sell a mental institute, the Hospital Júlio de Matos, and its valuable estate for redevelopment, and to transfer patients to a network of thirteen new mental-health centres. Doctors were angered by her implication that they were too free with prescriptions, that they were at fault for aspects of slack hospital organization. Doctors resented their conditions of hospital service, the discouragingly low pay, in places – as one doctor told me – 'the awful pressure to keep going, the lack of time to be humane'.

Nurses, 24,000 of them – several thousand too few – were no happier than doctors. With state salaries miserably low, many, like doctors, were forced to take on private work in addition to hospital duties. Exclusivity – full-time state service – was itself an issue. Salaries were raised as an incentive. Exclusivity, except for postgraduate interns, remained optional. Critics of Leonor Beleza were quick to point to real or apparent wrongdoing in her ministry. They were scathing about a dozen delayed plans and broken promises, from incomplete vaccination that had failed to contain a measles epidemic to the absence of long-heralded computerized services. It was remarked, more than once, that Health is more important than Beauty. When Cavaco Silva was forced by Socialist gains in the December 1989 municipal elections to shuffle his government, Leonor Beleza was dropped. (So was the unpopular finance minister Miguel Cadilhe; in his place came Leonor Beleza's clever brother, Miguel Beleza.)

It is not entirely fair to say that the Portuguese enjoy bad health. Newspaper photos of fit and smiling centenarians celebrating among family and friends are common. Increasing, too, are rather less cheerful old people's homes. Cardiovascular diseases are the principal cause of death (though relatively few Portuguese drop dead of a heart attack). Cancer comes second. Tuberculosis still kills some 400 Portuguese each year. By mid-1990, over 460 people, more than fifty of them women, had contracted Aids – its initials SIDA in Portuguese (around one tenth of cases were the virus HIV-2). The slogan in an intensive educational campaign was '*Vida ou Sida – Decida*' ('Life or Aids – decide'). By a quirk of language, a condom is a *preservativo*. Girls at a disco, I heard, were not at all shy to be seen dropping coins in a vending machine to buy what they lightly called *camisinhas* ('little shirts'). In the discreet homosexual community – there are gay bars and saunas in Lisbon and elsewhere – the jokes are edged with anguish.

Statistically far more significant is death on the road, with 108 deaths per 100,000 vehicles in Portugal. By comparison Spain has 61, France 48, Italy and West Germany 31, and the British 27. In an average year there are over 90,000 traffic accidents on Portuguese roads, close on 3,000 people are killed, over 13,000 seriously injured and 50,000 more slightly hurt.

In the public-health system, treatment is free, as are all essential medicines. Discounts of at least 50 per cent are given on prescriptions for non-essential medication. Doctors in private practice and in the increasing number of private health-centres and clinics – very often the same doctors attending patients in state hospitals – are paid a fee for consultation and treatment. What private patients are paying for (often from private insurance) is immediate individual attention. The worst feature of the public system is the waiting. Everyone can tell you a shocking story. Sandra França, a schoolgirl, won a prize from *Diário de Notícias* for hers – about an unlucky witch called Bruxilda who decided to visit the city and look for a job. Her tussles with employers and bureaucracy were frightful. Forced to face a new life with a plastic broomstick in the polluted air of the city, she became ill. She was quickly carried to hospital but – *coitada*! poor thing! – the hours passed as she waited for attention and, sadly, she died.

Sandra's modern fairy-tale is caustically on target. Merely to make an appointment may take months. To see a specialist, more months. Waiting for an operation, years. For emergencies, if you can walk and talk you wait your turn. It may take several hours. In the vast hospitals like Santa Maria in Lisbon (1,300 beds, over 500 emergencies a day) or Oporto's São João which treats over 235,000 patients a year, the standard practice is to keep incoming stretcher cases for observation in the busy corridors. The sounds and smells are of pain and misery, the scene pure Dickens. But this awful limbo is not Dickens, but infrastructure.

Doctors are not indifferent to the failings of the infrastructure. It is not medical skills that are missing but maintenance, not surgeons but sound organization. The surgeon Gentil Martins, a celebrated expert in the separation of Siamese twins, revealed after yet another successful operation in Lisbon's Dona Estefânia hospital that he and his team had had to 'pirate' equipment from other hospitals. The hospital had even, for two weeks, been without toilet paper. (The deprivation would appear to be national: *Eurobusiness* magazine, reporting on consumer habits, noted that, according to a Euromonitor survey, Portugal had the lowest per capita consumption of toilet paper in Europe.)

Medicine was being taught in Coimbra's Santa Cruz monastery as early as 1130. A large Lisbon hospital, All Saints, built in 1504, was destroyed in the 1755 earthquake. Medicine has always attracted brilliant minds. The life of Professor António Egas Moniz – born in 1874, he lived to be eighty-one – provides a glimpse of how things were quite recently. From a doctorate at Coimbra he headed a new neurology section in Lisbon's Faculty of Medicine. To an American specialist, his work on cerebral leucotomy was 'the discovery of the century' on the functions of the human brain. Egas Moniz's achievements in cerebral medicine and neurosurgery won him the Nobel Prize. From an interest in politics he developed a new career as orator, deputy, diplomat – he became ambassador to

Madrid, then foreign minister. Losing interest in the political whir-
ligig, he dedicated himself to his clinic and to scientific and literary
works. Medicine was clearly more an intellectual exercise than
social service.

In Portugal's literature the country doctor is an oddly prominent
figure – Miguel Torga and Fernando Namora, especially, both
small-town general practitioners, are beloved literary giants. Doctors
today would seem to have little time for reflection. The health
services are in a perpetual race to meet a rising tide of expectations.
A reflection, perhaps, of new times, the first case of homicide by
medical negligence arose only in 1989. The current condition of
medicine ranges from the latest skills in heart surgery, *in vitro*
fertilization and plastic surgery (many Portuguese women want big
breasts to be smaller) to rural health centres and even village
treatment by *bruxas*. Hospitals vary from handsomely appointed
establishments and well-equipped new clinics to gaunt buildings
juggling permanent overcrowding with perpetual renovation –
Lisbon, trying to cope, was adding new emergency services to four
major hospitals as the 1990s began. One image shows immaculate
intensive care, another the reeking and decrepit. Lisbon's huge,
archaic São José hospital was angrily described as 'a desperate
case'. Daily, doctors restore the sick to health, defeat death and
disease through their medical skills. Yet a cure has still to be found
for the medical structure itself, too often 'a desperate case'.

In the chequered saga of Portuguese health a crucial role is played
by the *bombeiros*, the fire brigade, whose ever-ready *voluntários* battle,
year after year, against the relentless fires of summer, the sudden
conflagrations in village, town and city. But firefighting is not all
that they do. How dependent I was, before I possessed the luxury
of a borehole, on the water delivered by the Loulé fire brigade!

Every important town has its own small permanent brigade on
emergency call – men and, increasingly, women, who have had
first-aid training. (There was a time when they treated venereal
disease, raising surreal images of victims getting a forceful hosing
down.) *Bombeiros* respond to home emergencies. Their ambulances
take the sick and injured to hospital. When birth pains begin, it is

the *bombeiros* who are called to take labouring mothers to hospital – often with no time to spare. 'Born in an ambulance,' the papers announce, again and again. Volunteer fireman Jorge Pécurto of Carnaxide arrived, one damp March evening, at a humble *bairro de lata* outside Lisbon and unexpectedly found himself delivering twins. Jorge, a student aiming for a career in administration, was only seventeen.

The *bombeiros* number some 2,000 professionals and 38,000 unpaid volunteers. The armed forces, their heyday over, their historic authority impaired by bureaucratic grumbling and discontent, sigh for a similar public spirit. These days, when opportunity knocks within a peaceful economic union, few see any appeal in a military career. In 1978 candidates to the Military Academy numbered close on 2,000; by 1989 the figure was 332. So low had the fortunes of the armed forces sunk fifteen years after the 1974 revolution and the end of the African wars that the armed-forces chief (and one-time presidential candidate) General Soares Carneiro felt obliged to remind everyone, as he pressed for enhanced rights, rewards and privileges for the forces, that it was thanks to military action that the country had been restored to a true path. At the beginning of 1990 the armed forces appeared to have been pushed even further down in the pecking order when, in a government reshuffle, Cavaco Silva replaced the defence minister Eurico de Melo with a failed municipal candidate with no experience whatsoever of military affairs. (Within weeks his place was taken by the capable young minister of justice, Fernando Nogueira.)

The armed forces – the army particularly – are suffering from a touch of schizophrenia. In one of their personalities they are the guardians of history: installed in the great coastal forts and solid former convents, they ceremonially celebrate the glories of the past, the anniversaries of ancient battle victories. On the other hand, they are also active members of NATO, jockeying for prestige positions in CINCIBERLANT – the Iberian–Atlantic area of NATO, now including Madeira and the Açores, with its headquarters in Oeiras on the outskirts of Lisbon – and participate regularly in training exercises for nuclear, biological and chemical warfare. In fact, the Portuguese, only partly due to their experience of earthquakes, distrust nuclear power intensely. With no nuclear power stations in Portugal, they watch Spain's with fear and suspicion – but at least Spain has rejected nuclear arms. When the Portuguese government pompously announced, in April 1989, that it would not evade its responsibilities to NATO and would, if it were necessary, permit nuclear installations in Portugal, the only reason there was no great outcry was the wonderful new sense, as perestroika bloomed, that there was no threat.

As the eastern Communist regimes collapsed like a house of cards at the end of 1989 the Portuguese were busily adapting their defence systems to planned requirements. The air force, its main base at Monsanto, was eagerly modernizing its structure and communications (a part of the system called POMBAL, for Portuguese Maritime Buffer and AEW Link), even if its squadrons of aircraft, mainly A-7P Corsair, Fiat G-91, P3 Orion, C-212 Aviocar and the heavy C-130, were not the world's newest models. The United States, with whom Portugal maintains a bilateral agreement on the use of the Lajes base in the Açores, was to supply twenty new, latest-model F-16s. Renegotiation with Federal Germany over the base at Beja included the supply of Alpha-Jet advanced training aircraft. For small arms and munitions Portugal has its own manufacturing company, INDEP.

The navy, like the air force, was active in the continent–Madeira–Açores triangle, winning public relations points for courageous sea-rescue services. Its fleet was modest: four small frigates and three ageing submarines headed a list of sixty-odd assorted craft. Three Meko 200 frigates, German-financed through the Beja agreement and built in Hamburg, equipped with British Sea Lynx helicopters, would add muscle. Modernizing was a key word but, to keep down costs, the helicopters would be serviced by the air force – whose workshops in Alverca handle a wide range of servicing, repair and construction.

Cost was another, and crucial, factor. For a total mobilized force of about 70,000, the military budget was around £700m – and almost no one was satisfied. Heading a *Quadro Permanente* of around 22,000, some 6,300 senior and junior officers were well paid but embittered by politicians' lack of interest in the services – particularly in their protests that their funds were inadequate even to keep the equipment functioning. Sergeants, almost 9,000 of them throughout the services, campaigned rancorously for improved career conditions. Contract personnel were another group – among them junior officers – whose status, seniority rights and advanced opinions had been, in the pre-revolutionary forces, emotional issues. Last of all came the endless thousands of youths on obligatory military service, from 1990 being cautiously reduced from twelve to four months. I never met one youngster who said he liked it.

Military matters and questions on the modern role of the military are publicly aired in Portugal's energetic and determinedly free press. After Salazar's menacing PIDE was destroyed, nobody cared to admit to chasing spies or keeping secrets. Cautiously, ten years after the revolution, a new law permitted three separate information services: SIED, strategic and defence, outside the country; SIS, information and security, within the frontiers; and SIM, or DINFO, military information. The judicial police force, Polícia Judiciária, has a rival combat force, DCCB; the security police, PSP, has its Special Operations group. Completing the martial muster are the little-loved Guarda Nacional Republicana, the Guarda Fiscal – customs – and around 8,000 security guards in numerous city-based private security companies. If such an array of bristling authority seems formidable, the old axiom applies: try and find a policeman when you need one.

These forces protect and defend, moreover, a near perfect peace. Portugal's colonial wars are in the past, world war seems happily remote, national banditry is minimal, riots virtually non-existent, violent crime far below the level of countries, like the United States, with the death penalty. It was a reassuring sight to watch Mário Soares on his travels, on his 'open presidency' tours of Portugal. No nervous bodyguards pressed close on brief walkabouts. Soares, besieged by the eager *povo*, mingled with the crowd, ate and drank among them, listened, consoled, responded – 'He got us a bus service,' a villager in Rio de Onor in the far north told me. On a trip to the USSR, he laughed away a suggestion that he should include a security guard in his party – which always includes personalities from all political spheres. 'It would,' he said, 'be like taking bananas to Madeira' – an expression equivalent to taking coals to Newcastle or ice to the Eskimos. From a trip to the Açores came the image – on a day of televised death and disaster across the world – of a serene and solitary President Soares in a small boat rowed by island fishermen.

Portugal wears the countenance of a good-news country. It is bland rather than exotic, pleasing rather than dispiriting. Once, Turditania was here. Now, travellers see a smiling Ruritania – with stability, security, democracy, justice. There are times when the Portuguese seem like one big happy family – when Amália Rodrigues, the great lady of *fado*, celebrated a fifty-year career with a spectacular concert in Lisbon, President Soares and the prime minister, Cavaco Silva, were there among the adoring crowds to pay homage. She was, in her seventies, Portugal's own still glamorous star, the show a sell-out. An international committee of honour included a king, presidents, a cardinal, world-renowned personalities. But it seemed like a family occasion.

Glamour and celebrity, instant worldwide recognition, the superstar lustre of the rich and famous, have eluded the Portuguese. Carmen Miranda grew up in Brazil. The Portuguese fisherman Spencer Tracy played in *Captains Courageous* – what was he called? In the ranks of big money, in the art auctions, in art, even in literature, no Portuguese name transcends all others. With a confidence bestowed by an immense culture and a long history, most Portuguese pretend not to care. But they do. Listen to the loud rejoicing when a Portuguese is a winner, is noticed and praised across the world. Observe the frustration when hopes are destroyed. Sport or scientific prowess, the Eurovision song contest, an EEC, NATO or UNESCO post – the context is irrelevant. Disguised occasionally with wit and self-mockery, a fierce patriotism prevails.

A journalist once said of Mário Soares, whom the press like to lampoon as a modern monarch, 'You can say anything you like about him, he can take it.' Then a foolish young woman, the niece of a maverick general, said that Mário Soares at a London demo during his exile had trampled on the flag of Portugal. He promptly sued. (Later, his honour untainted, the gesture made, he dropped the case.) An actor in a children's television programme – its theme nationalism and patriotism – was banned from performing, the programme was suspended and a charge made of 'lack of respect for the national anthem', which was performed for the kiddies in an 'accelerated' version. A popular comedian, Herman José, whose dedicated vulgarity and burlesque versatility has won him national fame, suffered a long suspension for satirizing a nationally sacred theme: Portuguese history.

'I want to say to the Portuguese,' Jacques Delors once said encouragingly, 'that they must never forget they are Portuguese before they become Europeans.' The advice was met with barely concealed hoots of laughter. It is inconceivable that a Portuguese could ever be unmindful of origin, of nationality. Top business through the Associação Industrial Portuguesa strives to present a European face in its dealings with, say, the United States (the AIP also operates an advisory European office). The Luso-American Foundation for Development (FLAD) aims to promote Portuguese business, cultural and educational links with the US. The question was, as editor Vítor Direito put it in *Correio da Manhã*, will the Portuguese, with all his virtues, but above all with all his faults – the ordinary fellow, the little guy – ever be a European?

In ordinary daily life patriotism and national glory are not uppermost. A Discoveries Commission earnestly propagates the achievements of the past. Most flag-waving is in local colours for club teams – football is not so much a sport as a component of the national psyche. At any pivotal league match, fan fever is high. Flags compete in size, flares fly and smoke rises as in some holy, bloodless war. When Benfica charged Porto with poaching, war was the word used – by the press, at least. 'In terms of actual power,' wryly observed journalist Miguel Sousa Tavares, 'it is incontestably more important and more rewarding to be president of Sporting [a club rooted in Lisbon and national life for more than eighty years] than to be a European deputy.'

The burdens of the rich are not those of the poor. Rural concerns are not those of the city. The preoccupations of Oporto are not those of Lisbon. *Lisboetas* weep for their burned Chiado; country folk have never been there. The picture of one big happy family gathered to honour Amália, the stars of football or a shining heroine like marathon champion Rosa Mota, is a collective expression of national pride. In smaller gatherings, too, the Portuguese, sensitive, under-appreciated, honour their prophets.

Wine-makers pay tribute to renowned enologists like Manuel Vieira, Nicolau de Almeida and Amândio Galhano. Intellectuals eulogize artists, musicians, writers and poets – scores of them. The sciences esteem the estimable. Portuguese awards and prizes for distinguished national achievement proliferate. Some folk aspire to the singular eminence of *The Guinness Book of Records*: human statues, stilt-walkers, endurance disc jockeys and dancers, the cyclist who pedalled non-stop for 191 hours, fryers of the world's biggest steak, bakers of the world's tallest cake. An Algarve magician, Professor Herrero, beat Paul Daniels's record by performing sixty-four tricks in 3 minutes 47 seconds. To Portugal, in 1987, came a Japanese TV team to film – together – a Guinness-listed world's tallest man, Moçambican-born Gabriel Monjane (245.7 cm, 8 ft $\frac{3}{4}$ in) and the shortest man, António Ferreira (75 cm, 29$\frac{1}{2}$ in). Ferreira, a drummer in a group called the Pop Kings, was a cheerful, outgoing man, immensely popular. (Both died within a couple of years.) *The Guinness Book of Records* had already listed King Afonso Henriques as the longest-reigning European monarch, poor Luís Filipe, the son of the assassinated King Carlos, who barely survived him, as having the shortest reign in history and Salazar as the dictator who lasted longest. The Portuguese take pleasure in their own national quirks and unforgettable characters, praise their own national skills and successes, rejoice in their splendid literature and language, art and architecture – on the unstated principle that hardly anyone else does. And the individual success all Portuguese celebrate, the bright flame round whom all Portuguese joyously gather, contrasts all the more powerfully with failure, frustration, contention, yearning – *saudade* – the word that expresses a state of mind.

In the nature of a people so divided between urban and rural, issues that seem urgent in Lisbon mean little or nothing further afield: polls taken on subjects like an interest in politics or the importance of NATO show that only a small youthful group is enthralled and aware, the majority indifferent. Election fever strikes few other than those desiring to be elected. An enterprising minor party built, in an imaginative echo of Oporto history, a bridge of boats across the Douro. In Lisbon, a candidate made every paper when he entered the lion's cage at a circus. Neither won. The rural Portuguese correctly judge election periods to be almost the only moment when government notices their opinions. And if not voting may seem an odd way to say what you think, in Portugal boycotting elections is a guarantee of national publicity.

Small communities are suddenly in focus. The mood is agitated. Voices and tempers are raised. Roads and railway lines are blocked. The causes are various. Vizela in the north fought for years to be independent from the Guimarães municipality. In Barqueiros the issue was a widely disliked kaolin mine in the centre of town. As simmering indignation grew to anger, the GNR gathered and a young man was shot dead by a GNR bullet. Elsewhere, villagers wanted a new fire station. The people of Pernes and Vaqueiros, near Santarém, demanded a clean-up of their factory-polluted river. Culatra, an island off Faro, wanted electricity. On election day some parishes voted, some did not. Some won their point. Some did not. Until the next elections no one, except the frustrated *povo*, much cared.

Old resentments simmer on – the nineteenth and twentieth centuries were periods of passions and hates, Oliveira Marques reminds us. At a certain social level questions of personal honour were resolved by duels – in 1912 a youthful Dr Egas Moniz and Major Norton de Matos clashed swords over a political difference. Monarchists still ardently argue with Republicans. Even as whole towns compete increasingly sharply for investment and for tourists old, odd issues persist. Relations between Ourique, in the Alentejo, and Vila Chã de Ourique near Santarém remain hostile as each determinedly claims to be the site of the crucial battle of Ourique won by Dom Afonso Henriques in 1139.

Enhanced status, a better life, are not unreasonable expectations. Can EEC funds and government budgets ease the troubled hearts and minds of the Portuguese? The statistics tell a cold, colourless story. How does one weigh the prospects for these profoundly self-analytical people, absorbed by their own past, challenged by change, burdened with bureaucracy and defective services, pressed by low income, rising costs, high taxes? The opinions of foreign specialists, economists and eminent visitors are sought at times, foreign press news and comment quoted in the Portuguese press. How much of what they say carries any weight with the Portuguese? Vasco Pulido Valente in *O Independente* deftly dismissed outside opinion even as he caught the nuance of a national complex with his tart remark that no foreigner who studies Portugal could be any good as no erudite foreigner would, anyway, study Portugal.

A well-crafted joke frames with delicious melancholy a false humility. Clever wordsmiths on the quality newspapers display in artful columns their inventive gifts. As it happens, inventiveness in Portugal, if not one of the characteristics you read of in tourist brochures, is not at all uncommon. Portuguese inventors are always winning international prizes for designs that range from civil engineer Martins de Oliveira's economic vertical drain to dentist António Roseiro's robot to assist him when he works with children – a walking, talking, singing, smiling, wonderfully diverting, fully functional, dental assistant.

My favourite among a host of ingenious contrivances is the one I found in a diminutive jewellery and watchmender's shop in the small town of Tabuaço on the high southern banks of the Douro river. Amândio Ribeiro had spent years crafting a prodigal clock, its data-crammed face as high as himself, which does far more than tell the time. It can look back, and forward, 6,000 years. It can tell you what were the solar and lunar cycles on your day of birth, the sign of the planet and more, much more. And it is a speaking clock, piping the hours in Sr Ribeiro's own gentle voice.

The Portuguese, you will hear again and again, have little sense of time, are never in a hurry: *amanhã* does not mean tomorrow but any time (though try telling that to a farmer or a clock-punching factory hand). A Portuguese journalist fretted that this lassitude in the society could, untreated, turn fatal. He need not be alarmed: the Portuguese have survived far worse maladies. Perhaps it is that the Portuguese, with so much time behind them – like the great, engaging clock in Tabuaço – hold a unique mental measure of time to come. By this measure, their limitless tolerance, their resolute scepticism, their durable pessimism, are the strongest weapons in the national armoury. The poet Fernando Pessoa closed his visionary work *Mensagem* ('Message') with a resounding cry of hope: '*É a hora!*' ('The time has come'). Maybe it has. Forget the statistics. The Portuguese are unrushed, unbowed, unconquerable.

11 Treasures of heaven
and earth

To most Portuguese, *terra natal*, the place where they were born, is the sweetest in the world. The decay and dilapidation in old Lisbon grieves *lisboetas* but is trifling compared with their beloved city's grace and elegance. Is her beauty wrinkled, her elegance faded, the ribbons of her finery ripped away in builders' frenzy? The *grande dame*, the Tejo at her feet, still has all her powers of seduction. Although not, in truth, for *portuenses* singing the praises of their ancient, moody, river-misted Oporto, her veins 'streets with a thousand lives', who love her so dearly they would put 'a diadem on her head'. Across Portugal, each city, every town and village, as magnetic as Lisbon and Oporto, as obscure as A-do-Barbas and Zouparria, has the homely light that beckons to staunch citizens and to some emigrant somewhere.

The rest of us, for ever foreign, lacking the granite pride of the Oporto *tripeiro*, 'tripe-eater', or the sophisticated self-mockery of the Lisbon *alfacinha*, literally 'little lettuce', can pick from the Portuguese jewel-box, invitingly thrown open for our delectation, the gems that please us most. But how to choose? There are so many centuries, so much genius, so many marvels and enchantments scattered across the map. For a particularly intriguing conjunction of history with art, of church and sword, of the spectacular with the enthralling, take as an example Tomar, headquarters of the Knights Templar and their successors, the Order of Christ.

In one pleasant town on the River Nabão are displayed not only the still-evident skills of the founding father, Gualdim Pais, Grand Master of the Templars, who began to build in 1162, but the whims and caprices of some of the cleverest and richest kings of

Portugal, their architects and artists. Tomar also received the occasional attention of Prince Henry the Navigator, head of the Order of Christ from 1417 to his death in 1460. He had a palace within the castle walls – his oldest brother, King Duarte, died there in 1438 – and saw to the building of two cloisters. His true impact came with the maritime wealth of his great-nephew, Dom Manuel.

In the Convento de Cristo, the twelfth-century Charola (rotunda) takes its inspiration from the Holy Sepulchre in Jerusalem. The paintings on wood in the ambulatory, with Jesus and Jerusalem as their appropriate theme, are attributed to Jorge Afonso, royal painter to King Manuel I from 1508. Others are the work of his equally renowned son-in-law Gregório Lopes. Dom Manuel's expansive urges are responsible for much fine building, typified by the ornate chapterhouse window, its plain grille elaborately framed in a fantasy of marine motifs, with Dom Manuel's own emblem, the armillary sphere, at the upper corners, the Cross of Christ at the top and an enigmatic bearded face at the bottom. The artist is unknown; the window was created while Diogo de Arruda was supervising, around 1510, the construction of part of the convent complex in which, across the years, many other hands and minds – and architectural styles – were involved. And if the window is the exotic, hallucinatory epicentre of the _convento_, calm is restored by the cool Renaissance design by Diogo de Torralva of the Great Cloister (built by order of Dom João III in the Italianate style) and, just down the hill, the church of Nossa Senhora da Conceição.

Tomar's Convento de Cristo is one of seven Portuguese sites on UNESCO's world heritage list (the others are the Batalha, Alcobaça and Jerónimos monasteries, the Belém tower, Évora's historical centre and, in the Açores, the historical centre of Angra do Heroismo). Tomar wears its distinction easily. As for windows, in Portugal there are astonishing and exquisitely proportioned windows – arched, rectangular, moulded, carved, lintelled, latticed, lavish, plain – almost everywhere you look. The Casa dos Coimbras in Braga looks out through Manueline windows almost as celebrated, just as accomplished, much less convoluted. In Évora, the palace window with a Moorish air named after Garcia de Resende, one of an eminent cluster of intellectuals who were born in Évora, or lived there, is among the gentler joys in Évora's cornucopia of religious, functional, defensive and decorative architecture.

The old farmhouses of southern Portugal were built with few windows, often with none at all. Sunlight enters through doors set in walls of stone two feet thick or filters down from a *clarabóia*, a small inset skylight or glass tile slotted into the clay roofing tiles above the cane ceiling. Inside, it is dark, cool, safe and private. Outside, beyond an outhouse for cooking, a privy – also, perhaps, an *armazém* (storeroom), with its thousand and one uses from storing dried figs and carobs to garaging a son's car or bed space for the family's old folk – are chicken enclosures, a rabbit run, a mule stable and cart shelter, and the fields. In villages, towns, even cities, light only enters the terraced houses from the front. Outside is sunshine and an infinite spectacle.

Climate, geography and custom dictated the basic architectural ground rules. In the north the need was to keep out the cold and the rain, in the south the fierce heat of the sun. The Alentejo, suffering both sharp winter wind and torrid summer heat, traditionally compromised with thick walls and few, small or no windows. Romans, with Mediterranean instincts, opened windows in Portugal. The Moors kept their women behind them – even now the world view for numerous folk is through the flap of a crocheted curtain. Christian faith, building to a greater glory than mere human need, looked to higher inspiration – and built so strongly and well that many early monasteries, like the São João de Tarouca church south of Lamego, the first Cistercian monastery in Portugal, completed in 1152, still stand. All the older cathedrals – Braga, Lisbon, Coimbra, Oporto, Viseu – have that robust, plain-spoken, fortified aspect to them. Stone was strong, the spirit stronger.

Faith was a mainspring in the evolution of independent Portugal, in winning (and losing) battles, in the adventure of discovery, in motivating an expanding empire, in the long horror of the Inquisition. Kings built great monasteries and churches, some of them sensibly defensive, in praise of God. That they were also durable symbols of royal power and prestige was scarcely a minor consideration. The lasting thrill is the creativity and imagination in so much construction. A tired eye blurs – mine, at least – and perception is blunted by all the gilded woodwork, by the limitless fecund baroque curl and flourish, by those humbling altarpieces, by too rich a diet of sacred paintings, sacred poses. But the striking individuality of each vigorous, buoyant, cathedral city, its past indissolubly linked to the present and the future, is the true surprise.

Skip the deformities, the ugly modern excrescences, the jumped-up apartment blocks, the useful and dull building growing fast on the fringes, the sudden outbursts of impresario enterprise. Vital expressions though they are of economic vigour, exalting treasure lies beyond. In places – Évora is one of them – there are no obstacles. Not even during the more heated gatherings to discuss agrarian reform were tourists disturbed from their meditation of its wonders. Évora's serene outline, in whites and greys, has a luminous glow even from a distance. Rising from the Alentejo fields, enfolded within high walls of different ages, Évora dazzlingly encapsulates all Portugal's dramatic history, cultural tastes, intellectual attitudes, even its streak of mordant humour.

The cathedral, Romanesque Gothic, dating to 1186, framed by two towers of mesmerizing dissimilarity, is warmed by the brilliant Alentejo sun. Steps away are the columns of the Roman temple of Diana – once I saw them, stark and disquieting, at full moon. Startling, too, are four muscular stone giants, quaintly dubbed *meninos* ('little boys') *da Graça*, perched on pediments of the Nossa Senhora da Graça church. In the museum is a splendid collection of sculpted, carved and painted treasures. In mansions, ducal and princely palaces, in the streets – in the arcades of the Praça do Giraldo and leading from it, in the *pousada*, cleverly converted from the Convento dos Loios (dine in the cloisters, sleep in a cell), in the university, in any of twenty-odd churches, is Portuguese architecture and artistry at its most illuminating.

Évora countryside is also rich in megalithic monuments: dolmens, tall, phallic menhirs jutting from olive groves. There, too, west of Évora, along a well-marked sandy lane through a cork forest, is an eerie Portuguese Stonehenge, the cromlech of Almendres. More than four thousand years ago, the experts say, the cromlech, an oval of elliptical standing stones, was a temple dedicated to a solar cult, an inscribed central rock where the rays of sunrise and sunset intersect its awesome 'stone of power'.

It is, though, to Évora's imposing São Francisco church that holiday crowds flock with expectant shivers. Deep inside is Portugal's most notable Capela dos Ossos, a macabre, vaulted chapel totally lined with matched bones and skulls from 5,000 skeletons recovered in the seventeenth century from – I read – forty-eight churches and thirty-two monasteries. Above the entry is a grim line, in rhyme: '*Nós ossos que aqui estamos pelos vossos esperamos*' ('We bones that are here await yours'). I record in passing that there are echoes of this morbid humour in the name of Lisbon's main cemetery: Prazeres ('pleasures'). Also that there are bone chapels in the parish church of Campo Maior, to the north-east of Évora, and, in the Algarve, modestly in Alcantarilha and, in Faro, in a neat arrangement of 1,245 skulls within the Nossa Senhora do Carmo church. Above the chapel door the inscription reads in translation: 'Stop here and think of this fate that will befall you!' It is not a lovely place. More people ponder on passing time and fate in the busy post-office building across the square.

Faro, too, is a cathedral city, its low sandstone tower dating to 1251. As Silves faded, Faro grew – to city status in 1540 and as seat of the Algarve diocese in 1577. Built, perhaps, over a Moorish mosque, the cathedral stands in the walled old town foursquare to peaceful space, orange trees, a former seminary and the bishop's palace. Behind it, a sixteenth-century convent with evocative cloisters, designed by an architect from Évora, Afonso Pires, houses an archaeological museum. Catastrophe – fire, earthquake, invasion – has left Faro with few treasures. My own frivolous favourite is the Lethes theatre inside a building that was once a Jesuit college and is today owned by the *Cruz Vermelha*, the Red Cross. It is a small gem of a theatre with a fetchingly painted ceiling and five rows of boxes, still on occasion in use. (Amongst other groups, the Faro film club uses the theatre; watching the films of Woody Allen, John Cleese, Almodóvar *et al.* from a dress-circle box undeniably adds to the pleasure.)

Coimbra, standing tall beside the Mondego river, its hilly poise as ancient capital and noble seat of learning marred by ill-considered building, manages to suggest invincibility. It even has two cathedrals, the Sé Velha, founded in 1162, with its solid Romanesque two-tier arched portal and contrastingly delicate Gothic cloister, and what is called the new cathedral, Sé Nova, originally a church begun by Jesuits in 1598 beside their Colégio das Onze Mil Virgens. The Jesuits were banished in 1759; the Sé Nova became the episcopal seat in 1772 – and the old bishop's palace has become the admirable Machado de Castro Museum, sculpture understandably its strong point as Joaquim Machado de Castro himself was a consummate sculptor. Born in Coimbra in 1732, he lived to be ninety. In the Santa Cruz church down the hill are buried the long-lived King Afonso Henriques and his son, King Sancho I. It was in this church that King Pedro enthroned the decomposing corpse of his lover, Inês de Castro, for his court to honour. Yet Coimbra, for all its old churches and a patriarchal university with a library so sublime it seems sacrilege to thumb the books, in the end is a city, in term time, anyway, of noisy streets and boisterous youth. You could never call it dull.

Guarda, on the north-eastern shoulder of the Serra da Estrela, with its dark fortress of a cathedral, is used to being called names. '*Forte, feia, fria e farta*' ('strong, ugly, cold and richly productive'), say the Portuguese of this Beira city that is the highest – at 1,056 m – in Portugal. Cold it can be – I was caught one January in a slow-moving line of traffic blocked by a thick fall of snow. Ugly is merely unkind. In Guarda, with abounding municipal pride, they describe their *cidade dos 'Efes'* as '*farta, forte, fria, fiel e formoso*' ('rich, strong, cold, faithful – and lovely'). To each his own. Certainly Guarda had a certain appeal for some Portuguese kings – from a liaison between Dom João I and the beautiful Inês Fernandes, the daughter of a deeply disapproving Jewish shoemaker in Guarda, was born a son who became the first Duke of Bragança and founder of the last line of kings. Guarda is a frontier city. It must have seemed appropriate in 1390, when building began, that the cathedral should have the fierce qualities of a fortress. Yet Boitac worked here, as did master builders from Batalha, and the mix of styles, the flying buttresses, the pinnacles, the odd, unexpected gargoyle, João de Ruão's hundred-odd carved figures high on the retable in the surprisingly light interior, give to a massive hulk an almost friendly character – the indefinable secret ingredient of Portuguese building.

Reconquest built cathedrals, reconstruction preserved them and changed them – Viseu twice at least. Its seventeenth-century façade, with its niches and statues and symbols, is an indulgent counterpoint to the twin-towered, equally remodelled Misericórdia church in the same square. Viseu was a Roman crossroads, Gothic kings were here, perhaps the Lusitanian hero, Viriato. Viseu's greatest treasure is not the cathedral's valuable *tesouro*, crosses and coffers and rare pieces from across the ages, but the artistry of a city son, the painter Vasco Fernandes (1475–1541), known as Grão Vasco ('the great Vasco'). Some of his most sumptuous work (and that of the school he led) hangs in the Grão Vasco museum in the former bishop's palace.

Silves in the Algarve is not the only cathedral city with a distinguished past to lose its status. The Manueline Igreja Matriz of Elvas, attributed to Francisco da Arruda, was a cathedral between 1570 and 1881. But unseemly squabbling between bishop and deacon – it inspired a comic poem – deprived Elvas of its episcopal status.

In a final flourish, in the reign of Dom João III (1521–57), three cathedrals rose in the style called *igreja-salão*, three naves to a spacious equal height, in the towns of Miranda do Douro in the north, on a high cliff beside the river, in Portalegre in the east and in Leiria in the west. Miranda's moment at the diocesan peak lasted a bare two centuries. In 1770, following Spanish invasion, siege, calamity, the bishop plumped for Bragança (where modern designs for a shining new cathedral have been in abeyance for years).

Miranda has no lack of rare characteristics, its bizarre folk dancers among them. They are called *pauliteiros*. They carry sticks, and they are a sight to be seen: tough men in petticoats and shawls, in striped socks and heavy boots, their broad-brimmed hats trimmed with flowers. When they dance, boots thump, sticks whack and skirts fly. The town has many treasures – in the *mirandês* culture graphically displayed in the museum, in the little town's quiet streets and churches, in the cathedral itself. Quite the most memorable is a tiny Christ child. Commemorating a seventeenth-century *mirandês* victory over Spanish forces, it is kitted out with a grand, if miniature, wardrobe – I counted seven embroidered shirts alone. This Menino Jesus da Cartolinha appears outside only once a year, on Miranda's patron saint's day in August. It is quite a moment. '*Jesu' sai*,' the crowd whispers; 'He is coming out.' And on a trestle borne by four children comes a doll-like figure in courtly costume, bow tie and top hat.

Portalegre's cathedral, its white twin pinnacles adding emphasis, is plainly at the core of a resolute community. Leiria, above the little river Lis, a small town rich in kingly activity, is different yet again. Dominated by the imposing broad-hipped castle with its crenellated towers and palace chambers – and fine view – the cathedral seems to lack impact. This is an illusion. The cathedral, designed by the architect Afonso Álvares (who afterwards worked on the outwardly severe São Roque of the Jesuits in Lisbon), with its plain exterior and soothing, light, vaulted interior, surveyed by an almost restrained retable, is the more elevating structure.

After the sixteenth century no more cathedrals were built. Traditionally, cathedrals reflect not only the spiritual tenets of their builders but also the needs of society. And Portugal's great churches do just that, in a sequence – the stalwart Romanesque of reconquest, Gothic for growth, ornament marking maritime expansion, the austerity of Counter-Reformation – that began in Braga. '*Tão velho como a Sé de Braga*,' they say in the Minho when they speak of times long past; 'as old as Braga Cathedral', which was consecrated in 1089, although additions, modifications and embellishments went on well into the eighteenth century. Nor has work ceased: as the cathedral's nine-hundredth anniversary was being celebrated, archaeologists were elatedly delving in the remains of a Roman temple to Isis and, in nearby Dume, finding evidence of a sixth-century basilica constructed by the influential São Martinho de Dume, an archbishop of Braga who died in 579.

Count Henry of Burgundy and his wife Teresa, parents of Portugal's first king, Afonso Henriques, commissioned the building of Braga cathedral and are buried there. The cathedral treasure is a large and immensely valuable collection. There has been talk of enlarged premises and remodelling. The part of it on display, when I saw it, seemed a strange jumble. For all the unburnished gold and silver, the ivory caskets and chalices, the cloth, the carving, a portable organ, the numbing knicknackery, I recall most of all – perhaps because of its simplicity – a slender, unadorned iron cross little more than a foot high. The cross was carried across the Atlantic by Pedro Álvares Cabral on his voyage of discovery in 1500 and used for the first mass celebrated in Brazil.

Braga's showpieces leap the ages: Roman ruins continue to be excavated, a prehistoric *fonte do ídolo* (fountain of the idol) continues to mystify – and, close by, luxuriant windows froth from the thoroughly baroque Casa do Raio. A sixteenth-century palace, the Casa dos Biscainhos, enfolds the city museum; the handsome and dignified archbishop's palace, with an elegant fountain in the forecourt, is part Minho University and part public library, one of the largest, oldest and finest in Portugal.

On a thickly forested hill above Braga, the sanctuary of Bom Jesus crowns the celebrated cascade of steps thought out by a tirelessly diligent archbishop, Rodrigo Moura Teles, in 1723. A hydraulically operated funicular, installed in 1882, glides helpfully beside the steps. Piety and Christ's passion are the stern motifs of Bom Jesus. Chapels and sacred statues flank the long zigzag of the stairway. On centre landings, as you climb, gruesome fountains hideously represent the five senses then, marginally less grim, faith, hope and charity. Yet Bom Jesus, in the down-to-earth Portuguese way, is a resort, a jolly place for picnics, with bright flowers in pleasant gardens, shady glades, a lake with boats and long-established hotels which take credit cards.

Like any successful theme park, Bom Jesus has been imitated – in miniature in Peneda, deep inside the National Park, and grandly in Lamego. Not at all outshone is Lamego's cathedral, blending Renaissance with Gothic, its façade balancing, like three Graces, a trio of elegant doors and windows. Prime treasures of Lamego's museum are a series of sixteenth-century Flemish tapestries and, from a panel of twenty that once adorned the cathedral, a glowing 'Creation of the Animals' and four other paintings by Grão Vasco.

*

For over a thousand years, allowing for heated opposition from Toledo, Santiago de Compostela, Moors, Leon and Castile, Braga was the religious capital of Portugal. Modern Braga, its mind on commerce and industry, looks outward and forward – and upwards, in places, to multi-storey building blocks. Traffic roars by day and *discotecas* blast by night. Braga's religious dominance in Portugal took a sharp knock when in 1716 King João V won from Rome the right of Lisbon to have its own patriarch. The anticlerical shocks of 1834, the end of monarchy in 1910 and revolution in 1974 further crushed church authority – although, if you were to see the fervent Holy Week processions in Braga or the Whitsun crowds at Bom Jesus you would never know it.

It was Braga's conservative archbishop, Dom Eurico Dias Nogueira, who once pointedly remarked that only a small part of the property expropriated from the Church by the 1911 Separation Law had been returned after the 1940 Concordat. The mountainous register of the Church's fortunes and misfortunes, assets and outlays, debts and obligations, sufferings and persecutions – over centuries, across an empire – comprises immeasurably more than relatively recent quarrels.

Today, the Catholic Church (though no other), thanks to the government's appreciation of its 'relevant social role' and the 'religious sentiments of the Portuguese population', has been absolved from paying IVA, or value added tax. The state provides funds for construction, repair and restoration of churches (in 1989 about Esc.390m, over £1.5m), and additional grants to the União das Misericórdias, some four hundred local charitable organizations and other private institutions, which run crèches, old people's homes, aid for the handicapped and other social programmes, and which altogether employ some 20,000 people. The Misericórdias, a body nearly five hundred years old, one of some sixty Catholic establishments and associations in Portugal, is also extremely affluent. In 1988, its income from lotteries and football pools was reported to be over 95m contos, about £380m.

The church hierarchy, although accepting the long-standing autonomy of the Misericórdias, each one headed by a local notable of considerable influence, began to redefine the relationship. A matter of some controversy was the setting up by some of the Misericórdias of a holding company for investment and finance purposes. Among its first acquisitions was a factory that made hospital furniture and coffins. There were reports of establishing a bank and insurance company. At about the same time as the venerable Misericórdias were absorbing the trendy attitudes and structures of high finance, the Lisbon Patriarchate announced that its parish priests, some 300 priests in 267 parishes, would for the first time be paid a salary. Braga, with roughly twice the number of priests, contemplated a similar course.

The affairs of the Church are followed with interest, not all of it devout. Among the national leaders, politicians of the centre and left, and professionals are many who practise no religion. Others, some 2,500, are members of the clannish, cryptic Opus Dei. In the Alentejo town of Monforte two French priests of the Fraternidade Sacerdotal São Pio X conduct daily Latin masses for a scattering of followers of the ultra-conservative French bishop Marcel Lefèbvre. The press treats Church activities as any other social or news event, with features on the work of several orders and congregations (one quaintly named Irmãs Adoradas – Adored Sisters) in helping the needy. *Correio da Manhã* won a rare interview, through a grille, with the Mother Superior of the Convento das Concepcionistas in Campo Maior, who had lived a cloistered life there for forty years 'without a moment of regret'. The Order of the Immaculate Conception, maintaining total seclusion, was founded by Portugal's only female saint, Santa Beatriz da Silva, born in Campo Maior in 1424. When a retired priest built a replica of his church beside his apartment on the topmost floor of a modern block of flats in Póvoa de Varzim, *Expresso* managed a gentle pun on 'Glory to God in the highest'. At times the papers report a call by the Cardinal Patriarch, Dom António Ribeiro, for more priests.

In all Portugal there are some 2,500 serving priests, many of them over fifty. Nor would you recognize them outside church: they dress like everyone else. Over five hundred priests have left the priesthood since 1974, a few on points of doctrine, most to marry – lamenting, in many cases, the Church's insistence on celibacy. (No longer unequivocal; the Lisbon parish of the Igreja das

Mercês is served by a priest, formerly Protestant, who is married and has children.) Parish response to their maverick priests varies from calling them traitors to doting on their children.

The Portuguese are not unaccustomed to large priestly families, a commonplace over the centuries – Oliveira Martins is richly sarcastic on the waywardness of nuns and priests. One of Portugal's great men, Nun' Álvares Pereira, Dom João I's constable and dearest friend, who died a monk, was one of the numerous children of Dom Álvaro Gonçalves Pereira, Grand Prior in Crato in the Alentejo of the Order of Hospitaleiros de S. João de Jerusalém. He built in 1356 the stoutly fortified church and monastery of Flor da Rosa in Crato, and lies there even now, in stately splendour, as workmen complete the transformation of 'the flower of Crato' to a comfortable *pousada*. In Crato two Portuguese kings were married to Spanish wives – Dom Manuel I to his third wife, Leonor, and Dom João III to Catarina. Now, its importance has shrunk to a small farming town, its roadside houses squeezed under big chimneys rising to the limitless Alentejo sky. Churches are still here, and a prior and – little treasures – frolicking children.

So much has gone – above all, with empire, Portugal's missionary role as *Alferes da Fé* ('standard-bearer of the faith'), the phrase of playwright Gil Vicente. Perhaps it is surprising how much has endured – a Church no longer fused with the state but an imperishable state within a state, with even the old military Orders of Christ, Santiago and Avis surviving in Portugal today as secular honours and decorations. And there are still small communities of the time-honoured holy orders, Dominican, Benedictine, Franciscan and Jesuit. One Dominican monk, Frei Elias, an accomplished illuminator of texts, embodies continuity of ancient skills: the first known works of Portuguese art (guarded in the national archives) were thirteenth-century manuscripts – the most famous aptly depicts grape-picking from a mighty vine – illuminated by monks at Lorvão.

Religious faith in Portugal today freely encompasses complexities of belief and doctrine. Among them Jews, Muslims, Buddhists, Hindus, Roman Catholics, Christian Scientists, Friends, American

Episcopalians, the Church of Scotland, the Church of England, Lusitanians, the Salvation Army, Baptists, Methodists, the Evangelical Assembleia de Deus, Jehovah's Witnesses (conspicuous as conscientious objectors; several hundred young men have been permitted since 1985 civic instead of military service) and the Church of Latter-day Saints (Mormons).

Not a single law pronounces Portugal as Roman Catholic. There is no bloody battle for souls. Tolerance rules. At the intellectual level Catholics challenge convinced atheists to debate the future of God – as happened when Carlos Macedo, a devout doctor, took on virtuoso Vasco Pulido Valente during a weekend gathering at the Centro Universitário Padre António Vieira to discuss the world in change. In the streets, on the land, at the seashore, at all the teeming fairs, in the rollicking *festas* and rituals of pilgrimage, there is no debate. Few talk of doubt or devotion. For the vast majority of Portuguese, there is one faith, and it is immutable.

Or is it? The spiritual comfort, the electric charge so many Portuguese derive from their Church is due not so much to its essential doctrines but to what they themselves have made of it. The cathedrals, the great churches – Jerónimos, Alcobaça, Batalha and others – reflect national pride at its peak. In Lisbon's São Roque church the chapel of St John the Baptist, sumptuously ornamented with lapis lazuli, ormolu, porphyry and agate, was commissioned by King João V in 1742, built in Rome, blessed by Pope Benedict XIV, taken apart and brought piece by piece to Lisbon. The huge cost of it, as with Mafra, as with the resplendent church of the Convento de Arouca, up in the hills north-east of Aveiro, with its baroque golden choir, or the grandiose refurbishing at ancient Lorvão itself in its green valley near Coimbra, the gold and glitter the length of the land, enhanced the magnificence of the Church, the renown of the king, the glory of Portugal.

By marked contrast, shaped and cut into the rock above Sintra in 1560, the mossy, cork-lined Convento dos Capuchos with its tiny cells famously illustrates faith at its least grandiose. (You can also see countless simple chapels across Portugal.) When the Marquis of Pombal demanded a post-Earthquake account of properties, the Sintra register listed forty-four hermitages apart from

churches and monasteries. One of the monks – all were Franciscan
– Frei Honório, believing himself confronted by the devil in the
form of a young and lovely girl seeking confession, spent thirty
years expiating temptation in a penitentially horrid cavern. He died
in 1596, no doubt still atoning, aged ninety. Philip II, his vast
monastery-palace, the formidable Escorial, freshly built, pronounced
Capuchos the poorest convent in his kingdom. Yet it was not
poverty that gave humble Capuchos its lasting significance but
individuality. In Portugal, ordinary folk did things – do things –
their way.

They humanized their Church, made it friendly, here and there
brought it up-to-date – little Alcoutim, beside the Guadiana,
decided to equip four neighbourhood church towers with micro-
computerized clocks so that the bells would ring on time. At
Christmas, in the chilly Beira Baixa, every town and village lights a
log fire – huge sections of tree trunk – outside or near the church,
and keeps it burning until Twelfth Night. They bring their ex-
votos, pray to Our Lady and the saints, especially their own. They
have even made their own. In Aveiro, Joana, the sister of Dom
João II, retreated to the Convento de Jesus (today the regional
museum) and died there in 1490. Legend has flowers and leaves
falling in grief on her coffin. Beatified in 1693, she is, to the
Portuguese, their Princesa Santa Joana. Arouca reveres its Rainha
Santa (holy queen), in the princess Mafalda, born in Coimbra in
1195, the daughter of Dom Sancho I. When a childhood marriage
to the youthful heir to the throne of Castile was annulled, she
devoted her life, and her wealth, to Arouca, and was buried there
after a long, full life. In 1616 nuns found her body incorrupt in its
tomb and at the end of the eighteenth century she was beatified. In
Rome she numbers among the waiting cases. Not in Portugal's
green northern valleys. Favours are asked of her every day. Girls
are named after her. And in Arouca, on the first Saturday of May,
they celebrate the *festa de Santa Mafalda*.

Popular religion, uncontemplative and emotional, responds to
mystery, magic, legend and tradition. On a hill above Arganil, east
of Coimbra, the Santuário do Monte Alto, like Miranda, has its
own image of Jesus as a boy in a modish outfit topped by a cocked

hat. He, too, has a wardrobe of new clothes, and touching tributes of children's worn hats and caps. Commemorating the retreat of French troops, he carries a silver-topped cane in one hand, a blue globe and cross in the other, and is said, with an admirable lack of logic, to represent the vanquished Napoleon. In tiny Lapa, north-west of Trancoso, in a church where boulders form the altar, a doll is *Nossa Senhora da Lapa* who, according to legend, brought speech to a deaf and dumb child.

In the Açores, scarcely a village is without its diminutive house beside each chapel, the mysterious empire at the heart of the cult of the *Espírito Santo*. With echoes of the messianic fervour of Padre António Vieira for a fifth empire of the spirit – evoked by Fernando Pessoa in his *Mensagem* – the cult, through emigration, is strong in many countries. In the Albano Sardoeiro museum in Amarante two black statues, male and female, are associated with worshipping, or appeasing, the devil. (The Archbishop of Braga, in 1870, alarmed at their popularity, ordered them to be burned. Instead, the male devil's rampant penis was severed and, some years later, the statues were sold to a buyer in England. Amarante outrage led to their return.) Amarante's handsome church and monastery of São Gonçalo, beside the São Gonçalo bridge, contains the tomb of the saint, so celebrated as marriage-maker that his effigy is worn smooth by the touch of hopeful spinsters and bachelors. In the Santuário de Nossa Senhora do Bom Despacho, in Cervães, near Braga, the uterine form of two great rocks, a holy image in the cleft, could scarcely be a more explicit symbol of fertility. Each sanctified spot, each corpse, each cult, has its annual pilgrimage.

Ritual has a prominent place in Portuguese life. Solemn proce-dure reflects not only the long, close links of the people with the Catholic Church, but also superstition bred of ignorance, fear, credu-lity and old habit. On dark and stormy nights when the wind howls malignly through bleak mountains, it is the voice, some will still say, of *lobishomens* (werewolves). According to the Portuguese, only the great constellation of saints and, above all, Santa Maria – Holy Mary, mother of God – can protect you, your animals and your possessions, from harm. It is a belief usually expressed with an open and unaffected simplicity and a comfortingly cheerful mix of sacred and profane, sublime and ridiculous.

Cure my pig, prays a woman on her knees to São Luís, patron saint of animals and, for emphasis, to *Nossa Senhora* (Our Lady). When it recovers, she leaves a little wax model of her pig in her village church. Come saint's day, the band of the fire brigade plays, rockets are fired – a lighted cigarette sending them whooshing to the skies – a mass and procession solemnly honour the saint, whose image is supported on the shoulders of the faithful. In streets and squares, bedspreads hang like banners from open windows where the leaning townsfolk watch: a gesture of respect. Then comes, perhaps, an auction (the proceeds to the church or an old folks' home) or home-made liquor, cakes, *chouriço* and *chouriça*, sausages masculine and sausages feminine – stick straight or gently rounded – from, who knows, the selfsame pig. There rises the powerful odour of sardines grilling and sausages aflame in the potent brandy, *bagaceira*: the time has come for feasting, drinking, jokes and poetry.

In variations as manifold as the calendar of saints the saint's day *festas* enliven the spirit, comfort the flesh and soothe the soul. And in this country with its Marian cult, its profound feeling for the mother as protector, more than a thousand *festas* across the country, exploding with noise and colour or modestly low-key, invoke *Nossa Senhora*. She is *Nossa Senhora da Boa Hora*, *de Bom Sucesso*, *da Boa Morte* – of incipient birth, a happy event, a worthy death. She is *Nossa Senhora da Boa Viagem* and *dos Navegantes*, of a safe journey and of seamen.

In Viana do Castelo, venerable capital of the high Minho region at the mouth of the River Lima, she is *Nossa Senhora da Agonia*. They tell you in Viana that in ancient times the city was Diana and the tranquil Lima the legendary Lethe, river of forgetfulness. It is there, each August, that the Portuguese flock in great multitudes for the queen of the folk fairs. Serene brides are in black, wearing a fortune in gold. Scores of smiling young women parade in costumes the colour of flame and of flowers. The city resounds with the noise of pandemonium as thousands of pilgrims joyfully celebrate in the name of Our Lady of Agony. Everywhere, on painted hanging panels, stitched in hearts on fancy garments, the message is *'amor'* (love). No riddle, these are the curious highlights of a spectacular festival.

In Lisbon, huge amounts of money and a great deal of time and effort go into the preparations for the *festas dos Santos Populares* from the middle to the end of June. *Bairros* are decorated, costumes stitched, marches rehearsed. For Sant'António, born in Alfama, a special affection is demonstrated – in a heavy consumption of grilled sardines and wine, and loud, nightlong song, dance and fireworks. In Oporto, on the feast of São João (24 June) the most gripping spectacle is a jolly and entirely secular regatta on the River Douro of *barcos rabelos*, the flat-bottomed, high-bridged sailing boats that once braved rapids to carry casks of port wine downriver. The regatta is a new tradition, begun in 1983 to keep the boats alive.

In the neighbourhood of Graça in Lisbon the annual procession on the second Sunday of Lent of the brotherhood of Santa Cruz dos Passos dates to 1634. Across the Tejo river, the people of Cacilhas devoutly join the procession held each 1 November, All Saints' Day, to celebrate the town's escape from the Great Earthquake of 1755.

More informal processions are taking place across the land, all ending at the local cemetery. Beggars and flower-sellers keenly await them, knowing it is the day of the dead. Inside the walls, most graves, marble scrubbed clean, are already blooming with jars of chrysanthemums. Along the rows of tall stone tombs, each like a miniature rococo mansion, a door is open here and there, lace curtains blowing in the breeze. Women are arranging flowers, shaking out the cloth coffin covers, chatting with neighbours. They are well-dressed and look prosperous. A few women weep, with genuine or effortlessly practised tears. The graveyard is convivial, flowers everywhere, lit candles in tiny lamps. At one grave, a woman is absorbed in prayer, rosary in hand, her handbag hanging from the cross. Her prayer concluded, she crosses herself, collects her bag and briskly departs. I almost expected her to punch a card on her way out.

There is nothing morbid about these holy day activities. The wax ex-votos, bleeding images, crucifixes, robed brotherhoods, cemetery visits and numberless religious processions are accepted custom and procedure in this well-ordered society where sacred, sociable, profane and pagan coalesce in ways of uncertain origin. For the launching of a boat a Portuguese owner will wisely arrange ancient pagan rites, a church blessing with a sprinkling of holy water, and champagne to break on the hull. The motives are sound, the provenance obscure, the show colourful.

Then there is Fátima, unarguably Portugal's paramount devotional spectacle, most of all on 13 May and 13 October, the dates of the first and last appearance of the Virgin to three shepherd children in 1917. Hundreds of thousands of pilgrims make their way to the sanctuary of Fátima, 'altar of Portugal'. Days before, you see on every highway, with strained faces and bandaged legs, many of the 20,000 or more who go on foot. (The first time I saw a group, with expressions of anguish, freshly bandaged legs, carrying staves, I thought there had been a dreadful road accident.) They wear tracksuits and neon shorts, ordinary trousers, skirts, overalls, sweaters. There are elderly women in their regulation black who have made the pilgrimage many times before. You see open summer sandals, a few sensible shoes or sturdy trainers, and penitentially bare feet. Like Lourdes, the phenomenon of Fátima has grown from the fairly common mystical idea of a vision. On 13 May 1917 three children, Lúcia dos Santos, aged ten, and her cousins, Francisco and Jacinta Marta, he nine and she seven years old, were in a field at Cova da Iria, close to the small town of Fátima, where they saw a shining figure in a tree, a holm oak. She told them she had come from heaven and ordered them to return to the tree six times, at the same hour and on the same day of the month. In October she would reveal who she was and what she wanted.

Republican policies, in 1917, were anticlerical. The Church was not at all pleased when news of the apparition spread. On 13 August the three children were arrested and interrogated; the fourth vision appeared to them on the 19th instead. On 13 October, 70,000 pilgrims waited eagerly with the children and many attested afterwards that the skies suddenly cleared and that, in what was soon called the miracle of the sun, a brazen sun shot beams of light upon them – curing long illnesses and opening the eyes of the blind. No one but the children saw the shining lady, who now left with Lúcia, the only child who heard her clearly, a message containing three prophecies, the 'secrets of Fátima'.

The first concerned peace and a fiery hell. The second anticipated the Bolshevik revolution and the Russian threat to world peace and the Church – or perhaps, as was suggested recently, the promise of perestroika. The third, never divulged, so that it grew in frightful import, was alleged by various newspapers to warn of disaster so great that millions would perish and those that remained alive 'would envy the dead'. In 1981, a man who had been a Trappist monk hijacked an Aer Lingus jet and threatened to blow up the aircraft with its 123 passengers if the Pope did not immediately reveal the third secret. The man was subdued, the secret kept. When, a few days later, on 13 May itself, Pope John Paul II was shot in an assassination attempt in Rome, many people assumed this was the earthshaking event prophesied by the third revelation.

Lúcia, who had taken her vows as a nun in 1934 and later joined a Carmelite convent in Coimbra, was among the throng who welcomed the Pope to Fátima on his pilgrimage of thanks in 1982. She was the only survivor of the three children. Francisco died in April 1919, and his sister, Jacinta, less than a year later, in the widespread epidemic of flu. In 1928 the first stone of the basilica was laid – on 13 May. In April 1929 the cult of *Nossa Senhora de Fátima* was authorized by the Church. In May 1967, the fiftieth anniversary of the first apparition, Pope Paul VI came to Fátima. In May 1989 the bishop of Leiria announced to the throng that, by papal decree, Jacinta and Francisco, for their heroic virtues, were to be beatified.

In church terms, they were unusual candidates. For one thing, the massive pilgrimages to Fátima had given them a universal renown that had not been accorded to other worthy cases. Additionally, although a canonization commission of eleven cardinals unanimously agreed that the two little children could properly be venerated, there remained the question of a confirmed miracle, a standard qualification for canonization. There were hundreds, thousands, of witnesses that miraculous cures had occurred. Portuguese church leaders felt it advisable to seek expert medical opinion: a commission of ten specialists was formed to analyse selected case histories and decide if there was, or was not, a scientific explanation for the extraordinary recoveries. But a year later no cases had been presented. As things turned out, the papal decree of beatification resolved this logistical problem. It also raised Portugal's ranking of *santos* and *beatos* – low in this respect, as in others, compared with Spain and Italy, a commentator dourly noted.

The shrine of Fátima's colossal congregations inevitably invite the attentions of commerce. Unsightly souvenir shops peddle images of Our Lady of Fátima, various representations of the newly beatified Francisco and Jacinta, mementoes of Sister Lúcia and a vast range of trinkets. For 250 escudos or thereabouts you can buy a squashily translucent Virgin-shaped plastic flask of holy water. Or you can help yourself, as I did, from a tap in the Sacred Heart monument mid-esplanade. An uneasy infidel in this rite, made at the request of a faraway friend, I have to say that the rest of my journey went remarkably well. Nothing should be made of this: I saw that the entire town was unlucky enough to run out of water once when 300,000 pilgrims were there for the holy 13th.

Fátima to a critical eye is architecturally obnoxious, yet another failure of Salazar in whose era the basilica with its 65 m (213 ft) tower was built. Portugal's greatest art is in the building of its churches. It is astonishing that, as pilgrims for centuries to the extraordinary and beautiful shrine of Santiago de Compostela in neighbouring Galicia, at Fátima they seem to have learned no lesson from it, nor from their own church architecture.

The stupendous evolution of Fátima, after the apparitions to the three children in 1917, is phenomenal only because of its scale. The surface ritual may be Christian; the roots are deeper. In Portugal, in small northern villages, you can still come across boars' heads in stone, crudely sculpted and venerated by Celts between about the sixth century BC and the first century AD. The *porca de Murça* in Murça's main square, a great totemic granite boar, probably dates to the very beginning of that period. In Bragança, beside the castle keep, a stone boar is pierced through by the shaft of the *pelourinho*, the city's emblematic pillory. The children of a Douro fisherman led me to a riverside cliff below Mazouco in the Trás-os-Montes to show me a figure they called *o carneiro* (sheep). Engraved in rock, part sheep, part horse, it is to expert eyes the first Paleolithic art discovered in the open air in Portugal. Ancient doodling? Great art? Object of veneration? In Portugal, all symbols – of God, the devil, man or nature – end in poetry. The magical beasts are poetry in stone.

'The winter is past, the rain is over and gone; the flowers appear on the earth.' So it is in the Song of Solomon. In Portugal the wild flowers, given exuberant life by the winter rains, bring enchantment to a land already greatly endowed with beauty. The new year has barely begun when a gorgeous lacework of pink and white blossom drapes the south and sunbursts of yellow mimosa give an incandescent glow to the north. A long unfolding spring extending to June lays gaudy seasonal counterpanes upon the earth: first the yellow oxalis of January, later the scarlet glory of a field of poppies – for an Alentejo farmer a pernicious raider in his wheat – and great hillsides speckled with rock roses, the familiar evergreen cistus.

Between the mountainous Peneda-Gerês in the north and the hills, woodland and sand dunes of the Algarve are fifty-nine known species of endemic wild flowers and more than a hundred very rare flowers. The flora of the Peneda-Gerês alone includes twenty-six very rare species and fifteen existing only in the park, among them a purple iris (*Iris boissieri*). In the forest and lowlands of the charmed world of the Arrábida Natural Park south of Lisbon are more than a thousand plant species, ranging from giant heather to tiny, exquisite wild orchids. In the Serra do Caramulo, in the Beira Alta, the Cambarinho Natural Reserve exists to protect the *Rhododendron ponticum*, a vivid mauve in May and June, known there as *loendro*, or oleander.

The flowers of the earth, the characterful trees, the wild creatures, which are protected at least within the parks and reserves, the birds that fly overhead, feed in the wetlands or, like thousands of seagull chicks in the Berlenga islands in June, wander underfoot while swooping adults bark and yap in parental cacophony, are all conjoined through a finely balanced, immensely thrilling, combination of climate and landform. But climate alters in onrushing highs and lows and the seasons roll. The ultimate treasure beyond price lies in the rocks and forms of the landscape – the granite and schist of the north, the limestone which predominates in Coimbra, Leiria, Tomar and Lisbon, the central Algarve's sandstone – the folds, the faults and phenomena that shape and colour the land. From its own dependable stone were carved all Portugal's great castles, cathedrals, palaces and town and country houses. And, with infinite architectural grace, the simplest of dwellings.

No master composed the granite or schist houses of the Beira interior, many with great, single-stone lintels, door-frames and steps. Form, texture, colour grew from the land and the basic needs of the people who lived on it. In the isolated village of Piódão, tucked into a valley among the bald-headed hills of the Serra do Açor, schist houses three storeys high, with dark stony walls and darker, irregularly tiled, pitched roofs, cluster protectively on a slope around a startling white sugar-plum church. A tarred road goes there now (via Arganil, Côja, Porto de Balsa) and stops. In the village, the pathways, too, are dark brown stone.

To the east, below the south-eastern flanks of the Serra da Estrela, Monsanto's granite houses snuggle into, over, under and around the tumbled boulders of a hill topped by a medieval castle where once there was the fortified settlement of a Lusitanian *castro*. Chickens roost on granite, dogs drink from bowls gouged in granite, minuscule gardens are sunk in granite. Broad red tile roofs, the farms and green fields below, soften the grey chill of stone, but across the Beira region stone is a brooding, dominating force. In Idanha-a-Velha, south of Monsanto, once the Roman Egitania, birthplace of Wamba, king of the Goths, all Portuguese history is marked on the stones – original, discovered, collected, stored – in the restored paleo-Christian basilica.

Monsanto, in 1938, after a national contest, was declared the most Portuguese village in Portugal. The contest brought Monsanto lasting national fame but raised the question of how so singular a village could win so incomprehensible a title. From the cold Atlantic north to the warm south there is a striking diversity of folk architecture. Nine villages from across Portugal reached the finals. Alte, in the Algarve, was one of them. A village of white-washed, thick-walled Moorish houses on a mountain slope, it has a sparkling stream, shady walks and its own home-grown poet, Cân-dido Guerreiro, to sing its praises.

Roman-tiled pyramid roofs are Tavira's distinguishing feature and, in Olhão, cubes. The flat rooftop terraces (*açoteias*) with a narrow access stairway, that you see on so many Algarve houses, are still used to dry fruit in summer and as water catchment in winter. Marking the architectural transition from the simplest small house with its fringe of tiles to the sophisticated urban style is the descriptive *platibanda*, the plain or decorated fascia.

The low, white farmhouses of the Alentejo plains, clay layered on rock and stone, many rimmed in blue to ward away the devil, are squeezed and modified in compact towns like Serpa or Moura in the eastern Alentejo. Streets of solid white, where even the shadows are white, have a perfect, linear elegance. In the islands of the Açores is the opposite: the black on black of volcanic rock.

On the west coast, at Carrasqueira on the Sado estuary, a few fishermen still live in rectangular thatch houses bound with cane. (Madeira's conserved thatch houses are neat triangles.) Near Mira on the coast north of Figueira da Foz, there are still a few of the colourfully striped wooden houses called *palheiros*. In the small towns and villages of the Minho the plainspoken house is sturdy granite with broad steps to a second level edged with a veranda. More prominent, like tombs on stilts, with a cross fixed to the shallow pitched roof, are weathered granite *espigueiros* (corn stores). At Soajo, north-west of Ponte da Barca, not far from the gaunt *pelourinho* with its odd graven image and the church whose clock I swear I heard strike twice, assembled *espigueiros* rise in stark sil-houette from a great boulder. At Lindoso, near by, close to the Spanish frontier, even more *espigueiros* drift funereally up the hill towards the castle, sometimes with lyre-horned cattle ruminating among them. Each structure, joining earth to sky, stands in its own right. None is alien. All the homes enclose small living spaces, and at times squalor and misery. For the Portuguese, each style of house is a true *casa portuguesa*.

*

Cultivated men and women, with wealth as well as a gift for rhapsody, built remarkable houses, furnished them with taste, filled them with precious things and at times, with a final flourish, left them – or their families did – to the nation. An architectural jewel in Alpiarça, across the Tejo from Santarém in the Ribatejo, lightly juxtaposing arched with rectangular windows, galleries with stairway and striped spire, is the Casa dos Patudos. The Sintra architect Raul Lino designed it at the end of the nineteenth century for José Relvas, landowner, politician and – briefly – premier, renowned in Portugal as the man who proclaimed the Republic in Lisbon on 5 October 1910. Today the house is a museum reflecting Relvas's eclectic interests – Arraiolos carpets, furniture, porcelain, clocks and assorted paintings: sixteenth-century religious art, a still-life by the seventeenth-century woman painter known as Josefa de Óbidos, and several works by notable nineteenth-century Portuguese naturalists such as Columbano – the brother of Rafael Bordalo Pinheiro – Carlos Reis, Silva Porto and the redoubtable José Malhoa.

José Relvas was the oldest son of Carlos Relvas (1838–94), aristocratic, godfather to King Carlos (father and son, holding radically opposed political views, quarrelled fiercely), an intellectual with an all-embracing curiosity. Above all, he was a skilled enthusiast in the brand-new art of photography. By 1869 he was a member of the Society of Photography in France and winning prizes around the world. (Another photographer from Golegã, Frederico Bonacho, also won awards for early colour photos using the gum bichromate process.) Carlos Relvas's house in the horse-loving town of Golegã north-east of Santarém, the Casa-Museu de Fotografia Carlos Relvas, not only contains in his atelier some 13,000 glass negatives, various cameras and lenses, but is itself an exquisite flourish, by architect Henrique Carlos Afonso, of art-nouveau design.

Not every luminary home is architecturally elegant. In São Mamede de Infesta, Oporto, an unpretentious suburban house records the life and work of Guimarães-born Abel Salazar (1889–1946), artist and scientist, who lived there. West of Guimarães, in São Miguel de Seide, you can see, in the uncompromising Casa de Camilo – the house actually belonged to the husband of the woman he loved – the very chair in which the great writer, Camilo Castelo Branco, shot himself. In Caramulo, in the *serra* west of Viseu, the Museu Abel Lacerda presents a medley of fine paintings, furniture, collected antiques and a fleet of vintage cars that keen owner-drivers of what the Portuguese call Dona Elviras have had their eye on for years.

'. . . it can be argued,' writes Nicolas Sapieha in his introduction to *Country Manors of Portugal*, 'that the most perceptive interpretation of a country's history is derived from its domestic architecture. House or palace, a domestic building chronicles a way of life.' The effortless beauty of the simplest *casa portuguesa* is a sure sign, to a mind fixed on money, of economic poverty. How different then are the *solares* and *quintas* and, as they are called in the eastern Alentejo, the *montes*, that reflect old wealth, the possession of land, title, rank and authority. You might still see, lying on a table here and there, the *Livro de Oiro da Nobreza* ('The Golden Book of the Nobility'), the Debrett-style record of past eminence. The society is altered, fortunes dissolved, yet scores of austere, finely crafted or utterly flamboyant manor-houses still enrich the land – although in an uneven pattern. The Minho and Douro, oldest Portugal, are flush with grand houses – and you can stay at some of them. In the far south, only one – the statue-studded eighteenth-century Palácio in Estói with its elaborate, multi-layered gardens – electrifies the connoisseurs. (Long closed and abandoned by all but a single gardener, the palace now belongs to the Faro municipality which, in 1990, was still not admitting visitors to the palace rooms.)

Impressive country houses cross centuries and styles. Watchtowers, once crucial, still stand – among them the Torre dos Azevedos in Barcelos, its wings stretching from a tower dated 1536, and the Torre de Ribafria at Sintra. The towers appear in the Minho's eighteenth-century unflustered baroque Paço da Glória, whose remarkable history includes ownership by a *minhoto* who married the widow, and fortune, of the inventor of the Stetson hat. The *paço*, English restored and owned, welcomes guests. Nasoni's Solar de Mateus, at Vila Real, is baroque at its most sublime, its chapel set back to one side, part of the integrated whole. Nearly all the noble houses have a private chapel, some separate, others joined or within, a symbol, perhaps, of the harmony between daily life and religion – or, as a visiting marquis suggested in 1738, 'husbands' jealousy is so strong they construct chapels to prevent their wives from attending church'. Many houses also, like Mateus, incorporate water and formal gardens into one grand concept.

The Moorish Gothic fantasy of eccentric Englishmen in the Quinta de Monserrate at Sintra, crowning faultlessly landscaped gardens, still dazzles and provokes. The Paço dos Duques de Bragança at Vila Viçosa proves a suitably kingly country retreat with its long façade, great enfiladed rooms, costly furnishings and tapestries, a dining-room that seats thirty under three heavily antlered chandeliers, a kitchen that contains – I was told – 609 copper pots and pans that weigh over 2,000 kilos. You can still hear peacocks cry, wonder at the royal crib with its blue silk canopy, crown and golden angel beside the bed of Queen Amélia, admire paintings of and by her unlucky husband, King Carlos, and – as in any home – look at family snapshots.

Behind the high walls of the Quinta da Bacalhoa in Azeitão, south of Lisbon, soothingly peaceful despite the bus station opposite the tree-shrouded entrance, you can look upon one of the earliest and finest tile panels in Portugal. Dated 1565, 'Susanna and the Elders' is set above a doorway in an arched pavilion, the Casa do Tanque, lined with tiles in a cheerful snowflake pattern, overlooking and reflected by a large square pool. The Renaissance house, with gently domed towers and cool arcades, belonged from 1528 until his death in 1581 to the son of Portugal's first, empire-expanding viceroy, Afonso de Albuquerque. The house, changing hands as centuries passed, quietly faded. In 1937, an American, Elizabeth Scoville, bought the property and slowly and carefully restored its original grace. By the mid-1980s, Bacalhoa, now welcoming visitors, was almost as well known for its wine as for its simple country elegance and the striking Susanna.

Outside, the Casa Anadia, at Mangualde south-east of Viseu, displays poised arched arcades and a pear-shaped entry dividing curving flights of steps. Indoors, blue tiles illuminate the great stairway, exploding in baroque scrolls on the landings and into the rooms. In the opulent Palace Hotel at Buçaco the battles of Wellington's forces against the might of Napoleon are monumentally re-fought in armies of tiles. At the Palácio dos Marqueses de Fronteira, at Benfica, Lisbon, the many-splendoured seventeenth-century gal-leried tile panels are held to outshine the mansion's numerous architectural merits.

The great authority on *azulejos*, Santos Simões, describing the evolution of Portuguese style from the Mudéjar tradition that entered from Andalusia, noted that this *monumentalidade* was a prime characteristic of Portuguese *azulejos*, together with a capacity to adapt to architecture. Tiles, flaunting or discreet, sacred or secular, are a vital art form: ubiquitous historical and hunting themes, biblical and natural themes, enthralling documentary tiles, often by Jorge Colaço, at railway stations – those at Pinhão on the Douro, among others made at the Fábrica Aleluia in Aveiro, were copied from photographs by Domingos Alvão (1872–1946). Many Metro stations are decorated with the work of Maria Keil; newer stations display tiles by Vieira da Silva, Júlio Pomar, Manuel Cargaleiro and Sá Nogueira.

The shifts in pattern, and colour, of *azulejos* are summarized in the Museu do Azulejo in the Madre de Deus convent at Xabregas in Lisbon. In Lisbon's city museum, the Museu da Cidade, in the early eighteenth-century Palácio Pimenta, of all the decorative tiling it is the kitchen I remember best, for its household themes of the time – cats, fish, flowers, fruit, pigs, ships and, in the middle, a black slave cleaning fish. As a museum, the house holds a rich and vivid record reaching back to Roman times. Its beguiling per-sonality comes from its design as a congenial country house.

Not only in Lisbon and Oporto, but in every major city and most of the towns as well, palaces, convents, *quintas* and lordly houses have become effective, often deeply impressive, museums. Some, moving on from a static role as treasure chest of Portuguese history, operate as dynamic cultural centres with changing art exhibitions, film seasons, displays and discussions. Typifying the new thrust is the thoroughly 1930s Casa de Serralves at Oporto, a pale pink two-storey building with eighteen hectares of gardens, fountains and park, acquired by the state only in 1987 to be the Museu Nacional

de Arte Moderna. Oporto already has several important museums
– the Soares dos Reis museum, named after the nineteenth-century
sculptor, in a former palace; the Guerra Junqueiro museum, named
after the poet, in a baroque mansion; a museum of sacred art; and
military, ethnographic and other museums. Serralves, attracting
young people and wide attention, has acted on the ancient city like
a tonic.

Below Oporto's granite cathedral, where rowdy crusaders were
cajoled into joining King Afonso Henriques in the siege of Lisbon,
where King João I and his English bride Philippa were married in
1387, and their son, the Infante Dom Henrique – Henry the Navigator – was christened, narrow streets press one on another, their
rattling trams and rushing traffic in endless contest. Oporto is a
city of tumbling red roofs, a city of steps, of fine bookshops,
crowded cafés, grand churches, showy palaces and cramped *bairros*
where fluttering laundry signals above the silvery Douro.

The city of close on 400,000 people and its satellite towns form a
congested triangle of factories and crowded workshops that is the
biggest, busiest industrial zone in Portugal. No vast industry domi-
nates. But shipping, textiles, timber and cork products, metalwork,
furniture, fireworks, agriculture, table wines and *vinho verde* as well
as the classic port add up to around 60 per cent of Portugal's
economy. Oporto is itself an art form, demanding, frustrating,
generous, lively – and with a steadily growing number of art
galleries, as well as Serralves.

A lively art scene, with Lisbon the animated capital as its natural
centre, implies lively artists. Art follows certain specified rules and
disciplines; the artists themselves are unrestrained and vigorous.
With Vieira da Silva, Júlio Pomar and Paula Rego in the forefront
of Portuguese living artists as the 1990s began (echoed by prices
paid for their work), other major artists ranged from Artur Bual, a
powerhouse painter of fiercely dramatic canvases, and the eclectic
art professor, Gil Teixeira Lopes, to the playful, painted sculptures
of José de Guimarães in their bold primal colours. Sculpting in
stone and marble, moons away from the great, grand tombs, were
the *alentejano* João Cutileiro, with his lovely nubile figures, José
Pedro Croft, Manuel Rosa, Clara Menéres, João Duarte and the

eminent António Duarte, much of whose work is bestowed on the Atelier-Museu in his name in his culturally conscious home town, Caldas da Rainha. The town was also the *terra natal* of the nineteenth-century master painter, José Malhoa, and it was there that Rafael Bordalo Pinheiro, the brilliant perpetrator of caricatures in sketches and ceramics, set up his factory. A leading ceramicist and sculptor today, working with his wife, Janet, in the Algarve, is Jorge Mealha, whose pieces often reflect the earthen colours and creatures of his Moçambique background.

Among established painters of widely varying inspiration and expression are Eduardo Batarda, António Dacosta, Graça Morais – with all the natural force of her beloved Trás-os-Montes – Helena Almeida, Júlio Resende, Manuel Baptista, David de Almeida, Artur de Cruzeiro Seixas, António Pimentel, Lima de Freitas, João Vieira, Júlio Quaresma, António Sena, Álvaro Lapa, Margarida Lagarto (among a talented group from Évora), another woman, Menez, and Pedro Proença, Pedro Portugal and a third Pedro, Cabrita Reis, from Lisbon. (And of the long-resident foreigners who paint Portugal with feeling and acuity I submit two: an Englishman, Glyn Uzzell, not quite abstract, not at all figurative, and the Flemish Jules Heyndels, for his wry, precise comments on his own rural neighbourhood – and mine.)

Portuguese artists, responding to the country's new mood, new money and new optimism, do not ignore external trends any more than they did in the past. Artists who work or live abroad are undiminished in the eyes of their compatriots delighting in their success – 'brilham lá fora', the expression goes ('shining out there'). António de Holanda, a sixteenth-century artist, father of the seminal Francisco de Holanda, won commissions in Italy and Spain. Cultural interchange merely restates the habit of centuries.

In 1428, the Flemish master Jan van Eyck was invited to Portugal by King João I to paint his only daughter, the Infanta Isabel, two years before her wedding to the Duke of Burgundy, Philip the Good. Some say Van Eyck was the mentor of Nuno Gonçalves, royal painter to Dom João's grandson, King Afonso V. To Gonçalves is attributed Portugal's supreme masterpiece, once the retable in the São Vicente de Fora church, now in the Museu Nacional de

Arte Antiga. Six panels, the foremost colours deep crimson and glowing gold, depict the adoration of São Vicente, Lisbon's patron saint, and honour by implication the early discoverers. The genius of the painting lies in the resonant portraiture of the sixty figures, many of them identified. Prince Henry the Navigator himself is plainly there, in dark robe and broad-brimmed *bolonhês* hat. Or is he? It has been suggested that all the royal personages were living relatives of King Afonso. Prince Henry, by then, was dead. The academics, as usual, argue. In the corner of the same panel is – perhaps – Nuno himself with a lined face, intelligent and quizzical.

The museum, a low stone palace on the Rua das Janelas Verdes ('green windows') built in the seventeenth century by the Condes de Alvor, houses collections of art, national and international, of startling range. Of the great painters, Dürer is here with a vibrant St Jerome, and Hieronymus Bosch with his terrifying 'Temptations of St Anthony'. Romney and Reynolds are represented. Velázquez appears with a portrait of the second wife, Mariana of Austria, of his great patron, Philip IV of Spain. Spain's greatest master, a Portuguese profile will tell you, was born in 1599 in Seville of a Portuguese father, a *fidalgo* from Oporto by the name of Juan Rodriguez de Silva. Velázquez, for whatever reason, adopted, and immortalized, the name of his mother, Jerónima Velázquez.

An impressive selection of sixteenth-century art is credited to the Portuguese School (whose masters included Gregório Lopes, Cristóvão de Figueiredo and Francisco Henriques). Among them is the horrific 'Inferno', a ghastly rendering of boilings, chainings, throttlings and burnings of upside-down womanhood, the victims heavily outnumbering the busily engaged winged goblins and tailed devils. How benevolent after this seem the seventeenth-century artists Domingos Vieira and Josefa de Óbidos – actually Josefa de Ayala (1630–84), the daughter of an Óbidos painter and his Spanish wife and known especially for her religious paintings in Óbidos and her still lifes. How tender, too, are the portraits of children by the prodigious Domingos António de Sequeira (1768–1834), who spent much of his life abroad.

Ramalho Ortigão, in 1900, contemplating the eighteenth century, wrote in melancholy mood that it had been the most *inactivo*, the

most *infecundo* in all the centuries of Portuguese nationhood. The
nineteenth century made up for it with a flourish, which became a
surge of naturalist and portrait painting, pushing romanticism aside.
Miguel Ângelo Lupi (1826–83) led the first great wave, followed
by António Silva Porto (1850–93), and José Malhoa (1855–1933)
and his contemporary, Columbano Bordalo Pinheiro (1857–1929).
Their work is well represented in Lisbon's Museu Nacional de
Arte Contemporânea (founded in 1911). Malhoa is also the shining
light of the Museu José Malhoa in Caldas da Rainha, though it has
few of his best paintings.

They formed a group of artists – the Grupo do Leão, whose
lions Columbano presents in one of his wittier paintings. An artist
whose dynamic skills lay in studio craft, in shaping light for his
portraits, he left humour's cutting edge to the caricatures of his
brilliant older brother, Rafael Bordalo Pinheiro. But Malhoa, too,
for all his portraits, landscapes, sensual and dramatic scenes from
Camões, could pinpoint as sharply – as in the lavish surrender to
song of '*o Fado*' and the lush celebration, to the last drop, of
'*Festejando o São Martinho*' – the joys, follies and weaknesses of
humankind.

For a link with the present – and the future – there was the
short-lived Amadeu Sousa Cardoso and, above all, José Almada
Negreiros (1893–1970), nonconformist and theatrical, and of immense cultural range, imagination and energy. Of all his multifaceted output, the portrait in Lisbon's city museum of his friend,
Fernando Pessoa, painted in 1954 long after the poet's death, is
closest to the heart of the Portuguese. Admirers of art are not
averse to eccentricity in a fine artist, or to a touch of mystery and
perversity, as in the 1930s work of Ofélia Marques, or to investment
potential: when the individualistic artist João Hogan died in 1988,
every single one of his paintings then on show at a Lisbon gallery
– strong, autumnal forms of a transfigured landscape – was snapped
up.

Hogan appeared to ignore in his paintings the city in which he was
born, raised and died – Lisbon. Few others do. In countless ano-
dyne water-colours, in photographs, in every *lisboeta*'s eye, are

fixed images of the venerable city on seven hills sloping down to the Tejo. Low in the centre is the Rossio square and the Baixa, the grid of well-formed eighteenth-century houses built to the order of the Marquis of Pombal. High on the west side the Bairro Alto is a shadowy warren of tall, seventeenth-century town-houses and perilously narrow streets. Here are murky *tabernas*, snug grocery stores, antique shops and many, many restaurants, some of them echoing in the night's darkest hours with the sweetly doleful sounds of *fado*. Rising steeply to the east – the medieval *bairro* of Alfama, a labyrinth of narrow alleys, whitewashed houses and bright flowerpots, of sudden stairways, old churches and enclosed courtyards. Beyond is the neighbourhood of Graça, whose grander town-houses still have the gates where carriages used to enter. Above Alfama, looking across the valley of small, staggered houses from the Graça hilltop where Dom Afonso Henriques surveyed the siege, sits the castle of São Jorge – at night I have stared at its embattled outline, hypnotically bright with floodlighting, lamps twinkling in the valley, the sky sliding under a great buttery moon. A revelatory view from its ancient walls encompasses all Lisbon, the river and the majestic concrete Christ beyond the suspension bridge linking Lisbon with the south.

Lisbon packs on to its crowded hills, in the suburbs rising around them and the problematic *bairros de lata* a population of around a million voluble people who, rich or poor, delight in music – loud disco, trad *fado* or the shrill folk music that is the country-and-western of Portugal. They love wine and food and plenty of both. In Lisbon are a large number of restaurants, some almost as long-lived and aristocratic as the peerless Tavares Rico (founded 1784), many cheap and satisfying. There are nameless bars, smoky dives, trendy discos, *botequins* (night clubs) where the familiar face across the room is probably that of a minister. Theatres range from the bulk of the D. Maria II to the Ritz-Clube, the Casa da Comédia to the revived Maria Vitória, where revues are presented. Lisbon is enlivened further with tantalizing food shops, genteel tea-rooms, led by the elegant Versailles, full of gossiping women eating sweet pastries, and cafés providing a quick drink, a meal, hours of talk; the Nicola, in the Rossio, the haunt of Bocage and his poet friends, was said by an *habitué* to represent 'an honourable testament to civilization'.

Trendy commercial centres in plump and elderly neighbourhoods are crammed with well-designed shops, galleries, cinemas and snack-bars. The largest, Amoreiras, looms like a gigantic tinselled toy-box to the north-west of the city. A vastly disproportionate, architecturally controversial, post-modern complex of some three hundred shops and mock medieval towers of apartments and offices, it was described by its architect, the notorious Tomás Taveira, as neo-modern. Others choose other epithets. Kids and young couples love it. No one is indifferent. It is a commercial success. Its architectural gewgaws were instantly imitated, its very gigantism inspired further colossal construction. '*Amoreiras*' means mulberry trees. In Lisbon, there were once leafy groves of mulberry trees, planted by order of the progressive Duke of Ericeira and, afterwards, the Marquis of Pombal, to feed the silkworms on which the silk industry depends.

Past intertwines with present and future. Cities grow and change. The Marquis of Pombal sought to construct a modern city, as did Duarte Pacheco in the early years of Salazar. More recently the city experienced the heavy hand of Nuno Krus Abecasis, whose urge for gargantuan construction as at Amoreiras remains the most prominent aspect of his tenure as mayor, which ended in 1989. Almost his last act in office was the forcing through of yet another controversial project: a Hilton hotel and congress centre. His view that a Hilton would raise Lisbon to the ranks of top cities ('the cities of this world are divided into two categories: the ones which have a Hilton Hotel and the ones that do not') was disputed, particularly as the substantial construction was to be within a nominally protected city park.

What would become of Lisbon? Would Lisbon, as commentators feared, become unrecognizable? Would the city's treasures disappear? For investors, savagely competing, Lisbon as building site was the ideal. Yet in the streets of Lisbon there are still buildings of infinite grace in a delicious medley of styles from dignified neoclassical to the seductive curves of art deco. Churches of radiant grandeur shape the skyline – the mannerist São Vicente de Fora guarding the Bragança tombs, the great domed Santa Engrácia, the national pantheon (begun in 1690, completed 1966), the imposing Basílica da Estrela raised by Queen Maria I, inaugurated in 1789. (She was buried there in 1816.) There are churches, still beautiful, that precede the founding of the nation, and Carmo, casualty of the 1755 earthquake, standing in roofless tribute to a fourteenth-century national hero.

In luminous, lovely, indulgent Lisbon some buildings vanish, others are cleaned and renovated, and new ones grow with well-watered speed. A new Chiado is rising in the ashes of the old, the project of the architect Siza Vieira. His international eminence in no way deters the Portuguese from questioning the merits of his design every brick and pane of the way. But *lisboetas* still have their familiar neighbourhood markets and bargain-filled fairs – Cascais on Wednesday, Carcavelos on Thursday, the anything-goes thieves' fair, *Feira da Ladra*, in the Campo de Santa Clara on Tuesday and Saturday. In the Baixa they still have their streets named for the goldsmiths and silversmiths, drapers and cobblers who used to work there. In the crowded *bairros populares*, even in exclusive Lapa, there are still bakers and shoemakers, button and broom makers, cramped and busy haberdashery and hardware stores.

There are still tin-hat street kiosks, and Maluda's stamps to keep them in memory, still electric trams and stately *elevadores* – Eiffel's vertical Santa Justa and the funicular Bica, Lavra and Glória – tirelessly shuttling *lisboetas* up and down their precipitous hills. Look down at the pavements at the intricate mosaics of cobbled art, the *calçada* patterns created by brawny *calceteiros*, look out to the river to see the ships and ferryboats, look both ways at every corner for hurtling traffic, for the taxis contemptuously treating the streets as race track, look up at the houses for their quirky wrought-iron balconies and symphonies of tiles.

Some of the famous factories that made *azulejos* have vanished, but others survive – the Fábrica Sant'Anna (founded 1741) and the Fábrica Cerâmica Viúva Lamego (founded 1849), in its prodigiously tiled building in the Largo do Intendente, close to a tawdry, low-life district that would deeply have grieved the energetic Intendant-General of Police to Pombal (and subsequently Dona Maria II) for whom the square was named, Diogo Ignácio de Pina Manique. He is renowned for bringing street lighting to Lisbon, for founding the Casa Pia, a charitable institution for girls and – hoping profits would accrue to his charity – for achieving the construction of the São Carlos theatre in an astonishing seven months.

Mystery, history, secrets, treasures – every ancient city has them. Lisbon, for all its challenging problems, its crisis of identity, invites exploration – in every street, along the riverside, in gardens as admirable, educative and agreeable as the Jardim Botânico, the Estufa Fria, the cool, covered greenhouse-park in the Parque Eduardo VII, or in scores of other peaceable green spaces. Some museums are enhanced by gardens – the Traje, a costume museum, lies within the Parque do Monteiro-Mor out at Lumiar. A soothing landscaped garden is the calm setting for the rich and varied pleasures of the Calouste Gulbenkian Museum and the separate Centro de Arte Moderna, which displays the works of modern Portuguese artists.

The main Calouste Gulkenkian museum, low-level and discreet, contains an astounding range of European, oriental and classical art – paintings, sculpture, ceramics and porcelain, manuscripts and books, furniture and furnishings, coins, medals and superlative silver and, in a dark cool room, a display of René Lalique's art-nouveau jewellery, as fantastic and magical as dewdrops in a fairy glen – all of this, and more, the personal collection of one extraordinary man.

The foundation established and named after Calouste Gulbenkian plays a crucial role in Portugal's art world and across the nation's entire cultural and social framework. Gulbenkian, born in Istanbul to Armenian parents in 1869, studied at King's College, London, gaining a degree in engineering and applied sciences. He lived mainly in Paris, where he built up and maintained his renowned collection of fine art – his taste so sure that, for instance, he acquired most of his 169 pieces of Lalique jewellery between 1900 and 1903, when he was barely in his thirties and long before the 1928 petroleum deal in the Middle East gave him the nickname 'Mr Five Percent' and enormous wealth. In 1942, during the Second World War, he came to live in Portugal. He was seventy-three. He died in Portugal, aged eighty-six, in 1955.

He liked Portugal, and the Portuguese. He had considered setting up a foundation to house his collection in London, for which he had much affection. He was, moreover, a British citizen from 1902 until his death. His fondness faded when a British government clerk made the dreadful mistake of calling him a 'technical enemy'. Gulbenkian willed his entire collection and immense fortune to Portugal – a document legalized, according to Portuguese law, by his thumbprint. Through the foundation, headed by his friend and adviser, José de Azeredo Perdigão, a distinguished lawyer, he gave Portugal his incomparable art collection, concert and exhibition halls, a symphony orchestra, ballet and choral companies, and libraries of books as well as a travelling library service. He provided equipment for hospitals and social services, rehabilitation centres for the handicapped, grants and subsidies for restoration of historic buildings. Many of the Portuguese artists who exhibit successfully today studied on a Gulbenkian bursary. He was a philanthropist of immense stature in modern Portugal, a Rockefeller and Guggenheim rolled into one. The foundation's annual expenditure is larger than some ministries – yet, nurtured by his executors, its assets, some $60m in 1956, were well above $1bn before the 1980s ended. He was himself a treasure, pure gold, for Portugal.

12 Poetic pleasures and the joys of woe

It is not coincidence that conspicuous among Portugal's best-loved writers are men of a passionate and complex nature who have travelled adventurously, suffered stormy love lives and died young. The Portuguese are rightly proud of their illustrious explorers and discoverers, but the feeling they hold for their great poets and novelists and historians is closer: they revere and honour them with an intense devotion. Above all else, the Portuguese worship a glorious flow of words, a fervour all the more ardent if their golden-tongued idol has led a full, turbulent and tragic life.

Love for their language is the one absolute of Portuguese identity. Early kings – Dom Sancho I, son of founding father Afonso Henriques, and the indefatigable Dom Dinis, grandson of the learned Alfonso X of Castile – found time to write poetry. The seventy-six *cantigas de amor*, fifty-two *cantigas de amigo* and ten *de maldizer* – love, friendship and curses – counted by scholars put Dom Dinis as troubador in tender perspective.

> *Un tal ome sei eu, ai ben-talhada,*
> *que por vos ten a sa morte chegada;*
> *vedes quen é seed' en nembrada:*
> *eu, mia dona.*
>
> A certain man I know, fair one,
> Is dying of love for you.
> See who I mean and remember
> It is I, my lady.

Cossantes, these lyric poems are sometimes called. From them surged the river without end that is Portuguese poetry. Nor are they lost in its flood: on bookshop shelves, beside the ranks of national names, you will find collections – *cancioneiros* – of popular, anonymous poetry that echoes the themes and rhythms of the Middle Ages.

Then poetry sang of love and death and faithlessness; the universities springing up across Europe spoke the language of scholarship. The turgid works in Latin of the pedantic Pedro Hispano of Lisbon include a lengthy *Summulae logicales* on Aristotelian logic. Scarcely of wide appeal, they must have won respect in discerning pedagogic circles once, since for a year, from 1276 to 1277, he was pope: João XXI, the only pope Portugal ever had. By a twist of literary history, another scholar shines more brightly. A student at Bologna, João das Regras, had barely settled back in Portugal after completing his studies before he was arguing, in 1385, the right of Dom João of Avis to the Portuguese throne. His role as clever and loyal friend to King João I, the dramatic saga of João's assertion of Portuguese independence and the opening of the era of discoveries come to life in the colourful prose of Fernão Lopes, first of the observant, seemingly ever-present royal chroniclers. Fernão Lopes, appointed chronicler a generation after the events he describes, was not only the first writer of gripping Portuguese prose but an indefatigable down-to-earth reporter with a snappy turn of phrase. For Lopes the reign of Dom João I was 'the seventh age of the world'. His *Crónicas*, to the Portuguese, the heroes of the stirring story, are unalloyed rapture.

New chapters of discoveries unrolled in the lively chronicles of Gomes Eanes de Zurara, Rui de Pina, Garcia de Resende and Damião de Góis, who was the official recorder to King Manuel. From Brazil, in a letter from Pêro Vaz da Caminha in 1500, came news of its discovery with first impressions of a 'people of such innocence', the 'fine bodies and good faces' of the men and the beauty of the girls, with 'their privy parts so high, so closed and so free from hair that we felt no shame in looking hard at them ...' The appeal of the noble savage rapidly faded. Portuguese enchantment with the 'people of good and pure simplicity' changed all too soon to chagrin, disgust and qualmless cruelty.

Gaspar Correa, seventeen years old in 1512 and secretary to Afonso de Albuquerque, governor of India, wrote – and illustrated

– a vivid chronicle, *Lendas da Índia* ('Stories of India'), rich in unrestrained detail of all that he saw and all that he learned of the Portuguese conquest of India. Clear-eyed, and as thorough as the most hardened journalist, he describes the barbarous ferocity of a splenetically angry Vasco da Gama. In 1539, João de Barros (1494–1570), among the notable humanists, began his series of *Décadas* for a mammoth work, *Ásia*. He had been governor of the São Jorge fort at Mina and treasurer of the immensely wealthy Casa da Índia, Mina e Ceuta. The colonizing King João III had awarded him Maranhão, a huge area of Brazil, and reappointed him factor of the India House. He had all the right connections, every source of information was available to him and if, as even contemporary critics charged, he occasionally omitted an uncomfortable fact, he left for posterity a work that is read as history, philosophy, literature and – what else? – poetry.

Further *Décadas* were added by Diogo do Couto (1543–1616), whose career as soldier and chronicler mainly in India began as a page in the court of Dom João III. It was odd how often, across Portugal's sprawling empire, paths crossed. Couto, in Moçambique in 1569, bumped into Luís de Camões, penniless, desperately trying to get back to Lisbon, deeply depressed that a volume in which much of his lyric poetry was written had been stolen. Couto and his friends helped pay Camões's passage home to Lisbon. A year earlier, in 1568, the youthful King Sebastião, destined to inflict calamity on Portugal, had come of age.

Luís de Camões (1524–79), a near contemporary of Cervantes and Shakespeare, was what the Portuguese admire most: a man of passionate temperament and bold, adventurous spirit. A penniless *fidalgo* of the minor nobility with a solid education in the classics and a taste for the fast lane, he fell unsuitably in love, was involved in a brawl and was banished from court and capital. He sailed for Ceuta and active service as soldier in 1547, returning to Lisbon two years later minus an eye but with undiminished ardour for the joys of life. Another brawl earned him nine months in prison. A condition of pardon and early release was that he remove himself to India in the service of the king.

Of the fleet that sailed to India, his ship, the *São Bento*, was the only galleon to survive the stormy seas, one of the few strokes of good fortune in his life; it indubitably enhanced the realism of his poetry and his admiration for Portuguese seamanship, which is so gloriously extolled in *Os Lusíadas*. A hard life in India, a wretched stay in Macau, a shipwreck and more years in Goa left Camões physically shattered. His desire to return to Lisbon, to see his long poem published, was finally achieved in 1572.

Censors, installed soon after the Inquisition, found nothing objectionable in the poem but warned against Camões's use of fictitious gods and goddesses. Of the grandeur of the enterprise, of the expression of national history in epic verse, of the entirely modern suggestion of irrationality within human destiny or the positively carnal revelry of nymphs and seamen on the mythical Island of Love, the censor had nothing to say. Camões won a nod and a small pension from Dom Sebastião, dying unnoticed in 1579 less than a year after the catastrophe of King Sebastião's defeat at Alcácer Quibir. It was the enthusiasm of Spain's Philip II as king of Portugal in 1581 which raised the status of the poem, little noticed on publication, to that of the noble voice of Portuguese nationalism. Camões wrote three plays and other lyric poems. His *Lusíadas* stands apart, a symbol of Portugal.

With the discoveries, intellectual excitement had burst across Europe. Sciences, art, literature bloomed and flourished. The Renaissance flowered belatedly in Portugal but Erasmus and humanism had cast their light across the land. From a stay in Italy, the poet Francisco Sá de Miranda (1481–1558) returned to his northern homeland at Amares with a verve in his step and the new sonnets at his fingertips. At the court of King Manuel the scores of plays by Gil Vicente, salty farces, skittish comedies, mysterious tragicomedies as well as contemplative pieces with religious undertones took theatre to extraordinary heights. *Autos* (plays) flowed from his pen in a stream that lasted from 1502 to 1536. He is also, it is thought, the same Gil Vicente from Guimarães who crafted the celebrated monstrance from Vasco da Gama's first shipment of gold.

Until the Counter-Reformation and the full force of the Inquisition struck, knowledge itself was golden. Duarte Pacheco Pereira, captain and pilot to Dom Manuel, wrote *Esmeraldo de Situ Orbis*, a navigational treatise on the African coast that embraced reflections on the earth and its seas. The last of the great Indian viceroys, Dom João de Castro, had been a student of the renowned cosmographer and mathematician, Pedro Nunes (*c*. 1502–78), who had refined the astrolabe to a precision instrument and whose great published work was *Tratado da Esfera*. Castro's own contributions included sailing directions from Goa to Suez, *roteiros* that became the basis for Red Sea geography and all chart-making afterwards. The maps, like so many others by the Portuguese, are pure art. Pure science came from the hand of a Portuguese physician, Garcia da Orta; enthralled by the plants he found in India, he produced in 1563 an illustrated compendium called *Colóquios dos Simples e Drogas da Índia* ('Dialogue on Indian Herbs and Drugs'). The Portuguese hardly noticed it for some time, but others in the growing science of botany did. Pirated and translated into several languages, the book was the first Portuguese bestseller.

Orta survived the Inquisition. His bones did not. They were dug up by the Holy Office and burned, along with those of his elderly sister. The industrious chronicler Damião de Góis, an enthusiastic humanist and friend of Erasmus, for a time an administrator in Flanders, was another victim of the Inquisition, denounced and charged with heresy by an old antagonist, the Jesuit Padre Simão Rodrigues. Not even the support of Inquisitor-General Cardinal Henrique could save him from prison in his old age. From time to time the Inquisition issued a list of censored works. Its own grandest monument to censorship was the *Index auctorum damnatae memoriae* – any author who was anybody was in it. But the diffusion of knowledge and the printed word could only be delayed, not stopped.

Among the numerous books relating to the voyages of discovery which have recently been published or republished under the auspices of the national commission for their commemoration is one that is particularly hard to classify. Like so many others, *Peregrinação* ('Pilgrimage'), by Fernão Mendes Pinto, encompasses exploration and navigation, the perils of sixteenth-century travel the excitement of discovery, enthralling adventures, shocks and horrors. The book is Mendes Pinto's stirring life story, a priceless record of Portugal's early ties with the Orient. Mendes Pinto, born around 1510, travelled extensively for some seventeen years (1537–54). As a merchant, he made fortunes and lost them; as a shipmaster, he sailed ships and was shipwrecked. He was a vagabond and prisoner, a pirate perhaps. He was moved by friendship and admiration for the Jesuit saint, Francis Xavier, to join the Jesuit Order, and then without explanation to leave it. Finally, back in Portugal and living peaceably in Almada, he wrote of his experiences, of the amazing sights he had seen and of the strange things he had heard.

Peregrinação is an extraordinary work, full of truths and insights – and fantasies and lies. The Portuguese have never quite known what to make of their own venturesome Marco Polo. A schoolgirl told me a joke on his name: '*Fernão! Mentes?*' '*Minto.*' ('Fernão, are you lying?' 'Yes, I am lying.') For historians Mendes Pinto is a nuisance. So much of his sharp observation on the manners and morals, of Portuguese and others, is patently authentic. But how to pinpoint the fantasy and fiction? Rebecca Catz, who in 1989 produced a version in English, *The Travels of Mendes Pinto*, makes a valid case for Mendes Pinto as corrosive satirist in a separate book, her doctoral thesis, *The Social Satire of Fernão Mendes Pinto*.

Portuguese intellectuals did not lack the spirit of investigation. Among mysteries that enthral and tantalize modern students are illustrations by Francisco de Holanda (1517–84), a Renaissance architect – as well as artist, writer and humanist – in the service of King João III. In one of his books, *Livro das Idades do Mundo* ('Book of the Ages of the World'), among depictions of the Old and New Testament and the Apocalypse, are drawings that not only show the globe as seen from space but the birth of the universe in a vivid and dramatic Big Bang. Weary of the critics that assailed him, he retreated to think and write in the peace of Sintra.

Portuguese scholars achieved eminence in European universities and often, like the Beja-born humanist António de Gouveia (1505–65), were safer abroad. Francisco Sanches, born in Braga in the mid sixteenth century, taught several sciences as well as philosophy at

Toulouse University. His treatise *Quod nihil scitur*, presenting the view that nothing can be known, led to the school of thought called constructive scepticism but failed to outlive the impact of that 'smasher of all things', Kant. His descendant, António Ribeiro Sanches (1699–1783) from Penamacor, and of Jewish origin, was acclaimed for his enlightened views on education. He lived in Russia from 1731 to 1747 as physician to the family of the tsar; Catherine II, whom he had cured as a child, as queen awarded him a pension which he never actually received.

A priest, the Jesuit António Vieira, with his oratorical *Sermões* ('Sermons') and a diplomat, Dom Francisco Manuel de Melo, with a deluge of poetry and plays, history and commentary, letters and literary criticism, were the roaring lions of the seventeenth-century classics. By the eighteenth, neo-classicism and a heightened ardour for the Portuguese language for its own sake led to the poetry, romantic and satirical, of the tempestuous and irreverent Manuel Maria of Barbosa du Bocage – still toasted nightly in the Nicola café. Bocage's life held echoes of Camões's: born in Setúbal in 1765, at twenty he sailed for India and a posting as *tenente* (lieutenant), suffering as Camões had the full fury of the oceans – and finding in them inspiration for his first great lyrical poetry. His wild ways were too much for a shocked Goa, so he was deported to Macau and was even, like Camões, shipwrecked. A generous governor allowed Bocage to return to Lisbon.

Bocage's life was frenetic. From brief domesticity with a sister, he hurled himself into the whirlwind of reckless living and writing – and, to earn money, translation. His sonnets sang with lyrical beauty, the satire steamed with wit and venom. To the group of poets, the New Arcadians, poetry was no light distraction but excoriating war. The Inquisition, its old ferocity dimmed to toothless frailty, briefly imprisoned him, then placed him in penitential restraint in a monastery whose cordial friars allowed his muse to run free. The life of Bocage, wrote Pinheiro Chagas, was a fire. But the fire consumed him: barely forty, Bocage sickened and died, writing tormented sonnets to his last breath.

Poetry crossed pretensions and class. Bocage rocked the Nicola with his ripe extemporizing. In high society, the Marchioness of

Alorna wrote rippling verse under the pen name of Alcipe. Born in 1750, wealthy and beautiful in youth, she lived to a hearty eighty-nine, witnessing the birth of romanticism and a shining new era in Portuguese literature.

An energetic liberal, Almeida Garrett (1799–1854), wrote numerous lively plays, descriptive poetry and novels – his chatty *Viagens na Minha Terra*, published in English as *Travels in My Homeland*, the most notable of these. Before he was twenty, ambitiously planning a name for himself and seeing no dazzle in his own, Leitão da Silva (*leitão* means sucking pig), he adopted a maternal name, Almeida, and his grandmother's, Garrett. Agitated politics, a kindly bishop uncle who helped him get a Coimbra education, his own ardent temperament – leading to an early and unhappy marriage, true love and the birth of a daughter outside it – did the rest. Garrett and a fellow liberal, the very different Alexandre Herculano (1810–77), were both at the forefront of the heady romantic movement in Portugal. Herculano, as well as being a consummate poet, was a historiographer and historical novelist of the highest order.

On a towering second wave of glittering talent soared Camilo Castelo Branco (1826–90), inventive, socially aware, romantic, caustic. The best known of his novels and short stories is *Amor de Perdição*, but throughout a convulsive life plagued by scandal he was a prodigiously productive writer and journalist. At one crowded Camiliana seminar, a noted writer declared his affection for Camilo because he made him laugh out loud – bittersweet tribute to a man who was always short of cash, whose great love for a married woman provoked her enraged husband to hound them both, and who, when at last a contented marriage was theirs, went blind and, in racking despair, shot himself. (It was a black year: the romantic writer Júlio César Machado and the famous explorer Silva Porto also committed suicide in 1890.)

That edge of tragedy, the sigh of pain and woe, adorns Portuguese literature even when it is least expected. How delightful are the novels of yet another Oporto writer, Júlio Dinis, born in 1839 – and how awful that he died, coughing his lungs out, at only thirty-two. As the nineteenth century unrolled, with its urge towards realism, reassurance that life was not all pessimism and doom emanated from the solid figure of Teófilo Braga. Born in 1843, he was a highly visible Coimbra student who became a university professor and president of the republic. He was a thinker, battler and voluminous writer, ranging from folk-tales to poetry, from journalism to the history of Portuguese law. He lived to be over eighty, and died with dignity. A doom-laden fate awaited the friend of Braga's youth, Antero de Quental; he was just a year older, a poet, essayist, idealist and philosopher. To his friends, with whom he corresponded at length, he was Santo Antero, a brilliant mind overcoming the affliction of neurasthenia and depression. One day – he was forty-nine – overwhelmed by an intense mental agony, he purchased a revolver, asked the shopkeeper to load it, sat on a bench in a Ponta Delgada square and killed himself.

The shock was profound. Intellectuals sought explanations – and still do: the discovery of a new hoard of letters in 1989 put academe in a whirl. His friends could only mourn, and write. A photograph taken in 1884 shows five friends together – Antero in the centre, and with him the historian Oliveira Martins, Eça de Queiroz, Ramalho Ortigão and the poet Guerra Junqueiro, each one a luminary of Portuguese literature, the pre-eminent bards of 'the generation of the seventies'. Had Antero, with his death, consigned his followers to defeat? Not exactly. They called themselves the *Vencidos da Vida* ('Life's Vanquished') and with a twirl of a dashing moustache, carried on.

In the novels of José Maria Eça de Queiroz (1845–1900) the prose glides like a polished stone, characters are insistently alive, plots tingle with surprise and tension, wit shimmers. And some of them, including *The Maias*, with its sexual passion and taboo in a skewering portrayal of upper-class life, and *The Crime of Father Amaro*, are among the far too few Portuguese books of universal appeal that can be read in English – if you can find them. Eça de Queiroz knew England well himself. A Coimbra degree in law led to a diplomatic career: he was in Havana as consul, then Bristol; he worked in London – his second child was born in Ladbroke Gardens – and, to the envy of his colleagues, Paris. A dandyish bachelor until his forties, he fell ardently in love and was accepted in marriage – she was twenty-nine – by the cool, reserved daughter of the Count of Resende. Tender towards his family, despite his wife's perennial inability to live within his income, he kept his mordant irony for his prose. He more than anyone would have relished death's little joke, the farcical postscript to a life of accomplishment.

He died in Paris in 1900, was brought back to Lisbon and ceremoniously buried – his wife surviving him, on a government pension, until 1934. The family was dispersed. He had no one in Lisbon. For eighty-eight years, while his books were read by generations of spellbound readers, the unmarked grave was forgotten – until the Lisbon municipal council, in a general reordering, declared it abandoned. It seemed as if the mortal remains of Eça de Queiroz would disappear into a common grave of the lonely and unloved. In the subsequent brouhaha the *Câmara* denied it would do any such thing, President Mário Soares said Eça's remains belonged in the national pantheon, descendants who had not until now demonstrated loving concern were consulted. And in a final twist, the bones of the great Eça, after a mass at the Estrela basilica attended by embarrassed dignitaries, were transported to Santa Cruz do Douro and buried near the house which had become the fictional Tormes in his *A Cidade e as Serras*. He had thought the house, when he first saw it, very ugly.

Poetry, influenced by the rush of events, literary trends, public stimulus, private vision, now flowed in torrents. Pride of *algarvios* is the gentle poet-teacher from São Bartolomeu de Messines, João de Deus (1830–96) – named after the adventurer-saint, founder of the Hospitallers Order, who was born in 1495 in Montemór in the Alentejo. Cesário Verde, Gomes Leal, Eugénio de Castro, Camilo Passenha and others are among the classics. That the often depressed António Nobre, born 1867 – a 'decadentist poet of tedium' – is a cherished national poet reveals facets of Portuguese nationalism as well as an abiding fondness for evocative language. He had, I should add, every reason to be depressed: the abysmal state of the nation – *'Que desgraça nascer em Portugal!'* he sighed ('What a disgrace to be born in Portugal') – and the tuberculosis that finally killed him at thirty-three. The sound and essence of the language, as well as emotion, fill the many volumes of Vitorino Nemésio (1901–78) and, with tortured intensity, the passionate poems of Florbela Espanca. Her exalted anguish mirrored her life. Born illegitimate in 1895, she wrote a poem at eight entitled '*A vida e a morte*', she was three times unhappily married, she suffered a syphilitic miscarriage and the death of an adored younger brother. She died – of depression, neurosis and two jars of Veronal – at thirty-five.

In the passionate sonnets of Florbela you know where you are. With Fernando Pessoa and his multiple masks you can never be sure who he is. Of Portugal's most prominent and tantalizingly cryptic modernist poet, only the surface is cloudless. He was born in Lisbon in 1888, and at seven was taken by his mother to live in Durban, South Africa – a widow, she remarried a diplomat. He returned alone to Portugal at seventeen, stayed with aunts, then in rented rooms, enrolled briefly in a literature course, earned a living as translator in a commercial office and contributed poetry – 'not a profession, a vocation' – to the literary magazines of his day. The literary review *Orpheu*, marking the launch of the modernist movement, gave him national stature. He became a familiar figure, in his glasses, bow tie and fedora, in the Baixa café, Martinho da Arcada, and the Brasileira – where, in Lagoa Henriques's sculpture, he still sits. He wrote with silent emotion, smoking cigarette after cigarette, methodically and recklessly ravaging his liver with escalating tots of *aguardente*. In 1934, his epic *Mensagem* appeared, the only book published in his lifetime. He died in a Lisbon hospital in 1935.

Pessoa's first juvenile poems, simple or obsessional, were in English, as were his last written words – 'I know not what tomorrow will bring.' His spiritual mentors, his muse, his finest work, his yearnings, his soul and the dominant characters within his multiform persona, were quintessentially Portuguese. In the personality of Fernando Pessoa three other distinct and dissimilar poets – Alberto Caeiro, Ricardo Reis, Álvaro de Campos – came to imperishable life, as well as a prose writer, Bernardo Soares, in whose name appeared *Livro do Desassossêgo*, the fictional 'Book of Disquiet'. Pessoa devised these heteronyms and they in turn elevated and altered him. Researchers, delving into a rich archive kept in a chest, discovering a gallery of odd, literary characters, wondered who else they would meet. Pessoa's name means person or individual. But who was he? What was he? At thirty-two he fell in love with a nineteen-year-old girl, Ofélia Queiroz, and wrote more than fifty letters to her and love poems about her. She responded warmly but, confused, he stood back. The affair remained platonic. Was he perhaps homosexual? Some critics conclude that he was. No, not Pessoa himself, said an analyser of his work at the Instituto de Estudos Modernistas, but his *alter egos* Ricardo Reis and Álvaro de Campos. Pessoa's vision embraced human love, Portuguese destiny, all Europe. Widely read and studied in several languages, he remains an enigma.

'*Decadente*' was the label pinned to himself by the prose writer José Fialho de Almeida (1857–1911). His was a life with a rare happy ending – son of a poor Alentejo schoolmaster, treated in Lisbon like dirt, and raised by marriage to a rich woman to lifelong bourgeois comfort. His writing was much admired by his contemporary Raul Brandão (1867–1930), a popular writer enjoyed for his lucid style. Ferreira de Castro (1898–1974) won double distinction for social realism in *Emigrantes* and *A Selva*, and for unusual success with translations abroad.

Literary expression, intelligent opinion – words and thoughts – burst on to the intellectual scene of the early twentieth century through journals and reviews like *Águia*, founded in the first throes of republican idealism by Teixeira de Pascoaes (1877–1952), whose metaphysical poetry and nostalgic philosophy, called *saudosismo*, inspired Pessoa and his free-thinker friend, Leonardo Coimbra (1883–1936). Jaime Cortesão (1884–1950) was associated with them in the aspiring review *Renascença Portuguesa*; fourteen years later, in 1924 – after shattering experiences as a volunteer doctor in the First World War – he turned to another review, *Seara Nova*, together with António Sérgio (1883–1969). These dedicated liberals and those who thought like them in opposing Salazar and the Estado Novo were to find themselves effectively silenced. Another distinguished review, *Presença*, started in Coimbra in 1927, the arm of a second generation of modernists who included the eminent literary critic, João Gaspar Simões (1903–87), José Régio, a major poet, and Miguel Torga, born 1907 in the small village of São

Martinho de Anta in the Trás-os-Montes. A doctor and humanitarian, a resolute opponent of the Salazar regime, Torga wrote with grief in the preface to a 1945 edition of short stories of what he had seen on his return to his *terra natal* – 'more hunger, more ignorance, more despair'. Poet, playwright, essayist, above all vivid descriptive writer of rural life, he was still quick-witted and intransigent, ready 'to fight with everything and with everybody', as the 1990s began.

The landmark work fifty years earlier – and in its seventeenth reprinting in 1990 – was *Gaibéus* by Alves Redol. His much later novel, *Barranco de Cegos* ('Ravine of the Blind'), was deemed the better book, but *Gaibéus* – about the hardship of migrant harvesters – appeared at the start of the neo-realist era in Portuguese literature. A ten-volume anthology of neo-realist poetry, *Novo Cancioneiro*, was published in Coimbra (conveniently pruned since to a single volume by Alexandre Pinheiro Torres). One of those poets was Fernando Namora, born 1919 in Condeixa, near Coimbra. As a newly qualified young doctor, he lived and worked among abjectly poor communities – miners at Tinalhas, the boulder hill town of Monsanto, Pavia in the Alentejo. The worlds that he saw filled books that are still avidly read in Portugal – like *O Trigo e o Joio* ('Wheat and Chaff'); *Domingo à Tarde* ('Sunday Afternoon'); *Retalhos da Vida de um Médico*, printed in English as *Mountain Doctor*, and *Os Clandestinos*. For some years, until the income from his books gave him his freedom, Namora worked at the cancer institute in Lisbon – a *camponês* exiled in the city, he called himself. The pain that he witnessed there ultimately became his own. He died in 1989.

Such – in part – are the antecedents of Portugal's modern writers and poets. Generations overlap – Vergílio Ferreira, born in 1916, his first work neo-realist, changed step and viewpoint, enhancing his stature as a grand figure of Portuguese letters. Major poets a few years younger were Sofia de Melo Breyner Andresen and Eugénio de Andrade. Their generation includes Jorge de Sena (1914–78), of wide-ranging creativity and immense influence. In my town, Loulé, they honour their own António Aleixo (1899–1949). An extraordinary pride of literary lions was born in the 1920s: the novelists Agustina Bessa-Luís and Urbano Tavares Rodrigues, the poets Alexandre O'Neill, Mário Cesariny de Vasconcelos, António Ramos Rosa and David Mourão Ferreira, the multi-talented Natália Correia, the best-selling novelist José Cardoso Pires (*O Delfim*, *Balada da Praia dos Caes* ('Ballad of Dog's Beach'), *Alexandra Alpha*) and, dominating the 1980s, the dazzling sorcerer José Saramago, whose novels include *Memorial do Convento* (published in English as *Baltasar and Blimunda*), *O Ano da Morte de Ricardo Reis* and *História do Cerco de Lisboa*. Saramago has the gift of surprise: in his many years of Communist politics – dating to an era when all aspiration and rebellion was channelled through the clandestine Communist party – in his indifference to offers (from Spielberg and Fellini) to film *Convento* (he agreed to an opera, *Blimunda*) and most of all in his lusty, free-roving and eloquent prose.

Younger novelists sparkling in the Portuguese firmament of 1990, plots and characters often crafted from an experience of revolution, decolonization or social injustice, include António Lobo Antunes, Almeida Faria, Maria Velho da Costa (moving forcefully on from the 1972 notoriety of the *Novas Cartas Portuguesas*), Baptista-Bastos, *algarvia* Lídia Jorge, João de Melo, Clara Pinto Correia, Ângela Caires. Prominent among poets in a nation dedicated to the cadences of its language: Nuno Júdice, the principled Manuel Alegre – voice of liberation in times of trial – and, a fitting continuum, the cultivated Vasco da Graça Moura, executive head of the National Discoveries Commission. Closing a circle, the art of the chronicler is back – with a humour and panache uncommon in Portuguese writing. Miguel Esteves Cardoso's *A Causa das Coisas*, *Os Meus Problemas* and *As minhas Aventuras na República Portuguesa*, collections of pieces which appeared in *Expresso* or *O Independente*, of which he was also editor and assistant editor, not only present a mordant vision of a changing Portugal – in which he is both tender conservative and damning iconoclast – but are delectably quirky in their wit, heady, light and dry.

A recent exhibition to promote Portuguese books was attended by nearly two hundred Portuguese writers. Fifty Portuguese publishers were represented (from over 250, most of them small family businesses), who publish some 4,000 titles a year. Clearly, hosts of writers are excluded, nor have I touched on the literary accomplishments of so many eminent professors, philosophers, historians, scientists. To pass over the intellect of Eduardo Lourenço, Luís Lindley Cintra, Orlando Ribeiro, José Augusto Seabra, Eduardo Prado Coelho, Agostinho da Silva, José-Augusto França, António Quadros, José Mattoso, Luís de Albuquerque, Vitorino Magalhães Godinho, António José Saraiva, Joel Serrão, A. H. de Oliveira Marques and scores of other eminent figures in Portuguese culture will emphasize the general view of purblind *estrangeiros*. I pinpoint a few Portuguese, not their beloved language. Literary genes can pass laterally – even Brazil, huge, urgent, voluble, is ruled out. In Portugal, schools are named after the great Portuguese writers. Bulhão Pato, contemporary and antagonist of Eça de Queiroz, has achieved immortality for a clam dish. Numerous prizes are awarded for outstanding literary achievement. Poets figure on bank notes. But how many Portuguese, you might wonder, actually read their distinguished literature?

A poll in May 1989 – a book fair was on – showed that 33.2 per cent of the population over fifteen read books. Just over 5 per cent read extensively. Another 5.6 per cent read one or two books a year. The rest were in between, with a few books a year. Book fairs are successful: everyone loves a fair, and books are sold at 20 per cent off their cover price. What sells most? School books. Newspapers list current bestselling fiction and non-fiction. Portuguese preoccupations were clear enough the week that a tax guide topped the list; a translation of Stephen Hawking's *Brief History of Time* was in third place. A spirited book club, Círculo de Leitores, boosts book sales with a bright catalogue, its own editions and a chatty magazine. Publishers are not at all unimaginative. All the notable foreign authors are sold in translation, from the thrilling spy novels of Charles McCarry to the Austrian writer Peter Handke and James Joyce's *Ulysses*.

Being published at all seems to console most Portuguese writers; very few can afford to live off their books. A *Semanário* poll on contemporary literature revealed that Fernando Namora was the best-known author – his name was recognized by 21 per cent. No one over forty-six could name the authors of certain specific current books. And 52.7 per cent of the group polled could not think of any book at all. Everyone knows the reasons, said one publisher: they begin at school and end with the price of books. A writer wondered if figures in other countries were much different. João Aguiar, author of action-packed historic novels – *A Voz de Deuses* ('The Voice of the Gods') is lively reading on Lusitanian times – refused to be depressed; the figures are a salutary exercise in humility, he said. Moreover, there was cause for optimism: more than half of the poll – 50.8 per cent – could name a Portuguese author. Nor, lately, has a single author killed himself.

Almost everyone I have talked to can tell a story and recount a legend such as the story of *A Moura Encantada*, about a Moorish princess. You will hear of the *trovador* of Trancoso, of the mysterious Zé do Telhado. But according to the 1989 poll, the best-known poet (5.1 per cent) was Natália Correia – perhaps, it was suggested, because as a Member of Parliament as well as a queen bee of culture, she is frequently on television. Television, a state monopoly with two channels until 1990, allotted slots to art and culture featuring authors reading from their own books, but you would have to care deeply to watch. The RTP channels (Radiotelevisão Portuguesa) dish up a menu uneven in quality, unimpeachably diverse and inexcusably unpunctual. Sport rules; football, frequently unscheduled, Byronically fills 'the glowing Hours with flying feet'. Many programmes, some of them exquisitely filmed, highlight aspects of heritage: cities, countryside, the islands. Game shows entrance millions. Crisply presented news too often breaks up into slabs of talking heads. Day and night the *telenovelas* chatter – Brazilian soap is a national addiction; the *crème de la crème* keep track with their videos. You will see shepherds in rustic bars staring transfixed at the box on the wall; all Portugal watched the tempestuous *Roque Santeiro*. The screen consumes dusty American favourites like *General Hospital*, *Mission Impossible*, *Maude*, *Murder She Wrote*. A Portuguese novelist declared Archie Bunker his favourite foreign television character. Portuguese shopping centres and village cafés call themselves Dallas. The trendy *Twin Peaks* arrived. *Sesame Street*, cleverly adapted, became a captivating *Rua Sésamo*.

Some imports – environmental films among them – are shown with voice-over in Portuguese. But all other foreign shows, the low comedy and high quality British serials, movies old and not so old, have made it to the Portuguese screen, subtitled for Portuguese viewers, with their original sound-track.

Like all else, television is changing. Never a medium for the cultivation of language, the choice of entertainment is broadening almost by the hour. Multiplying parabolic dishes seem in places like an invasion of flying saucers. Installation itself is hotly competitive. By the end of the 1980s the Portuguese could view twenty-four channels emanating from five satellites. Pirate stations flourished. The prospect for the 1990s: many more satellites, a multiplicity of channels and, at last, private Portuguese television. In radio, bitter squabbling marked the opening of the air waves. Finally, a radio commission allotted licences, from 457 proposals, for 402 frequencies. With television more was at stake. The amount spent on publicity in 1988 was 40m contos (about £160m); television earned 16m contos, two fifths of the total; Portugal, lowest in terms of advertising expenditure, was expanding faster than any other EEC country.

The prime minister, Cavaco Silva, proposed that in the two new private channels a minimum of 50 per cent of programmes should be in Portuguese, no company could hold social capital greater than 25 per cent (foreigners no more than 10 per cent) and, the burning issue, that the Catholic Church should have space within a channel. This suggestion was hotly contested. Sections in the Church demanded more than a space. Members of Cavaco Silva's own PSD party piously reminded him that his mentor, Sá Carneiro, had in 1980 promised the Church a channel. Constitutionalists saw illegalities in the mix of harvesting profits and harvesting souls as well as in the absence of public concourse. A candidate company, the large publishing concern SIC (Sociedade Independente de Comunicação), led by *Expresso* owner Francisco Pinto Balsemão, declared that if the Church wished to enter commerce in the private sector it should do so on the same footing as any other applicant. In the heat of argument – *intenso verbalismo*, as one paper put it – arose the charge that the Church was confusing that which is

Caesar's with that which is God's. Polls were taken, but the results proved contradictory. A farce, an objector raged. Certainly, as impassioned Portuguese polemic, it had all the elements of sparkling theatre.

For true, live theatre, which lacks for nothing in plays and – in Lisbon especially – players, survival is a struggle. A handful of groups, sustained by subsidies and grants, keep the spark alive. The stage has grand dramatic stars like Luís Miguel Cintra or Eunice Muñoz, born of a pre-television travelling family of performers. Some actors – Cintra himself or Raul Solnado – have gained wider fame in films and television. For most, lack of recognition, low pay and long periods of unemployment are the reward. What's on in Lisbon at any time can include plays by Sophocles, Shakespeare, Molière, Jean Cocteau, Ionesco, Lorca, Tennessee Williams, Neil Simon and Alan Bennett. Portuguese playwrights are well represented – perhaps by Francisco Manuel de Melo, Almeida Garrett or Raul Brandão, by Bernardo Santareno, Luís Sttau Monteiro or Natália Correia. Almost certainly one or more of Gil Vicente's plays is on. Hits, unpredictable as anywhere, are scarce. One Portuguese comedy, by Filipe La Féria, played to packed houses month after month, had the odd title *What Happened to Madalena Iglésias?* Suddenly, theatre-going was the rage. The author, delighted with the new crowds of theatre-goers, ascribed the show's success to its links with traditional revue, always close to the *lisboeta*'s heart.

In film, António Pedro Vasconcelos's 1984 modern, edgily mysterious *O Lugar do Morto* ('Place of Death') beat all box-office records in Portugal. More than 130,000 people went to the cinema to see it. In 1990 Vasconcelos made *Aqui d'El Rei*, a Luso-Spanish-French co-production in two versions, for cinema and television. Anticipated audience: 150 million. Since the first Portuguese film in 1896, movies have been a passion for a handful of determined film makers. Determination, as vital as creative skill, overcame (still continuing) pettifoggery and raised the cash. Virtually all Portuguese films are heavily subsidized and, these days, internationally funded.

In the thirties and forties the prime successes were social

comedies made by Leitão de Barros. In 1931 a twenty-two-year-òld actor from Oporto, Manoel de Oliveira, borrowed money to buy a camera and made a film about the Douro. Nearly sixty years on, vigour, cinematic art and enthralment with Portuguese identity intact, he had completed *Non ou a Vã Glória de Mandar* ('The Vain-glory of Command'), a film about battles Portugal had fought, and lost, and was moving on to a new film, *The Divine Comedy*. To his credit across the decades were such critical successes as *Aniki-Bobó* (1942), *O Pão* (1959), the 1970s trilogy of frustrated love, *O Passado e o Presente, Benilde* and *Amor de Perdição, Francisca* (1981), *O Sapato de Cetim* (1985), *O Meu Caso* (1987) and *Os Canibais* (1988). Are they under-appreciated? The themes obscure? Manoel de Oli-veira, Portugal's most eminent film maker, has never attained the Oscars, recognition and fame of the grand Italian directors. Even in Portugal, for all its national pride, and the multi-theatre opening of his 1990 'Vainglory', he has rarely drawn a crowd. Film makers traditionally despair at the peculiarities of distribution. In Portugal, although enthusiasts organize regular film festivals, not every town has a cinema or wants one – in some cities even architecturally stylish cinemas are disappearing.

The urge to make movies is strong. There is no stopping direc-tors like José Fonseca e Costa, João César Monteiro, João Mário Grilo and João Botelho. Cinematographers whose work appears on television, among them Brandão Lucas, Carlos Alberto Estevão and José Medeiros in the Açores, enhance small-screen viewing.

Portuguese settings and themes have been used by foreign direc-tors as well as Portuguese. Scenes from *The Russia House* (from John le Carré's spy story) were filmed in Lisbon. To Wim Wenders, Lisbon was a perfect 'old Europe'. For the Portuguese external trade secretary, briskly promoting in Hollywood images of smogless sunshine, varied landscapes, picturesque castles and quaint villages, low costs and high cinematic skills, all Portugal has a thrilling potential – as a film set.

The arts are blood brothers and, in Portugal, never tongue-tied. For the revered guitar player Carlos Paredes music is 'a language, a world of sensations'. From earliest times the Portuguese immersed themselves in this world. Music was a course in the university Dom Dinis founded in 1290. King Pedro the Justicer soothed his rages by dancing in the streets of Lisbon as trumpets played. King Duarte was a notable patron of arts, letters and music in the fifteenth century. King Manuel the Fortunate adored music – 'For his chamber music and for his chapel he collected famous performers from all parts of Europe,' the chronicles report; 'he had the best choir of any of the kings and princes then alive.' Even when he went hunting musicians went with him 'to play and sing to him out in the field or during his repose'.

In the seventeenth century, the first Bragança king, Dom João IV, owned an extensive musical library, inherited from his father and grandfather, and employed an English music teacher and choirmaster. He wrote knowledgeably of liturgical music and was also a keen composer of masses, motets, psalms and madrigals. King João V, joyfully spending Brazilian gold, brought Italian singers to his court and Domenico Scarlatti as music master and tutor to his children. His court organist and harpsichord player, Carlos Seixas (1704–42), composed cascades of sonatas and toccatas that enchant audiences today. From the enthusiasm for opera of Dom João's son, King José, rose no fewer than five opera-houses. At one of them, in the Bairro Alto, the Setúbal-born Luísa Todi (1753–1833) made her first appearance; her lyric singing later brought her ovations around the world. Luísa Todi came home and died in Lisbon. In the New World, John Philip Sousa (1854–1932), of Portuguese origin, was bandmaster, inventor of the sousaphone, a great bass tuba, and composer of such surpassing works as 'Semper Fidelis' and the rousing, all-American 'Stars and Stripes Forever'.

The distinguished musician appointed director of the newly created Conservatory of Music in Lisbon in 1835 had the tuneful and appropriate name of João Domingos Bomtempo (1771–1842). He brought the works of Mozart, Beethoven and Haydn to Portugal, and wrote estimable compositions of his own. At the end of the nineteenth century the pre-eminent composer was Alfredo Keil (1850–1907). Notable recent composers include Luís de Freitas Branco (1890–1955), his disciple José Manuel (Joly) Braga Santos (1924–88), whose widely performed works include six symphonies and three operas – he was also a much-loved teacher and orchestra director – and Fernando Lopes Graça, born in 1906, a militant Communist celebrated for his wide musical range, who was still composing in his eighties.

Opera survives in brief seasons at the São Carlos, whose company includes an admirable soprano, Helena Vieira, and one of the few national symphony orchestras. In dance, the versatility and choreography of dancer Olga Roriz sustains ballet and dance enthusiasts. *Música antiga*, baroque and earlier still, is performed from time to time. Álvaro Cassuto, as creator and maestro of the itinerant Nova Filarmonia Portuguesa, brings music to people who have never heard a live orchestra. Patrons are no longer kings but private industry, allowed tax-deductible sponsorship under the imaginative *Lei do Mecenato Cultural. Mecenato*? Maecenas. Concerts are frequently performed in stunning settings – cathedrals, the Jerónimos cloister, the roofless Carmo ruins, the great monastery at Mafra, the palaces of Queluz and Ajuda, and the Sociedade de Geografia, as well as universities, town halls and churches across the land.

Festivals of music flourish in the long summer months in Estoril, Sintra, Lisbon and the Algarve. None are amateurish make-believe. Dance and instrumental groups, and soloists including such giants as Mstislav Rostropovich, come from across the world to join Portugal's own chamber and dance groups, orchestras, choirs, soloists. Besides Maria João Pires, the idol of Portugal, compelling pianists include José Carlos Sequeira Costa, his brilliant pupil Artur Pizarro, 1990 winner, by unanimous jury vote, of the prestigious Leeds International Piano Competition, and Pedro Burmester. Portugal's modest profile, it has been suggested, is not due to lack of musical skills – Miguel Graça Moura, for instance, is but one of several gifted conductors – but of hubris. And money. Without the cultural vision of Calouste Gulbenkian and the Gulbenkian Foundation's thrust in creating, and funding, an orchestra, choir, ballet company, festivals and countless innovative musical happenings (organized for several years by Madalena Perdigão through a programme called Acarte), the sound of music would be positively *pianissimo*.

Acarte brings youthful vitality, the new and unexpected, and, every August, jazz. There are other regular jazz festivals – Lisbon's is an annual treat. City folk are not unfamiliar with jazz: the Hot Clube in Lisbon, engendered by Luís Villas Boas and his engineer, doctor and architect friends, has been going strong for more than forty years. António Pinho Vargas and his jazz sextet have won themselves a reputation abroad. You might even hear a jazz beat at a country fair. Certainly you will hear rock. Leading groups like Xutos e Pontapés can find subsidies, just as classical musicians do. Mild-looking, bespectacled Rui Veloso, Portugal's top rock guitarist and a versatile performer, is a national celebrity. Young musicians may have one ear listening to the new sounds on the airwaves of the world, but they are also keeping a close watch on national fans, markets and tastes. Among the reverberating rhythms on the first disc released by the heavy-metal group V12 was a Jorge de Sena poem.

On his own, an *alentejano* is reticent. In a group, he sings. The soul music of the Alentejo is the strong, stirring harmony of men singing in a field, in a *taberna* – the groups (*ceifeiros*) of Cuba and Serpa renowned across generations. Their songs, simple and unfrivolous, about pain and loss and death, have three vocal elements: *ponto*, *alto* and the *segundas vozes*. A single voice rises, perhaps improvises, a phrase lingers and is taken up by other voices, without accompaniment. The rich cadences are quite different from the bouncy rhythms of popular folk music, or *fado*. The origins of each are mysterious. Academics argue, composers find inspiration, singers sing.

Earthy and emotional songs throb sweetly in Portuguese ears. The simple song of brotherhood, '*Grândola, vila morena*', played on the radio in April 1974, the signal for revolution, remains a deeply moving symbol of protest. For many Portuguese, its composer, Zeca Afonso, represented his generation's struggle against fascism. For thirty years he sang and wrote songs, often in aid of left-wing causes – he sang, he once said, because the Salazar regime had stopped him from teaching. After a long battle with muscular sclerosis he died, aged fifty-seven, in 1986. At the funeral Manuel Alegre observed: 'The country was one thing before him and another after.'

Zeca began his career by singing the *fados* of Coimbra where he studied in the 1940s. *Fado*, a word meaning fate or destiny, embodies more than any other music the Portuguese spirit of *saudade*, of yearning, of homesick longing. The soaring, haunting sounds of *fado* are descended, perhaps, from a melancholic dance of Congolese slaves shipped to Brazil. Or perhaps from the *cantigas* of the Middle Ages – like the Coimbra *fado* sung by black-cassocked students, an expression, as a historian put it, of masculine sentiment. The instruments: the twelve-stringed Portuguese guitar and what the Portuguese call *viola*, or Spanish guitar.

In Lisbon, in the Bairro Alto and Alfama, women as well as men sing *fado*. One of the most famous *fadistas* was Maria Severa, the daughter of a gypsy. Her admirers were legion – sailors, bull-fighters, a count. She died in 1846. She was twenty-six, a legend overnight. *Fado* comes in several styles – all of them profound. Straight from the heart is the singing, intense and woeful, you can hear in unpretentious Lisbon *tascas* – the informal, nonprofessional, spontaneous *fado vadio*. For her innumerable fans, the most thrilling of all *fadistas* is Amália Rodrigues. Hers is a classic rags-to-riches story, and she survived the political changes of the years un-perturbed, always unaffected and likeable. Even in old age, adored and scintillating, she ruled audiences with her personality and *sensibilidade*.

Not at all glamorous but nevertheless a popular Portuguese winner, like the ineffable Amália, of the record industry's platinum disc for multi-sales (in Portugal 40,000) is a singing monk, Frei Hermano da Câmara. That songs on Jesus of Nazareth are top sellers says a good deal about Portuguese taste. There are those who think it a pity that so much of the music blaring from loud-speakers during country fairs and other public gatherings is from foreign Madonnas rather than from their own friar.

It is easier to understand a nation by listening to its music, someone said, than by learning its language. What can an *estrangeiro* do? The music, with its echoes of Babel, is increasingly diverse. Visual humour? The Portuguese enjoy riddles and rude jokes. Fancifully illustrated homilies are painted fore and aft, port and starboard, on the long-necked *moliceiros* of the Aveiro lagoon. A painting shows a soldier wooing a young woman. 'You're not to be trusted,' it says below. A crude painting of a man, his wife and his ox-cart beside the lagoon quips: 'Let the rushes grow, I want to make some money.' *Larachas*, these paintings are called. Sometimes the joke is ruder and craftier. It is folk art and humour far from the savage wit and sophisticated draughtsmanship of newspaper cartoonists like *Expresso*'s António or Rui Pimentel in *O Jornal*. But even the papers carry earthy jokes. As for photographs, the *Expresso* photographers led by Rui Ochôa are a shining example of quality photojournalism. Elsewhere in photography, barring such magicians as Eduardo Gageiro and Eduardo Nery, and occasional riveting exhibitions, I observe with regret a trend towards sterile flimflam.

Words rather than music or humour or the universe of photography? Seeking illumination, we struggle in the spires and shadows of a shimmering language, lacking easy familiarity with Camilo and Ramalho, with Cesariny, or Sofia, or Agustina. Newspapers and magazines, competing with a new urgency, flash and flutter from racks and stacks. For a purchasing population that is much the lowest in Europe there is a spectacular choice of newspapers and magazines: a dozen or so dailies and eight major weeklies, whose irrepressible and lively journalists and contributors discuss Portugal's government, and its problems and prospects at length. There is also a broad specialist range, starting with sport, women's interests, business. Far ahead of any other publications in the circulation battles are a sports paper, *A Bola*, and a pocket-size women's magazine, *Maria*, its pages of letters more intimately revealing and celebrated than the classic *Cartas de Amor duma Freira Portuguesa*, the letters written by a seventeenth-century Beja nun to her French lover. There are numerous worthy regional and local papers and, for a parochial perspective in English, a handful of publications for residents and tourists.

There is more English spoken in Portugal than ever before. Youngsters learn it at school. Tourism, the economy, cannot expand without it. But you might, if you persist, find in the far north-east people who still speak *mirandês*, the language neither Portuguese nor Castilian that once was widely spoken around Miranda do Douro. Up there, Rio de Onor and Guadramil, a mere five kilometres away, also had their own *língua*. The north-west, where Portugal began, is home to a *galego* dialect. In Brazil, over 140 million people speak Portuguese – and academics lament that Portuguese is the only language with two official orthographies. Portuguese is the official language of Angola and Moçambique, Guinea-Bissau, Cape Verde and São Tomé and Principe. It lingers across all Africa – Zaïre uses *matabiche* to mean gift, or bribe. Here, *matar o bicho*, literally to kill the beast, means a reviving nip. Should a minister be heard to speak at international gatherings in any language but Portuguese, expressions of national outrage follow. UNESCO recognizes Portuguese as one of nine official languages (the United Nations works with six; NATO two; the EEC – expensively – with all the twelve languages of its members). They speak Portuguese in Macau. In the Açores, in Madeira, even in the Algarve, old folk speak a Portuguese that matches hardly at all the smooth Lisbon pronunciation. And you will hear mysterious intrusions of *inho* (a diminutive, pronounced een-yoo) and *eh, pá* (close to 'hey, pal' in sound and meaning), without which much of informal speech would falter. The floods of language resonate at times like the buzzing of busy bees. Surely only in Portuguese is there a place – *Freixo de Espada à Cinta*, the Trás-os-Montes town – with a name which means 'Ash Tree of the Belted Sword'.

We can contentedly explore, converse with the elderly, who are patient, listen to the talk of the market-place and the cafés, follow the fast-changing fads of the young. We find they frequent discos with names like Banana Power, Stones, Springfellows, Whispers, Jet-Set, Ad-Lib, Kremlin, Plateau, Trumps, Twins and T-Club. (Even a municipal streetsweeper I saw wore a T-shirt shouting STREETBEAT.) While a bossy civil governor in the Algarve – anxious to defend the national culture, or perhaps to distract citizens from their numerous grievances – was tearing down English-language publicity, the newspapers were full of words and phrases like *know-how, handy size, turn-around, short-selling, leverage buy-out, joint venture, cash flow, price book value, boom, splits, hot money, star quality, bright young things, software and hardware do futuro*. Sometimes there are slip-ups. *Death Wait?* They meant dead weight. For destination, I once saw the infinitely preferable *destiny station*. Where to, Portugal?

Where, indeed? If this is the most insistent, the biggest national question, it is one that appears to vex neither the confident cliques of the rich, smelling of money, the men in well-tailored suits, their women partying in elegant black-and-white, nor the fatalistic, eternally tolerant poor. The Portuguese – rich and poor – have proved themselves skilled across centuries in the arts of survival. Unfortunately, most modern judgements are not made on abstract virtues but on productivity. Jumping the train to destiny station are the able legions of self-made men and women entirely aware of the dangers on the line. 'The problem is not the lack of resources, but the lack of organization,' the cork king Américo Amorim sighs.

Not everything is quite as it should be. Even the shiniest new post office is equipped with little pots of glue. In this country, which conquered empires and is bounding towards the future, the postage stamps do not stick, their cost at times appears to accord with the mood of the postmistress, mail to many localities goes no further than the village store and may lie there for ever. But, as always, there is a proverb: *'Depressa e bem, não faz ninguem'* – 'more haste, less speed'. It will come right in the end. The popular joke is that the Portuguese put off until the day after tomorrow what they should have done the day before yesterday – and those are the fast ones.

Such glib stereotyping is facile. National and multinational companies profit from skilled, cheap, Portuguese labour. Generalizations on the Portuguese character can be just as easily refuted. Are the Portuguese cruel? Vasco da Gama's awful butchery of the crews of Muslim ships and the Zamorim's messenger, the casual cruelty to Amerindians of the settlers in Brazil (and of latter-day Brazilians), the exploitation and repression of African peoples in the long colonial era, all contribute to a picture of a ruthless, brutal society far from the one every traveller to Portugal encounters. Are they racist? Professor Boxer has described the historic class and administrative imperatives of *limpeza*, of *pureza de sangue* (purity of blood), the contempt for *raças infectas.* But practice, human urges – 'the Portuguese have adopted the vices and customs of the land without reserve,' wrote a shocked priest in India in 1550 – Pombal's anti-discrimination measures, the colonial experience and post-colonial relationships point to a healthy absence of bigotry. Are they courteous? Salazar in print was *senhor professor doutor*. I have heard a mini-skirted functionary in the electricity company addressed as *Vossa Excelência* (Your Excellency), as are all Members of Parliament, a formality that extends to letter-writing. But my neighbour calls me *amiguinha* (little friend), you hardly ever hear an apology, the Portuguese talk volubly, listen with difficulty and interrupt without qualm.

Are they honest? The chronicles relate how Dom João de Castro, governor of India, borrowed money from merchants to rebuild Diu on the security of a single hair plucked from his beard. The current scene in crime and corruption is little different from that of any other rapidly changing society. Are they bold, brave, moral, truthful, generous . . .? You can pick examples from a thousand eventful years that confirm or deny traits of national character and temperament. You will discover countless tics and quirks and looks and customs that seem pure Portuguese. But nothing is fixed. Are all women called Maria? Fewer then ever before, as young mothers break from tradition. Do the Portuguese like noise? Fog sirens wailed, Alan Villiers wrote, as the cod fleets departed. Mule bells jingle, dogs bark, motor bikes scream down country roads, farmers shout across the fields, train-drivers blast repeated warnings – which no one seems to hear. Yet ears are sharp for a joke and earthy gossip, especially over good wine and food – great servings of fresh seafood along the coast, the lamprey and salmon of the Minho, tasty *caldeiradas* (the *bouillabaisse* of Portugal), cod (*bacalhau*), the national dish, in one of its manifold forms, rustic soups, suckling pig, the splendid meaty stews (*ensopados*) of the Alentejo, fowl and game, hams and sausages (*chouriços*), cheeses and sweets – regional and convent recipes – made from many eggs and much sugar. Are they food fanatics? Few go as far as the woman owner of a country restaurant who hanged herself over a case of food poisoning in her establishment. There are Portuguese who dislike *bacalhau*, who have no interest in football, never go near Fátima, and cannot abide *fado*. There are contradictions in the traditional respect of Portuguese for authority: democracy tolerates the old generals' praise of the Salazar regime, provokes the firing of ministers whom *o povo* finds arrogant, perpetuates *personalismo* in the popularity of Mário Soares as president.

Above all, the Portuguese are nationalistic. Portugal's role in a fast-changing Europe is much discussed. Geography places Portugal on the periphery of western Europe, a position which is being accentuated as eastern European countries open up for business. (Madeira and the Açores were being described as 'ultraperipheral'.) It is an inconvenient position but scarcely fatal; peripheral vision would be worse. A maritime periphery, after all, served the Portuguese well in the era of discovery, in its links with Brazil and Angola, and has advantages for enterprising companies reaching out for new ties with Africa, a *novo atlantismo*. The failings of decolonization and fratricidal war will soon, they hope, be a distant memory. Treading lightly, Portugal backs every move towards peaceful democracy. But whatever African, European or global restructuring takes place, the most alluring, the most desirable destiny, for which all Portuguese yearn, is a Portugal for the Portuguese.

Political stability and fast economic growth are the obvious Portuguese assets in confronting the ever-changing challenges of western and eastern Europe, and government leaders, company administrators and economists endlessly rethink their strategy as the sharp winds of rivalry blow from the east. The great strides which Portugal has made since the turmoil of revolution win credit in international circles. Portugal changes as you watch. You will still see wooden ploughs in remote inland fields; the farmers' sons take smartcards and intelligent buildings for granted. Convenience foods, hotly competing pet foods, wine in cartons, are on the supermarket shelves. Along with zonephones there is tele-shopping. My neighbour José, who always had a weather eye to the sky, now takes his forecasts from TV. Not all his attitudes are altering though: he will never believe that gardening is pleasure and sitting indoors work.

If there is a national delusion, it is that Portugal, once great and wealthy, will stand as tall in the eyes of the world again. Status is seen as crucial. Every individual win or loss counts. Pessimism is howled down, a positive outlook cheered. The decision to instal the Council of Europe's Centro Norte–Sul (North–South Centre) in Lisbon was met with rejoicing. Portugal declared itself a candidate for the headquarters of the international Court of the Sea, for a European centre of oceanography, the European Environment Agency, EXPO-98 and the World Cup in 1998, the five-hundredth anniversary of Vasco da Gama's great voyage. Suddenly the Portuguese, so proud of their past, are alert to their future. Lisbon would become, said a planner, 'a city of the twenty-first century'. Win or lose, there would be other projects, other yearnings.

Whatever the Portuguese make of their country, it will arouse argument. If I am sure of anything, I am sure of that. All of us who pass by seek a glimpse into the soul of this likeable people. They can infuriate with stubborn or slow-moving ways. They can be cautious and complaining, or tender and warm and generous. They have shown a peculiar mastery in activities that require foresight, courage and endurance. They have patience, a measure of discipline and all the time in the world. Their problems are numerous and challenging. They face them with equanimity. They have reached out before, after all, and won.

Sources and further reading

Much of my material I have gathered in fields and streets, in homes, shops, villages, at *festas* and fairs, in general conversation, by interview, by observation, by eavesdropping. I have also read many, many newspapers, mainly the daily papers *Diário de Notícias*, *Correio da Manhã* and, as I was completing my text, *Público*; at the weekend, *Expresso*, *O Independente*, *O Jornal*, *Semanário* and the magazine *Sábado*.

It is hard to pick names from a press of eloquent journalists but I would note particularly the acerbic political comment of Paulo Portas in *O Independente* and the wry touch of Joaquim Letria in *Sábado*. I learned much about literature and the arts from the newspapers' culture sections, about forts and castles from Carlos Pereira Callixto's articles in *Correio da Manhã* and *Diário de Notícias*. The anecdote on the American diplomats on the night of revolution comes from José Freire Antunes's text in *Semanário*, on the Jewish Lopes Suasso family, bankers to William III, from the research of Joel Cahen of Amsterdam, described in Michael Davie's column in the *Observer*, 22 May 1988.

Of other English-language publications, I found the *Financial Times* supplements on Portugal useful and Diana Smith's stories especially instructive. I have also valued seeing the business magazine, *EuroBusiness*, and their annual *Europe Review* (World of Information, Saffron Walden). Stories by Jill Jolliffe in the *Guardian* and elsewhere, as well as news stories and features in the *International Herald Tribune* supplements and other publications by Peter Wise, Ken Pottinger, Martha de la Cal, Peter Collis and Paul Ames, have been helpful. Of English-language papers in Portugal, the *Algarve News*, *Portugal Post* and their sister colour magazine and, in Lisbon, the *Anglo-Portuguese News* inform and entertain the foreign resident.

Additionally, I have delved into works of history, poetry, commentary, review, art and architecture, travel, food and fiction. Some of these are listed below. The more academic and specialized books provide their own often extensive bibliography.

General history

IN ENGLISH

History of Portugal by A. H. Oliveira Marques (Columbia University Press, 1976); *A New History of Portugal* by H. V. Livermore (2nd ed., Cambridge University Press, 1976); *A History of Spain and Portugal*, by William C. Atkinson (Penguin Books, 1960); *A History of Spain and Portugal* by Stanley G. Payne (University of Wisconsin Press, 1973); *Portugal* by Charles E. Nowell (Prentice-Hall, 1973); *Aspects of European History* by Stephen J. Lee (Methuen, 1978). The British Historical Society of Portugal, in Lisbon, have published two helpful booklets: *The Lines of Torres Vedras* by A. H. Norris and R. W. Bremner (1986); and *The Lisbon Earthquake of 1755: Some British Eye-witness Accounts* (1988).

IN PORTUGUESE

História de Portugal by A. H. Oliveira Marques (Palas Editores, 1981), and his *A Sociedade Medieval Portuguesa*; *História de Portugal* by J. P. Oliveira Martins (Guimarães Editores, 1987); multi-volume histories by Joaquim Veríssimo Serrão, edited by José Hermano Saraiva (Verbo); the *Dicionário de História de Portugal* by Joel Serrão.

The discoveries and expansion

IN ENGLISH

The Discovery of the Sea by J. H. Parry (Weidenfeld & Nicolson,

1975); *The Portugal Story* by John Dos Passos (Robert Hale, 1970); *The Discoverers* by Daniel J. Boorstin (Penguin Books, 1986); *The Portuguese Seaborne Empire 1415–1825* by C. R. Boxer (Hutchinson, 1977); *The European Discovery of America* by Samuel Eliot Morison, 2 vols., *The Northern Voyages* and *The Southern Voyages* (New York, OUP, 1971 and 1974); *Prince Henry the Navigator* by John Ure (Constable, 1977); Hakluyt Society publications; *Men, Ships and the Sea* by Capt. Alan Villiers (National Geographic Society publication). See also *The Quest of the Schooner Argus* by Alan Villiers (Hodder & Stoughton, 1951), on the Portuguese cod-fishing voyages. Portugal's appearance in Africa features in *The River Congo* by Peter Forbath (Secker & Warburg, 1978). *In the Wake of the Portuguese Empire* is a photographic record of Portugal's presence across the world by Michael Teague (Carcanet Press, 1988). Also *Africa Explored* by Christopher Hibbert (Penguin Books, 1984); *Portugal in Africa: The Last Hundred Years* by Malyn Newitt (C. Hurst, 1981); *East Timor: Nationalism and Colonialism* by Jill Jolliffe (University of Queensland Press, 1978).

IN PORTUGUESE

Os Descobrimentos e a Economia Mundial by Vitorino Magalhães Godinho; *Os Descobrimentos Portugueses* by Jaime Cortesão, among a considerable list, including editions of the chronicles, published under the auspices of the National Commission for the Commemoration of the Portuguese Discoveries, Casa dos Bicos, Lisbon; see also their quarterly journal, *Oceanos*. Notable facsimile map collections are: *Portugaliae Monumenta Cartographica* by Armando Cortesão and Teixeira da Mota (Imprensa Nacional); the *Atlas* of the Visconde de Santarém (Admin. do Porto de Lisboa) as well as the *Roteiros* of Dom João de Castro (Ed. Inapa). Commemorative editions also include *Peregrinação e Cartas* by Fernão Mendes Pinto (Afrodite); among books sponsored by the Instituto Português do Livro e da Leitura is *O Impacto Português Sobre a Civilização Japonesa* by Armando Martins Janeira (Dom Quixote, 1989).

Modern history

IN ENGLISH

Republican Portugal, a Political History 1910–1926, by Douglas L. Wheeler (University of Wisconsin Press, 1978); *Portugal: A Twentieth Century Interpretation* by Tom Gallagher (Manchester University Press, 1983); *Contemporary Portugal* by Richard Robinson (Allen & Unwin, 1979); *Oldest Ally, a Portrait of Salazar's Portugal*, by Peter Fryer and Patricia McGowan Pinheiro (Dobson, 1961); *Portugal: Fifty Years of Dictatorship* by Antonio de Figueiredo (Penguin Books, 1975); *Portugal's Struggle for Liberty* by Mário Soares (Allen & Unwin, 1975); *Fascism and Resistance in Portugal* by D. L. Raby (Manchester University Press, 1988); *Portugal in Revolution* by Michael Harsgor (Washington Papers, Sage Publications, 1976); *In Search of Modern Portugal*, ed. by Lawrence S. Graham and Douglas L. Wheeler (University of Wisconsin Press, 1982).

IN PORTUGUESE

See under General History, including the multi-volume *História de Portugal* edited by José Hermano Saraiva; *Portugal Contemporâneo*, vols. I and II, by J. P. Oliveira Martins (Europa-América); *História da República*, in five volumes, by Raul Rêgo; *Diário de Uma Revolução* (Mil Dias, 1975). Among books on the end of empire and decolonization are: *Os Anos da Guerra*, the Portuguese in Africa between 1961 and 1975, ed. by João de Melo (Dom Quixote, 1988) and *Timor, terra sangrenta* by Jill Jolliffe (O Jornal, 1989).

Geographical and social

IN ENGLISH

The Individuality of Portugal, a study in historical-political geography, by Dan Stanislawski (University of Texas Press, 1959); *A Portuguese Rural Society* by José Cutileiro (Oxford, 1971).

IN PORTUGUESE

Portugal, o Mediterrâneo e o Atlântico by Orlando Ribeiro (Coimbra, 1945); *Geografia de Portugal* by Orlando Ribeiro, Hermann Lautensach and Suzanne Daveau; *Atlas de Portugal* (Selecções do Reader's Digest, 1988); *Rio de Onor, comunitarismo agro-pastoril*, by Jorge Dias (Presença, 1953); *Construções Primitivas em Portugal* by Ernesto Veiga de Oliveira, Fernando Galhano and Benjamim Pereira (Dom Quixote, 1988); *O Povo Português nos seus Costumes, Crenças e Tradições* by Teófilo Braga (Dom Quixote, 1989); *Jogos Populares Portugueses* by António Cabral (Domingos Barreira, 1990).

Literature

IN ENGLISH

Major writers from Eça de Queiroz to José Saramago, translated into English, are noted in my text. *The Maias* and *The Sin of Father Amaro* by Eça de Queiroz, *Ballad of Dog's Beach* by José Cardoso Pires, *South of Nowhere* by António Lobo Antunes are among English translations that should not be difficult to find. Saramago's *Memorial do Convento* appears as *Baltasar and Blimunda* (Ballantine, 1988). Portugal's great epic by Camões is available as *The Lusiads*, translated by William C. Atkinson (Penguin Books, 1952); and *Luís de Camões: Epic and Lyric* by L. C. Taylor (Carcanet, 1990). Of the masterly chronicles, *The English in Portugal, 1367–87* by Fernão Lopes, is translated by Derek Lomax and R. J. Oakley (Aris & Phillips). See also *The Times Literary Supplement*, 9–15 December 1988, articles by Kenneth Maxwell, Alexandre Pinheiro Torres, Hélder Macedo, José Saramago, Peter Rickard, Michael Freeman, Luís de Sousa Rebelo, C. R. Boxer, R. A. H. Robinson; *Portuguese Studies*, a literary journal published by the Department of Portuguese, King's College, London; *Tales and Legends of Portugal* by Emily George (Alves de Oliveira, 1981).

IN PORTUGUESE

I mention a few leading writers and poets in my text. I have quoted a poem by Dom Dinis included in the *Antologia da Poesia – Trovadoresca Galego-Portuguesa* edited by Alexandre Pinheiro Torres (Lello & Irmão, 1987); another fine anthology, on Oporto, is *Daqui Houve Nome Portugal*, organized by Eugénio de Andrade (O Oiro do Dia, 1967); my quote from Sá de Miranda came from an edition published on the five-hundredth anniversary of his birth by the Câmara Municipal de Amares. Fernando Pessoa is published by Ed. Atica in paperback; Júlio Dinis's *Uma Família Inglesa* by Simões Lopes. Miguel Torga's *Contos* are published by Coimbra. Another storyteller, the criminologist Artur Varatojo, is published by Civilização. Many of the classics are published in paperback by Europa-América. Oral literature – riddles – appear in *Adivinhas Populares Portuguesas* by V. Moutinho (Domingos Barreira, 1988) and proverbs in *Pequeno Dicionário de Provérbios* by Helena Duarte Silva and José Luís Quintão (Moraes, 1982). The Calouste Gulbenkian Foundation publishes literary and art journals, *Colóquio/Letras* and *Colóquio/Artes*. For topical publishing and news of reprints, see the journal *Ler – Livros & Leitores*, published by the Circulo de Leitores, Rua Eng. Paulo de Barros 22, 1599 Lisboa. Tel. (01) 709215/709221.

Cultural and literary history

IN PORTUGUESE

História do Romantismo em Portugal, vols. I and II, by Teófilo Braga; *História da Literatura Portuguesa* by António José Saraiva and Oscar Lopes; *História da Cultura em Portugal* by António José Saraiva (Lisbon, 1962); *O Crepúsculo da Idade Média em Portugal* by António José Saraiva (Gradiva, 1988); *Fontes Remotas da Cultura Portuguesa* by Moisés Espírito Santo (Assírio & Alvim, 1989); *Portugal – Razão e Mistério* (on megalithic civilization) by António Quadros.

Travel and travellers

IN ENGLISH

They Went to Portugal by Rose Macaulay (Cape, 1946; Penguin Books, 1985) is the handiest and most entertaining account of the way it was. You will find early editions of original accounts in the great, or private, libraries; and editions of exploration and travel books show up from time to time in the antiquarian bookseller lists. (*A Journey from London to Genoa* (1770) by Joseph Baretti, on a trip through Portugal, Spain and France suggested by his friend, Dr Johnson, I saw in a Francis Edwards, Hay-on-Wye, catalogue at £150. *How I Crossed Africa: From the Atlantic to the Indian Ocean* (1881) by Major Serpa Pinto, was listed at £300.) Fortunately many classics like William Beckford's *Recollections of an Excursion to the Monasteries of Alcobaça and Batalha* (1835), are still in print and can be had for very little.

Early modern guides include *The Selective Traveller in Portugal* by Ann Bridge and Susan Lowndes (Chatto & Windus, 1963) and *Algarve: a Portrait and a Guide* by David Wright and Patrick Swift (Barrie & Rockliff, 1965). *The Algarve* by Charles Wuerpel (David & Charles, 1973), with its list of flowering plants, is still relevant in some ways. After the 1974 revolution came Anthony Hogg's *Travellers' Portugal* (Solo Mio Books, 1983), Ian Robertson's Blue Guide *Portugal* (3rd ed., A.&C. Black, 1988), Fodor's *Portugal*, *Portugal* by Susan Lowndes (2nd ed., Thornton Cox, 1987); the Collins Independent Travellers' Guide *Portugal* by Martha de la Cal (1988); *The Rough Guide to Portugal*, edited by Mark Ellingham and John Fisher (3rd ed., Harrap Columbus, 1990), an Insight Guide, a Birnbaum Guide, Berlitz Travel Guides, *The Penguin Guide to Portugal*, and more. There are guides to the *pousadas* – *Pousadas of Portugal* by Sam and Jane Ballard (Moorland, 1986), is one. *Algarve*, by Frank Cook, is a guide to the distractions of the area.

Michael Howard's books of photos hold an older Algarve in memory. Other photographic books include *The Algarve: The Land, Sea and People* by José Adragão (Presença, 1988). There are also several for Sintra, among them (with colour photos and in four languages) *Sintra and its Farm Manors* by Arturo D. Pereira, Felipa Cardoso and Fernando Correia (published by the authors, 1983). I hardly touch on the islands, Madeira and the Açores. The rugged beauty of the Açores is handsomely portrayed in books by Willy Heinzelmann (1980) and by Bob Silverman, both called *Açores*.

All the great early journeys have been published and republished. Serpa Pinto's account of his journey across Africa, *Como Eu Atravessei a África* is published in paperback by Europa-América, as is the journey of Capelo and Ivens – *De Angola à Contracosta*.

For present-day travel *À Descoberta de Portugal* (Selecções do Reader's Digest) covers all mainland Portugal, Madeira and the Açores. José Saramago wrote *Viagem a Portugal* in 1981. The classic Portuguese guide is the *Guia de Portugal* in several detailed sections by several authors. Many small towns have also been treated separately – my own neighbourhood is represented in the *Monografia do Concelho de Loulé* by Ataide Oliveira (Algarve em Foco). (From the same author and publisher is a collection of popular poetry, *Romanceiro e Cancioneiro do Algarve*.) There are many monographs on local history. For Sintra, for instance, see *Velharias* written by José Alfredo da Costa Azevedo or *Sintra na Literatura Romântica Inglesa* by J. Almeida Flor (published by the Sintra Câmara). New and beautiful books appear regularly on Lisbon, Oporto, Sintra, the Algarve, the ancient towns, the land, the coast, the rivers, the boats, the trains, the people.

English novels

The Man from Lisbon by Thomas Gifford (Futura, 1978), like *The Man Who Stole Portugal* by Murray Teigh Bloom (Secker & Warburg, 1967), tells the vivid story of Alves Reis and the banknote case, 'the greatest swindle of all time'. *The Judas Code* by Derek Lambert (Hamish Hamilton, 1983) thrillingly links the spies and intrigues of wartime Lisbon to the mysterious Hitler–Stalin pact. Kingsley Amis set *I Like It Here* (Gollancz, 1958; Penguin Books, 1968) in the false sunshine of Salazar's Lisbon. Spies, sunshine and Lisbon appear again in John le Carré's *The Russia House* (Hodder & Stoughton, 1989; Coronet, 1990). The Douro is the setting for an evocative port-wine saga in Charles Gidley's *The River Running By* (André Deutsch, 1981). In *The Viceroy of Ouidah* Bruce Chatwin told the story of a Brazilian slaver who made his fortune in Dahomey (Picador, 1988). (A Portuguese translation calls it *O Vice-Rei de Ajuda*.) *Foucault's Pendulum* by Umberto Eco mystically, mysteriously, involves the Knights Templar (Secker & Warburg, 1989).

Art and architecture

IN ENGLISH

The Art of Portugal, 1500–1800, by Robert C. Smith (Weidenfeld & Nicolson, 1968). J. B. Bury's chapter on the subject in the Blue Guide to Portugal is helpful and concise. So is Ruth Rosengarten in the *Insight Guide* (APA Publications, 1988). For manor-houses see *Country Manors of Portugal* by Marcus Binney with photos by Nicolas Sapieha and Francesco Venturi (Difel, 1987); *The Finest Castles in Portugal* by Júlio Gil, photos by Augusto Cabrita (Verbo, 1988); also *The Finest Churches in Portugal* by Júlio Gil, photos by Nuno Calvet (Verbo, 1988) and *Churches of Portugal* by Professor Carlos de Azevedo (Difel).

IN PORTUGUESE

Tesouros Artísticos de Portugal (Selecções do Reader's Digest, 1976); *Por Terras de Portugal* (Selecções do Reader's Digest); *Solares Portugueses* by Carlos de Azevedo (Horizonte, 1988); *Casas Nobres de Portugal* by Marcus Binney (Difel, 1987); *Os Mais Belos Castelos de Portugal* and *As Mais Belas Igrejas de Portugal* by Júlio Gil (both Verbo); *Dicionário da Arte Barroca em Portugal*, ed. José Fernandes Pereira (Presença, 1989); and *Itinerário do Barroco no Algarve* by Francisco I. C. Lameira with photos by Nany Santos-Costa (Del.

Regional do Sul da Sec. de Estado da Cultura, 1988); *A Arquitetura Manuelina* by Pedro Dias (Civilização, 1988); *Dicionário de Pintores e Escultores Portugueses* by Fernando de Pamplona (Civilização, 2nd ed., 1988); *Estudos de Pintura Maneirista e Barroca* by Vítor Serrão (Caminho, 1989); *Desenhos da Prisão* by Álvaro Cunhal (Avante, 1975); *Azulejaria Portuguesa* by José Meco (Bertrand, 1985); *Azulejos em Portugal nos Séculos XV e XVI – Introdução Geral* by J. M. dos Santos Simões (Fundação Calouste Gulbenkian, 1990).

Food and wine

IN ENGLISH

Portuguese Cookery by Ursula Bourne (Penguin Books, 1973); *Traditional Portuguese Cookery* by Maria de Lourdes Modesto (Verbo); *The Food of Portugal* by Jean Anderson (Robert Hale, 1986); *The Cooking of Spain and Portugal* by P. S. Feibleman (Time-Life Books, 1970); *The Taste of Portugal* by Edite Vieira (Robert Hale, 1988; Robinson Publishing 1989); *The Englishman's Wine* – the story of port – by Sarah Bradford (Macmillan, 1969); *Port Wine* – notes on its history, production and technology – published by the Instituto do Vinho do Porto; *Vinho Verde* by Amândio Galhano (Comissão de Viticultura da Região dos Vinhos Verdes, 1986); *The Wines of Portugal* by Jan Read (Faber, 1987); *The Wines of Spain and Portugal* by Charles Metcalf and Kathryn McWhirter (Salamander, 1988). Hugh Johnson's *Pocket Wine Book* (Mitchell Beazley, 1989); *The Sunday Times Handbook of Wine*, adapted by Joanna Simon.

IN PORTUGUESE

Cozinha Tradicional Portuguesa by Maria de Lourdes Modesto (Verbo); *O Livro de Bem Comer* by José Quitério (Assírio & Alvim, 1987); *Tesouros da Cozinha Tradicional Portuguesa* (Selecções do Reader's Digest); *A Cozinha Descoberta pelos Portugueses* by Maria Odette Cortes Valente (Círculo de Leitores, 1989); *O Trivial* – easy recipes by Filipa Vacondeus – (Area, 1986); *A Boa Mesa do Alto Minho*, a collection of recipes published by the Região de Turismo

of the Costa Verde; *Roteiro Gastronómico da Região dos Templários*,
recipes published by Fábrica Mendes Godinho, Tomar; *O Livro dos
Vinhos* by José A. Salvador with photos by Luís Ramos (Frag-
mentos, 1989); *Vinhos de Portugal* by Jan Read (Quetzal, 1989).
Very useful, too, are the wine supplements published in *O Jornal*
and every second Friday in *Diário de Notícias*.

Flowers, gardens, birds, animals, environment

IN ENGLISH

Flowers of South-West Europe: A Field Guide, by Oleg Polunin and
B. E. Smythies (Oxford, 1973); *Reader's Digest Encyclopaedia of
Garden Plants and Flowers* (Reader's Digest Association, 1978); *Wild
Flowers of the Algarve* by Mary McMurtrie (published by the author,
1973); *Gardens of Portugal* by Patrick Bowe, photos by Nicolas
Sapieha (Quetzal); *Country Life Guide to the Birds of Britain and
Europe* by Bertel Bruun (2nd ed., Newnes, 1986); *A Field Guide to
the Birds of Britain and Europe* by Roger Peterson, Guy Mountfort
and P. A. D. Hollom (Collins, 4th ed., 1983); *Mammals of Britain
and Europe* by Richard Orr and Joyce Pope (Pelham, 1983; Peerage,
1986).

IN PORTUGUESE

Tratado da Grandeza dos Jardins em Portugal by Hélder Carita and
António Homem Cardoso (published by the authors, 1987); *Palácio
de Queluz – Jardins* by Simonetta Luz Afonso and Angela Delaforce,
photos by Nicolas Sapieha (Quetzal, 1989); *Jardins de Portugal* by
Patrick Bowe, photos by Nicolas Sapieha (Quetzal). *O Meu Primeiro
Livro de Aves* (ICBP Migratory Birds Programme with the Serviço
Nacional de Parques, Reservas e Conservação da Natureza); *O
Homem e o Ambiente* by José Batista and Luís Palma (Texto, 1984);
Flores do Parque Nacional (de Peneda-Gerês) by Georgina Macedo
and Maria Helena Tiago (1985).

Music, cinema, photography, the press

IN PORTUGUESE

História do Fado by Pinto de Carvalho (Dom Quixote); *Dicionário do Cinema Português de 1962 a 1988* by Jorge Leitão Ramos (Caminho, 1989); *Anuário Português de Fotografia*, published annually by Fotojornal; *História da Imprensa Periódica Portuguesa* by José Tengarrinha (Caminho, 1989).

Women

IN ENGLISH AND PORTUGUESE

Literature on many themes related to women's status is published by the Comissão da Condição Feminina, Av. da República, 32–1°, 1093 Lisbon. Still relevant is *New Portuguese Letters* by the 'three Marias', Maria Isabel Barreno, Maria Teresa Horta and Maria Velho da Costa (Paladin, 1975; in Portuguese, *Novas Cartas Portuguesas*).

Business, finance

IN PORTUGUESE

Exame, the monthly business magazine; economic supplements in *Diário de Notícias*, *Expresso*, *Semanário* and other newspapers. *Os Grandes Patrões da Indústria Portuguesa* by Maria Filomena Mónica (Dom Quixote, 1990).

Kings, queens, presidents of Portugal: a chronology

Kings and Queens

First dynasty (*Afonsina*), House of Burgundy

REIGNED		LIVED
1128/39–85	Afonso (Henriques) I, *o Conquistador*	1109–85
1185–1211	Sancho I, *o Povoador*	1154–1211
1211–23	Afonso II, *o Gordo*	1186–1223
1223–48	Sancho II, *o Capelo*	1209–48
1248–79	Afonso III, *o Bolonhês*	1210–79
1279–1325	Dinis, *o Lavrador*	1261–1325
1325–57	Afonso IV, *o Bravo*	1291–1357
1357–67	Pedro I, *o Justiceiro*	1320–67
1367–83	Fernando, *o Formoso*	1345–83

Second dynasty (*de Avis*), House of Avis

REIGNED		LIVED
1385–1433	João I, *de Boa Memória*	1357–1433
1433–38	Duarte, *o Eloquente*	1391–1438
1438–81	Afonso V, *o Africano*	1432–81
1481–95	João II, *o Príncipe Perfeito*	1455–95
1495–1521	Manuel I, *o Venturoso*	1469–1521

1521–57	João III, *o Piedoso*	1502–57
1557–78	Sebastião, *o Desejado*	1554–78
1578–80	Henrique, *o Casto*	1512–80

Third dynasty (Filipina), Castilian usurpation

1580–98	Filipe I, *o Prudente* (Philip II of Spain)	1527–98
1598–1621	Filipe II, *o Pio* (Philip III of Spain)	1578–1621
1621–40	Filipe III, *o Grande* (Philip IV of Spain)	1605–65

Fourth dynasty (Bragantina), House of Bragança

1640–56	João IV, *o Restaurador*	1604–56
1656–67	Afonso VI, *o Vitorioso*	1643–83
1667–1706	Pedro II, *o Pacífico*	1648–1706
1706–50	João V, *o Magnânimo*	1689–1750
1750–77	José, *o Reformador*	1714–77
1777–1816	Maria I, *a Piedosa*	1734–1816
1816–26	João VI, *o Clemente*	1767–1826
1826	Pedro IV, *o Libertador*	1798–1834
1828–34	Miguel, *o Usurpador*	1802–66
1834–53	Maria II, *a Educadora*	1819–53
1853–61	Pedro V, *o Esperançoso*	1837–61
1861–89	Luís, *o Popular*	1838–89
1889–1908	Carlos, *o Martirizado*	1863–1908
1908–10	Manuel II, *o Desventuroso*	1889–1932

Presidents

Presidents of the First Republic

1910–11	Teófilo Braga	1843–1924
1911–15	Manuel de Arriaga	1840–1917
1915	Teófilo Braga	1843–1924
1915–17	Bernardino Machado	1851–1944
1918	Sidónio Pais	1872–1918
1918–19	Admiral João do Canto e Castro	1862–1934
1919–23	António José de Almeida	1866–1929
1923–5	Manuel Teixeira Gomes	1862–1941
1925–6	Bernardino Machado	1851–1944
1926	Commander José Mendes Cabeçadas	1883–1965
1926	General Manuel Gomes da Costa	1863–1929
1926–51	General António Óscar de Fragoso Carmona (with António de Oliveira Salazar as premier 1932–68)	1869–1951
1951–8	General Francisco Craveiro Lopes	1894–1964
1958–1974	Admiral Américo Tomás (with Marcelo Caetano as premier 1968–74)	1894–1987

Presidents of the Second Republic

1974	General António Spínola	1910–
1974–6	General Francisco da Costa Gomes	1914–
1976–86	General António Ramalho Eanes	1935–
1986–	Mário Soares	1924–

Travel advisory

Where to go, when to go, how to go, where to stay, where to eat, what to eat, what to see and do, what to buy? Language problems? Money, banks, credit cards? Doctors and pharmacies? The traveller's natural questions demand an answer. My text provides few of these details, except that where I have written of a place not widely known I have usually included the name of the nearest town or city. The index and maps will help you link themes I have touched on with places to see.

Your nearest **Portuguese National Tourism Office** can provide guidance and information. In **England**, their office is at 1/5 New Bond Street, London, W1Y 0NP (tel. 071-493 3873; telex 265653). In the **United States**, they are at 548 Fifth Avenue, New York, NY 10036; in **Canada** at 1801 McGill College Avenue, #1150, Montreal, Quebec. In **Portugal**, the head office is: Direcção-Geral do Turismo, at Av. António Augusto de Aguiar, 86, 1000 Lisbon (by mail to Apartado 1929, 1004 Lisbon; tel. (01) 575086; telex 13408 Portur P; fax (01) 556917).

How to go?

You can get to Portugal **by air** with several major airlines or charters. TAP Air Portugal, the national airline, and its subsidiary, Air Atlantis, operate a wide range of flights. International airports are at Lisbon, Oporto and Faro (as well as Funchal in Madeira and Ponta Delgada in the Açores). There is air access across country by regional flights. You can go **by road**, with a choice of routes that include ferries. From England, several ferry services link the Eng-

lish coast with France. Brittany Ferries additionally links Plymouth
to Santander in northern Spain twice-weekly, a twenty-two-hour
journey in their new flagship, the 23,000-tonnes *Bretagne* (580 cars,
2,030 passengers). From Santander to the Algarve is about sixteen
hours' driving. You could also travel **by coach**. Or you could go
by train. There are special youth and pensioner fares. In England
there is an InterRail system for young people under twenty-six; in
the United States and Canada EurRail passes. A Lusitania Express
connects Madrid and Lisbon, a Sud Express Lisbon and Paris, both
with sleeper cars. (These are not to be confused with the exquisite
and elegant Andalusian Express, operated by the Spanish rail company Renfe, which tours southern Spain.) France operates the
ultra-fast TGV (*Train à Grande Vitesse*); the TGV in Spain and
Portugal in 1991 was at the planning stage.

When to go?

The weather follows the European pattern of hot summers and
wet, chilly (though never extremely cold) winters, yet even in small
Portugal there are distinct variations between north and south –
and coast and inland. The Algarve glows with 3,000 hours of
annual sunshine; it hardly rains at all between June and late September but in November and December especially it can rain heavily.
Lisbon and the Alentejo, too, are hot in summer – I never drive
without a very large flask of iced water. The mountains of the
north and centre create their own sometimes disconcerting mi-
croclimates. The north, fairly wet, is never uncomfortably hot. To
me, the most beautiful months across the land are April, May and
June, but travelling is still a pleasure at any other time. Golfers
come in winter, sun-worshippers in summer – though scarcely a
winter passes without bared bodies on a beach somewhere. **Cloth-
ing?** A swimsuit, light clothes, a sweater, a rain shield in summer;
in winter, warmer clothes, especially for the north.

Where to go and how to get there?

Taste, time and pocket decide that. A sunny beach? Cool mountains? Ancient towns with glorious monuments? The grand churches and museums? Nightlife? Bird life and the great out of doors? You need not only specific information but a really good up-to-date map (the roads are changing and extending as I write). *Turismo* offices across Portugal are generous with information and with maps. In **Lisbon** the tourist office is centrally situated in Palácio Foz, Praça dos Restauradores (tel: (01) 3463624; hours 9 a.m.–8 p.m., Sundays and holidays 10 a.m.–6 p.m.). They can provide national as well as specifically Lisbon information, and will advise on the availability of hotel accommodation.

All the larger towns and most small towns have a *Turismo* office. Bear in mind that tourism defines areas differently from an administrative or regional map. Where I have written of the Minho and Trás-os-Montes, for instance, they have Costa Verde and Montanhas; for the Beira Baixa and Alentejo they say Planicies. (See maps on pages xii–xvi, showing the administrative and tourism areas; the main wine regions and parks, reserves and other protected areas are also shown.) Large-scale maps for walkers can be purchased from the Instituto Geográfica e Cadastral, whose head office is in the Praça da Estrela, Lisbon (tel. (01) 609925).

Driving everywhere, except Lisbon and Oporto, is easy: stay on the right, watch out for dangerous drivers, keep within the speed limits (60 k.p.h. in built-up areas, 90 k.p.h. on open roads; 120 k.p.h. on motorways). Car hire is cheaper than in most other countries, Portuguese companies on the whole cheaper than the international ones. A national, or international, driving licence is required. You categorically must be insured. There is an Automóvel Club de Portugal with offices in Lisbon, Oporto and Faro. It has links with motoring organizations in other countries and operates an emergency service. Service stations are widespread, petrol among the priciest in Europe. Lead-free is sold at the newer stations. Some of these, on main roads, take Visa cards (for a tax, written in, of 100 escudos). All major towns have taxis, still cheap – so add a tip of around 15 per cent. Lisbon and Oporto have colourful trams – *eléctricos* – as well as a bus service. Lisbon has an underground metro system (watch out for pickpockets).

A public company, Caminhos de Ferro Portugueses (CP), runs the **railways**. Medium-fast Rápido trains (with air-conditioned coaches, a bar and restaurant car) link Lisbon to Oporto, medium-slow (though cheaper) trains operate on the rest of the national network. You cannot pay as a rule on the train; you must get your ticket in advance. Often, there is a queue. Theoretically, you can get almost anywhere by train. In fact, many stations are situated miles from town. A good service links Lisbon (from Cais do Sodré station) with Estoril; another, from Rossio station, Lisbon and Sintra. Scenic routes on classic lines – the Douro, the Vouga, the Minho, have been the delight of patient travellers and train buffs. Incessant strikes and closed routes as new investment takes hold have tended to take the pleasure out of train travel. Up on the Douro, the line ends before the Spanish border. There is no one at Alegria to sell you a ticket, although the train will still stop for you there. (Alegria, which has won prizes for its prettiness, means 'Happiness'.)

You can also travel across Portugal **by bus**. Tour coaches, with refreshments and toilet, run the main routes, the main bus company, Rodoviária Nacional (RN), goes almost everywhere. Bus stations are nearly always in town centres, the service reliable, reasonably comfortable and safe.

Boats, increasingly, can give you illuminating views of Portugal. On the Tejo at Lisbon, apart from the regular ferry boats leaving from near the Praça do Comércio or Cais do Sodré, you can take day or night cruises. A car ferry south of Lisbon links Tróia to Setúbal across the Sado river estuary. In Oporto, tourist boats can carry you upriver to port-wine country or on mini-cruises. They depart from the Ribeira, the waterfront. (You may hear of a Duque da Ribeira – a jaunty boatman who, into his eighties, was a well-known Douro personality.) In Faro, José Vargas (tel. (089) 21376) or Isabel Vicente at Viagens Elena (tel. (089) 801691) can show you the bird life on the offshore islands. Ria Formosa cruises has a range of tour boats (tel. (089) 818541). Many river and sea ports have boats for hire (for fishing, too). Check with the nearest *Turismo*.

Where to stay?

Hotels are rated from 5-star to 1-star. I list a few below. *Estalagens* (inns) and *pensões* are rated from 4-star down. There are also the state-run *pousadas*, an ever-increasing selection of private owned manor-houses within an officially encouraged scheme, *Turismo de habitação*, as well as camp-sites (a handy pamphlet and information from *Turismo*) and rooms – *quartos*. Telephone numbers, I have to warn you, may change. (Dial 166 for information; some operators can speak English.)

Pousadas

Some *pousadas* are more historic and architecturally thrilling than others. All are comfortable. None is truly cheap; prices vary according to standard and historical glamour – in the Alentejo, for example, the modest mansion at Serpa is much cheaper than the castle in Estremoz. The food is variable, often very good, with regional as well as international dishes. Some of the mansions have swimming-pools. *Turismo* can provide a detailed list, with low, middle and high season prices. Reservations can be made through Enatur, Empresa Nacional de Turismo, Av. Santa Joana a Princesa, 10, 1700 Lisbon. Tel. (01) 881221/889078; telex 13609 or 63475 Enatur P; fax (01) 805846. They are listed below, alphabetically by place.

Águeda (mansion at Serém, just off main road north of Coimbra and Águeda): Pousada de Santo António, tel. (034) 521230.
tel. (059) 95467.
Almeida (within the walls of a star-shaped fortification): Pousada Senhora das Neves, tel. (071) 54290.
Amarante (mansion in the Serra do Marão some 25 km up a winding road to the west of Amarante); Pousada de São Gonçalo, tel. (055) 461113.

Batalha (mansion beside the monastery): Pousada Mestre Afonso Domingues, tel. (044) 96260.

Bragança (mansion overlooking the castle and old town): Pousada São Bartolomeu, tel. (073) 22493.

Caniçada (mansion overlooking a man-made lake south of Peneda-Gerês. The village is off the main road some 36 km north-east of Braga): Pousada de São Bento, tel. (053) 647190.

Caramulo (mansion with a valley view): Pousada de São Jerónimo, tel. (032) 86291.

Elvas (mansion): Pousada de Santa Luzia, tel. (068) 62128.

Estremoz (thirteenth-century castle): Pousada de Rainha Santa Isabel, tel. (068) 22618.

Évora (fifteenth-century convent): Pousada dos Loios, tel. (066) 24051.

Guimarães (a vast monastery on the outskirts): Pousada Santa Marinha da Costa, tel. (053) 418465.

Guimarães (historic building in the city centre): Pousada de Nossa Senhora de Oliveira, tel. (053) 412157.

Manteigas (mansion high in the Serra da Estrela): Pousada de São Lourenço, tel. (075) 98150.

Marvão (in the old town below the castle, within the city walls): Pousada de Santa Maria, tel. (045) 93201.

Miranda do Douro (mansion overlooking the Douro river): Pousada de Santa Catarina, tel. (073) 42255.

Murtosa (mansion on a spit of land at the water's edge overlooking the Ria de Aveiro): Pousada da Ria, tel. (034) 48332.

Óbidos (castle within the walls of the medieval town): Pousada do Castelo, tel. (062) 95105.

Oliveira do Hospital (mansion in the village of Póvoa das Quartas, north-west of Oliveira do Hospital): Pousada de Santa Bárbara: tel. (038) 52252.

Palmela (fortified monastery on a high escarpment): Pousada do Castelo de Palmela, tel. (01) 2351226.

Sagres (mansion on a cliff beside the sea): Pousada do Infante, tel. (082) 64222. The *pousada* manages, as an annexe, the cliff-top, four-room Fortaleza do Beliche close to Cape St Vincent; tel. (082) 64124.

Santa Clara-a-Velha (mansion overlooking a man-made lake in the western Alentejo): Pousada de Santa Clara, tel. (083) 98250.

Santiago do Cacém (mansion near the historic town): Pousada de São Tiago, tel. (069) 22459.

São Brás de Alportel (mansion in inland Algarve): Pousada de São Brás, tel. (089) 842305.

Serpa (mansion with a vista of olive-studded plains): Pousada de São Gens, tel. (084) 90327.

Setúbal (castle on heights above the sea with a stone-stepped tunnel entrance): Pousada de São Filipe, tel. (065) 23844.

Tomar (mansion at Castelo do Bode overlooking a dam beside the lake on the Zêzere river, some 14 km east of Tomar): Pousada de São Pedro, tel. (049) 381159.

Torrão (hunting-lodge south-west of Alcácer do Sal beside a man-made lake): Pousada de Vale de Gaio, tel. (065) 66100.

Valença do Minho (within historic fortified town often crowded with shoppers from Spain): Pousada de São Teotónio, tel. (051) 22242.

Vila Nova de Cerveira (castle and quiet buildings overlooking the Minho river): Pousada de Dom Dinis, tel. (051) 795601.

Turismo de habitação

The manor-house scheme includes *solares* and *casas antigas, quintas* and water mills, town houses and rural modern. You might get a crown-embroidered pillowcase in the Conde de Calheiros's ancient *paço* near Ponte de Lima, an ancient *pelourinho* outside your door at the Casa do Adro in Soajo at the edge of the Peneda-Gerês national park. Under the *Turismo de habitação* scheme, visitors can stay in rooms in historic houses as guests of the owners. Breakfast is always included; other meals can sometimes be arranged, and there is always some kind of restaurant fairly close. All rooms are government-checked; all have private bathrooms. Tourist offices in each area can provide local information. At present, there are two associations: Turihab, with its office in Ponte de Lima, has a wide range in the green north; PIT, based in Cascais, has a countrywide list. Prices and booking conditions vary. Generally, they like you to book in advance and stay for at least three days.

Associação de Turismo de Habitação (Turihab)
Praça da República (in the Tourist Office)
4990 Ponte de Lima
Tel. (058) 942729; telex 32618 PTPL; fax (058) 941864.

Tradition of Portugal (PIT)
Alto da Pampilheira
Torre D-2, 8° A
2750 Cascais
Tel. (01) 2844464/4867958; telex 43304 PITSA P; fax (01) 2842901.

Hotels and other accommodation

In LISBON and OPORTO there are numerous hotels. Among several 5-star hotels in Lisbon is the Ritz-Intercontinental (tel. (01) 692020), the august Avenida Palace (tel. (01) 3460151) or the Hotel Tivoli on the Avenida da Liberdade (tel. (01) 530181). There is a Sheraton and Meridien in both Lisbon and Oporto. My favourite 5-star in Oporto is the older, plusher Hotel Infante de Sagres (tel. (02) 2008101).

The 4-star range is even wider. In LISBON the Hotel Tivoli Jardim (tel. (01) 539971) is next door to the five-star hotel Tivoli. In OPORTO, the Grande Hotel de Batalha (tel. (02) 2000571) is in the city centre. Among 3-star hotels in LISBON is the Hotel Bôtanico (tel. (01) 320392) and the Hotel Eduardo VII (tel. (01) 530141). Very popular in Lisbon for character and situation is the Pensão Residência York House in the Rua das Janelas Verdes (tel. (01) 662435). My own choice, for its incomparable view over Alfama and the São Jorge castle to the river – King Afonso Henriques stood here during the siege of Lisbon in 1147 – is the Albergaria Senhora do Monte in the Graça neighbourhood (tel. (01) 866002).

Every town has its *pensão* (pension), or several, its hotel, or several, a guesthouse, a room for the night. Some have restaurants, some do not, but a *residencial* offers only *pequeno almoço* (breakfast). Some establishments are full of character, known for their style, comfort and good food – like the Hotel Palácio dos Seteais in SINTRA (tel. (01) 9233200); the Hotel do Guincho on the surfy

Atlantic shore beyond Cascais and Estoril (tel. (01) 2850491); the Hotel Albatroz in CASCAIS (tel. (01) 4832821). Further afield there is the architecturally inimitable Palace Hotel at BUÇACO (tel. (031) 93101), in the far north the Estalagem da Boega (tel. (051) 795231) at GONDARÉM off the main road a little south of Vila Nova de Cerveira, or the Estalagem do Caçador (tel. (078) 42356) in MACEDO DE CAVALEIROS in the Trás-os-Montes. No grand hotel but, in MOGADOURO, to the south-west in the same rugged region, is the A Lareira (tel. (079) 32363), a restaurant with rooms, owned by a French-trained Portuguese chef and his brother.

Hotels are rising all the time, as I have written. Some are horrible, ugly and misplaced. Some, like the little Bela Vista on Praia da Rocha beach, PORTIMÃO (tel. (082) 24055), try to keep their stylish character as new blocks rise around them. (It has no restaurant. Best dining in the neighbourhood is at the restaurant A Lanterna, on the eastern outskirts of Portimão on the Ferragudo turn-off – tel. (082) 23948). With rare and special qualities in the Algarve, too, are the hotel and restaurant, La Réserve at SANTA BÁRBARA DE NEXE near Faro (tel. (089) 90474); Vila Joya, a small hotel at PRAIA DA GALÉ, west of Albufeira (tel. (089) 591795); and Vilalara, discreetly designed apartments set among pools and gardens above a snug beach near ARMAÇÃO DE PÊRA (tel. (082) 314910). Other hotels are wonderfully convenient for inland travel – like the Estalagem da Neve with its own restaurant in FUNDÃO (tel. (075) 52215), just south of the Serra da Estrela. Or, in north-eastern Guarda, the sturdy, if dated, Hotel de Turismo, with its excellent food and service (tel. (071) 22205). Or the 3-star *residencial* (bed-and-breakfast) Hotel São Gens in ARGANIL (tel. (035) 22959) for visiting the Serra do Açor, inland from Coimbra. North of Tomar in quiet wooded country at Cernache do Bomjardim, SERTÃ, over-looking the Castelo do Bode lake, is the Estalagem Vale da Ursa, with good regional cookery (tel. (074) 67511). In the Berlengas, a magnificent fort surrounded by crystal clear waters, is a cheap hostel (check with *Turismo* in Peniche: tel. (062) 72271). Close to Peniche, across the causeway dividing two moon-white beaches at BALEAL I have delighted in the peace of the Casa das Marés (House of the Tides) owned by three sisters, all named Maria, set

above a fisherman's cove (tel. (062) 76371). As in many such *casas*,
there is no restaurant. PENICHE, a fishing port, has many. I can
recommend Oh Amaral, next to São Pedro church.

What and where to eat?

The hotels and restaurants I have already mentioned barely skim
the surface of where to eat in Portugal. There are restaurants (and/
or snack-bars) in every town and neighbourhood. The Portuguese
love their food – lots of it, flavoursome and succulent. Sophisticated
men and women tuck contentedly into great helpings of hearty
stews. Vasco Graça Moura, the cosmopolitan head of the Discoveries Commission, asked his favourite   dish by *Olá*, replied,
'*Feijoada com tripas e pézinhos de coentrada*' – three dishes, pork and
beans, tripe, and pig's trotters with coriander, all rustically savoury.
Cuisine nouvelle, or *cuisine minceur*, would never get a look in here.
Even the good little French restaurant in LOULÉ, Aux Bons Enfants,
serves healthy portions. In Loulé, for good steaks and fish on an
international menu that includes Portuguese dishes, we go to the
Avenida. Seafood, fresh and tastily prepared with a variety of
herbs, is to be had all along the coast. In ERICEIRA, of several
seafood restaurants, I urge you to try the back-street Painel do
Mar. Quite often, you will find good fish inland too – I have eaten
a pleasing plaice and chips (*solho e batatas fritas*) at an Alentejan
road-house restaurant, A Lanterna, on the main Lisbon/Algarve
highway south of GRÂNDOLA. Sometimes, I have wondered why
there was such a hunger for spices when herbs grow in variety and
abundance – thyme and parsley, coriander and fennel, and more.
With heavenly seafood, meat dishes various and sometimes glorious, desserts colourful, distinctive and very sweet, you have to
beware only of one thing: those generous quantities, especially in
unsophisticated establishments. For the food itself, use a dictionary
or phrasebook (although many restaurants have English-language
menus). You might need to know that a half portion is *meia dose*.

For visitors, the food – or the order in which it is served – can
at times seem somewhat odd. For example, it is not unusual to start

a meal with cheese – small rounds of soft white or hard yellow goat cheese – and to finish, in some rural areas, with a bowl of soup. Even port, by tradition a *digestif*, a perfect end to a perfect meal, also comes in a pleasing dry white aperitif.

You can eat magnificently with the help of an attentive waiter anywhere. Linguistic problems may arise only in the unpretentious, resolutely no-star restaurants where a meal, starting with chewy bread and olives, can cost, with wine, a startlingly modest sum.

All Portugal likes its soups – *caldo verde*, made from cabbage leaves, is commonplace. In the Alentejo, soup (like stew) has bread in it, gusts of garlic – an *açorda* often appears with a raw egg floating in it. A popular soup, too, is *sopa de pedra* (stone soup) – a thick, filling, meat and vegetable soup in the depths of which is a large white stone. Legend describes its origins like this: a pedlar (a priest in some versions) arrives at a village house and begs water. His thirst quenched, he says to the woman of the house: 'I am hungry but, if you give me a stone, I shall prepare a wonderful soup that will satisfy us both.' The woman hands him a stone which he puts in a pot of water, and places the pot on the fire. Both wait. 'A few beans,' the pedlar says, 'would make the stone cook faster. And do you have a potato or two?' The woman gives him a handful of beans and some potatoes. Soon the pot begins to bubble. 'Some meat, a slice of *chouriço* [garlic sausage], salt, a little parsley, would soften the stone,' the man says. The woman gives him all he asks. The pedlar stirs the pot and soon pleasant aromas arise from it. The soup impresses the woman of the house and the pedlar, for his part, eats his fill. 'You see,' he says as he leaves with her praises in his ears, 'how easy it is to make a soup with just a stone.'

Dried cod (*bacalhau*), the national dish, the national passion, can be cooked – tradition has it – 365 ways (after soaking in several changes of cold water for at least twenty-four hours). Fine restaurants serve *bacalhau à brás* where the fish is flaked into a savoury mix of potatoes, onions, black olives and beaten eggs. Of all the recipes, this is probably the most palatable to the initiate, unless you count the puff pastry and rissoles made with *bacalhau*.

In the north you will find fresh salmon, trout, lampreys, eel and *rojões* (tasty chopped braised pork), and the famous *tripas* (tripe) of Oporto. The Beiras like their *cozidos* (stews). Try *chanfana* (braised lamb), if you see it. Virtually everywhere, vegetables are freshly picked. In my neighbourhood in early spring the land is green with *favas* (broad beans) – often lightly cooked with a flavouring of spicy *chouriço*. The Algarve also has its *cataplana*, a casserole of diced pork and clams with onions, *presunto* (smoked ham), a touch of paprika and a spoonful of *piri-piri* (powdered dried red chillies) cooked in a wok-like covered container. The Restaurante Dois Irmãos in FARO does a splendid version.

One of the classic sweets in Portugal is *Pudim Molotov*. I have not yet heard a likely explanation of the name – one wit alleged that, before the 1974 revolution, it was called *Pudim Salazar*. It looks like a giant *crème caramel* but, at its best, is infinitely lighter: a cream soufflé with caramel sauce and a touch of liqueur. Names of the sweets of convent origin are odd, too: *papos d'anjo* (angel puffs), *orelhas de abade* (abbot's ears), *línguas de bispo* (bishop's tongues), a rich dessert called *barrigas de freira* (nun's belly). Even rice pudding sounds better as *arroz doce*. At BOM JESUS, above Braga, in the Hotel do Elevador, I ate the simple and delicious *rabanadas*: bread soaked in milk and egg, fried golden and dipped in cinnamon sugar. For some of the convent sweets – and for first-class cuisine altogether – I enthusiastically recommend the Restaurante Conventual in LISBON.

You will find coffee everywhere – with various names for small, large, with/without milk, weak or strong. Most Portuguese drink tea without milk – country folk also make herb teas from lemon balm (*erva cidreira*) and the elder tree (*flor de sabugueiro*). Older hotels might serve you *marmelada* for breakfast – not marmalade but a quince jelly as solid as Turkish delight, most frequently eaten at lunch with cheese. Jams are *doces*.

The Restaurante Conventual is among the few restaurants in Portugal to have won a Michelin star. In an article in *Expresso*, José Quitério, a Portuguese gourmet and food-writer, deplored Michelin's chauvinism, their idiosyncratic selections, ratings and exclusions. Portuguese cooking wholly lacks the subtlety and mystique attached to French cuisine. For the Portuguese this detracts not at all from its satisfying taste. They do not worship food. They enjoy it.

Any gourmet who comes to Portugal already has à list of restaurants selected for their food and elegant setting. On it will be, for LISBON, the Tágide, Casa da Comida, Conventual, Aviz, António Clara, Tavares Rico, Clara – but there are also numerous cheerful *bairro* restaurants where you can eat cheaply and well.

In OPORTO, the top restaurants include Portucale and Casa Aleixo. I have always liked the Gambamar. José Quitério describes O Fialho in ÉVORA as the cathedral of Portuguese gastronomy; you may well prefer the *pousada*'s wider-ranging menu, lighter touch and smoother service. In VILA NOVA DE FAMALICÃO he admires the Iris; a friend of mine raves over As Filhas do Tanoeiro (The Tanner's Daughters), in the same town. In BRAGA he admires O Abade de Priscos, in BARCELOS Bagoeira, on the outskirts of LEIRIA (near Nazaré) the Casarão. Like A Lareira in MOGADOURO, Trás-os-Montes, Maria Rita of ROMEU, near Mirandela, and Gabriela in SENDIM are nationally known. In VISEU Quitério, author of *O Livro de Bem Comer*, chooses O Cortiço and Trave Negra, in SEIA the Camelo, in TOMAR O Chico Elias.

Restaurants have a basic tourist menu, and house wine. There is food, and a restaurant, to every taste and pocket. There are guides to help you find them. One is *Recommended Restaurant* (Pascoal & Palanque, Lisbon) with a countrywide listing. (Who was it who said ask a fat policeman?) Many restaurants accept credit cards. Mealtimes are roughly 12.30 to 2.30 for lunch; 7.30 to 9.30 for dinner. As they say here: *bom apetite*!

Shopping, banking, post-office and museum hours

Most **shops** are open Monday to Friday, 9 a.m.–1 p.m. and 3–7 p.m.; on Saturdays in the morning only (except supermarkets which are often open all day). Most businesses have the same hours. Factories may start earlier, and end earlier. **Main Banks** are open Monday to Friday, 8.30–3 p.m. (A few Lisbon banks operate longer hours, airport banks are open up to 24 hours.) **Post-office** hours vary across the country. Some close at lunch, some do not. Some are open Saturday morning, some are not. Generally, they open weekdays 8.30 a.m.–6.30 p.m. In LISBON, the post office at Restauradores is open until midnight; the one at the airport is open 24 hours. **Museums**: variable; roughly, 10 a.m.–1 p.m. and 2.30–5 p.m. Some are closed on Mondays and public holidays. Try to check with *Turismo*. In the countryside many **churches** or **monuments** are kept closed, the key at a house close by. (Ask for the *chave*, pronounced 'shaav'.)

Public holidays

The first of January, New Year's Day; 25 April, Revolution anniversary; 1 May, Labour Day; 10 June, Camoẽs and Portugal Day; 15 August, Assumption; 5 October, Republic Day; 1 November, All Saints' Day; 8 December, Immaculate Conception; 25 December, Christmas Day. **Moveable holidays:** Carnival in February, Shrove Tuesday, Good Friday, Corpus Christi and local saints' days across the country – in Lisbon, 13 June, Sant'António; in Oporto, 24 June, São João. When a holiday falls on a Tuesday or Thursday some establishments close for long weekends.

Money, medical services, emergencies, electricity

The currency is the escudo. There is no need to declare how much you bring in or take out. Credit cards are accepted in numerous establishments, as are Eurocheques. Traveller's cheques and the main foreign currencies are also easily changed. **Tipping:** service is often allegedly included in bills. A tip of 10–15 per cent should still be left for good service.

Sunbathers be warned: the sun is much hotter than you think it is. Start cautiously with filtering lotions. **Pharmacies** – *farmácias* – are open during normal business hours and every town has a night service. Most pharmacists speak some English. English is also spoken by doctors and nurses at the British Hospital in Lisbon, a private hospital (tel. 602020/603785). The nationwide **emergency telephone number** is 115.

Electricity voltage is 220 AC. Plugs are continental 2-pin.

Sports, libraries, entertainment, language, photography

Turismo offices have pamphlets; newspapers list what's on and where – especially the weekly *Sete*. Films are shown in their original language. In Lisbon there are several libraries, the Biblioteca Nacional at Campo Grande, the Calouste Gulbenkian Foundation, the British Institute, the American Cultural Centre among them. Hours vary. A phrasebook is useful, although English and French are widely spoken. Portuguese words and pronunciation can be frustrating – I can still forget that *puxe*, on a door, means pull. **Photos:** if you want to take a close-up, you should ask; you will hardly ever be refused.

Index